Murder Among Friends

Murder Among Friends

Violation of Philia
in Greek Tragedy

ELIZABETH S. BELFIORE

New York   Oxford
OXFORD UNIVERSITY PRESS
2000

Oxford University Press

Oxford   New York

Athens Auckland Bangkok Bogotá Buenos Aires Calcutta
Cape Town Chennai Dar es Salaam Delhi Florence Hong Kong Istanbul
Karachi Kuala Lumpur Madrid Melbourne Mexico City Mumbai
Nairobi Paris São Paulo Singapore Taipei Tokyo Toronto Warsaw

and associated companies in
Berlin Ibadan

Copyright © 2000 by Elizabeth S. Belfiore

Published by Oxford University Press, Inc.
198 Madison Avenue, New York, New York 10016

Library of Congress Cataloging-in-Publication Data
Belfiore, Elizabeth S., 1944–
Murder among friends : violation of philia in Greek tragedy /
p.   cm.
Includes bibliographical references and index.
ISBN 0–19–513149–5
1. Greek drama (Tragedy)—History and criticism.
2. Friendship in literature.   3. Murder in literature.
4. Family in literature.
5. Love in literature.   I. Title
PA3136.B45   2000
882'.0109355—dc21   99–13051

1 3 5 7 9 8 6 4 2

Printed in the United States of America
on acid-free paper

In Memory of Louise and John

> . . . ἀλλ᾽ ἓν γὰρ μόνον
> τὰ πάντα λύει ταῦτ᾽ ἔπος μοχθήματα.
> τὸ γὰρ φιλεῖν οὐκ ἔστιν ἐξ ὅτου πλέον
> ἢ τοῦδε τἀνδρὸς ἔσχεθ᾽, οὗ τητώμεναι
> τὸν λοιπὸν ἤδη τοῦ βίου διάξετον.

Ὀρέστης. εἰ σόν γ' ἀδελφόν, ὦ τάλαιν', ἀπώλεσας.
Ἰφιγένεια. . . . παρὰ δ' ὀλίγον ἀπέφυγες ὄλεθρον ἀνόσιον ἐξ
  ἐμᾶν δαϊχθεὶς χερῶν.

ORESTES: If you had killed your brother, wretched woman.
IPHIGENEIA: You escaped by little an unholy death, struck by
  my hands.

(Eur. IT 866–73)

Acknowledgments

Among the many scholars to whom I am indebted for reading drafts, discussing relevant issues, and encouraging me to complete this project are Alan Boegehold, Peter Burian, Christopher Carey, Christopher Gill, Patricia Easterling, Michael Ewans, Michael Haslam, Eva Keuls, Nita Krevans, David Konstan, Nicholas Lowe, Daniel Ogden, Douglas Olson, Seth Schein, John Wilkins, and Sumio Yoshitake. Two in particular, Richard Seaford and Mae Smethurst, gave me their enthusiastic support from beginning to end of this project. The anonymous readers for Oxford University Press provided valuable criticisms that helped me to improve this book. I am indebted to Susan Chang of Oxford University Press, and to Angela Blackburn and Barbara Norton of Invisible Ink, for efficient and judicious editorial assistance. I also benefited from helpful discussions provided by audiences at the annual meetings of the American Philological Association (1997) and of the Classical Association of the Middle West and South (1996, 1998), and at the Universities of Cambridge, Exeter, Minnesota, Oxford, Pittsburgh, and Stanford. I am grateful to Mark Griffith for allowing me to see a draft of his *Antigone* commentary prior to publication. The Beazley Archive, Ashmolean Museum, Oxford, generously provided me with a database on Greek vases. Special thanks are due to my husband, Peter, for editorial assistance, literary discussions, and encouragement, to my son, Michael, for dramatic examples, and to Vincent Truitner for the cover illustration. This book is dedicated to the memory of my parents, John and Louise Stafford, who introduced me to Greece, to literature, and to *philia*.

Research for this book was supported by several grants from the University of Minnesota—a sabbatical leave and Bush Sabbatical Supplement in 1994–95, a Single Quarter Leave in 1997, and travel grants in 1996 from the Institute of International Studies and Programs and from the McKnight Arts and Humanities Fund for International Travel—and by an Honorary Research Fellowship from the University of Exeter in 1994.

Earlier versions of parts of this book have been published previously. A shorter version of chapter 1 was published as "Harming Friends: Problematic Reciprocity in Greek Tragedy," in *Reciprocity in Ancient Greece*, ed. C. Gill, N. Postlethwaite, and R. Seaford (Oxford 1998), 139–58, reprinted by permission of Oxford University Press. An earlier version of parts of chapter 4 was published as "*Xenia* in Sophocles' *Philoctetes*," *CJ* 89 (1993–94): 113–29, reprinted by permission of the Classical Association of the Middle West and South.

Contents

A Note on Spelling
and Abbreviations

There is no standard way of referring to Greek names and titles in English. I adopt the following rules. For Greek names, I transliterate according to the rules of *The Chicago Manual of Style*, 14th ed. (9.131): Greek υ is transliterated as y, except in diphthongs, where it is transliterated as u (for example, Hippolytos, Oidipous, Eumenides). For the titles of fragments, I use transliterated Greek, giving the English translation after the first occurrence. For titles of the extant tragedies, which have passed via Latin into common English usage, I use a combination of English, Latin, and transliterated Greek, as listed below.

Abbreviations and Titles

For ancient authors and works, I follow the abbreviations listed in the *Oxford Classical Dictionary* (*Chicago Manual* 15.299). The most commonly used are listed below.

Tragedies

For abbreviations of the titles of extant tragedies, I follow the Latinized forms listed in *Oxford Classical Dictionary*:

Aiskhylos:	Agamemnon	Ag.
	Libation Bearers	*Cho.*
	Eumenides	*Eum.*
	Persians	*Pers.*
	Prometheus Bound	*PV*
	Seven Against Thebes	*Sept.*
	Suppliants	*Supp.*

Sophokles:	*Aias*	Aj.
	Antigone	Ant.
	Elektra	El.
	Oedipus at Kolonos	OC
	Oedipus the King	OT
	Philoktetes	Phil.
	Women of Trakhis	Trach.
Euripides:	*Alkestis*	Alc.
	Andromakhe	Andr.
	Bacchae	Bacch.
	Children of Herakles	Heracl.
	Elektra	El.
	Hekabe	Hec.
	Helen	Hel.
	Herakles	HF
	Hippolytus	Hipp.
	Iphigenia in Aulis	IA
	Iphigenia in Tauris	IT
	Medea	Med.
	Orestes	Or.
	Phoenician Women	Phoen.
	Rhesos	Rhes.
	Suppliants	Supp.
	Trojan Women	Tro.

Other Ancient Works

Aristotle:	*Eudemian Ethics*	EE
	Magna Moralia	MM
	Nicomachean Ethics	NE
	Poetics	Po.
	Rhetoric	Rhet.
Hesiod:	*Works and Days*	Op.
Homer:	*Iliad*	Il.
	Odyssey	Od.

Modern Works

DK	Diels and Kranz 1935–37
LSJ	Liddell and Scott 1996
M	Mette 1963
MW	Merkelbach and West
N	Nauck 1964
R	Radt 1977 or 1985
RE	Pauly and Wissowa 1894–

Journals

AJA	*American Journal of Archaeology*
AJP	*American Journal of Philology*
BICS	*Bulletin of the Institute of Classical Studies, University of London*
BMCR	*Bryn Mawr Classical Review*
CA	*Classical Antiquity*
CJ	*Classical Journal*
C&M	*Classica et Mediaevalia*
CP	*Classical Philology*
CQ	*Classical Quarterly*
CR	*Classical Review*
CW	*Classical World*
GRBS	*Greek, Roman, and Byzantine Studies*
G&R	*Greece and Rome*
HSCP	*Harvard Studies in Classical Philology*
ICS	*Illinois Classical Studies*
JHS	*Journal of Hellenic Studies*
PCPS	*Proceedings of the Cambridge Philological Society*
REG	*Revue des études grecques*
RhM	*Rheinisches Museum*
TAPA	*Transactions of the American Philological Association*
WS	*Wiener Studien*
YCS	*Yale Classical Studies*
ZPE	*Zeitschrift für Papyrologie und Epigraphik*

Introduction

Greek tragedy represents many terrible deeds among kin: patricide, incest, matricide, child-murder, fratricide. In Aristotle's view, these events are central to the plots of the best tragedies: "When the terrible events take place within kinship[1] relationships, for example, when brother kills or is about to kill brother, or does something else of this kind, or when son does this to father, or mother to son, or son to mother, these things are to be sought" (*Poetics* 1453b19–22). Like Aristotle, modern scholars have often noted that many tragedies have plots in which *philos* (kin or friend) harms or is about to harm *philos*, or have called attention to the importance of *philia* (kinship or friendship) in such aspects of Greek tragedy as characterization and social context. For example, Mary Whitlock Blundell's influential study *Helping Friends and Harming Enemies* documents the immense importance of *philia* in Sophokles' plays.[2] Neither ancient nor modern scholars, however, have fully appreciated how prevalent is the plot pattern praised by Aristotle. I argue in this book that harm to *philoi* is in several respects characteristic of Greek tragedy as a genre. It is, first, a central element in the plot structures of nearly all of the extant tragedies. An act in which harm occurs or is about to occur among *philoi* who are blood kin is central to the plots of more than half of the thirty-two extant tragedies. In the major events of most of the other extant plays, such an act occurs within relationships that bring outsiders into a *philia* group: marriage, *xenia* (the host-guest relationship), and suppliancy. Harm to *philoi* is also important in less major incidents of nearly all of the extant tragedies, as well as in the language and imagery of all these plays, in the mythological background alluded to, and in the social world of the dramatic figures. Finally, an awareness of the roles played by kinship and by formal reciprocal relationships similar to kinship is crucial to an understanding of the tragedies. The many different aspects of tragedy—characterization, imagery, language, ideas, religion, ritual, formal structure, and historical and social context—are best appreciated when studied within the framework of the kinship relationships that are essential to the tragic plot. The tragedies of which only fragments remain, to judge from the scanty evidence, were no exception, and harm to *philoi* was of great importance here also.

The emphasis in tragedy on violation of *philia* reflects the concerns of this genre with problems of reciprocity. As just noted, the violence in tragedy to which Aristotle draws attention occurs between those who are *philoi* in a larger sense (suppliants and *xenoi*) as well as between family members. In the normative pattern assumed by the plays, reciprocity plays a crucial role in all of these relationships. Suppliancy and *xenia* are initiated and maintained by reciprocation of favors, and family relationships, while based on blood kinship or marriage, are also characterized by reciprocation of favors or benefits. In tragedy, the norm is that "favor always produces favor" (χάρις χάριν γὰρ ἐστιν ἡ τίκτουσ᾽ ἀεί: Soph. *Aias* 522). Tragedy emphasizes, however, the portrayal not of this norm, but rather of its violation. In some cases, two *philoi* engage in reciprocal violence (e.g., Eteokles and Polyneikes); in others, only one *philos* violates the norm (e.g., Agamemnon kills Iphigeneia, who has done him only good).

I argue in this book that the focus on the reversal or problematization of the normal is characteristic of the tragic genre. In contrast, as Richard Seaford has recently pointed out, violence between *philoi* does not have the same central role in Homeric epic that it has in tragedy.[3] The subject matter of epic is κλέα ἀνδρῶν, famous deeds of men, in which heroes win glory by fighting enemies; for example, Akhilleus kills Hektor, and Odysseus slays the suitors. The epic plot, however, tends to avoid the portrayal of the bloodshed between relatives that figures so largely in tragedy. To take only one example, the sacrifice of Iphigeneia by her father Agamemnon—the subject of Euripides' *Iphigenia in Aulis* and an important issue in Aiskhylos's *Agamemnon*, Sophokles' *Elektra*, and Euripides' *Iphigenia in Tauris*—is never mentioned in Homer.

The existence of these generic differences raises intriguing historical questions about the relationship between the rise and development of tragedy and that of the polis. The predominance in tragedy of violation of *philia* may reflect a period and social context (fifth-century democratic Athens) in which reciprocal relationships between family members and other kinds of *philoi* had become problematic, in a way that they were not in Homer, because of the emergence of new modes of social and economic life. In this book, however, I do not explore a historical line of explanation for the predominance of violence among *philoi* in Greek tragedy, but instead attempt to provide a typology of this aspect of tragedy.

The following chapters explain and demonstrate the validity of this approach to tragedy. Chapter 1 uses Aristotle's theory of tragedy as a starting point for an overview of the nature of *philia* relationships in Greek society and of the differences between tragic and epic treatments of *philia*. Chapters 2–6 analyze five plays in detail, showing how *philia* relationships figure in major and minor events and in the language of the plays. Chapter 2 studies Euripides' *Iphigenia in Tauris*—a play Aristotle takes to be paradigmatic, citing it as one of the "best" plays—in which sister is about to kill brother but does not do so because recognition occurs. Close analysis shows how kin murder and the averting of harm to kin not only is central to the main incident of the plot but also figures in many other comparatively minor events that either take place on stage or are alluded to by the dramatic figures. The other four plays—Aiskhylos's *Suppliants*, Sophokles' *Philoktetes* and *Aias*, and Euripides' *Andromakhe*—are hard cases for my view, since they are not concerned with harm to kin in as direct and obvious a way as is the *Iphigenia in Tauris*. I argue that in each of these plays, nevertheless, harm to those within reciprocal relationships that are similar to blood kinship is a crucial issue. Chapter 3 shows how supplication, marriage, and blood kinship are intimately connected in Aiskhylos's *Suppliants*. In this play, the Danaïds are threatened with harm by their cousins, who want to marry them by force. The women flee to King Pelasgos, from whom they claim protection both as suppliants and as kin. They claim protection from Zeus on the same grounds, for he is the god of suppliants and their ancestor through his marriage with Io, the mythological prototype of the Greek bride seen as respected suppliant. A focus on *philia* and its violation in the *Suppliants*, instead of on the psychology of the Danaïds, helps to explain many difficulties. Although harm to blood kin does not take place in Sophokles' *Philoktetes* (chapter 4), violation of the reciprocal relationship of *xenia* is of central importance. Neoptolemos's threatened abandonment of Philoktetes is represented not merely as the betrayal of a stranger, but as violation of a divinely sanctioned *xenia* relationship that is established by means of definite rituals in the course of the play. Euripides' *Andromakhe* (chapter 5) is concerned with Neoptolemos's harm to his kin by marriage. He injures not only his legitimate wife, Hermione, and her relatives, whom he insults by bringing a concubine into the same house with her, but also his slave wife Andromakhe, an enemy Trojan whose husband Hektor was killed by Neoptolemos's own father, Akhilleus. These specific acts in violation of the marriage relationship lead to disaster. Chapter 6 focuses on another kind of *philia* relationship: that with oneself. The Greeks believed that the self is one's closest *philos*, and that suicide is therefore like the killing of close blood kin. It is, therefore, in accord with Greek beliefs to see Aias's suicide as an instance of kin murder. This approach also helps to explain some puzzling features in Sophokles' play.

The appendixes contain evidence demonstrating the prevalence of the pattern of harm to *philoi* within tragedy as a whole. I present this material in the form of a database rather than as a unified narrative, providing brief analyses of each of the twenty-seven extant tragedies that were not discussed in detail in chapters 2–6 and summarizing the information available about harm to *philoi* in the lost tragedies through the fourth century B.C.E. While these sections are very different from the narrative chapters, they are an especially important part of this book, providing the data that support my argument that emphasis on harm to *philoi* is characteristic of Greek tragedy as a genre. Although the appendixes can be read straight through, many readers may find them more useful as reference material, to be consulted on individual plays, categories of relationships, or myths about particular subjects, or for statistical summaries.

Appendix A gives a brief analysis of the role of kinship and kinship-like relationships in each of the extant tragedies. Appendix B studies *philia* in the tragic fragments and testimonia of Aiskhylos, Sophokles, and Euripides, and appendix C surveys the evidence for harm to *philoi* in the lost plays of the minor tragedians through the fourth century B.C.E. While conclusions about the lost plays must be somewhat tentative, I argue that this material provides further evidence for the view that harm to *philoi* is an important characteristic of tragedy as a whole, not merely of the plays that happen to have survived in more or less complete form.

This book, then, is a comprehensive survey and analysis of instances of violations of *philia* relationships in the tragedies. While other scholars have given partial lists of plays in which harm to kin occurs,[4] no one, to my knowledge, has ever completed an exhaustive study of this topic in all of the tragic corpus. My study, then, fills a gap and contributes to a greater understanding of an important aspect of Greek tragedy. I hope that it will also help to stimulate further research. My approach does not exclude but rather complements other ways of studying tragedy. An awareness of *philia* relationships can greatly increase our understanding not only of the plots, but also of many other aspects of the plays, such as the motives of the dramatic figures, the mythological background, and the staging. The nature of these relationships in the tragedies can provide clues to many puzzles in the overall structure of the plays, in individual scenes, and in the text. I offer here a framework, a database, and some detailed examples and analyses that seek to demonstrate the fruitfulness of this approach. My hope is that the reader can return to the plays themselves with greater awareness of the biological and social relationships with which they are centrally concerned.

In beginning with Aristotle's insight that tragedy is centrally concerned with terrible deeds (*pathê*) among *philoi*, my approach has the advantage of adopting an ancient rather than a modern perspective. It can thus help us to read the plays as artifacts of a culture very different from our own. Moreover, Aristotle's insight is validated by the evidence of the plays themselves, which give us reason to believe that his statement can be interpreted as not merely prescriptive, but normative, serving to characterize tragedy as a genre. Although an analysis of the *Poetics* is beyond the scope of this book, the fact that Aristotle was right about this point has important consequences for an understanding of both Greek tragedy and the *Poetics*. Closer attention to the philosopher's ideas might provide other important insights into aspects of the plays that have been neglected by modern scholars. In addition, Aristotle's views on the centrality of harm to *philoi* in tragedy might help us to understand his own ideas on such important topics as generic differences, pity and fear, and the best tragedies.

Although this book is primarily addressed to specialists who read the plays in the original Greek, every effort has been made to make it accessible to others with an interest in Greek tragedy. While the frequent necessity to quote passages in the original Greek makes it impossible to translate every word, I translate or paraphrase almost all of the Greek (with the exception of a few technical passages that are not essential to the main argument), and provide a glossary of frequently transliterated Greek words and of technical terms. Brief explanations of Greek concepts and institutions are given, and chapters 2–6 begin with short plot summaries.

Unless otherwise noted, all translations are my own and I use the following texts: for Aiskhylos, Friis Johansen and Whittle 1980 (*Supp.*), West 1990 (other plays); for Euripides, Mastronarde 1994 (*Phoen.*), Diggle 1981–94 (other plays); for Sophokles, Lloyd-Jones and Wilson 1990; and for tragic fragments, the four volumes of *Tragicorum Graecorum Fragmenta*.

Murder Among Friends

Philia Relationships and Greek Literature

This chapter provides an overview of the role of *philia* relationships in tragedy (sections 3 and 4) and contrasts the importance and prevalence of this pattern in tragedy with its absence or lack of emphasis in epic (section 2). First, however, section 1 contains a brief discussion of *philia* in Aristotle's *Poetics* and of *philia* relationships in Greek society generally.

1. *Philia* in Aristotle and Greek Society

"When the *pathê* take place within *philia* relationships, for example, when brother kills or is about to kill brother, or does something else of this kind, or when son does this to father, or mother to son, or son to mother, these things are to be sought" (*Po.* 1453b19–22). In discussing plot patterns in tragedy, I begin with Aristotle's explicit statements in the *Poetics* about *philia*, *pathos*, and recognition.[1] Aristotle does not define *philia*, but he frequently mentions it in connection with *pathos* (for example, in the passage quoted above) and, in the passages cited in the next paragraph, in connection with recognition. He defines *pathos* as "a destructive or painful event [πρᾶξις φθαρτικὴ ἢ ὀδυνηρά], for example, deaths vividly represented, and great pain, and wounds, and all things of this kind" (*Po.* 1452b11–14). *Pathos* is one of the three parts of the tragic plot. Aristotle's account in chapters 10 and 11 implies that *pathos*, unlike recognition and reversal, is part of all tragic plots, simple as well as complex. Although a tragedy may have more than one *pathos*, the major *pathos* is an important event in the plot, one that arouses pity and fear and has important consequences for the good or bad fortune of the dramatic figures.

Recognition, in Aristotle's account, is closely connected with both *philia* and *pathos*. In the best plots, *philos* harms *philos*, or is about to do so, in ignorance of the relationship. Recognition either occurs after the act, as happens in Sophokles' *Oedipus the King,* or it prevents the act from occurring, as in Euripides' *Iphigenia in Tauris* (*Po.* 14). According to Aristotle, then, there are four basic plot patterns (14.1453b27–54a9): (1) the act may be done by those who know of their *philia* relationship, as happens in Euripides' *Medea*; (2) it may be done in ignorance of this relationship, with recognition of *philia* coming after the act, as occurs in Sophokles' *Oedipus the King*; (3) the action may be about to occur but be prevented by recognition, as happens in Euripides' *Iphigenia in Tauris*; (4) someone may be about to harm a *philos* with knowledge of the relationship, but fail to act, as happens when Haimon in Sophokles' *Antigone* tries to strike his father but misses. Such events in themselves arouse pity and fear, even without being staged (14.1453b1–7).

According to Aristotle's definition, "Recognition is . . . a change from ignorance to knowledge, either to *philia* or to enmity, of those marked out for good or bad fortune" (*Po.* 1452a29–32). It is important not to confuse what Aristotle terms "recognition to *philia* or to enmity" (ἀναγνώρισις . . . ἢ εἰς φιλίαν ἢ εἰς ἔχθραν), that is, recognition leading to a state of *philia* or enmity, with "recognizing *philia*" (ἀναγνωρίσαι τὴν φιλίαν: 1453b31). In the case of Oidipous, Aristotle's example of "recognizing *philia*" (1453b30–31), Oidipous recognizes that Iokaste and Laios are his parents. On the other hand, "recognition to *philia* or to enmity" must involve more than knowledge of identity. Since harm to an enemy does not arouse pity in the best way (1453b17–18), recognition of the identity of an enemy plays no role in Aristotle's theory of tragedy. Unlike simple recognition of identity, then, "recognition to *philia* or to enmity" is the realization that one is in a state of friendship or enmity with one's *philoi*, because one's actions are, were, or will be those of a friend or enemy. For example, Orestes discovers that Iphigeneia is his sister (recognizing *philia*) and that she is ready to act as his friend (recognition leading to a state of *philia*), but Oidipous finds out that he has acted as an enemy to his own kin (recognition leading to a state of enmity).

The *philoi* in Aristotle's examples are all close blood kin—parents, children, and siblings—and some scholars, for example Gerald Else, hold that Aristotle excludes non-kin relationships.[2] In the case of *pathos* also, Aristotle emphasizes death and physical pain. However, there is good reason to hold that his examples of both *philoi* and *pathê* are paradigmatic rather than restrictive. In defining *pathos,* he writes, "for example . . . and all things of this kind" (1452b12–13), and in giving examples of the best tragedies, he states, "for example . . . or does something else of this kind" (1453b20–22). This suggests that other kinds of relationships and events would count as instances of *philiai* and *pathê.*

Evidence that events other than death and woundings count as *pathê* is provided by the fact that Aristotle cites the *Hellê* as an example of the best kind of plot, one in which a *pathos* between *philoi* is prevented by recognition. In this play, "son, being about to hand over [ἐκδιδόναι] his mother, recognized her" (1454a8).[3] Since the *pathos* here is not murder with one's own hand but betrayal to an enemy, failure to protect a *philos* or suppliant would seem to count as a *pathos*. Another category of *pathos* would include sexual acts. Rape is a painful and socially destructive act that occurs or is threatened in a number of plays. For example, in Sophokles' lost *Tereus*, mentioned by Aristotle at 1454b36–37, Philomela reveals by means of a woven picture that she was raped by her brother-in-law Tereus, who then cut her tongue out to prevent her telling what he had done. It is reasonable to count not only the wounding but also the rape as a *pathos*, especially since it is so central to the story. It also makes sense to count Oidipous's incest as a *pathos*. This act is not physically painful, but it is destructive (φθαρτική), in a social and religious sense, and in fact it directly causes Iokaste's suicide. Moreover, Oidipous's relationship with Iokaste is explicitly said to be central to the reversal of the *Oedipus*, in which the messenger comes "to free Oidipous from his fear concerning his mother" (1452a25–26). The incest would also count as a *pathos* because it causes ὀδύνη in the common sense of "pain of mind" (LSJ s.v. ὀδύνη 2), as do other terrible acts among *philoi*. For example, Pelias is said to have died in the "most painful" (ἄλγιστον) way, because he was killed by his own daughters (Eur. *Med.* 486–87).

There are also reasons to believe that *philia* in the *Poetics* includes more relationships than Aristotle's paradigmatic examples of siblings, parents, and children. Aristotle divides all human relationships into only three categories — that of *philoi*, enemies, and neutrals (1453b15–16) — and he uses the plural in stating that the best *pathê* take place "within *philiai* relationships" (ἐν ταῖς φιλίαις: 1453b19). Greek kinship included many more blood relationships than those within the modern "nuclear family." In fact, the Greek concept of kinship (*ankhisteia*) included relatives to the degree of children of cousins.[4] In the *Nicomachean Ethics*, Aristotle notes the similarity between the relationship of cousins and that of brothers, and he draws no strict line between more and less distant relationships (1161b35–1162a1–4). In many tragedies — for example, Aiskhylos's *Suppliants* — cousinship or descent from a common ancestor is represented as a strong claim to kinship. All of this gives us reason to believe that *philia* in the *Poetics*, as in Aristotle's other works, includes a wide range of blood relationships.[5]

Tragedy also represents *pathê* between spouses and *xenoi*, and between suppliant and supplicated. Which of these, if any, would count as *pathê* among *philoi*? Although Aristotle does not mention spouse murder in his discussions of the house of Atreus, it is reasonable to count Klytaimestra's murder of Agamemnon (referred to as an attack on *philoi* in Ais. Ag. 1234–36) and Deianeira's poisoning of Herakles as the killing of a *philos*. Even though spouses are not usually blood relatives, they are an integral part of the household (οἰκία), and at *Poetics* 1454a12, Aristotle writes of households in which terrible deeds occur. It is less likely that the text justifies the inclusion of *xenoi* and suppliants as *philoi*. The *Poetics* is silent on these categories of relationships, as it is on marriage, and *xenoi* and suppliants are not part of the household. On the other hand, Aristotle's concept of *philia* is much broader in his ethical works. For example, *NE* 8.12 lists three categories of *philia* relationships: community *philia* (κοινωνική), including *xenia*; companionship *philia* (ἑταιρική); and family *philia* (συγγενική), which includes the marriage relationship.⁶ The ethical works also include self-love as a kind of *philia* (*NE* 9.4 and *EE* 7.6–7). Aristotle's broad concept of *philia* in these works gives some support to an interpretation of the *Poetics* according to which *philia* is centered on, but not restricted to, blood kinship. In the *Poetics* Aristotle stresses the closest blood kin—parents, children, and siblings—not because *philia* is limited to blood kinship, but because this kind of relationship is exemplary and paradigmatic of *philia*. Just as in the *NE*, he leaves open the possibility that *philia* can be extended inwards, to include one's relationship with oneself (self-love), and outwards, to include more distant relations such as cousins and spouses, suppliants, and *xenoi*.

In any case, Aristotle's views merely serve as a useful starting point. It is fruitful for a study of Greek tragedy to adopt broader concepts of *philia* and tragic recognition than the text of the *Poetics* explicitly warrants. According to the broader view adopted in this study, the *philia* relationships within which *pathê* take place in the best tragedies include not only close and more distant blood kinship, but also the formal reciprocal relationships of marriage, *xenia*, and suppliancy. Recognition, in turn, is not limited to the treatment of blood kin as *philoi*, but includes the acknowledgment and acceptance of outsiders as parties to these reciprocal relationships. This broadening of the concept of *philia* makes sense, because marriage, *xenia*, and suppliancy are all formal relationships involving reciprocal rights and obligations and are in many ways similar to blood kinship. These are, in John Gould's words, "social institutions which permit the acceptance of the outsider within the group and which create hereditary bonds of obligation between the parties."⁷ To include formal reciprocal relationships as well as biological kinship is not only useful for a study of Greek tragedy, it is also consistent with Greek ideas about *philia*. Biological kinship normally also involves positive reciprocity; moreover, formal non-kin relationships initiated and maintained by acts of positive reciprocity—marriage, *xenia*, and suppliancy—are assimilated in turn to kinship in Greek thought.⁸ On the other hand, it is reasonable to exclude from the relevant *philia* relationships those between *philoi* who are merely "friends" outside of these biological and reciprocal relationships.

Blood kinship differs from relationships initiated by reciprocal acts in that people do not choose their blood kin and may even be ignorant of the identity of their kin. However, because biological kinship is in most cases also a social relationship, it can be strengthened by acts of positive reciprocity or weakened by negative reciprocity. That Aristotle is concerned with the social aspects of biological kinship (the kind of *philia* represented by the paradigmatic examples in the *Poetics*) is apparent not only in the ethical works, but also in his definition of recognition in the *Poetics*, discussed above. In the paradigmatic cases, "recognition [leading] to [a state of] *philia* or to [a state of] enmity" is not merely the attainment of cognitive knowledge of the identity of one's biological kin ("to recognize *philia*"), it also involves acting as a *philos* or enemy. Because recognition leading "to [a state of] *philia*" is the acknowledgment of another as someone toward whom one has obligations of positive reciprocity, people may "become *philoi*" even when they are already *philoi* in the sense of biological kin. On the other hand, recognition leading "to [a state of] enmity" involves the discovery that one has acted as an enemy to one's biological kin. Reciprocity, then, plays a central role in the social relationships of blood kin, as it does in all kinds of *philia*.[9]

Of the three reciprocal relationships, marriage is closest to blood kinship. Although the bride retains important ties to her family of birth and is "foreign" (ὀθνεία) to her husband's family, spouses are members of the same household.[10] And although spouses are not usually blood kin, their relationship is like kinship in having its basis in "nature" (*NE* 1162a16–17). Moreover, marriage leads to an indirect biological tie between two spouses after children are born. As well as being a "natural" relationship, marriage creates important reciprocal relationships not only between the individual spouses, but also between their two families, who exchange gifts and services.[11] Homer's Alkinoos says that "father-in-law and brother-in-law are nearest after one's own blood and race" (*Od*. 8.582–83). On the negative side, conflicts may take place between spouses and in-laws, and tensions can arise when one man has children by two different women. When a man keeps a concubine, as well as when he has a legally bigamous household, the birth of children with the same father and different mothers (*amphimētores*) is an important cause of tensions within the household (amphimetric strife) as mothers and children compete with one another for legitimacy, favors from the father, and recognition by the polis. In similar ways, tension is created by the presence of stepchildren.[12] This kind of conflict does not occur in Homer, but it is important in tragedy, for example, in Euripides' *Hippolytus*, where Theseus's bastard son Hippolytos lives in the same household with his legitimate wife and her children.[13]

Although *xenia* and suppliancy are less close to blood kinship than is marriage, both are relationships that are "expressed in terms of the language of kinship."[14] According to Homer, "a *xeinos* and a suppliant are like a brother to a man" (*Od*. 8.546–47). *Xenia* in the sense relevant here is a formal, hereditary relationship of "ritualized friendship" initiated by specific actions.[15] The *xenos* in this sense differs from both the stranger toward whom one has no obligations and the temporary guest or host toward whom one has only temporary and limited duties.[16] Not every gift exchange or instance of hospitality establishes formal *xenia*. The exchange between Hektor and Aias in the *Iliad* is merely a token of temporary cessation of fighting,[17] and the reception of Priam by Akhilleus does not make them *xenoi*, as is clear when Hermes warns Priam not to sleep among "enemy men" (*Il*. 24.683–84).[18] *Xenoi* have many of the same reciprocal obligations toward one another that blood kin do, including the giving of mutual aid and acting as foster parents for each others' children.[19] On the other hand, reciprocity is essential to *xenia* in a way in which it is not to blood kinship. Kin may fail to keep their obligations and still remain kin, but *xenoi* must engage in reciprocal benefits if they are to become and remain *xenoi*.[20]

Supplication, of course, may take place within an already existing *philia* relationship. The kind of supplication with which I am most concerned here, however, is that which seeks either to initiate a *philia* relationship where one did not previously exist at all, or to gain for the suppliant acknowledgment as a *philos* on the basis of a previous relationship that was dubious or tenuous (for example, distant kinship). This kind of supplication is *hiketeia* in the etymological sense of supplication by an "arriving stranger" (*hiketês*). Suppliancy, like *xenia*, is a reciprocal relationship, although this is not so obvious to us. A suppliant always has obligations to reciprocate if possible[21] and may offer substantial benefits to the person supplicated, like those, for example, that Oidipous offers Theseus (Soph. *OC*, 576–78). However, just as the person supplicated has the power to harm the suppliant by a refusal, so the suppliant also has the power to harm if rejected. All supplication creates a strong obligation, supported by social and religious sanctions. In fact, because the suppliant is protected by Zeus, supplication carries with it an implicit threat to the person supplicated. Once successful, a *hiketês* enters into a reciprocal relationship with the person supplicated, becoming a dependent *philos* or, if the two are social equals, a *xenos*.

These three reciprocal relationships are similar to one another as well as to kinship. The *xenos* in the sense of "stranger" who seeks to be accepted as a *philos* is in many ways indistinguishable from the suppliant,[22] and *xenia* may be initiated by supplication. The marriage relationship can be seen as a particular form of *xenia* and suppliancy, because a wife is a *xenê* who comes to the hearth of her husband as a suppliant.[23] The close connections among all of these relationships are also apparent from the fact that all arouse similar emotions. Violence to a suppliant or *xenos* is as shocking as kin or spouse murder, incest or cannibalism, crimes that tend to go together in Greek thought.[24] Usually, however, *aidôs* ("respect," "reverence") prevents harm to kin, spouse, *xenos*, or suppliant. Even before being formally accepted as a *philos*, a suppliant has *aidôs* for the person supplicated and has strong claims to be treated with *aidôs* in return.[25] This fact has important consequences for an interpretation of suppliant plays. If *aidôs* is characteristic of both *hiketês* and supplicated at the time of supplication, and if, as Gustave Glotz claims, *philoi* are those who are united by a feeling of *aidôs*,[26] then the suppliant is already in some respects like a *philos* even before being fully acknowledged as such. Thus, even before being accepted, a *hiketês* is an outsider who nevertheless has strong claims to be treated as a *philos*. Correspondingly, to accept a suppliant is much like what Aristotle calls "recognition [leading] to [a state of] *philia*": recognition of identity that involves acting as a *philos*.

These similarities between biological kinship and relationships based on reciprocity are strongly emphasized in tragedy. In this genre, harm to distant kin, and to suppliants, *xenoi*, and spouses has a dramatic function similar to *pathê* among close blood kin, and the acceptance of outsiders as *philoi* toward whom one has reciprocal obligations is represented as similar to the recognition of the identity of a blood relative that involves acting as a *philos*.

2. *Philia* in Epic

A brief survey of Homer's very different treatment of violation of *philia* can illuminate the distinctive role played in tragedy by *pathê* among *philoi*. Although this discussion is confined to Homer, there are indications in the fragments of the Epic Cycle that Homer's treatment of *pathê* among *philoi* was not exceptional.[27] Although *pathê* are important in epic as well as tragedy, in epic they tend to take place between enemies rather than *philoi*. This may be one reason why, in Aristotle's view, tragedy develops out of and is superior to epic: tragedy has discovered that *pathê* among *philoi* best arouse pity and fear.[28]

Problematic *philia* relationships, of course, are important in epic as well as in tragedy. The Trojan War begins with Paris's violation of *xenia* in Menelaos's house, and the quarrel between Akhilleus and his friend[29] Agamemnon occasions the wrath that is the subject of the *Iliad*. Akhilleus's revenge on Hektor for the death of Patroklos, the friend whom Akhilleus accuses himself of failing to protect, is another central event in the poem. In the *Odyssey*, the marriage relationship between Penelope and Odysseus is threatened by Odysseus's long absence, and proper *xenia* behavior is neglected by the Kyklops and by the suitors in Ithaka.

Epic differs significantly from tragedy, however, in its treatment of these relationships. First, an act of direct, physical harm among blood kin, spouses, *xenoi* or suppliants is not central to epic plots as it is to the plots of most tragedies. Akhilleus's wrath results in harm to the Greeks, and he even asks that they be killed beside the ships (*Il.* 1.410–11). However, Akhilleus in the *Iliad* is not related by blood to Agamemnon or to Patroklos, and his suppliancy relationship with the latter is barely mentioned.[30] Moreover, his role in the death of even unrelated Greek friends is the indirect one of refusing to fight. That the *Iliad* goes out of its way to stress that he commits no act of violence against them is apparent from the scene in *Iliad* 1 in which Athena appears precisely in order to avert physical violence between Agamemnon and Akhilleus. Akhilleus does not curse the Akhaians, as Theseus curses his son in Euripides' *Hippolytus*, nor does he pray directly to Zeus asking him to kill the Akhaians, as happens in *Iliad* 1.37–43 when Khryses prays to Apollo to punish the Akhaians and is immediately answered. Instead, Akhilleus takes a more indirect route, asking Thetis to ask Zeus to aid the Trojans and punish the Akhaians (*Il.* 1.407–10). Zeus's will is carried out in a series of complex actions over the course of many books, so that Akhilleus's responsibility is further diluted in the narrative. Nor is Akhilleus's refusal to fight portrayed as direct harm to his friends, like murder or betrayal to an enemy. Indeed, his wrath is not blamed by his friends until he refuses the gifts in Book 9 (see 9.515–18, 523), and even after that point, no one holds him personally responsible for the deaths of his friends. Akhilleus blames himself for failing to protect Patroklos and his other friends (18.98–106), but he never suggests that he is a kind of murderer. Those responsible, according to Patroklos himself, are Zeus, Apollo, Euphorbos, and Hektor (16.844–50).

Central to the plot of the *Odyssey* is Odysseus's restoration of order in his troubled household. He both renews his marriage with Penelope, which was threatened in his absence, and kills her suitors. However, Odysseus's marriage is threatened not by Penelope, who is frequently contrasted with the faithless Klytaimestra, but by the suitors, and these men are not *philoi* who betray him, but simply his enemies (see *Po.* 1455b22). Instead of offending against an existing *xenia* relationship with Odysseus, the suitors refuse to enter into any positive reciprocal relationship in the first place, engaging in a purely "negative reciprocity."[31] Far from being his *xenoi*, the suitors have consistently refused to share a table with the disguised Odysseus.[32] One exception proves the rule. Antinoös, whose father fled his own people and was protected as a suppliant by Odysseus, is the only one of the suitors who is guilty of ingratitude to Odysseus as hereditary suppliant or *xenos*. This fact, however, is mentioned in only a single brief passage (16.418–33) and is not alluded to when Antinoös is killed. Yet, an emphasis on Antinoös's violation of *xenia* would have helped to underline his other defects. He is the ringleader of the suitors (17.394–95), and his faults are recounted frequently and at length. He plots the ambush against Telemakhos (4.663–72), advises the suitors to kill the young man in another way when this fails (16.364–92), is the only one of the suitors who does not give food to the disguised Odysseus, and is the first to attack him physically, an act condemned by all the others (17.409–504). Fittingly, he is the first to be killed (22.1–30).

In more minor events also, epic either lacks or fails to emphasize violent events among blood kin or spouses.[33] There is no mention in Homer of a sacrifice of Iphigeneia by her father, and Oidipous continues to rule in Thebes after he discovers that he has committed patricide and incest (*Od.* 11.271–80). The brothers Atreus and Thyestes, notorious enemies in tragedy, appear to be on good terms in Homer (*Il.* 2.106–7).[34] The murder of Agamemnon by Aigisthos (who is not said to be his kin) is mentioned many times in the *Odyssey*, but Klytaimestra's killing of her husband is only rarely alluded to. Usually she is represented as merely helping to plan the murder of Agamemnon.[35] In contrast, it is Klytaimestra who does the deed in Aiskhylos's *Agamemnon* and Aigisthos who helps in the planning (1614, 1627, 1634–35, 1643–46). In the tragedy, moreover, the kinship between Agamemnon and Aigisthos is stressed (*Ag.* 1577–1611). Furthermore, epic society is not centered around large, organized kinship groups, so that there is no kinship between Odysseus and the Ithakans he slaughters.[36] In tragedy, on the other hand, all inhabitants of a polis tend to be seen as kin, so that civil war is a kind of kin murder.[37] In tragedy, even the opposition between Greeks and barbarians may be seen in terms of kinship. As a barbarian, the Trojan Hektor is kin (ἐγγενής: *Rhesos* 404) to the Thracian Rhesos, and the "barbarian race" (γένος) is opposed to that of the Greeks.[38] Epic even avoids violence among friends related by marriage (*Od.* 10.438–42) or unrelated friends: the quarrel between Akhilleus and Odysseus (*Od.* 8.75–77), like that between Akhilleus and Agamemnon, is conducted in words only.

The epic treatment of the suppliant-exile also differs markedly from that of tragedy. The most famous suppliant-exile in tragedy is Oidipous, who seeks asylum in Kolonos after committing patricide and incest (Soph. *OC*). Euripides' Medeia and Herakles also take refuge in Athens after murdering their children, and the supplication and trial of the exiled matricide Orestes is the subject of Aiskhylos's *Eumenides*. In contrast, violence against kin is unimportant in the common epic pattern of the suppliant-exile. Often, the epic *hiketês* is an exile because he has killed someone and flees retribution from the dead person's kin. In his story to Athena (*Od.* 13.259–75), Odysseus claims to be an exile from Crete who fled because he killed the son of Idomeneus and who escaped by supplicating the Phoinikians. In the *Iliad*, Lykophron (15.430–32) and Patroklos (23.85–88) were both exiled because they killed a man. Sometimes the person killed happens to be related to the murderer-exile. Tlepolemos (*Il.* 2.662–63) killed his father's uncle, Medon (*Il.* 13.694–97) killed a kinsman of his stepmother, and Epeigeus (*Il.* 16.571–74) came as suppliant to Peleus and Thetis after killing his cousin. The prophet Theoklymenos fled Argos after killing a "relative" or "fellow tribesman" (ἄνδρα ἔμφυλον: *Od.* 15.271–78). In these cases, however, kin murder is merely mentioned in passing, and does not become an important issue. When two disputants are very closely related, murder is avoided altogether. Phoinix, who, at his mother's urging, slept with his father's mistress, quarreled with his father and was forced to flee his country. Thus, like the typical suppliant-exile, Phoinix fled his own country because of a quarrel, but, unlike the typical exile, he did not actually commit murder. On the contrary, Homer is careful to tell us that he refrained from patricide (*Il.* 9.458–61).[39] In Euripides' *Phoinix*, in contrast, Phoinix is falsely accused and then blinded by his father.

Epic also differs from tragedy in that it does not represent harm to *xenoi* and *hiketai* as similar to harm to blood kin. Although *hiketai* in tragedy are frequently kin, however distant, this is not the case in epic. An epic *hiketês* may be a god in disguise (for instance, *Od.* 17.483–87) but is never suspected of being a distant cousin. The disguised Odysseus invents many stories to engage the sympathy of those he meets, and he tells Penelope that he once entertained Odysseus as a *xenos*; but he never claims to be a relative, as a tragic figure might be expected to do. Indeed, the function of Zeus Hikesios in epic is precisely to care for those who have no other claims to protection: "beggars and suppliants" (for example, *Od.* 6.207–8).

Homer, moreover, tends to portray offenses against *xenia* as refusals to enter into a reciprocal relationship in the first place rather than as betrayals from within an existing *philia* relationship. While the Kyklops in the *Odyssey* offends against the rules of *xenia* in the most extreme manner possible—by eating his guests—one thing he is not guilty of is betrayal of a *philos*. Actual betrayal within a preexisting *xenia* relationship is either avoided in epic or given much less emphasis than in tragedy. As noted above, the suitors in Ithaka (with one exception) are not Odysseus's *xenoi*. Aigisthos kills Agamemnon after inviting him to a feast at his house, but this incident is passed over in two lines (*Od.* 11.409–11), and the story of Herakles' murder of his guest Iphitos is mentioned only briefly (21.24–30). In the *Iliad*, the Greek Diomedes gets the better of his Trojan *xenos* Glaukos in taking gold for bronze but never considers killing him (6. 212–36). Although Akhilleus kills a suppliant, Lykaon, who claims to have received food from him, this act is not portrayed as a violation of *xenia* or *philia*. Akhilleus had previously spared Lykaon's life only in order to sell him as a slave (*Il.* 21.75–79).[40]

Scenes of supplication in epic also differ significantly from those in tragedy. In epic as in tragedy, Zeus Hikesios punishes those who fail to protect *xenoi* and *hiketai*, and the fear of his anger is explicitly or implicitly appealed to by the suppliant.[41] Tragedy, however, gives a dramatic and emotional emphasis to this fear that is absent from epic. In tragic supplication scenes, acceptance of a suppliant often has very serious consequences—war, for example—and the dilemma faced by the person supplicated is typically emphasized in the dramatic action. In epic, in contrast, the decision is usually swift and without painful consequences.[42] A partial exception underlines this rule. When Thetis supplicates Zeus, asking him to show favor to the Trojans, Zeus briefly hesitates before agreeing, saying that this will cause conflict with Hera (*Il.* 1.517–27). Among the gods, however, such conflict never has serious consequences, but is easily resolved in Zeus's favor, as we are reminded at the end of Book 1. Moreover, references to pollution, absent from epic, add an entirely new dimension to tragic supplication. In tragedy, to harm a suppliant is to pollute and defile (μαίνειν) the suppliant's wreaths, the gods, and human laws (Eur. *Heracl.* 71, 264; *Supp.* 378). The suicide of a suppliant, especially at an altar or other sacred place of refuge, creates extremely harmful pollution.[43] The threat of pollution in tragedy helps to make harm to a suppliant just as pitiable and terrifying as harm to blood kin. In addition, the emphasis given to supplication scenes in tragedy gives initial hesitation followed by acceptance of a suppliant a dramatic and emotional impact similar to that produced by the recognition and acknowledgment of blood kin that prevents a *pathos* in tragedy.

Two epic examples show particularly clearly how epic supplication differs from the tragic examples discussed below. In *Iliad* 9.502–14, Phoinix supplicates Akhilleus and warns him against rejecting the Litai,[44] daughters of Zeus, lest their father send Atê to punish the transgressor. Neither in this parable, however, nor in Phoinix's subsequent story of the supplication of Meleagros, nor in Akhilleus's reply is there any mention of fear of Zeus. The emphasis is instead on the positive results of yielding: honor and gifts from other people

(*Il.* 9.515–19, 598–99, 602–5). Far from fearing Zeus, Akhilleus replies, "I think that I am honored by the decree of Zeus" (608).

Another important supplication takes place in *Iliad* 24, when Priam asks Akhilleus to give back Hektor's body. The danger to Priam is emphasized in many ways. Zeus himself seeks to allay the old man's very natural fear, by sending Hermes to guide him and by reassuring him (152–58, 181–87). Hekabe fears for her husband's life (201–8), and he is escorted out of Troy by his kin "lamenting much, as if he were going to his death" (327–28). In the actual supplication scene, the danger to Priam is again stressed in the characterization of Akhilleus's hands as "terrible and murderous" (479). Even after the supplication is successful, Akhilleus warns Priam not to push him too far (568–70), and after Priam has gone to sleep in Akhilleus's tent, Hermes wakes the old man and tells him to leave, warning him not to sleep among "enemy men" (682–88). On the other hand, there is little suggestion of any possible danger to Akhilleus from the anger of Zeus Hikesios. True, Akhilleus is ordered to give back Hektor's body by Zeus himself, who is angry with him for his treatment of the dead man (113–16, 134–36), Priam tells Akhilleus to respect the gods (503), and Akhilleus says that he fears offending against the orders of Zeus (570). Nevertheless, the threat to Akhilleus has no significant emotional impact. It is implicit rather than explicitly dramatized, and failure to accept supplication is not represented as a real possibility, considered and debated by Akhilleus. Instead, he agrees immediately, in two lines, to obey Zeus (139–40).

3. *Philia* in Tragedy: Overview

Pathê among *philoi* are of much more central importance in the plots of tragedies than they are in Homer. In arguing for this view, I begin, in this section, with an overview of the different kinds of relationships within which a *pathos* occurs or is about to occur in the major events of the plots of the thirty-two extant tragedies. My groupings of plays according to *pathê* within categories of relationships are based on the broad concept of *philia* and recognition explained in section 1. They are intended not to be rigid or absolute but merely to serve as one convenient way of grouping tragedies with similar plots.

I. In seventeen plays, the central *pathos* is a violent act, actual or threatened, against a *philos* who is a blood relative. In the majority, the *philoi* are parent and child.

    A. Parent harms child in seven plays. In Aiskhylos's *Eumenides*, mother, in the guise of her Furies, torments son. Six plays of Euripides also focus on violence of parent against child. Mother kills child in *Bacchae* and *Medea*, and in *Ion*, mother is about to kill son. Father kills child in *Herakles*, *Iphigenia in Aulis*, and *Hippolytos*.

B. In five plays, child harms parent. In Aiskhylos's *Libation Bearers*, son kills mother, in Sophokles' *Oedipus the King*, son kills father and marries mother, and in the *Elektra* plays of Sophokles and Euripides, children kill mother. The consequences of matricide are the subject of Euripides' *Orestes*. The stage action of this play represents many *pathê* about to take place among kin. Grandfather (Tyndareos) harms grandchildren (Orestes and Elektra) by urging the Argives to punish them. Uncle (Menelaos) harms nephew and niece (Orestes and Elektra) by refusing to protect them. Nephew and niece (Orestes and Elektra) attempt to kill aunt (Helen), and cousins (Orestes and Elektra) threaten to kill cousin (Hermione).

C. Fratricide is the subject of three plays. In Aiskhylos's *Seven Against Thebes* and Euripides' *Phoenician Women*, brother kills brother, and sister is about to kill brother in Euripides' *Iphigenia in Tauris*.

D. Harm to other blood kin takes place in two plays. In Aiskhylos's *Prometheus Bound*, Zeus tortures his uncle Prometheus,[45] and in Sophokles' *Antigone*, Kreon condemns his niece Antigone to death.

II. Central to a group of nine plays is a *pathos* among those in reciprocal relationships by means of which outsiders are brought within formal reciprocal *philia* relationships: marriage, *xenia*, and suppliancy.

A. In two plays, Aiskhylos's *Agamemnon* and Sophokles' *Women of Trakhis*, the central *pathos* is the murder of husband by wife.

B. Violation of the *xenia* relationship is central in three plays. In Sophokles' *Philoktetes*, Neoptolemos is about to betray and abandon Philoktetes, his *xenos* and suppliant. In Euripides' *Hekabe*, Polymestor kills his *xenos* Polydoros and is killed in turn by Hekabe while being entertained as a *xenos* by her. In Euripides' *Helen*, Theoklymenos threatens to harm Helen, the hereditary *xenê* who was entrusted to his father by Zeus (see below, section 4). Violation of *xenia* is an important, though not central, issue in other plays. For example, in Aiskhylos's *Libation Bearers* and in Sophokles' *Elektra*, Orestes kills his mother after being received as a *xenos*, and in Euripides' *Elektra* he kills Aigisthos while he is a guest at the latter's feast.[46]

C. In four plays, the central *pathos* that is averted is harm within a suppliancy relationship: Aiskhylos's *Suppliants*, Sophokles' *Oedipus at Kolonos*, and Euripides' *Children of Herakles* and *Suppliants*.[47] Supplication is also a minor event in most of the other extant tragedies.[48]

III. This leaves only six of the extant plays that do not at first appear to have a plot centering on harm to blood kin, *xenos*, spouse, or suppliant: Aiskhylos's *Persians*; Sophokles' *Aias*; and Euripides' *Alkestis, Trojan Women, Andromakhe,* and the *Rhesos,* attributed to Euripides. Violation of *philia* nevertheless plays an important role even in a number of these plays. Xerxes' defeat in *Persians* is dramatized as an act by which he has harmed his own *philoi*, the Persians; Aias kills himself, his own closest *philos*, and in *Andromakhe,* Neoptolemos injures his *philoi* by bringing a concubine into his house.[49]

According to my interpretation of the plays, then, the central *pathos* occurs among *philoi* in twenty-six of the thirty-two extant tragedies. Only six plays may be classified as exceptional. The table at the beginning of appendix A summarizes the central *pathê* in the tragedies according to the categories of relationships listed above. Harm to blood kin occurs, or is threatened, in seventeen, or 53 percent, of the thirty-two extant tragedies, and harm to people in formal reciprocal relationships occurs in nine plays. This brings the total of plays in which harm to *philoi* occurs to twenty-six, or 81 percent of the total.

Although the evidence for the tragedies that have not survived in complete form is scanty and difficult to evaluate, it points in the same direction as the more complete record for the extant plays. Tables in asppendix B, section 6, and appendix C, section 4, provide summaries. In the fragments of Aiskhylos, Sophokles, and Euripides, harm to blood kin occurs in sixty-nine, or 49 percent, of the 141 plays in which the kind of *pathos* can be determined with some likelihood. Harm to spouses, *xenoi*, or suppliants occurs in an additional thirty-seven plays, raising the total to 106, or 76 percent of the total. The evidence for the fragments of the minor tragedians suggests a similar pattern. Harm to blood kin is likely to have occurred in seventy-four plays, or 53 percent of the 139 plays in which the kind of *pathos* can be determined with some likelihood. Harm within reciprocal relationships occurs in an additional twenty-nine plays, bringing the total to 103, or 74 percent of the total.

4. *Xenia* and Suppliancy in Tragedy

A closer look at some plays in which *pathê* occur among *xenoi* and suppliants will help to justify their inclusion within the same category as tragedies in which harm to blood kin occurs. In tragedy, to a much greater extent than in epic, harm to suppliants and *xenoi* is represented as similar to harm to blood kin. Tragic *hiketai* typically supplicate people who are in fact kin, however distant, and they typically flee violence threatened by their own kin. Unlike epic, tragedy also portrays offenses against *xenoi* as betrayals of an existing *philia* relationship, represented as similar to kinship. Moreover, the tragic supplication plot as a whole resembles the tragic plot pattern of harm among kin averted by recognition.

Although *hiketai* are complete strangers in epic, in all but one of the four suppliant tragedies, suppliants are related by blood to those whom they supplicate, and they cite this relationship as a basis for their claim to protection. The Danaïds in Aiskhylos's *Suppliants* claim protection from Pelasgos on the basis of kinship, stressing their Argive origin in supplicating the king of Argos (for instance, 274–75). They also claim protection from Zeus Hikesios on the basis of their kinship with him as descendants of his son Epaphos (531–37; cf. "Zeus Forefather" [γεννήτωρ]: 206). In Euripides' *Suppliants*, the Argive women supplicate Theseus on the basis of kinship, since they, like him, belong to the race of Pelasgos (263–64). In addition, Theseus's own mother, Aithra, joins the women as suppliant (32–33, 93), and it is to her personal appeal as their representative that Theseus responds (359–64). In Euripides' *Children of Herakles*, the children supplicate their kin Demophon (207–13, 224, 240). Only in Sophokles' *Oedipus at Kolonos* are the primary suppliant and supplicated (Oidipous and Theseus) not related by blood. Even in this case, however, Theseus's sympathy for Oidipous is increased by the fact that the two men have had a common life as *xenoi* (562–68), and it is noteworthy that Antigone supplicates the Chorus (ἱκετεύομεν: 241), asking them to pity her as if she were kin (245–46). This play also has a minor supplication between kin: Polyneikes supplicates his father Oidipous.

Suppliant-exiles in epic only rarely flee relatives who attempt to harm them. However, this pattern occurs in three of the four suppliant plays. The Danaïds flee harm from their cousins in Aiskhylos's *Suppliants*, and in Euripides' *Children of Herakles*, the children are pursued by Eurystheus, a cousin of their mother, Alkmene. In Sophokles' *Oedipus at Kolonos*, Oidipous is pursued by his uncle, Kreon. Moreover, unlike the typical suppliant-exile of epic, Oidipous has fled his own country because he harmed his closest relatives. In Euripides' *Suppliants*, Adrastos and the Argive women do not flee harm from their own kin; however, their alliance and kinship by marriage with Polyneikes, Adrastos, and the other Argives give them a familial concern in his fratricidal death and in the harm done to him by his kin Kreon, who forbids his burial. All, as the Chorus state, have shared in the fate of Oidipous (1078).

The tragic suppliant plot in all of these plays is similar to the plot pattern of the *Iphigenia in Tauris*, in which harm to kin is averted by recognition. Tragedy, unlike epic, dramatizes the danger of pollution to the person supplicated as well as the danger of physical harm to the suppliant. Those supplicated experience *aidôs* for the suppliant and fear of Zeus Hikesios so strongly that they are willing to risk war in order to protect a suppliant. Their very hesitation is an acknowledgment of the strength of the suppliants' claims and an implicit recognition that the suppliant is already in some respects like a *philos*. To fail to protect a suppliant, we are made to feel, is like harming a *philos*, and to hesitate fully to acknowledge a suppliant is like being about to harm a *philos* who is not yet fully recognized as such. When a suppliant is at last accepted, this act is dramatically and emotionally similar to the recognition of *philia* that averts harm in plays like the *Iphigenia*.[50] These similarities are, in most cases, heightened by the fact that there is actual blood kinship of a distant kind between suppliant and supplicated.

Aiskhylos's *Suppliants* provides the clearest example of this pattern, as will be seen in detail below in chapter 3. In this play, the dramatic focus is on the relationship between suppliant and supplicated, instead of that between suppliant and pursuer. The altar at which the women supplicate is the center of attention throughout the play, and the action moves from the Danaïds' bad fortune as suppliant-exiles to their good fortune as successful suppliants and accepted residents of Argos. The main threat in the dramatic action represented on stage is that Pelasgos (and Zeus Hikesios) will reject their supplication and hand them over to their enemies. This is the central *pathos*. The danger is twofold: Pelasgos would harm the Danaïds by allowing them to fall prey to their cousins, and they in turn would harm him by arousing the wrath of Zeus and creating pollution.

The act of supplication gives the Danaïds strong claims, recognized by Pelasgos, to be treated as *philai*, and their distant blood kinship with him strengthens these claims. Pelasgos's initial hesitation is a failure fully to acknowledge and recognize these claims by acting as a *philos* and according them protection. In pressing their claims, the Danaïds give proof of their kinship by relating the story of their Argive ancestor, Io (291–324), in a recognition scene very similar to that in the *Iphigenia in Tauris*, in which Orestes gives his sister proof of his identity by recounting family history (806–26).[51] Kinship figures prominently in the final decision of Pelasgos and the Argives, because it helps to create the possibility of the "double pollution" against which Pelasgos warns the Argives (618–19). While Pelasgos's recognition that a relationship of blood kinship exists (325–26) does not, as in the *IT*, lead immediately to full acknowledgment and acceptance of the Danaïds as *philai* who must be protected, it helps to assimilate the threat of harm to suppliants to threat of harm to close blood kin. Aiskhylos also uses explicit threats of suicide made by the Danaïds to increase and dramatize the serious consequences of a rejection. The Danaïds first threaten to go to the underworld to bring charges against Zeus himself, their divine host and kin (154–74). Next, by threatening to hang themselves from the city's altars, the Danaïds threaten Pelasgos with pollution for the entire city that will call down the wrath of Zeus Hikesios (473–79, 615–20). When Pelasgos finally yields to their threat (478–79), he fully acknowledges *philia* (that is, a recognition leading to a state of *philia* occurs) by acting as *philos* and giving them protection. Danaos explicitly appeals to Pelasgos's recent acknowledgment of himself and his daughters as *philoi* in the speech in which he requests an escort to protect him from possible harm by the citizens: "For before now someone has killed a *philos* because of ignorance" (καὶ δὴ φίλον τις ἔκταν᾽ ἀγνοίας ὕπο: 499). In *Suppliants*, as in the *Iphigenia*, harming a *philos* in ignorance is averted by recognition and acknowledgment of *philia*.

In the three tragedies that focus on *xenia*, harm to *xenoi* is represented as the violation of an existing reciprocal relationship. In tragedy, in contrast to epic, a reciprocal relationship is first established, and then betrayal either occurs or is averted by recognition and acknowledgment of *philia*.

In Sophokles' *Philoktetes*, the *xenia* relationship plays an essential role in the interactions of Neoptolemos and Philoktetes, as I argue in detail in chapter 4. In acquiring Philoktetes' bow, Neoptolemos completes with the older man many of the acts that initiate *xenia*. If Neoptolemos fails to return the bow, as he at first threatens to do, he will in effect injure a *xenos* and declare hostilities with him by refusing to reciprocate in the exchange. When Neoptolemos at last keeps his promise to Philoktetes, he recognizes and acknowledges the older man as a *philos* by acting as a *xenos*. The assimilation of *xenia* to blood kinship in this plot is evidenced by Sophokles' representation of the relationship between the two men as similar to that between father and son. Philoktetes' friendly feelings toward Neoptolemos are in large part due to his previous friendship with Akhilleus. Although we are not told in this play that Akhilleus and Philoktetes were *xenoi*, this is certainly possible, especially since Philoktetes acts like a *xenos* in treating Akhilleus's son as his own child. He calls the young man "the son of the dearest father" (242) and addresses him as though he were his own son.[52] This assimilation of *xenia* to kinship helps to make Neoptolemos's acknowledgment of Philoktetes as a *xenos* dramatically and emotionally similar to a recognition between blood kin that averts a *pathos*.

Euripides' *Hekabe* represents betrayals of *xenia* that actually take place. Hekabe suffers as a slave after the Trojan War, which was caused by Paris (629–56, 943–51), who violated his *xenia* relationship with Menelaos. When she discovers Polydoros's corpse and realizes that her *xenos* Polymestor has killed her son (681–720), a recognition thereby occurs that a *philos* has acted as an enemy (recognition leading to a state of enmity). Hekabe persuades Agamemnon to allow her to punish Polymestor, "the most impious of *xenoi*" who did "the most impious deed" (790–92). She takes an appropriately reciprocal revenge on Polymestor by pretending to receive him as a *xenos*. She lures him to her tent and appears to treat him as a friend (ὡς δὴ παρὰ φίλῳ: 1152). Instead of wine, however, Hekabe offers Polymestor blood, killing his sons and blinding him.

In Euripides' *Helen*, the relationships among Zeus, Proteus, and Helen are much the same as those among Priam, Polymestor, and Polydoros in the *Hekabe*.[53] Zeus gave Helen to Proteus, king of Egypt, to keep her safe for her husband while he was away at Troy fighting to regain the phantom Helen (44–48, 909–11, 964). This *xenia* relationship between Helen and Proteus has been inherited by Proteus's son Theoklymenos, who, however, attempts to violate it by forcing Helen to marry him.

This brief survey has introduced evidence that tragedy, in contrast to epic, is characterized by its focus on harm among *philoi*. Kin murders and violations of formal reciprocal relationships are notably either absent from epic or, if mentioned, are little emphasized. On the other hand, violation of *philia* is an important element in most of the extant tragedies. To judge from them, violation of *philia* occurs not only in those tragedies Aristotle calls "best"; rather, it can also can be said to be a defining characteristic of tragedy as a whole. More detailed support for this view will be given in later chapters.

Appendix to Chapter 1: David Konstan on *Philos* and *Philia*

I have followed common practice in translating the word *philia* as "kinship" or "friendship" and the word *philos* as "kin" or "friend." However, since the traditional interpretation of these terms has recently been challenged by David Konstan, this practice requires some justification.[54] Konstan argues that the Greek term *philos* "designates a party to a voluntary bond of affection and good will, and normally excludes both close kin and more distant acquaintances" (1997, 53). He holds that in the classical period and later, the noun *philos* (usually with the article) has a restricted sense, referring to a friend who is not a relative, while the abstract noun *philia* and the adjective *philos* (without the article) have a wider range and can also be used to refer to kin.[55] Konstan also disagrees with the view of most scholars that *philia* refers to objective obligations, arguing instead that it "refers to friendly actions or treatment, whether of friends who behave attentively or of kin whose feelings and conduct are appropriately warm and loyal" (1996, 89).

Konstan has done a great service in reopening the question of the meaning of these important terms, in calling attention to their wide range and frequent ambiguity, in demonstrating that *philos* often means "friend" or "dear," and in showing that *philia* often refers to "affectionate sentiments" and not merely to "objective obligations"(1996, 71). He has also amassed a wealth of evidence that will be of great use to future scholars, and he has presented it with admirable fairness, taking into account exceptions and cases that are problematic for his interpretation.[56] Nevertheless, his arguments are not entirely convincing.[57] In the first place, although *philia* can indeed refer to affectionate sentiments, Konstan's account does not give sufficient emphasis to the objective obligations that *philia* relationships entail. In ancient Greece, more than in most modern societies, people in close relationships have ethical and legal obligations to help one another, although they may also be motivated by affection to fulfill these obligations. Moreover, Konstan's thesis that the term *philos* "normally excludes . . . close kin" either fails to take important passages into account or requires some very strained interpretations.

One important passage not discussed by Konstan is *Poetics* 14. Here, as noted in section 1, Aristotle begins by dividing human relationships into three exhaustive categories: *philoi*, enemies, and neutrals (1453b15–16). He then states that in the best plots terrible deeds take place within *philia* relationships, citing relationships within the nuclear family. Aristotle goes on to give examples of plays in which blood kin harm or are about to harm blood kin. For example, Sophokles' Oidipous does the terrible deeds and only later happens "to recognize *philia*" (1453b29–31), that is, he recognizes that he has killed his father and married his mother. In *Poetics* 14, then, the noun *philos* surely has the same range as *philia*, and both refer primarily, if not exclusively, to relationships among close blood kin. Aristotle also uses *philos* (with the article) in the sense of "kin" at NE 8.12.1162a31–32: "[Justice] does not appear to be the same for a *philos* to a *philos* [τῷ φίλῳ πρὸς τὸν φίλον], and to an outsider, and to a companion, and to a schoolmate." Here, the contrast between *philos* and companion (*hetairos*) clearly indicates that the word must mean "kin."[58]

In a number of passages in tragedy also, it is very difficult not to give *philos* (with or without the article) the sense of "kin."[59] For example, in Aiskhylos's *Seven Against Thebes* 971, the fratricide is lamented: "You perished at the hands of a *philos*, and you killed a *philos*" (πρὸς φίλου ἔφθισο. καὶ φίλον ἔκτανες).[60] When the Erinyes say that they punish the murderer of the *philos* within the house (Ais. *Eum.* 354–59), the word must refer to blood kin,[61] especially since they later explain their failure to punish Klytaimestra by saying that she was not guilty of killing someone related by blood (604–5). In Euripides' *Elektra* 1230, Elektra says of the mother she and her brother have just killed, "*Phila* and not *phila*" (φίλα τε κοὐ φίλα). Konstan's interpretation—"Though dear as a mother, Clytemnestra is an enemy"— is hardly the most natural; since the play has continually emphasized Elektra's hatred, the only way in which Klytaimestra is *phila* to her is by virtue of kinship.[62] A frequently cited example of *philos* in the sense of "kin" is Euripides' *Phoenician Women* 1446, where the dying Polyneikes says of his dead brother, "*Philos*, he became an enemy, but was still *philos*" (φίλος γὰρ ἐχθρὸς ἐγένετ', ἀλλ' ὅμως φίλος).[63] Konstan also denies that *philos* can mean "kin" in Sophokles' *Antigone* (1996, 89–91). However, his claim (1996, 91) that "the issue of his [sc. Kreon's] relationship to Polyneices is never raised" in this play misses an important irony. Just before Kreon redefines *philos* to exclude kin, and proclaims his decree against burying Polyneikes, he states that he holds the rule in Thebes because he is next of kin to Oidipous's dead sons (ἐγὼ κράτη δὴ πάντα καὶ θρόνους ἔχω / γένους κατ' ἀγχιστεῖα τῶν ὀλωλότων: 173–74). Kreon's power to deny Polyneikes the obligations due to kin depends, ironically, on his kinship relationship with the young man. Moreover, Kreon's emphasis on this relationship at the beginning of his speech ensures that the audience will be aware of the sense of "kin" that Kreon excludes when he subsequently speaks of counting people as *philoi* or of making *philoi* (182–90). For all of these reasons I continue to translate *philos* as "kin" or "friend" and *philia* as "kinship" or "friendship."

Averting Fratricide: Euripides' *Iphigenia in Tauris*

In the background of the play's action but kept always in the foreground of attention is the sacrifice at Aulis. Iphigeneia is thought to have been sacrificed by her father Agamemnon at Aulis, at the command of Artemis. She was, however, secretly rescued by Artemis and brought to the Taurian land, where she was made the priestess of rites in which *xenoi* are sacrificed to the goddess. When the play opens, Iphigeneia, having just had a dream which she interprets to mean that Orestes is dead, mourns for her brother. Orestes, however, is still alive and has just arrived in the Taurian land with his cousin and brother-in-law Pylades. After killing his mother, Klytaimestra, in obedience to Apollo's oracle, Orestes received a second oracle from the god, telling him that he would find release from his mother's Erinyes by taking Artemis's statue from the Taurian land to Athens. When Orestes has an attack of madness caused by Klytaimestra's Erinyes, he and Pylades are captured by the Taurians and brought for sacrifice to Iphigeneia.

The priestess learns that the young men are from Argos and agrees to help one of them escape if he will take a letter to her friends in that land. While she goes to get the letter, each of the young men offers his life for the other. They finally agree that Orestes will die while Pylades will carry on the family name as husband of Orestes' sister Elektra. When the priestess returns to give Pylades the letter, she reveals that she is Iphigeneia. Orestes joyfully recognizes and embraces his sister, and, after he correctly answers questions about their family, Iphigeneia also recognizes her brother and rejoices with him.

The siblings then plan their escape. Iphigeneia tells Thoas, king of the Taurians, that the young men are matricides, who must be purified in the sea along with Artemis's statue, which their presence has polluted. Pretending to conduct secret purification rites, the three put to sea in Orestes' ship, taking the statue with them. They almost escape, but a wave pushes the ship back to shore, and Thoas orders pursuit. All is not lost, however, for Athena appears *ex machina* to assure a happy ending. She calms the sea, tells Thoas to call off the pursuit, prophesies a safe return to Greece, and establishes rites in honor of Orestes at Halai and in honor of Iphigeneia at Brauron.

As is apparent from this summary, the play is centrally concerned with the avoidance of bloodshed. In the central *pathos*, Iphigeneia, who has almost been sacrificed by her father, Agamemnon, is about to sacrifice Orestes, in ignorance that he is her brother. Recognition prevents fratricide and allows the rescue and purification of Orestes, who has killed his mother and is pursued by her Erinyes. This averting of bloodshed in the central event of the plot is also reflected in many more minor incidents. Iphigeneia not only rescues her brother, she also forgives the father who tried to murder her, and she refuses to attack Thoas, the Taurian *xenos* who holds her captive. For his part, Orestes redeems his house from its bloody past by refusing to save his own life at the expense of those of his sister, Iphigeneia, and cousin, Pylades, and by avoiding bloody conflict with the Taurians. The gods are also involved in averting bloodshed. Artemis, who was implicated in the human sacrifices at Aulis and in the Taurian land, comes to preside instead over rites in which sacrifice is avoided. Similarly, Artemis's brother Apollo, who ordered Orestes' matricide, later orders Orestes to go to the Taurian land, where a bloodless rescue takes place.

The averting of fratricide ends a series of *pathê* among five generations of kin in the house of Tantalos and restores good fortune to individuals and house alike. In this plot, Iphigeneia and Orestes end the chain of terrible events in the house of Tantalos by actively turning away from bloodshed and by accepting the obligations of *philia*, acting as *philoi* not only to each other but to others as well. In addition, both humans and gods make use of previous evils in order to bring about good. Orestes' matricide leads to his going to the Taurian land at Apollo's command, and his pollution is used by Iphigeneia to contrive the rescue. Similarly, Iphigeneia's misfortunes, as victim and perpetrator of human sacrifice to Artemis, become the means of rescue from bloodshed for both woman and goddess. In the *Iphigenia*, good does not simply triumph over evil, as the Chorus of Aiskhylos's *Agamemnon* pray (αἴλινον αἴλινον εἰπέ, τὸ δ᾽ εὖ νικάτω: "Say woe, woe, but may the good win": 121 = 139 = 159); good fortune actually arises out of the events that contributed to previous bad fortune. As Pylades says, "It is possible for great bad fortune to give rise to great changes" (721–22).

1. The House of Tantalos

In the prehistory of the *Iphigenia* are five generations tainted by violence against *philoi*. "Pelops" is the first word of this play, which begins with a genealogy of the unhappy house of Agamemnon: Tantalos's son Pelops begot Atreus, who was the father of Menelaos and of Agamemnon, Iphigeneia's father (1–5). In each succeeding generation of the house of Tantalos, the penalty for previous crimes had to be paid (197–201).[1]

Tantalos began the chain of evils, for he, according to legend, gave a feast to the gods at which he served them the flesh of his own son, Pelops. This story is mentioned only once in the play, in a passage in which Iphigeneia states that she does not believe such tales:

> ἐγὼ μὲν οὖν
> τὰ Ταντάλου θεοῖσιν ἐστιάματα
> ἄπιστα κρίνω, παιδὸς ἡσθῆναι βορᾷ,
> τοὺς δ' ἐνθάδ', αὐτοὺς ὄντας ἀνθρωποκτόνους,
> ἐς τὸν θεὸν τὸ φαῦλον ἀναφέρειν δοκῶ·
> οὐδένα γὰρ οἶμαι δαιμόνων εἶναι κακόν. (386–91)[2]

> Indeed, I judge the feast given to the gods by Tantalos to be unbelievable,
> that they took pleasure in food consisting of his son.
> It seems to me that people here on earth, themselves being murderers,
> blame the foul deed on the god,
> for I think that no divinity is evil.

What Iphigeneia questions is not the story of Tantalos in its entirety, but only the role of the gods in this legend of child-murder and cannibalism.[3] In her speech just before the Tantalos story, Iphigeneia states unequivocally that Agamemnon sacrificed his daughter (360). Earlier, she had also stated on her own authority that her father sacrificed her (6–8, with 27), but she attributed to Kalkhas the idea that this was demanded by Artemis (16–24). Her speech at 380–86 also indicates that humans are responsible for the bloody rites in the Taurian land, but that they slander Artemis in holding that the goddess takes pleasure in human slaughter. In the passage quoted above (386–91), then, Iphigeneia's point is that just as humans blame Artemis for the murders they commit in the Taurian land, so Tantalos was guilty of doing evil to his son while blaming the gods for his own acts. Within this context, "those here" (τοὺς δ' ἐνθάδ': 389) does not refer exclusively to the Taurians, but also to other humans here on earth, who blame "the god" for their own evil deeds.[4]

In the second generation, Tantalos's son Pelops killed a *xenos*, Oinomaos, with a spear in order to marry his daughter, Hippodameia (παρθένον Πισάτιδα ἐκτήσαθ' Ἱπποδάμειαν, Οἰνόμαον κτάνων: 824–25).[5] Although in other versions of this story Pelops bribed Oinomaos's charioteer Myrtilos to damage his master's chariot and then killed Myrtilos, whose dying curse troubled succeeding generations, in the *Iphigenia* there is no reference to Myrtilos.[6] Some scholars believe that Euripides removes the evil aspects of Pelops's victory by eliminating the story of Myrtilos.[7] This view, however, ignores the fact, not noticed by scholars, that the curse is replaced by something worse. In Euripides' version, Pelops marries Hippodameia after killing her father with his own hand, thereby becoming *authentês*, killer of a relative, to his wife. Marriage with an *authentês* is one of the greatest of evils in Greek thought, and in Euripides it is sometimes linked to further disasters within the relationship. Klytaimestra's terrible marriage with Agamemnon began when he killed her husband and child (*IA* 1148–52), and Herakles, after killing his wife and children, traces the source of the evils in his own life to the marriage of his father, Amphitryon, to Alkmene after he had killed her father (*Her.*1258–62).[8]

In the third generation, the sons of Pelops, Atreus and Thyestes, quarrel over a golden ram, a story mentioned in two passages. At 193–202, unfortunately a very corrupt text, the golden ram is said to be a source of grief to the house, and an allusion is made to the story that the sun changed course as a result of the brothers' quarrel. Again, at 812–17, Iphigeneia and Orestes allude to the quarrel of Atreus and Thyestes over the golden ram and to the sun's change of course. Although our text of the *Iphigenia* does not mention the details of this story, they are given in other plays of Euripides. Thyestes stole the golden ram from his brother Atreus by seducing his wife, after which the sun changed course (*El.* 719–36). In revenge, Atreus killed Thyestes' children and served them to him as food (*Or.* 812–15).[9] Although the feast of Thyestes is not explicitly mentioned in the *Iphigenia*, the golden ram is said to bring about "murder upon murder" and to lead, in future generations of the descendants of Tantalos, to punishments coming "from the former dead" (φόνος ἐπὶ φόνῳ ἄχεα ἄχεσιν. ἔνθεν τῶν πρόσθεν δμαθέντων ἐκβαίνει ποινὰ Τανταλιδᾶν εἰς οἴκους: 197–201). These statements make the most sense when taken as allusions to the feast and to the subsequent violence in the house of Atreus.[10] Moreover, kin murders, such as those that take place in the house of Agamemnon, would be the most appropriate punishment for the kin murders committed by Atreus.

In the fourth generation, Agamemnon sacrifices his daughter Iphigeneia, a crime that is repeatedly emphasized in the play. Iphigeneia discusses the event at length in her opening speech (6–27), stating that her father slaughtered her (ἔσφαξεν: 8) and that she was killed with the sword (27). She again reflects on Aulis at 358–77, saying that the Greeks slaughtered her in a rite at which her father was priest (ἔσφαζον, ἱερεὺς δ᾽ ἦν ὁ γεννήσας πατήρ: 360). Even though she did not in fact die and Agamemnon only thought he was killing her (ὡς δοκεῖ: 8; cf. 176–77, 785), she holds her father to be her actual murderer: "My father killed me" (πατὴρ ἔκτεινέ με: 920). The divine rescue saved Iphigeneia, but not Agamemnon, who is guilty of murder even though his victim did not die.[11] Agamemnon's violence leads to more violence in the fourth generation. Although Euripides does not, like Aiskhylos, explicitly link Agamemnon's own murder by his wife Klytaimestra to the sacrifice of Iphigeneia, the association is suggested by line 553, "O cause of many tears, she who killed and he who killed,"[12] and by the use, in connection with Agamemnon's murder, of the word σφαγείς (552), which also referred to Iphigeneia's slaughter.

Finally, in the fifth generation, Orestes and Iphigeneia follow in the bloody steps of their ancestors. Orestes' matricide, a crime for which he is pursued by his victim's Erinyes (79–80, 285–91, 931), is frequently alluded to (e.g., at 79, 556, 924, 934, 957), and Iphigeneia sacrifices others just as her father sacrificed her. Moreover, like her ancestor Pelops, she is involved in the murder of *xenoi*. Iphigeneia has a "*xenos*-murdering craft" (τέχνην . . . ξενοκτόνον: 53), and she holds a "*xenos*-killing office" (ξενοφόνους τιμάς: 776), which she is eager to exercise, according to the Herdsman: "You prayed for the slaughter of *xenoi*" (336–37).[13] Her own words, expressing regret that Menelaos and Helen have not come to her as victims in retribution for Aulis (354–58), show that he is right. Even though Iphigeneia does not herself hold the sword (40, 621–22), in preparing people for sacrifice she is just as guilty of murder as if she actually struck the victims. If Orestes had been sacrificed, she says, he would have died an "unholy death, cut by my hands" (ὄλεθρον ἀνόσιον ἐξ ἐμᾶν δαϊχθεὶς χερῶν: 871–73). That is, she would have incurred the pollution of fratricide, just as Orestes has been polluted and maddened by matricide. By similar reasoning, Iphigeneia holds Agamemnon guilty of her own murder, even though she did not actually die.

All of these terrible events in the house of Tantalos have led to misfortunes so great that the house is as though dead, an idea dramatically represented by the apparent deaths of the two children of Agamemnon. Iphigeneia, herself thought to be dead by those in Argos (564) and believing, because of a dream, that her brother Orestes is dead, leads the Chorus in a dirge for the ancestral house (143–235).

The gods are implicated in the crimes committed in the house of Atreus. According to Kalkhas, Artemis demanded the sacrifice at Aulis (16–24), and, at least in the view of the Taurians, the goddess demands the human sacrifices over which Iphigeneia presides in their land. Iphigeneia herself states that Artemis saved her at Aulis only to establish her as priestess in the temple where the bloody rites take place (28–41).[14] Just as Artemis saved Iphigeneia at Aulis only to place her in another terrible situation, so Apollo saved Orestes from one danger only to put him in another. In obedience to the god's oracle, Orestes killed his mother (714–15), and as a result he was pursued by her Erinyes. Although Apollo then saved Orestes (μ' ἔσωσε: 965) by witnessing on his behalf at the trial in Athens, some of the Erinyes did not accept the verdict and continued to pursue the matricide. By threatening to starve himself in the god's precinct, Orestes compelled Apollo to save him once again (σώσει: 975) and obtained a second oracle, telling him that he would be freed from the Erinyes if he brought Artemis's statue from the Taurian land to Athens (961–78; cf. 77–94). When Orestes obeys the oracle, only to be captured and prepared for sacrifice, he complains that the god has led him back into the net (77–78) and lied to him (570–75, 711–15).

In these and other ways, the gods are characterized as bloodthirsty and vengeful. When Iphigeneia says that the gods are not responsible for evil (380–91), some scholars believe that she is telling the truth within the fictional world of the play.[15] Nevertheless, although Artemis is removed from her Taurian connection with human sacrifice at the end of play, there is every indication that both Apollo and Artemis not only approve of but even demand murder previous to the rescue. Apollo is shown to give true oracles at Delphi, just as the Chorus claim (1254–55), for Orestes is in fact saved after he obeys the second oracle telling him to go to the Taurian land. However, the same god who gave the second oracle, the one that leads to Orestes' salvation, also gave the first oracle telling Orestes to kill his mother. The bloodthirsty nature of this god and his oracle is also shown by the fact that Apollo took over the oracle at Delphi from Themis after killing Pytho (1245–52), thereby angering Gaia, mother of Themis and Pytho, and causing her to withhold her prophecies (1267–69) from the oracle.[16] Apollo won back his privileges only after Zeus sided with him (1270–82), thus giving implicit sanction to the murder of Pytho. Artemis might be expected to share Apollo's bloody nature, for she is his sister (86), and she loves the brother (1401) who does not give oracles that displease his sister (1012–15). Although Iphigeneia expresses doubts about Artemis's role in the sacrifices in the Taurian land, she does not question the belief that the goddess placed her in the Taurian temple (ναοῖσι δ' ἐν τοῖσδ' ἱερέαν τίθησί με: 34) where these rites take place, making it clear that she believes Artemis to be implicated, whether directly or indirectly, in the murder of *xenoi* in the Taurian land. The bloodthirsty nature of the goddess is even apparent in her "reformed" rites at Halai, in which human blood is still shed as a way of giving honor to the goddess (1458–61). Although the text leaves the question open, it would be in character for such a goddess to demand the sacrifice at Aulis, as Kalkhas claims she does.

Both gods and humans, then, are involved in a long history of bloodshed. Five generations of the house of Tantalos have been guilty of violence against kin and *xenoi*. Moreover, the role of Apollo in Orestes' matricide, and that of Artemis in bringing Iphigeneia to the Taurian temple and, perhaps, in demanding her sacrifice at Aulis, implicate the gods in these crimes. At the beginning of the play, this bloody history has culminated in the apparent destruction of the house of Tantalos. Agamemnon and Klytaimestra are dead, murdered by their own kin; Orestes and the other Argives believe that Iphigeneia has been killed by her father (563–64); Iphigeneia believes that her brother is dead and that her ancestral house has perished with this last male heir. The apparent destruction of the house is reflected in the destruction of friendly feelings in Iphigeneia. Her belief that Orestes is dead has made her savage and pitiless to the Greeks, those of her own tribe (θοὑμόφυλον), for whom she used to weep (344–50). She regrets not having been able to take vengeance on Helen and Menelaos (354–58), who are, after all, her aunt and uncle, and she recounts in detail her own slaughter by the Greeks and her father, dwelling resentfully on her useless supplication, and on the fact that Agamemnon brought her by a trick to a "bloody wedding" (359–71). Her statement that humans are murderers (ἀνθρωποκτόνους: 389) is applicable to herself as priestess of Artemis, to Agamemnon as priest at Iphigeneia's sacrifice, and to Tantalos, who committed crimes against his son.[17] The apparent destruction of her family has made Iphigeneia, like her forebears, "hardhearted" (δύσνουν: 350) instead of "mild" and "pitiful" (γαληνός, φιλοικτίρμων: 345).

2. Pylades as Savior and Kin

One of the descendants of Tantalos who is, exceptionally, untainted by the family history of bloodshed is Pylades, the son of Anaxibia, sister of Agamemnon.[18] Although he is kin to Orestes and Iphigeneia, Pylades was born after the terrible time of Iphigeneia's sacrifice (920), and although he shared Orestes' upbringing, he did not participate in the matricide. Pylades, being fortunate and pure, is exempt from the madness that afflicts Orestes, while Orestes himself is polluted and unfortunate (693–94). This youngest member of the house of Atreus, unpolluted by bloodshed and a model of *philia*, is the savior of Orestes and of the house of his grandfather. A figure of pure devotion, he mediates between past violence against *philoi* and future renunciation of violence.

Although he is important in his own right, Pylades' dramatic function is primarily that of *philos* of Orestes.[19] The relationship between the two young men exemplifies three kinds of ideal *philia*. In their roles as companions, brothers-in-law and, finally, blood kin, Pylades and Orestes provide a model of positive reciprocity that counteracts the negative reciprocities exemplified by previous generations of the house of Pelops and by Orestes and Iphigeneia themselves. The Pylades-Orestes relationship shows that *philoi* can benefit instead of harming one another and that ideal kinship *philia* can include both ideal companionship and ideal kinship by marriage.

Orestes and Pylades first appear as unrelated companions. When the two are attacked by the Taurians and Orestes has a fit of madness, Pylades risks his life to care for his sick friend, "doing good to a friend by tending him" (φίλον δὲ θεραπείαισιν ἄνδρ' εὐεργετῶν: 314). When Iphigeneia asks, "Are you brothers from one mother?" Orestes replies, "[Yes], in love [φιλότητί γ'], but we are not brothers" (497–98). Orestes speaks eloquently of this friendship when he says that it is most shameful to be saved at a friend's expense, and that Pylades is his friend, whose life is as precious to Orestes as his own (605–8). Pylades has proved his friendship in deeds by traveling with Orestes to share his troubles (600), and Orestes in turn shows his devotion by offering to die in his friend's place (605). In reply to this speech, Iphigeneia remarks that Orestes is τοῖς φίλοις τ' ὀρθῶς φίλος (610), an ambiguous phrase that means both "a true friend to your friends" and "truly dear to your friends."[20]

When the two men are left alone after Iphigeneia has gone to get the letter she wants them to take to Argos (657–722), Orestes and Pylades are represented as ideal kin by marriage. Pylades, who now reveals for the first time that he is married to Orestes' sister Elektra, fears that he will be accused of murdering his brother-in-law in order to become the husband of an heiress (680–82).[21] He says that he wants to die with Orestes, since he is his friend (φίλον γεγῶτα) and fears blame if he survives alone (686). Orestes rejects this offer, telling Pylades that he must become heir to the house of Agamemnon after Orestes' death. As husband of Elektra, Pylades is to "live as heir" in Agamemnon's house,[22] beget children who will preserve this house and name, and give Orestes funeral rites (695–705).

Orestes' speech assumes customs like the Athenian laws concerning the *epikleros* (heiress). If a man died without male heirs, his daughter became an heiress and was required to marry her nearest male kin, who became the man's adoptive son posthumously.[23] The adoptive son severed all legal ties with his natural father[24] to take on instead the rights and duties connected with maintaining and perpetuating the house of his adoptive father. He inherited property and begot heirs, and he was responsible for burying the family dead and tending to the family tombs.[25] A sister who survived her brother was probably regarded as the heiress of her father, not of her brother.[26] Orestes' speech indicates that Elektra will be *epikleros* of her father, Agamemnon, after Orestes' death; that Pylades, as her husband and nearest male kin, will become heir to this house; and that their children will belong to the house of Agamemnon. Thus, Pylades' connection by marriage (κήδη: 707) to Orestes is very close indeed, for in taking Orestes' place as heir, Pylades becomes, in social and legal fact, another Orestes.[27] The closeness of this social relationship of *philia* by marriage is paralleled by the emotional closeness of the young men as companions. After his testamentary acknowledgment of Pylades as heir, Orestes calls him "dearest [φίλτατον] of friends," recalling how Pylades was brought up with him, hunted with him, and shared his trials (708–10). This close companionship was actually the cause of the relationship by marriage, for Orestes betrothed his sister to his friend (696). In turn, Pylades, after agreeing to his adoption as Agamemnon's heir, tells Orestes, "You will be more my friend dead than living" (718). This is literally true, for after Orestes' death, Pylades will become Orestes, taking his friend's place in Agamemnon's house. Together with Elektra, who, like her husband, has not participated in the matricide in this play, Pylades will renew the house.

In his roles as companion and relation by marriage, Pylades mediates between Orestes and Iphigeneia, helping to bring about their recognition (see below, section 3). It is only after this recognition that Pylades appears in the play in his third role, that of blood kin. Orestes in turn mediates between Iphigeneia and Pylades as he identifies Pylades as their cousin, the son of Strophios and of the daughter of Atreus (916–19). Now at last all three kinds of *philia* are united in one person. Pylades is greeted by Iphigeneia as the husband of her sister (922); Orestes refers to him as "my cousin, my only sure *philos*" (σαφὴς φίλος: 919) and as "my savior [σωτήρ], not only my kin [συγγενής]" (923). The blood relationship between Orestes and Pylades acquires positive connotations through its association with the two other kinds of *philia* relationships shared by the men and through its close connection with the positive reciprocity of the siblings.

In proceeding from companionship to kinship in his portrayal of the relationship between Orestes and Pylades, Euripides, like Aristotle, inverts Homer's statement that a companion is not inferior to a brother (*Od.*

8.585–86) by likening the *philia* of brothers to that of companions. Aristotle states in *Nicomachean Ethics* 8.12 that brothers, like companions, are of the same age, and that the upbringing they share makes them as intimate as companions. In addition, brothers, cousins, and other blood kin have a greater identity (ταυτότης) with one another the more closely they are related (*NE* 1161b30–1162a4). Euripides' Orestes and Pylades have shared the same upbringing, the same pursuits, and the same ills (709–10), like the brothers Aristotle compares to companions. Ute Schmidt-Berger correctly notes that the Orestes-Pylades relationship in the *Iphigenia* is the earliest example of a vivid representation of the Aristotelian idea that brotherly *philia* and companionship *philia* are closely related.[28] However, this is not because the play portrays companionship as more important than relationship by marriage, which in turn is more important than blood kinship.[29] Instead, the dramatic movement of the play from the companionship of Orestes and Pylades to their kinship helps to portray this companionship as a model for kinship *philia* that is especially appropriate for the descendants of Atreus, whose troubled kinship relationships have deprived them of such an example. The ideal companionship between Orestes and Pylades leads to their relationship by marriage and mediates between Orestes and his sister, helping each to recognize the other's identity as *philos* and to act not only as kin but also as saviors (923). When Orestes and Iphigeneia offer to give their lives for one another (1002–11), they follow the example of Orestes and Pylades.

3. Recognition

Pylades, as savior of Orestes and of the house of Tantalos, and as ideal *philos*, helps to bring about the mutual recognition of Iphigeneia and Orestes that leads to the rescue of all three individuals and of the house they share. These recognitions of identity are so moving in this play—ἐκπληκτικόν, to use Aristotle's word (*Po.* 14.1454a4), because they are part of a process of renewal of *philia* between brother and sister, brought about by the very evils that caused their previous separation and other misfortunes. Iphigeneia's sacrifice by her father, at the command of Artemis, results in her being settled by the goddess in the Taurian land as priestess of Artemis, an office that leads to her meeting with Orestes, to the recognition, and to the mutual rescue of brother and sister. In turn, Orestes' matricide, in obedience to Apollo's oracle, results in his pursuit by the Erinyes, in his appeal to Apollo to save him, in the god's second oracle that sends him to the Taurian land, in the attack of madness that leads to his capture, and in his meeting with Iphigeneia during which the recognition takes place. The escape of brother and sister is then brought about by a ruse that makes use of Orestes' pollution by matricide (1031, 1034). Good results from evil in this way because at last both Iphigeneia and Orestes, as Pylades has always done, fully accept the positive obligations of *philia* and reject the crimes that have tainted their family for generations.[30]

At the time of Orestes' capture, Iphigeneia is savage and pitiless toward her victims, having willingly accepted, like her father, a priesthood as sacrificer of humans (342–91). However, a change is apparent as soon as she sees Orestes and Pylades, whom she addresses not with the harshness her previous desire for vengeance has led the audience to expect, but as "*xenoi* in distress" (ταλαίπωροι ξένοι: 479). Her statements indicate that this change occurs because the young men remind her of fraternal love in general and of her own brother in particular.[31] Orestes has been in her thoughts since the dream of his death recounted at the beginning of the play, and the impending sacrifice of the young men has just reminded her of her own sacrifice at Aulis (342–71) and of her failure to embrace her baby brother on that occasion (372–79). Iphigeneia's first questions reveal her continuing preoccupation with her own brother, for she departs from the formulaic inquiries about paternity and country to ask, "Who is your sister?" and to remark that this sister will soon be "brotherless" (473–75). Moved in part by the messenger's report of Pylades' brotherly care of Orestes during his madness (310–14), she goes on to ask whether Orestes and Pylades are brothers (497).

Iphigeneia also uses the same phrase to refer to Orestes' father, "the father who begot you" (499), that she had previously used, in the same metrical position, in mentioning her own father (360). Thus, Iphigeneia's own sufferings and the similar misfortunes of Orestes help to create the beginnings of sympathy in her.[32]

Iphigeneia's newly awakened sympathy soon finds a response in Orestes. At first he refuses to tell her what city he is from, saying that this can be of no profit (κέρδος) to him. He yields, however, when she asks him to give her the information as a *kharis* (505–8).[33] This first act of *kharis* changes their relationship from the hostile one of priestess and victim to that of people who have taken a first step toward *philia*. Iphigeneia's friendly feelings increase when Orestes reveals that he is from Mykenai, for she exclaims that he has come "longed for" (ποθεινός: 515) from Argos, and when she learns that they have the same enemy, having both been injured by Helen (521–26). Iphigeneia's questions finally lead Orestes to ask who she is and, on learning that she is a compatriot, to state that she rightly longs (ποθεῖς) to know about Greek affairs (540–42), thus echoing her word at 515.

Fraternal love for her absent brother causes Iphigeneia to sympathize with the Argive *xenos*, and this sympathy in turn leads to an awakening of her pity for the members of her family.[34] When she hears that Agamemnon is dead, she cries out in grief, "Wretched me!" (549). This leads Orestes to ask if this concerns her, using a word that often refers to the concern of kin for kin (προσῆκέ σοι: 550).[35] Again, on learning that Agamemnon has been slaughtered (σφαγείς: 552) by his wife, Iphigeneia exclaims, "O cause of many tears, she who killed and he who killed" (553),[36] words she echoes shortly after, in response to Orestes' report that Agamemnon's "slaughtered daughter" (σφαγείσης: 563) is considered dead: "Wretched is she and the father who killed her" (565). Iphigeneia's compassion, the dramatic importance of which is indicated by Orestes' later comment on her pity for Agamemnon and his family (ὡς ᾤκτιρ': 664), contrasts sharply with the horror she expressed, just before meeting Orestes, in recalling her own sacrifice, at which, she says, "the priest was the father who begot me" (360). Finally, Orestes tells Iphigeneia that her brother is alive, and she exclaims that her dream was false (567–69). Pity for her family has been followed immediately by hope that her troubled house (συνταραχθεὶς οἶκος: 557) has not, after all, completely perished, as she believed earlier (154–55). Her softened state of mind, by making it possible for her to gain this information, has actually produced a change in Iphigeneia's outward circumstances.

In contrast to the previous savagery caused by her dream of Orestes' death, Iphigeneia has now gone from pity for *xenoi* to a relationship involving *kharis* with one of them, to a sharing of common concerns, to pity for her family and the father who intended to kill her, to the realization that her dream of Orestes' death was false (569). The dream made her pitiless, but her pity, reawakened by the recollection of her previous sorrows and strengthened by her learning of further sorrows from a fellow townsman, has led to the discovery that the dream was false. Good has begun to come from evil.

The Chorus's two-line intervention and Iphigeneia's "Listen" (576–78) mark a new stage in the relationship between Iphigeneia and Orestes, one in which she begins to take positive action. In proposing to save Orestes if he will take a letter to Argos, she suggests a mutually benefiting gain: "a benefit [ὄνησιν] for you . . . and for me" (579–80). Orestes, who had previously been concerned only with profit (κέρδος: 506), now responds with an act of *kharis* to Pylades, refusing to save himself at his friend's expense (597–608). Orestes' act of generosity to an apparently unrelated companion becomes, for Iphigeneia, a model for ideal kinship *philia*. She exclaims, "You are a true friend to your friends" (610), and then at once thinks of her brother: "Oh how I hope that the one male survivor of my family is such as you are."[37] Moreover, she is now prepared to act as kin even to this unrelated *xenos*, offering *kharis* (631) for which there can be no return. When Orestes asks, "How might a sister's hand prepare me for burial?" (627), she promises to act as this sister in giving the young man funeral rites (630–35).

Iphigeneia's acting as kin to Orestes, prompted by his *kharis* to a companion, prepares the way for the recognitions of the identity of kin that immediately follow. Orestes' recognition of Iphigeneia results naturally from her request to Pylades to deliver a letter to Orestes from Iphigeneia: "Tell Orestes, the son of Agamemnon . . ." (769). This recognition dramatizes the interdependence of the three *philoi*, Iphigeneia, Orestes, and Pylades. When Iphigeneia asks Pylades to deliver the letter and he in turn asks for her oath that she will save him, both swear to keep their agreement on penalty of losing their return to Argos (735–52). Iphigeneia's letter not only asks Orestes to bring her to Argos, it also adds a threat, stating that if he does not do so she will be a curse to his house (778). These oaths and this curse bind the three together in a tight network of obligations and sanctions. Pylades' homecoming depends on his delivering Iphigeneia's letter to Orestes, while Iphigeneia's own rescue depends on her rescue of Pylades and on Orestes' granting her request. In turn, the salvation of Orestes and his house depends on his rescue of Iphigeneia, as requested in the letter delivered by Pylades. Each of the three can find personal *sôtêria* (salvation) only through providing *sôtêria* for the others. The recognition is brought about through the fulfillment of these obligations as Pylades mediates between brother and sister, keeping his oath to deliver Iphigeneia's letter, and as Orestes embraces his sister.

In contrast to Orestes' recognition of his sister, which follows straightfor-wardly from the incidents of the plot, Iphigeneia's recognition of her brother is more elaborate. This is not a defect in the play, as Aristotle thinks (*Po.* 16.1454b30–35), but serves an important dramatic function, linking the recog-nition to the bloody family history.[38] In response to Iphigeneia's skepticism about his identity, Orestes recounts the family genealogy: the daughter of Tyndaris bore him to the son (Agamemnon) of the son (Atreus) of Pelops (806–7). Since his sister still requires proof (τεκμήριον: 808), he mentions three pieces of tangible evidence that prove his knowledge of intimate family affairs: a picture woven by Iphigeneia representing the quarrel of Atreus and Thyestes, a lock of hair Iphigeneia gave to her mother as a memorial of her sacrifice by Agamemnon at Aulis, and the spear with which Pelops killed Oinomaos during his chariot race (811–26). Each of these three objects repre-sents a terrible event that took place in one of the generations mentioned in Orestes' compendious genealogy. Of the first two Orestes has heard from Elektra (811), but the spear he has seen for himself (822). Although the spear, like the other objects, is an entirely appropriate memorial of family history, its location, hidden in Iphigeneia's maiden chamber (826), is remarkable. Its presence in this incongruous place makes sense, however, in light of its his-tory and its status as family heirloom. It was in Agamemnon's house because Pelops gave it to his son Atreus, who gave it to his son Agamemnon, and it now rightly belongs to Agamemnon's son Orestes, who last saw it. Its presence in Iphigeneia's room has a dramatic function, serving to link Iphigeneia to the bloody inheritance of kin murder passed on to each generation of the house of Pelops. The spear is the tangible cause and memorial of the misfortunes that began with Pelops's killing of Oinomaos, a *xenos* and the father of his wife, that continued with Agamemnon, who killed and was killed by kin, and that have just ended in Iphigeneia's preparation of her brother for sacrifice and in her conditional curse on his house (778). Yet, it is also this spear that, by bring-ing about the recognition, finally ends the misfortunes that began with it.

The recognition ends the five-generation-long series of violent acts against kin, restoring brother and sister to a relationship of true kinship *philia*. Together, they lament the terrible deed that Agamemnon dared to commit in sacrificing Iphigeneia (τόλμαν ἦν ἔτλη) and the "unfatherly fate" that he gave her (862–63), and they shudder at Iphigeneia's own daring in having been about to sacrifice her brother (δεινᾶς τόλμας · δείν' ἔτλαν: 869–70). As they weep tears of sorrow and joy (832), they at last enjoy the embrace of which

Iphigeneia was deprived when she was taken to Aulis. Iphigeneia left the baby Orestes behind in Argos (231–35, 834–36) without picking him up or kissing him because she thought she was going to be married and would soon return (372–77). By restoring to the siblings the embrace interrupted by the events at Aulis, the recognition returns them to the time of innocence before Aulis, before Iphigeneia's service among the Taurians, and before Orestes' matricide, thus dramatizing the possibility of redemption through fraternal love.[39]

The siblings now work together as true *philoi* for mutual salvation. Orestes tells Iphigeneia that Apollo has marked out the way in which he is to attain salvation from the madness sent by the Erinyes (ὥρισεν σωτηρίαν: 979): he is to bring the Taurian image of Artemis to Athens. The young man asks Iphigeneia to join with him (σύμπραξον: 980) in bringing about this personal salvation, which will also bring about Iphigeneia's rescue and restore the house of Pelops. "Save our ancestral house, and save me," he asks her (σῶσον πατρῷον οἶκον, ἔκσωσον δ' ἐμέ: 984). Iphigeneia agrees, saying that she wants the same thing he does, to return to Argos (989–90) and to free Orestes and the house from trouble. As she acts as savior of house and heir, Iphigeneia also pardons Agamemnon for kin murder and escapes from the same crime herself:

θέλω δ' ἅπερ σύ, σέ τε μεταστῆσαι πόνων
νοσοῦντά τ' οἶκον, οὐχὶ τῷ κτανόντι με
θυμουμένη, πατρῷον ὀρθῶσαι θέλω ·
σφαγῆς τε γὰρ σῆς χεῖρ' ἀπαλλάξαιμεν ἄν
σώσαιμί τ' οἴκους. (991–95)[40]

I want what you want, to free you from trouble,
and, not being angry with the one who killed me,
I want to restore the sick house of my father.
Thus, I would free my hand from your slaughter,
and save the house.

By actively rejecting kin murder, Iphigeneia stops the pattern of bloodshed and pollution that has destroyed her house, and by pardoning her killer, and thereby freeing him from murder, she removes existing pollution.[41] Thus, instead of the curse she had threatened to become (778), Iphigeneia becomes the agent of salvation and purification. For his part also, Orestes now emphatically rejects even indirect kin murder, saying that he will not become the murderer of his sister as well as his mother by saving his own life and leaving Iphigeneia to die (1007–9). Just as Orestes rejects the crime of kin murder, of which he has been guilty, so Iphigeneia rejects her own previous crimes of xenocide. Although she prayed, before meeting Orestes, to be able to murder *xenoi* (ξένων σφάγια: 336–37, cf. 53, 776), now, when Orestes suggests killing King Thoas, she says that *xenos*-murder (ξενοφονεῖν) is a terrible thing and that she cannot do it even to save herself and her brother (1020–23). In this last passage, the *xenos* is a host,[42] while the *xenoi* in the earlier passages (336–37, 53, 776) were strangers. The similarity of language, however, underlines the similarity between the two crimes, as does the fact that the Greek strangers Iphi-geneia prepares for sacrifice are really "fellow tribesmen" (θοὐμόφυλον: 346).

At this point in the play a complete change in Iphigeneia and Orestes, and in their house, has been accomplished. Each of the siblings has undergone a resurrection from the dead in the eyes of the other, and the house, which Iphigeneia had lamented as dead, has been brought back to life in the form of its living male heir. Brother and sister have not merely avoided but actively rejected the bloodshed that polluted their family for many generations. They have done their part in their own rescue and in the restoration of the house: the rest depends on the gods.

4. Purification and Rescue

Just as the gods, Apollo and Artemis, have worked along with mortals to bring about the terrible events within the house of Tantalos, so divine brother and sister now work together with the human siblings to bring about rescue.[43] Artemis contributes to Iphigeneia's ultimate rescue by taking her to the Taurian land and making her priestess, for this enables her to meet her brother. She also assents, by her silence, to the removal of her image, for, as Orestes says, Apollo's oracle must have been pleasing to her as well (1012–15). This oracle, telling Orestes that he will find salvation if he takes Artemis's image to Attica, turns out to be true, for in going to the Taurian land, in being captured and almost sacrificed, Orestes meets his sister and thus achieves sal-vation. Apollo's protection is also evident to the audience in the Herdsman's account of the "incredible" escape from injury of "the gods' offerings," Orestes and Pylades (328–29), when they are attacked on the shore after arriving in the Taurian land.[44] Orestes doubts the oracle, saying that the "clever gods" are no truer (οὐδ᾽ . . . ἀψευδέστεροι: 570–71) than dreams. Yet, the play shows that Apollo indeed sits "on the throne of truth" (ἐν ἀψευδεῖ θρόνῳ: 1254), but that there is no truth for mortals in dreams (1279) such as the "false dreams" (ψευδεῖς ὄνειροι: 569) that deceive Iphigeneia into thinking that Orestes is dead. Iphigeneia's dream is true according to one interpretation, for Orestes indeed comes to Iphigeneia to be prepared for sacrifice, as happens in the dream.[45] But the dream is nevertheless deceptive because it is ambiguous, allowing Iphigeneia to misinterpret it, and because there are no sure criteria for interpretation. Apollo, on the other hand, gives clear oracles that admit of only one interpretation, the truth of which is validated by Athena at the end of the play (1438–41b).[46]

Nevertheless, it is misleading to say that the gods show their true natures by opposing human sacrifice. Just as the humans first engage in and then actively reject bloodshed, so the gods first accept and command and then actively reject and forbid murder. Euripides emphasizes this change in gods and humans in several ways. In his version of the Orestes story, in contrast to that of Aiskhylos, some of the Erinyes, dissatisfied with the verdict in Orestes' trial, continue to pursue the matricide (968–71), indicating that the series of bloody deeds cannot be ended by divinely sanctioned judicial fiat, as it is in Aiskhylos.[47] Instead, a more complete purification is required in the Taurian land, in the accomplishment of which Orestes and Iphigeneia reject murder of kin and *xenoi* and purify Artemis's image from the pollution of the murder Apollo had commanded.

One way in which Euripides dramatizes avoidance of bloodshed is by means of the wave that pushes the escaping boat back to shore (1391–97). This is not just a clumsy way of motivating Athena's appearance,[48] but a means of emphasizing the reconciliations among both gods and humans. Poseidon causes the wave to appear because he is opposed to the house of Pelops (1415), but he then calms it out of *kharis* to Athena (1444–45).[49] By her silence, Artemis also consents to the plan of the other gods, implicitly condoning the robbery of her own image from her own temple.[50] The wave also brings about human reconciliations. The Taurians take advantage of the wave to attack the Greeks (1407–34), but when Athena orders Thoas to cease pursuing the Greeks and tells him not to be angry (μὴ θυμοῦ: 1474), he obeys at once, telling Orestes that he is not angry with his sister (ἀδελφῇ τ' οὐχὶ θυμοῦμαι: 1478). Thoas, like Orestes and Iphigeneia, refrains from murdering *xenoi*. His words of forgiveness echo those of Iphigeneia when she stated that she was not angry with her murderer-father (οὐχὶ τῷ κτανόντι με θυμουμένη: 992–93): just as she absolves her father from polluting kin murder, so she is herself forgiven by the *xenos* whom she deceived. Moreover, as Christian Wolff points out, the wave and the sudden shift in wind that accompanies it (1394) recall the contrary winds at Aulis that led to Iphigeneia's sacrifice, and the subsequent calm without bloodshed is a "benign reversal" of the violence at Aulis.[51]

Another way in which the play represents the active avoidance of bloodshed is by means of the establishment of rites for Artemis. Athena tells Orestes:

νόμον τε θὲς τόνδ'· ὅταν ἑορτάζῃ λεώς,
τῆς σῆς σφαγῆς ἄποιν' ἐπισχέτω ξίφος
δέρῃ πρὸς ἀνδρὸς αἷμά τ' ἐξανιέτω,
ὁσίας ἕκατι θεά θ' ὅπως τιμὰς ἔχῃ. (1458–61)[52]

Establish this law: when the people hold festival,
in exchange for your sacrifice, let someone hold a sword
to a man's neck, and draw blood,
for piety's sake, and so that the goddess may have honors.

The Greek word ἄποινα means "ransom," "blood money"—that is, payment given in exchange for a life. In this passage, the idea is that the festival and the rite are substituted for human sacrifice.[53] Similarly, at Aulis, Artemis replaced human with deer sacrifice (28–29). Although this act saved Iphigeneia from death, it did not prevent Agamemnon's guilt, for he is repeatedly said to be a murderer, and Iphigeneia states, "I was killed by the sword" (27). At Halai, in contrast, a priest first draws real blood with a sword and then stops in the very act of killing, taking positive action to avoid human sacrifice. The rite, like its mythological *aitia* (cause), Orestes' averted sacrifice, is an avoidance of murder.[54]

While the rites at Halai are associated with Orestes, Iphigeneia, first as priestess of Artemis and then, after her death, as recipient of offerings of the clothing of women who died in childbirth, is central to a cult to be established at Brauron (1462–67). Euripides' Greek audience would have been reminded of another rite of Artemis at Brauron, the *arkteia*, the rite in which unmarried girls "played the bear" as expiation to Artemis for the death of a bear. The myths giving the *aitia* of the *arkteia* at Brauron and of similar rites at Mounichia resemble the story of Iphigeneia at Aulis, in which the sacrifice of an animal is substituted for that of a girl. In all of these myths, the essential element is the averting of human sacrifice.[55] Moreover, Euripides' mention of the establishment of a cult at Brauron may also contain a historical allusion, for an inscription at Brauron dated 416–15 suggests that the rites of the qua-drennial Athenian festival of the Brauronia were suspended during this period in the Peloponnesian War.[56] Therefore, this play, produced around 414, may look forward to a time of peace, during which killing in war is averted.

Finally, the purification rite by means of which salvation is accomplished also involves avoidance of killing. Iphigeneia tells Thoas that the image of the goddess has been polluted by contact with those guilty of matricide, and that it and the men must be purified in secret rites. As scholars have noted, she tells the truth in most respects,[57] praying to the goddess, "If I wash away the blood of these men and sacrifice where I must, you will dwell in a pure house, and we will be fortunate" (1230–32). One detail about which she lies, however, has not been noticed. Iphigeneia says that the purification involves the washing away of polluted blood by means of blood (φόνῳ φόνον μυσαρὸν ἐκνίψω: 1223–24), that is, by animal sacrifice. In the event, she only pretends to wash away blood with blood (ἵν᾽ . . . δοκοῖ: 1336; ὡς φόνον νίζουσα δή: 1338), giving out ritual cries to mask her escape in Orestes' ship.

Just as noteworthy as this avoidance of traditional animal sacrifice is the fact that no human being is killed when the Taurians attack the Greek ship. Both sides lack iron weapons, at first using only fists and feet, which wound but do not kill. When the attackers retreat to the hills and throw stones, they are kept at a distance by archers on the ship, and there are no deaths on either side (1366–78).[58] The absence of killing in the rescue episode of the *IT* is especially significant when contrasted with the bloody escape of Helen and Menelaos in Euripides' *Helen* (1581–1618). These plays have many similarities. In both plots, a Greek woman held captive in a barbarian land is rescued when her closest *philos* arrives. In both, the woman tricks her captor in order to escape by sea.[59] In the *Helen*, however, the rescue is marked by blood, both animal and human. As he sails away with his wife, Menelaos cuts the throat of a bull and prays to Poseidon while the blood streams into the sea (αἵματος δ᾽ ἀπορροαὶ ἐς οἶδμ᾽ ἐσηκόντιζον: 1587–88). Greeks and Egyptians then fight, so that the ship runs with blood (φόνῳ δὲ ναῦς ἐρρεῖτο: 1602) while Helen cheers on her compatriots. Of all the Egyptians, only the Messenger escapes to tell the tale.

Although Iphigeneia lies to Thoas about the means of purification, the escape brings about an actual purification, for Orestes is released from his madness, as we know from Athena's vindication of Apollo's oracle (1438–41b), and Artemis's statue is freed from its association with human sacrifice.[60] In contrast to the traditional homeopathic ritual of sacrifice in which blood is washed away by means of blood, in this new kind of purification blood is cleansed allopathically by the avoidance of murder, both animal and human. The ancient audience might well be reminded of Herakleitos's saying: "They vainly purify themselves of blood-guilt by defiling themselves with blood [καθαίρονται δ' ἄλλως < αἷμα > αἵματι μαινόμενοι], as though one who had stepped into mud were to wash with mud; he would seem to be mad, if any of men noticed him doing this."[61] In refusing to cause death, Orestes purifies himself of blood guilt and its consequent madness, and Iphigeneia purifies herself of the rites in which she has participated, as both victim and priestess. These purifications in the later part of the play reflect the avoidance of the pollution of fratricide in the main *pathos*. Artemis, who gives her tacit consent to the theft of her image from her temple, is also purified of her association with human sacrifice. Apollo participates in the purification too. He is the god of *katharmoi* (purifications): his oracle has commanded the theft of Artemis's image, and the Greek sailors defend themselves with his weapon, the bow. The voice that cries out from the escaping Greek ship (βοή τις: 1386) may well be his, for it has a mysterious, divine quality, like that of Dionysos in the *Bacchae*,[62] and it reminds the sailors that Apollo's oracle has been fulfilled: "We have that for which . . . we sailed" (1388–89). Thus Apollo, who murdered Pytho and commanded Orestes' matricide, oversees and approves a bloodless *katharmos*, and in so doing may be said to undergo it himself.

The bloodless rescue that purifies humans and gods ends the troubles of the house of Tantalos and Pelops. In the last words spoken in the play by a mortal, Thoas deliberately turns aside from murder: "I will stop the spear [παύσω δὲ λόγχην] that I raised against the *xenoi*" (1484). Humans and gods have worked together to reject the bloody inheritance of the spear of Pelops (λόγχην: 823) that was first raised against Oinomaos and was passed from generation to murderous generation of his descendants.

As the preceding analysis shows, the *Iphigenia in Tauris* provides excellent examples of many ways in which tragedy emphasizes kin murder. The averting of kin killing in the central *pathos* is highlighted and reinforced dramatically by other incidents in the play, for it is preceded by allusions to a whole series of acts of violence that have taken place against *philoi* and *xenoi*, and it is followed by representations of the avoidance of other bloody acts. Crimes against kin and *xenoi* stain the five generations of the house: those of Tantalos, of his son Pelops, of Pelops's son Atreus, of Atreus's son Agamemnon, and, finally, of Agamemnon's son Orestes. Pylades alone has escaped this bloody heritage to become a model of true *philia* for his kin. When the fratricide is about to take place, it is represented as the culmination of a series of acts of violence against *philoi*, and when it is at last averted, so are other acts of violence. Following the recognition, Iphigeneia forgives her father, thus helping to save his house and free it from pollution. In a reversal of the usual tragic pattern, in which harm to kin destroys a royal family,[63] in the *Iphigenia in Tauris* the house of Agamemnon is restored by the rejection of kin murder. Iphigeneia also refuses to kill Thoas, her *xenos*, who in turn spares her and Orestes. Human sacrifice is stopped in both barbarian and Greek lands when the gods cease to demand it. Even animal sacrifice and warfare against enemies are avoided in the escape.

In all of these ways, the minor events in this play strengthen the dramatic force of the central *pathos* of kin murder averted. In other tragedies also, as the next chapters will show, violence against *philoi* plays an important role, in minor events as well as in the central *pathos*.

The Suppliant Bride:
Io and the Danaïds in
Aiskhylos's *Suppliants*

The plot of Aiskhylos's *Suppliants* does not, like that of Euripides' *Iphigenia in Tauris*, center on a direct threat of kin killing. The Danaïds, the sons of Aigyptos, and Pelasgos are all related, however distantly, but no murder is committed or attempted among them, either with or without knowledge of their relationships. In this play, however, suppliancy creates a dramatic situation analogous to that in Euripides' tragedy. Pelasgos's initial reluctance to protect the suppliants makes a terrible and pitiable event appear imminent, and his subsequent agreement to shelter them averts this polluting *pathos* just as recognition averts fratricide in the *Iphigenia*.

In Aiskhylos's *Suppliants*, the fifty daughters of Danaos flee from Egypt to escape marriage with their cousins, the fifty sons of Aigyptos. They arrive in Argos and supplicate divine and human protectors: Zeus Hikesios (Zeus of Suppliants) and Pelasgos, the king of Argos. Pelasgos is at first reluctant because he knows that acceptance will involve war with the sons of Aigyptos. However, he is finally induced to act as advocate for the Danaïds, in large part as a result of their threat to hang themselves from the altars of the gods. Pelasgos then persuades the Argives to give Danaos and the women protection against their pursuers and to grant them formal status as *metoikoi* (resident aliens) in Argos. He defends them against the attempts of the representatives of the sons of Aigyptos to drag them from the altar by force and offers them asylum in the city. Here our play ends. It is clear from other sources, however, that the Danaïds marry their cousins in the lost plays of the trilogy, and that all but one, Hypermestra, murder their husbands on the wedding night.

The rather simple story of the Danaïds' flight and supplication in the extant play has aroused a great deal of controversy. One dispute concerns the reasons for the Danaïds' aversion to marriage with the sons of Aigyptos. Some believe that they are averse to all marriage, while others argue that they reject only marriage with their cousins, because of personal dislike, aversion to endogamy, a family quarrel, or for some other reason.[1] A second dispute concerns the relevance of the story of Io to the situation of the Danaïds. The myth of Io, the Danaïds' bovine ancestress, has an important role in the *Suppliants*. She is the basis for their claim to protection as kin of both Argives and Zeus; her situation as a fugitive pursued by an enemy parallels the Danaïds' own status as suppliants fleeing enemies, and the women pray for a release from pains like that given Io by Zeus (1062–67). In the version of Io's story presented in *Suppliants*, which differs in important respects from that of *Prometheus Bound*, Io, a priestess of Argive Hera, is tormented by Hera after a voluntary sexual union with Zeus. Hera turns the girl into a cow, sends a gadfly to torment her, and drives her from Argos to Egypt. There Zeus, by a breath and touch of the hand, at one and the same time releases Io from her torments and impregnates her with their calf-son Epaphos, ancestor of the Danaïds. Because Io is released from her pains by the very act that also engenders Epaphos, some scholars see an inconsistency in the fact that the Danaïds reject marriage yet pray for a release that is like hers.[2]

Discussions of these questions about the Danaïds' attitudes toward marriage often center on the sexual psychology of the Danaïds. Peter Burian writes of the women's "obsessive, hysterical fear of marriage."[3] Richard Caldwell provides a Freudian analysis, according to which "the Danaïds typify the oedipal situation: because of their excessive attachment to their father and their identification with a mother-substitute, they are unable to love other men and are therefore consumed by an incapacitating anxiety concerning sex and marriage."[4] Timothy Gantz writes, "[T]o deny that process [sc. sex], to refuse the sheer necessity of it, is a perversion of natural order."[5] According to Edmond Lévy, "Sexuality is rejected in a virginal concern for purity, that is manifested . . . in a particular devotion to Artemis."[6] Alain Moreau states, "Bodies of women and hearts of men, they represent, just like Clytemnestra, hybridism and the monstrous."[7] Robert Murray writes of the Danaïds' "death wish,"[8] of "the nearly pathological workings of the minds of the maidens" (28), of their "obsession" (29), and of "their curiously warped understanding" (70). He believes that they are "afflicted by a madness like that suffered by Io" (71). Reginald Winnington-Ingram holds that "the violent approach of the sons of Aegyptus has warped the feminine instincts of the Danaïds and turned them against marriage as such,"[9] and Froma Zeitlin believes that they have erotic feelings for Zeus.[10] However, the focus of these and other scholars on the alleged sexual abnormality of the Danaïds risks turning this play into a kind of case history of sexual dysfunction. Although sex, marriage, and fertility are important issues in the *Suppliants*, it is essential to place Aiskhylos's treatment of them within their ancient social context and within the literary context of the play as a whole.

Closer attention to one of the central issues of the play, supplication, can lead to a better understanding of the Danaïds, Io, and the parallels between their respective situations. Zeus Hikesios dominates the play, from the first three words, invoking Ζεὺς μὲν' Ἀφίκτωρ, Zeus the "super-suppliant."[11] There are frequent invocations of or allusions to Zeus of suppliants or of *xenoi* throughout, and the final words of the Danaïds (1062–73) call once more on Zeus to defend them. Zeus, in his role as Hikesios, not only presides over the suppliant action taking place on stage; he is also, I argue, an important figure in the story of Io, the mythological precedent to the Danaïds' story. Our text contains indications that Io, the bride of Zeus, is also a suppliant of Zeus Hikesios when she arrives in Egypt. She is thus the prototype of the Greek bride, who arrives as suppliant at her husband's hearth.

In order to show how the Danaïds, Io, marriage, and supplication are interconnected in this play, I analyze four significant relationships, those of the Danaïds and Pelasgos (section 1), of the Danaïds and Zeus (section 2), of Zeus and Io (sections 3 and 5), and of the Danaïds and the sons of Aigyptos (section 6). In order to shed light on the marriage of Zeus and Io, I include a discussion of the evidence for the Greek view that the bride is a suppliant (section 4). I conclude with some speculations about the trilogy as a whole (section 7).

1. The Danaïds and Pelasgos

In supplicating Pelasgos, the Danaïds claim protection on two grounds. First, they claim kinship as Argives. In the Parodos, the women state that they are Argives by race (γένος: 16), as descendants of Io, and that this is the reason for their seeking asylum in Argos: "At what land more kindly than this could we arrive with these suppliants' daggers?" (19–21). When Pelasgos arrives, they tell him that they are Argives by race (γένος: 274), and they explicitly base their request for asylum on this kinship (323–24). The Danaïds give proof of their kinship by relating in detail the story of their Argive ancestress, Io (291–324). These are the πιστὰ τεκμήρια (trustworthy proofs) of their Argive origin to which they allude in line 55, corresponding to the τεκμήρια (proofs) of his Argive kingship given by Pelasgos at 271.[12] Thus, the first episode contains a recognition scene very similar in some respects to the one in Euripides' *Iphigenia in Tauris*, in which Orestes gives his sister proof of his identity by recounting family history (806–26). Pelasgos notes that the story of Io related by the Danaïds coheres in all respects with his own knowledge of this history (310), and he concludes that they are "sharers from of old in this land" (325–26), thus admitting the validity of their claim to be blood kin. After this, the Danaïds invoke "Zeus of kinship" (402–3) in an allusion to the kinship between themselves and the Argives.[13]

The fact that Pelasgos does not agree to support the Danaïds' cause immediately after the women make their kinship-based request has led some scholars to argue that kinship plays no role in his final decision to accept the suppliants.[14] This cannot be right, for it is kinship that helps to create the possibility of "double pollution from both *xenoi* and townspeople" against which

Pelasgos warns the Argives (618–19; cf. ἀστοξένων: 356).[15] Moreover, after the Argives have voted, the suppliants praise them for respecting "their kindred suppliants of holy Zeus" (652–53). Kinship is also one reason for Pelasgos's hesitation to defend the women against their cousins: he fears ὅμαιμον αἷμα (449, cf. 474), the "kindred blood" he will shed if he fights the sons of Aigyptos, who are also of Argive origin. His dilemma, then, is not simply that he must choose between war and failure to protect suppliants. Pelasgos must choose between shedding kindred blood in war and failing to protect kin who are also suppliants.[16] The "double pollution" the latter course would involve greatly influences his choice and that of the Argive people.

The second basis for the Danaïds' claim is their status as suppliants, dramatized vividly by their position at the altar and by their suppliant branches. Pelasgos shows that he feels the strength of the suppliants' claims by the shudder (πέφρικα: 346) he experiences on seeing the altar with its suppliant branches. This shudder may, as Douglas Cairns suggests, be a physical manifestation of the *aidôs* (reverent fear) to which he later refers.[17] Pelasgos expresses the same emotion verbally by mentioning the "wrath of Zeus Hikesios" (347).[18] The suppliants play on this fear, by invoking the goddess Hikesia Themis (Established Custom for Suppliants), the agent of Zeus (360), by speaking of *aidôs* for the suppliant (362) and by warning Pelasgos of pollution (ἄγος φυλάσσου: 375), and of the "wrath of Suppliant Zeus" (385, cf. 427). They ask the king to have reverence for the gods (396), to become their εὐσεβὴς πρόξενος (reverent protector of *xenoi*), and not to betray the suppliants by allowing them to be dragged from the altar (418–27), and they warn Pelasgos of retribution that may fall upon his children and house (434–37).

When Pelasgos still hesitates, the Danaïds threaten to hang themselves from the altars of the gods (455–67). They thus threaten a particularly effective kind of vengeance suicide, for death at an altar greatly increases pollution.[19] Pelasgos calls it an "unsurpassable pollution" (μίασμ' . . . οὐχ ὑπερτοξεύσιμον: 473).[20] This threat of suicide, like the threats the women make against Zeus himself (154–75), has a function in the characterization of the Danaïds, revealing the intensity of their fears and showing them to be capable of violent acts. To view the threat as simply blackmail, however, is to ignore other important dramatic roles it plays.[21] In the first place, the suicide threat dramatizes and intensifies the threat of pollution implicit in all supplications. Supplication always has an aggressive aspect, which is stressed in this play from the first mention of the Danaïds' branches, called "suppliants' daggers."[22] The threat is also an effective way of emphasizing an important reason for the king's decision. In resolving to support the Danaïds, Pelasgos says that the highest object of fear for mortals is the wrath of Zeus of Suppliants, for which of necessity he must have *aidôs* (479–80). Danaos sums up Pelasgos's attitude by calling him *aidoion* (490–91). In showing Pelasgos to be ruled by *aidôs*, Aiskhylos represents him as the human agent of Zeus Hikesios, who is also called Zeus Aidoios (192). The suicide threat, finally, is very useful to

Pelasgos, since it gives him a powerful argument to use with the Argives: that there will be a pollution "before the city" (619) if they refuse.[23]

Since the gestures as well as the words of formal supplication are important for an understanding of what happens in this tragedy, it is essential to look closely at how the play makes use of supplication ritual.

Supplication may occur, as it does in this play, at a sacred place (an altar, a hearth, or a sacred ground), or it may occur at the knees of an individual. The suppliant carries *hiketêria*, suppliant branches, as a sign of suppliancy.[24] He or she sits or crouches and makes contact with the sacred place or object, or with the knees, right hand, or chin of the person supplicated. Scholars differ about whether or not the act is ritually valid when physical contact is not possible or desirable for some reason and the suppliant merely speaks such words as "I supplicate you by your knees."[25] In tragedy, however, where visual representation of supplication is possible, the representation of physical contact seems to be strictly required for ritual validity.[26] The person supplicated may reject the suppliant by trying to break the contact in some nonviolent way or by using force. To accept a suppliant, the person supplicated uses his or her right hand to grasp the suppliant's hand and raise him or her, performing what is technically called the *anastasis*.[27] For example, Alkinoös takes the suppliant Odysseus by the hand and raises him from the hearth (χειρὸς ἑλὼν . . . ὦρσεν ἀπ᾽ ἐσχαρόφιν: *Od.* 7.168–69).[28] After Odysseus has eaten, Alkinoös agrees (189–96) to grant his guest's request (151–52) for conveyance. For the person supplicated to grasp a suppliant's hand is the counterpart of the suppliant's gesture of touching the knees or chin of the person supplicated. In touching the suppliant, the person supplicated makes a reciprocal gesture expressing *aidôs*. Another action often accompanies the *anastasis*: the leading of the suppliant to a place suitable to a guest, for example, from a sanctuary to the house, or from the ground to a chair, as Alkinoös leads Odysseus from the hearth in order to seat him on a chair (*Od.* 7.169). Raising the suppliant and granting a request mark two separate stages in the acceptance of a suppliant.[29] This is especially clear in literary and historical cases in which the raising of suppliants is a temporary granting of asylum outside a sanctuary. In Sophokles' *Oedipus at Kolonos*, Oidipous at first intrudes into a sacred grove that the Chorus ask him to leave, promising that no one will force him from his seat outside it (176–77). Oidipous later calls this promise a pledge that he has received (ἐχέγγυον: 284),[30] and he states that they have raised him (ὥσπερ με κάνεστήσαθ᾽: 275). After this, Oidipous remains a suppliant, and the Chorus tell him to pray to the Eumenides (484–87). Oidipous's request to be taken into Athens is granted at a later stage, after Theseus's arrival (631–41). Oidipous's son Polyneikes is also granted safe conduct after being raised from an altar (1286–88). In a historical parallel, Kylon and his fellow suppliants are raised (ἀνιστᾶσι) from asylum, receiving a pledge (ὑπεγγύους) that they will not be killed (Herod. 5.71). They are not granted permanent immunity at this point but must still undergo a trial.[31] In Thucydides 3.28.2, some pro-Spartan Mytilenians take refuge at altars after the Athenian victory. Pakhes raises them with the promise that he will not harm them (ἀναστήσας αὐτοὺς ὥστε μὴ ἀδικῆσαι) and places them in Tenedos until the Athenians come to a decision about them.

Aiskhylos uses and adapts all of these rituals in the staging of the *Suppliants*.[32] During the Parodos, the Danaïds enter the orchestra holding suppliant branches bound with wool. The stage above them represents the sacred precinct containing the statues and altars of the gods. Danaos instructs his daughters on supplication etiquette, telling them to sit (προσίζειν: 189) on the mound where the statues are, and to hold the branches in their left hands (193). This will leave them free to stretch out their right hands in a gesture of supplication.[33] After instructing his daughters on how to speak as suppliants (194–203), Danaos probably seats himself, as is implied by his daughters' expressed wish to have a seat beside him (208).[34] The daughters finally do this when Danaos again tells them to sit (ἵζεσθε: 224). In addition to the branches they hold in their left hands, the Danaïds place other branches, mentioned by Pelasgos at 241–42, beside the statues of the gods. It is not clear exactly when they do this, but it may well occur at 223 ("be reverent": σέβεσθ᾽).[35] Thus, before the entrance of Pelasgos at 234, the Danaïds are in formal supplication position, seated in the sacred precinct, holding branches in their left hands while stretching out their right hands.

Pelasgos agrees to help the Danaïds at 478–79 when he says, "Nevertheless it is necessary to have *aidôs* for the wrath of Zeus of Suppliants." He addresses Danaos, telling the old man to take the branches that the Danaïds have deposited at the altar to other altars in the city (480–83), and he gives Danaos an escort (500–501). Then Pelasgos turns to the Danaïds, telling them to leave on the altars the branches they still hold in their left hands. After they do this, stating, "I leave them" (λείπω: 507), he instructs them to leave the sacred precinct. Pelasgos reassures them of his protection, saying that he will not betray them (οὔτοι . . . ἐκδώσομαι: 510), and the Danaïds agree that he has encouraged them in "speaking and acting" (515). Finally they leave the sacred precinct, probably after Pelasgos exits at 523. At this point, Pelasgos has granted the Danaïds the "raising" (*anastasis*) they asked for earlier (ἀνστῆσαι: 324).[36]

It is important not to confuse the *anastasis*, a personal promise to accord suppliant status to the women even after they leave the asylum, with the granting of their request for protection from the sons of Aigyptos. The latter occurs only after the vote by the Argive people, and until then the Danaïds and Danaos continue to supplicate. After he has agreed to support the Danaïds' cause, Pelasgos tells Danaos to take suppliant branches to the altars of the gods of the country as a proof of his suppliant status (ἀφίξεως τέκμαρ: 483). He also tells the Danaïds to continue to supplicate the gods in his absence (520–21). The branches that the women lay down (506–7) are also a sign that supplication continues. Only if the request is granted will the branches be taken from the altar.[37] Thus, supplication is not at an end at 506, when the Danaïds have gained an advocate.[38]

One characteristic gesture associated with raising a suppliant, however, is notably absent from our play: the taking of the suppliant by the hand. We would expect this gesture to be present in a play devoted to Zeus Hikesios, in which, moreover, every formal action connected with supplication is emphasized and made clear in the text. An allusion to a hand occurs at 507, but there is no explicit evidence that Pelasgos takes the women by the hand.[39] Because the suppliants' request has not yet been granted at the time of the *anastasis* (506–23), Aiskhylos displaces and modifies the gesture of touching with the hand, transferring it from Pelasgos, who raises the suppliants, to the Argive people, who formally grant their request by ratifying the king's decision.[40] Instead of physically touching the suppliants, the Argives raise their right hands in voting to grant their request (χερσὶ δεξιωνύμοις: 607; cf. χείρ: 604; χερσίν: 621). This vote is both the ratification by the people of Pelasgos's request and the ratification by Zeus of the decision to accept the suppliants (κεκύρωται τέλος: 603; κραινόντων: 608; ἔκραν': 622; Ζεὺς δ' ἐπέκρανεν τέλος: 624). By this decision, Danaos and the Danaïds are granted official status as *metoikoi* (μετοικεῖν), free and not to be seized (ἀρρυσιάστους), with sanctuary from every attacker (609–14).[41] The Danaïds are now fully accepted as *xenai*, under the protection of Zeus Xenios, whom they now invoke (627, 671–72).

2. The Danaïds and Zeus

The Danaïds seek protection from Zeus Hikesios on the basis of the same two claims they use in appealing to Pelasgos: kinship and suppliancy. They frequently invoke Zeus as protector of suppliants (e.g., Ζεὺς Ἀφίκτωρ: 1).[42] Just as the Danaïds threaten Pelasgos with the pollution their suicide would create, so they threaten Zeus with the unfavorable judgment against him that their suicide would cause (154–74). This threat, like the threats to Pelasgos, is a way of dramatizing and making explicit the implicit threats made by every suppliant to every divine and human object of supplication. A similar idea is expressed in Aiskhylos's *Eumenides*, where Apollo says that the wrath of a suppliant betrayed is terrible among mortals and gods (232–34), and where Athena states that she fears wrath if she does not protect suppliants (473–81).[43]

The Danaïds also appeal to Zeus on the basis of kinship, as "Zeus begetter" (Ζεὺς γεννήτωρ: 206), that is, father of Epaphos, their ancestor (15–18).[44] They ask him to "renew the kindly story" of Io in their case, reminding the god that they are of the race of Zeus (531–37).[45] Just as they recount Io's story to Pelasgos in giving proofs of kinship, so they also tell the story of Io to Zeus, this time emphasizing his own role (538–89). And just as the Danaïds begin the play by saying that they could come to no kindlier land than their ancestral Argos (19–20), so they state that there is no god whom they might more justly invoke than Zeus, the "planter" of their race (590–94). In their frequent allusions to Io, the Danaïds not only remind Zeus that he is their ancestor, they also appeal to Io's case as a precedent. In asking Zeus to "renew the kindly story" of Io and mentioning their own relationship to both Io and Zeus, the Danaïds employ the traditional argument used in prayers: You have done this before, to me or mine. The precedent in this case extends to specific details, for the Danaïds constantly represent their own situation as parallel to Io's. The women have literally followed in their ancestress's footsteps (538), and just as she was pursued by the gadfly, so the Danaïds are pursued against their will by the suitors. Hoping for the same kind of deliverance Zeus granted to Io, they pray Zeus to release them from their torments (λυτηρίοις μηχαναῖς: 1072–73), just as he released Io from her pains (πημονᾶς ἐλύσατ': 1065).

Zeus's reaction to the suppliants' pleas is much less clear to the audience than is Pelasgos's response. Since Zeus is represented in the play as the god of suppliants and the personification of *aidôs*, we are led to expect that he will help the Danaïds. However, Zeus's will, as the Danaïds state, is not easy for mortals to know (86–87, 93–95; cf. 1057–58), and when our play ends he has not yet revealed it. The Danaïds are still in danger, and they still call on Zeus to protect them. Of two things, however, the Danaïds are confident throughout the play—Zeus's justice and his benevolence—and we are given no indication that they are wrong. Zeus punishes wrongdoers (91–103), he weighs unjust and pious acts (403–4),[46] and by his will justice rules (437). In particular, he watches over suppliants and punishes those who do not respect them (381–86), while rewarding those who honor him as Xenios.

The end of the play represents, in effect, a benevolent alliance between Zeus Xenios and the Danaïds. After Zeus ratifies the Argives' decision (Ζεὺς δ' ἐπέκρανεν τέλος: 624) to accept the Danaïds' supplication, Zeus Xenios becomes increasingly important. The favorable result of the Danaïds' supplication leads them to pray that Zeus Xenios will bless the Argives (625–29), giving them fertility, among other good things (688–93, quoted in section 7 below). In the ode at 630–709, Zeus as Hikesios or Xenios is represented as the very basis for civilization. The women pray that Argos will receive the blessings of freedom from internal and external war, of good government passed on from one generation of good people to another, and of fertility of the earth and of herds. The Danaïds pray for these things because (οὕνεκ') the Argives have honored Zeus's suppliants (639–42). The blessings of all the gods, and of Zeus in particular, will not be given merely as answers to the Danaïds' prayers but will follow as effect from cause. The Argives' protection of suppliants means that their altars are pure, that their homes are not defiled, and that they have not incurred the anger of Zeus (646–55). Moreover, the good government the Argives will enjoy in the future is based on their giving highest honor to Zeus Xenios, whose ancient law is the source of good government (670–73). The Argives will continue to honor *xenoi*, gods, and parents (698–709), thus keeping the three commandments written in the *thesmioi* (ordinances) of Justice, that is, the laws of Zeus. Keeping the commandments leads in turn directly to the blessings invoked by the Danaïds. Honoring *xenoi* avoids external war (701–3), and internal war is avoided by obedience to gods and parents. We may also infer that honoring the marriage relationship, sanctioned by gods and parents, leads to avoidance of quarrels between husband and wife and between the fellow-citizens who are related by marriage. Avoidance of strife of all kinds is conducive to fertility of land, animals, and humans.

3. Io and Zeus Hikesios

Zeus's benevolence is also shown in his treatment of Io. The relationship between Zeus and Io is central to the play in two ways: as the basis for the Danaïds' claim to protection as kin of both Pelasgos and Zeus and as a mythological precedent for the Danaïds' present situation. In contrast to the account in *Prometheus Bound*, Zeus in *Suppliants* is portrayed as consistently benevolent toward Io. Even though we see Zeus's treatment of Io primarily through the eyes of the Danaïds, there are no suggestions that their account is partial or distorted, and it is in fact confirmed by Pelasgos (310). Io's relationship with Zeus begins in Argos and is explicitly said to be sexual (μειχθῆναι: 295; πελάζει: 300). There is no indication in the text that it is anything but voluntary on Io's part.[47] It is Hera who disturbs the original peaceful and voluntary union of Zeus and Io, turning Io into a cow, setting Argos to watch over her, and at last sending the gadfly to drive her from the land (296–309, 540–42). Hera's gadfly maddens and torments Io (562–64) and causes sickness (586–87), while it is Zeus who enchants her (571) and stops her pains with healing hand (1065–66). Zeus's begetting of Epaphos by gentle touch and breath (313, 17, 592) does not represent a change but is consistent with his previous benevolence as a lover.

In spite of the clear evidence in the text, scholars have frequently misunderstood the nature of Zeus's relationship with Io. Some assume that it is involuntary on her part, similar to the hostile relationship between the Danaïds and their pursuers or to the relationship between Zeus and Io in *Prometheus Bound*, where Zeus's lust for Io forces her father to drive her from her home against the will of both father and daughter (ἄκουσαν ἄκων: 671), and where the god becomes gentle only after Io arrives in Egypt (844–52).[48] In *Prometheus Bound*, in contrast to the version of *Suppliants*, Zeus is chiefly responsible for Io's sufferings, while Hera's role is minimized. The text of *Prometheus Bound* (673–77) does not say whether Zeus or Hera changed Io into a cow, and it does not state that the goddess sent the gadfly, although it is true that Hera's association with the gadfly is traditional, and she is said to have caused Io's sufferings at 592, 704, 900, and perhaps 600.[49] Scholars have misunderstood *Suppliants* in other ways as well. Robert Murray writes that it is Zeus who turns Io into a cow, ignoring the clear statement that it is Hera who does this (299), and he makes the argument, worthy of Euripides' Helen in *Trojan Women*, that Zeus is really responsible for the gadfly sent by Hera because, after all, he started the affair.[50] Froma Zeitlin appears to deny that the Argive union is sexual when she refers to Io as a virgin.[51] Christian Froidefond writes that Epaphos was conceived in Argos, ignoring line 313, which places the begetting (φιτεύει) after Io's arrival in Memphis (311).[52]

Some confuse the benevolent force of Zeus with harmful violence like that employed by the suitors. For example, Edward Whittle argues that the word ῥυσίων, used of Zeus's deliverance of Io at 315, has a connotation of violence.[53] The word indeed has negative connotations at 728, where Danaos characterizes the Egyptians as ῥυσίων ἐφάπτορες (seizers of plunder) of the Danaïds (cf. 412: ῥυσίων ἐφάψεται, 424: ῥυσιασθεῖσαν). However, the term and its cognates also have positive connotations in this play, particularly in connection with supplication. The verb ῥύοιτο is used of a grove protecting suppliants (509), and Artemis is asked to become ῥύσιος in saving the women from a hated marriage (150). Moreover, (ἐ)ῥύομαι and its cognates and compounds are frequently used in Greek literature to refer to the rescue of suppliants.[54] The term ῥυσίων surely has positive connotations at *Supp.* 315 also, where it is linked to Ἔπαφος ("Epaphos," a cognate of ἐφάπτωρ, "toucher," or "seizer"), also used in a positive sense. The positive sense is appropriate because Io's initial union with Zeus is voluntary, and, as will be shown in section 4, his deliverance of her has connotations of rescuing a suppliant. Aiskhylos uses cognates of the same words, ῥύσιος and ἐφάπτωρ, in both positive (315) and negative (412, 728) senses to call attention to the sharp contrast between Zeus's benevolent rescue by touch and the violent seizure of women by the Aigyptiads. The word *bia* (force) is also used of Zeus's powerful benevolence: "painless force" (βίᾳ δ' ἀπημαντοσθενεῖ: 576), "kindly force" (εὐμενῆ βίαν: 1067). These expressions are less paradoxical than Friis Johansen and Whittle believe.[55] The benevolence is directed toward Io, but the force is used to stop (παύεται: 578) or check (κατασχεθών: 1066) destructive evil. In contrast to Ares, who uses destructive violence (Ἄρη βίαν τ' ἔνδημον ἐξοπλίζων: 682–83, πρὶν ἐξοπλίζειν Ἄρη: 702), Zeus accomplishes his will and desire without armed violence (Διὸς ἵμερος . . . βίαν δ' οὔτιν' ἐξοπλίζει: 86, 99).[56]

It is a mistake, then, to see a parallel between Zeus in the Io story and the suitors who pursue the Danaïds. Zeus's human analog is instead Pelasgos, who rescues the Danaïds from the Aigyptiads. Danaos makes the general point that the Argives should be prayed to as one would to Olympic gods because of their role as saviors (980–82).[57] More specifically, Pelasgos resembles Zeus in his role as Hikesios: both are given the same epithet, *aidoios* (192, 491). This parallel is an especially close one, since Zeus Hikesios not only protects the Danaïds in the stage action, he also rescued their ancestress Io in the mythological precedent.

Taken together, several aspects of the Io story indicate that here also Zeus plays a role as protector of suppliants. After a long journey, Io "arrived" in Memphis (ἵκετο: 311) and "arrives" at the sacred precinct of Zeus (ἱκνεῖται: 556) in Egypt. In a play presided over by Zeus Hikesios, the verb ἱκνέομαι, often used of the arrival of a suppliant, cannot be without significance. In her bovine state, Io cannot make the physical gestures of supplication, but in rescuing and healing her by means of his hand, Zeus performs an act like that of accepting a suppliant. Just as the hands of the Argives, who vote to accept the Danaïds, give honor to the women, so Zeus's touch raises Io from animal to human and gives her an honored role as mother of his son and ancestress of a dynasty.[58] The *aidôs* experienced by Io when Zeus breathes on her is also in part connected with her suppliant status. When Io "lets fall mournful *aidôs* of tears" (δακρύων δ' ἀποστάζει πένθιμον αἰδῶ: 578–79) it is important to remember that she is a suppliant, and that *aidôs* characterizes the attitude of both parties in supplication.[59] In the *Suppliants*, Zeus Hikesios is called Aidoios (192), and as the personification of the *aidôs* felt toward a suppliant, Pelasgos is *aidoios* in accepting the suppliants (491). The very land of Argos will have *aidoion* breath (28–29) if it accepts the suppliants. In turn, the Danaïds as suppliants show *aidôs* toward Pelasgos. Danaos tells his daughters to speak *aidoia* words, without boldness or recklessness, and to exhibit *sôphrosynê* ("sound-mindedness") and quietness (194–99). In this context, when Io is said to "let fall mournful *aidôs* of tears" and expresses *aidôs* in tears, she is represented as manifesting the reciprocal emotion characteristic of the suppliant. Moreover, *aidôs* is a characteristically human emotion, and its presence in Io marks her change from animal to human.[60]

The *aidôs* of Io, however, is also closely connected with her role as bride of Zeus. Io is said to react with *aidôs* toward Zeus as sexual partner because this is an emotion especially appropriate for a bride, as is the mourning (πένθιμον) for her lost girlhood.[61] To understand fully the nature of Io's sexual relations with Zeus, it is first necessary to look in some detail at the evidence for the Greek idea that the bride is a suppliant.

4. The Suppliant Bride

Although the idea that the wife is a suppliant may be very ancient, there is no trace of it in Homer, where arriving strangers, *hiketai*, are always male.[62] In tragedy, on the other hand, female *hiketai* figure largely in the *Suppliants* of Aiskhylos and Euripides, and marriage and supplication are linked in imagery, language, and ritual.[63] This new association in literature between the two institutions, whether or not it is based on historical changes in marriage law and ritual, may reflect important changes in attitudes toward both marriage and supplication. The view that marriage is based on suppliancy implies that the household begins with and is based on the mutual respect (*aidôs*) of husband and wife. The stronger party, the husband, affords protection and maintenance to the weaker, the wife, who reciprocates by giving the greater share of honor to her husband and by making her own contribution to their shared life, especially in the form of children.

Three literary sources state explicitly that the bride comes as a suppliant to the home of her husband:

1. "One should not drive away one's wife, for she is a suppliant, for which reason we lead her from the hearth and [have the custom of] taking her with our right hand" (γυναῖκα οὐ δεῖ διώκειν τὴν

αὐτοῦ, ἱκέτις γάρ· διὸ καὶ ἀφ' ἑστίας ἀγόμεθα καὶ ἡ λῆψις διὰ δεξιᾶς: "Pythagoras," Iamblikhos, *Life of Pythagoras* 18.84);

2. "Moreover, one should consider that, since a man has taken his wife from the hearth with libations, like a suppliant before the gods, she has been led into his home" (ἔτι δὲ τὴν γυναῖκα νομίζειν ἀπὸ τῆς ἑστίας εἰληφότα μετὰ σπονδῶν καθάπερ ἱκέτιν ἐναντίον τῶν θεῶν εἰσῆχθαι πρὸς αὐτόν: *Life of Pythagoras* 9.48);

3. "Concerning a wife . . . the Pythagoreans say that one should least of all do wrong [to her, for she is] like a suppliant and one led from the hearth" (γυναῖκα . . . ὥσπερ ἱκέτιν καὶ ἀφ' ἑστίας ἠγμένην ὡς ἥκιστα δεῖν ἀδικεῖν: "Aristotle", *Oikonomika* 1344a10–12).[64]

All of these passages connect the suppliant status of the wife with the custom of leading the bride from the hearth. The first passage also mentions the groom's taking the bride with his right hand. As was noted above in section 1, similar actions occur when Alkinoös takes Odysseus by the hand and leads him from the hearth where he has been sitting as suppliant (*Od.* 7.168–69). These sources suggest, then, that three elements of the Greek marriage are connected with the suppliant status of the bride: a ritual at the hearth, the custom of the groom's leading the bride, and that of his taking her with his right hand. Examination of the literary and visual evidence for the Greek wedding ceremony supports this interpretation.[65]

There is good literary and visual evidence for a rite at the hearth of the new husband: the *katakhysmata* (showering). In a ritual of incorporation of the bride into her new home, bride and groom were seated at the hearth and showered with fruit, nuts, and coins.[66] The bride may have acted as a suppliant during or close in time to this rite.[67]

There is a much more evidence for the two other relevant elements of the wedding ritual: the custom of the groom's leading the bride and that of his taking her with his right hand. The words "taking with the right hand" (ἡ λῆψις διὰ δεξιᾶς, *Life of Pythagoras* 18.84)[68] recall an important part of the wedding ceremony, frequently represented in vase paintings, in which the groom leads the bride to his house in a gesture known as "hand on wrist" (χεῖρ' ἐπὶ καρπῷ).[69] No entirely satisfactory interpretation of this gesture has been given. According to George Mylonas, it indicates the sealing of the marriage contract between man and woman.[70] Since women could not make contracts, however, it is a mistake to conflate the "hand on wrist" gesture with the clasping of hands by two male equals.[71] Robert Sutton argues that the gesture signifies the legal transfer of the bride from father to husband.[72] If this were so, however, we would expect the gesture to occur at a single moment of the ceremony, as is the case with the modern exchange of rings. Not only is there no evidence for such a moment, but the gesture is most frequently represented in processions, which occupied a considerable period of time, from the house of the bride to that of the groom. It is also represented in a scene where the couple face one another in the marriage chamber, where, presumably, there were no witnesses.[73]

Whatever they may think about the legal significance of the gesture, most scholars believe that it indicates male dominance and possession of the woman or that it is connected with the idea of marriage as abduction.[74] Ample evidence for the reluctance of the bride is contained in many sources, including premarital myth and ritual and wedding songs expressing male-female conflict.[75] On the other hand, it is questionable whether this reluctance is represented in the wedding procession and in the "hand on wrist" gesture.

In the first place, this gesture is not peculiar to weddings or to men grasping women. The expression is used in Homer of mixed male and female dances (*Il.* 18. 594), of two men coming to an agreement (*Il.* 24.671), and of the violent seizing of one man by another (*Il.* 21.489).[76] Vase paintings show dancers holding each others' wrists. Also depicted is Aithra, mother of Theseus, being led "hand on wrist" by Demophon and Akamas, the grandchildren who rescue her from Troy.[77] When men do grasp women they often use gestures other than "hand on wrist," for example, grasping their clothes or hair, in what is more appropriately termed dragging (ἕλκειν) than leading (ἄγειν).[78] The differences between representations of weddings and images of abductions are readily apparent from a comparison of two examples. In one wedding scene, the groom lifts the bride into a chariot. While she stands somewhat stiffly, she faces straight ahead, resting her passive hand on that of the groom. In contrast, an illustration of the rape of Persephone shows the maiden standing in a chariot and turning back to stretch both arms out to her mother.[79] Nor is the pairing on some vases of nuptial rites with pursuit of a female by a male evidence that abduction and marriage are equated.[80] More plausibly, such juxtapositions represent two contrasting views of marriage.[81] Moreover, Sutton has shown that representations of wedding scenes in the fifth century present a "romantic view of marriage," emphasizing the emotional unity of the couple rather than male dominance. In the course of the fifth century, representations of the wedding procession on foot, in which the "hand on wrist" gesture typically occurs, replace depictions of the earlier type of procession, in which the couple ride in a chariot and the gesture is not used.[82] Typically, the groom leading the bride looks back at her with a glance "of reassurance and love."[83] This gaze, as François Frontisi-Ducroux has shown, indicates that the husband persuades rather than compels his bride.[84] Eros or erotes frequently appear in wedding scenes, and in one painting Peitho (Persuasion) also stands beside the bridal pair.[85] In a context stressing emotional unity, a gesture associated with abduction or male possession seems out of place.

Aside from these difficulties, many interpretations of the "hand on wrist" gesture fail to account for the fact that, in many cases, the groom does not lead the bride "hand on wrist." The term χεῖρ' ἐπὶ καρπῷ is rarely used in the context of a wedding. It is more accurate to say, with John Oakley and Rebecca

Sinos, that the groom takes either the bride's hand or her wrist: in many of their illustrations he leads her by the hand.[86] In Pindar also the bride is led by the hand: "he led the dear maiden, taking her by the hand with his hand" (παρθένον κεδνὰν χερὶ χειρὸς ἑλὼν ἆγεν: *Pyth.* 9.122–23).

It is important to note two additional features of this gesture. First, the groom lifts the hand of the bride. In Euripides' *Alkestis*, Admetos recalls that he walked in the wedding procession, "raising the hand of my dear wife" (φι-λίας ἀλόχου χέρα Βαστάζων: 917).[87] This is what many vase paintings seem to represent: the groom lifting the hand of the bride.[88] In one scene, the groom literally lifts the bride into a chariot, the lifting being chiefly represented in the gesture of the man, who places his right hand under that of the passive woman.[89] Second, the groom nearly always takes the bride's left hand or wrist in his right hand.[90] Thus, what we see in the vases is not "hand on wrist" but the gesture mentioned by "Pythagoras": "taking with the right hand" (ἡ λῆψις διὰ δεξιᾶς). "Pythagoras" connects this gesture not with male domination or legal agreements, but with the suppliant status of the bride: "she is a suppli-ant; *for which reason* we . . . [have the custom of] taking her with our right hand." This interpretation of the gesture deserves serious consideration.

Although we do not have descriptions or illustrations of the raising of a suppliant that would allow us to compare this gesture with that used in the Greek wedding,[91] it is probable that the gesture was similar to the "taking with the right hand" represented in wedding scenes. That is, in supplication ritual, the person supplicated used his or her right hand to grasp and raise the sup-pliant by the latter's left hand. The groom is said to "raise" the hand of the bride (Eur. *Alc.* 917), and the person supplicated also raises the suppliant by the hand. Literary sources indicate that the suppliant grasps the right hand of the person supplicated,[92] and "Pythagoras" suggests that the person suppli-cated touches the suppliant with the right hand, just as the groom takes the bride with his right hand. In contrast, it may be significant that the aggressor uses his left hand in *Il.* 21.489–90, where the phrase "taking by the wrist" is used of a violent seizing. On the other hand, it would have been appropriate for the suppliant to have been taken by the left hand. For the person suppli-cated to grasp the suppliant's right hand or wrist would have seemed, like the clasping of right hands in agreements and contracts, to indicate equality between the two parties.[93] The suppliant, however, was in a dependent and subordinate position that could be symbolized by a passive left hand, in con-trast to the active and authoritative right hand of the person supplicated. Indeed, the gesture of using the right hand to grasp another's left arm or hand was suitable to both groom and person supplicated, for both bride and sup-pliant were in unequal and dependent positions, but were also owed respect and protection. Just as the gesture of taking the suppliant by the hand indi-cated not dominance and aggression, but *aidôs* and protection, so the same gesture of the husband would have indicated respectful guardianship.

In addition to representing the suppliant status of the bride, the linking of hands of the married pair would also have been an excellent symbol of their metaphorical yoking in marriage. The Graces, often represented in sculpture as standing hand in hand, are said to be yoked (συζύγιαι), and when Herakles puts his arm around the neck of his friend Theseus, he calls this linking a "dear yoke" (ζεῦγος φίλιον), comparing it to his other "yoke" of marriage.[94]

Literary evidence other than the Pythagorean passages quoted above also indicates that the Greeks saw close parallels between raising a suppliant and leading a bride. Just as the suppliant is taken under a pledge of safety (ἐχέγ-γυος), so the bride is given by a pledge (ἐγγύη) to the groom.[95] Moreover, suppliants, like brides, are led to the homes of their protectors. Odysseus says of his successful supplication of Pheidon's son: "He led [me] to his house, having raised me by my hand" (ἦγεν ἐς οἶκον, χειρὸς ἀναστήσας: *Od.* 14.318–19). When Theseus agrees, at his mother Aithra's request, to help the suppliant Argives, he tells them to take their branches away from her "so that I may lead her to the house of Aigeus, applying my own hand" (πρὸς οἴκους ὥς νιν Αἰγέως ἄγω / φίλην προσάψας χεῖρα: Eur., *Supp.* 360–61).[96] Although Aithra is not actually a suppliant, her similarity to the suppliants whose part she takes is emphasized by her physical position: she sits at the altar (93, 290), encircled by suppliant branches (32–33, 102–3). Thus, when Theseus agrees to help the suppliants and leads his mother from the sanctuary to his house, his action is equivalent to the raising and leading of a suppliant. This scene, in which Aithra, like a suppliant, is led with Theseus's hand to the house of the son who is her guardian (*kurios*), would also have reminded the audience of the Greek wedding procession, in which the bride was led with the hand of the groom to the house of her new *kurios*, her husband.

Euripides provides still other examples of associations between suppliancy and marriage. In *Medea* 709–18, Medeia supplicates Aigeus, asking him to receive her at his hearth, in return for which she will help him to fulfill his *eros* for offspring by enabling him to beget children. Aigeus is like a husband receiving a suppliant bride into his home, except that this suppliant will give him children by means of drugs after killing her own offspring. This grim parody of wedding ritual is especially noteworthy in view of the fact that Medeia's marriage to Jason began, in a significant reversal of the traditional procedure, with his supplication of her.[97] In *Andromakhe*, Hermione supplicates Orestes, asking him to take her away from danger in Neoptolemos's house (892–95, 921–23). He agrees, saying, "I will lead you to your house and give you to the hand of your father" (984).[98] Hermione's reply, that her father will see to her marriage (987–88) comes as no surprise in light of the bride's suppliant status. Not only were Hermione and Orestes previously betrothed, as Orestes recalls bitterly (966–81), but Hermione as suppliant is now in the position of a bride about to be led away to her new home. When the two exit together, he surely leads her with his right hand. A supplication between former spouses occurs in *Trojan Women* 1042–48. Dressed in finery (1022–23) so that she resembles a bride, Helen supplicates Menelaos, who is determined to kill her. He immediately changes his mind, telling attendants to take her to the ships. Charles Mercier, citing *Andromakhe* 627–31, suggests that Helen has employed supplication as seduction, caressing Menelaos's knees.[99] If this is so, Euripides presents us with a travesty of the marriage ritual, in which the modest, suppliant bride is played by the shameless adulteress. In *Helen*, the long-separated spouses Helen and Menelaos meet and recognize one another while Helen is suppliant at Proteus's tomb (528–96). Again, at 1237–39, Helen supplicates Theoklymenos, asking him to allow a lavish burial for Menelaos, whom he supposes to be dead. She makes physical contact with him (ὠρέχθης)[100] immediately after she tells Theoklymenos that he may now begin (ἄρχε) a marriage with her (1231).

Especially close connections between supplication and marriage are evident in Euripides' *Herakles*. After Herakles has killed his family, he becomes like a suppliant in many respects. He is overcome by shame (αἰσχύνομαι: 1160, αἰδόμενος: 1199), and he covers his head, fearing to pollute Theseus with blood guilt (1159–62, 1199–1201). The literal meaning of the words he uses, προστρόπαιον αἷμα (1161), "blood that turns toward someone" or "suppliant blood," is appropriate here, for Herakles is in the moral position of the suppliant-exile who has committed murder and who turns to another for protection and purification. Herakles also sits in the position of a suppliant (θάσσοντα . . . ἕδρας: 1214).[101] Ironically, Amphitryon literally supplicates his son when he asks him to uncover his face (1206–10), but it is really Herakles who is in the physical and moral position of the suppliant.[102] For his part, Theseus, like the protector of the suppliant-exile, offers Herakles purification and a home (1324–25). In this context, when Theseus asks Herakles to rise (ἀνίστασ': 1226, 1394) and give him his hand (1398) the audience naturally thinks of the raising of a suppliant.

These allusions to suppliancy are all the more effective because they are combined with bridal imagery. Herakles, the mightiest of male heroes, has become not only like a helpless suppliant, but also like a woman, as Theseus indeed tells him (θῆλυν ὄντ': 1412). The shame he now feels is characteristic of a bride, as are the tears he sheds for the first time (1354–56). In these respects, Herakles resembles Io in Aiskhylos's *Suppliants* 578–79. Moreover, when Herakles is asked to uncover his head, the term used is that for the unveiling of a bride (ἀνεκάλυψας: 1231; cf. ἐκκάλυπτε: 1202, ἐκκάλυψον: 1226; cf. Eur. *Supp.* 111). Herakles implicitly compares his relationship with Theseus to a marriage when he speaks of his new "yoke" of friendship and compares it to his previous unfortunate "yoke" of marriage and children (ζεῦγός γε φίλιον· ἄτερος δὲ δυστυχής: 1403; cf. 1374–75: κἀποζεύγνυμαι τέκνων γυναικός τ'). The final scene of the play, in which Theseus leads Herakles to his new home in Athens (ὁδηγήσω: 1402) and Herakles says that he will follow like a small boat towed behind a ship (ἐψόμεσθ' ἐφολκίδες: 1424), is reminiscent of the leading of the bride in the wedding procession. It has often been noted that this scene is the reversal of an earlier one in which Herakles tows his children "taking them by their hands" (ἄξω λαβών γε τούσδ' ἐφολκίδας χεροῖν: 631).[103] In the staging, surely Theseus takes Herakles by the hand in the very same way. The fallen hero exits, like suppliant and bride, led to the home of his new protector.

5. Io as Bride of Zeus Begetter

As the preceding section has shown, there is ample literary and visual evidence for the idea that the Greek bride was thought to be a suppliant to her husband. It makes a great deal of sense to interpret Io's relationship to Zeus in *Suppliants* as that of suppliant bride. Seen in this light, Zeus's impregnation of Io is also connected with his role as Hikesios. Like a suppliant at the hearth of a human, Io "arrives" (556) in Egypt, "the sacred precinct of Zeus" (Δῖον ἄλσος: 558). Zeus's touch, like the touch by means of which a husband leads his bride to the marriage chamber, enables her to fulfill her primary duty as wife: becoming a mother. Just as the union of mortal husband and wife after the marriage ceremony produces legitimate heirs, so the Egyptian union of the suppliant Io with Zeus leads to the birth of Epaphos and founds the race of the Danaïds. Zeus's relationship with Io as suppliant bride, then, contrasts sharply with the relationship of pursuer to pursued, which is that of Hera to Io and of the Aigyptiads to the Danaïds. Far from being benevolent, Hera's gadfly drives Io from her native land (309), just as the sons of Aigyptos pursue (διωγμοῖς: 148; λυκοδίωκτον: 351) and seek to lead away unjustly (βίᾳ δίκας ἀγομέναν: 430) the women who flee them, thus violating the Pythagorean prescription that husbands should not "drive away" (διώκειν) or "wrong" (ἀδικεῖν) their wives.[104]

Just as Zeus's touch is connected with his role as husband of suppliant bride, the other means by which he impregnates Io, the breath (ἐπιπνοίας: 17, 44; cf. 577), also has traditional associations with fertility. Zeus in *Suppliants* is, among other things, a god of fertility, as the "life-producing" (φυσιζόου: 584) begetter of the race of Epaphos and the father who is the "planter" (φυτουργός: 592) of the race. Zeus also has a more general role in fertility, causing both fruit and cattle to thrive and increase (688–93). In this context, the breath by means of which Zeus begets Epaphos is the "breath of life," called *pneuma* in Aiskhylos's *Persians* 507 and *Seven Against Thebes* 981.[105] It is, both in Greek biology and in popular thought, the father's distinctive contribution to generation.

As early as Homer, mares are said to conceive by means of the wind (*Il.* 16.150). In *Generation of Animals*, Aristotle provides a philosophical account corresponding to this popular belief. According to Aristotle, the male's contribution to generation is the semen, a compound of water and *pneuma* (*GA* 735b37–736a2), which is a substance "analogous to the element of the stars" (736b37–737a1), that is, divine,[106] and which supplies the soul principle (737a7–8) to the offspring. Aristotle holds that "the male acts as a craftsman" (δημιουργοῦν: 738b21) and "completes" or "perfects" (ἐπιτελεῖ, ἀποτελεῖ: 741b5, 762b4) generation. The female, on the other hand, supplies the physical material to generation, just as the soil nurtures a seed (738b34–36). Aiskhylos uses the same metaphors from agriculture and craft that occur later in the works of the philosopher. In *Eumenides* (658–61), Apollo states that the mother is not the parent of the offspring but merely the nurse or nourisher (τροφός) of the embryo. The male is the parent, while the female, like a *xenê* for a *xenos*, guards the young shoot (ἔρνος). In *Suppliants* (282–83) males are compared to craftsmen (τεκτόνων), who stamp (πέπληκται) an impress (χαρακτήρ) onto female forms (τύποις). This account is similar not only to that of Aristotle, but also to that of Plato, who writes of the begetter who stamps an impress (ἐξομοργνύμενον ἐκτυποῦσθαι) onto the bodies and souls of his children.[107] In *Suppliants*, Zeus himself is said to be a "craftsman" (τέκτων: 594), or "planter" (φυτουργός : 592) who sows (φιτύει: 313) children. The agricultural metaphors for reproduction recur in the final play of the trilogy, the *Danaïdes* (see section 7).

The two means by which Zeus heals and impregnates Io—the hand and the breath—are, then, highly significant and appropriate. Just as the hand has associations with leading a suppliant bride, so the breath of the male is connected with fertility. By hand and breath, Zeus accepts and impregnates Io as his suppliant bride and provides a divine *aition* (cause) for the marriage ritual of taking the bride by the hand as a suppliant.

Thus, the union of Zeus and Io can be interpreted as the prototype of an ideal Greek marriage, in which the wife is a voluntary suppliant, respected, treated gently, and given honored status as the *xenê* to whom Aiskhylos compares her in *Eumenides* 660. This kind of marriage is not represented in the stage action of the extant play, but it is in some respects reflected in the status given the Danaïds in Argos. Like the Greek wife, they are accepted suppliants who are given protection and an honored place in the city, and the blessings they pray for the Argives to receive are those of fertility (688–93). As free *metoikoi* (609; cf. *Eum.* 1011), the Danaïds resemble the Greek wife, who is a free inhabitant of the city, with definite rights, but who does not fully participate in government.[108]

6. The Danaïds and the Aigyptiads

In contrast to the ideal Greek marriage prefigured by the relationship of Zeus and Io, the marriage sought by the Aigyptiad suitors is a barbarian one, characterized by lust and violence and by the pursuit and unjust treatment of wives. The Danaïds characterize the suitors as hubristic (30, 104, 426, 487, 528, 817, 845, 880–81), a view with which Pelasgos agrees (487), impious (422, 751, 757–59, 762–63), and lustful (741, 758, 762–63, 820–21), and they view the marriage as pollution (224–26), slavery (335), forced (39, 227, 1031–32), and a fate worse than death (787–90). The stage action shows these judgments to be correct. The Aigyptiads' *hybris* in this play is manifested in action primarily by the violation of suppliants committed by their representative, the Herald.[109] In what Simon Goldhill calls "perhaps the most violent scene staged in extant ancient tragedy," the Herald threatens to tear the clothes and hair of the Danaïds, to brand them and cut off their heads (839–41), and to drag them "willing or unwilling" (862) to the ship. At last he actually lays hands on the suppliants at the altar.[110] The Herald, identifying himself with the suitors, views the women as runaway slaves who are his property (918). In the kind of marriage the sons of Aigyptos seek, the wife is treated with *hybris* like a slave (δμωΐς: 335), rather than as an honored *xenê*. The Herald is not only hubristic toward the Danaïds, he is also impious, showing no fear of Egyptian gods (872), explicitly stating that he does not fear Greek gods (893), and offending Zeus Xenios by failing to act properly as *xenos* (917). His violence to suppliants, of course, is an offense against Zeus Hikesios.

If Pelasgos resembles Zeus in the Io story, the Aigyptiads are analogous to Hera and her gadfly. This association suggests that in this play the goddess of marriage represents the barbarian kind of marriage. Just as Hera drives Io from her land by means of the gadfly (309), so the suitors drive the Danaïds in flight from their country (350–51). Hera's jealousy leads to quarrels with Zeus (νείκη: 298), while the marriages sought by the suitors place them in opposition to Zeus Hikesios and may lead to a quarrel with the Argives and Pelasgos (νεῖκος: 358). Just as Hera turns Io into a cow, so the Herald treats the Danaïds like animals, threatening to drag them away by force (861–65, 884, 904, cf. ἱππαδόν: 431). The suitors also resemble the gadfly with which jealous Hera torments Io (16–17, 306–8, 541, 572–73) and maddens her (μαινόμενα: 562), making her a "maenad of Hera" (564). The gadfly is a "winged herdsman" (557) that torments Io with goads (563) and causes sickness (587). Similarly, the sons of Aigyptos, filled with lust, are driven by "the inescapable goad of maddened purpose" (109–10). They are compared to winged birds (226, 510) and are said to desire a "heart-tearing marriage" (798–99) to which death is preferable and to be the cause of the pains from which the Danaïds pray for a release like that given Io by Zeus's healing hand (1062–73). These parallels show that the gadfly is associated with the lust of the suitors and the sexual jealousy of Hera, and not, as Helen Bacon argues, with a sexual awakening experienced by Io or the Danaïds.[111]

The barbarian marriage associated with the suitors and with Hera is contrary to *themis* (established custom). When Pelasgos asks the suppliants whether they oppose marriage with their cousins because of enmity or because the union is contrary to *themis* (κατ᾽ ἔχθραν, ἢ τὸ μὴ θέμις : 336), he opposes two motives that are really one and the same. It is *themis* that forbids the barbarian marriage sought by the Aigyptiads, in which the bride is an unwilling partner. As the Danaïds state at the beginning of the play, they wish to avoid "entering into forced marriages that *themis* forbids" (λέκτρων ὧν θέμις εἴργει . . . ἀεκόντων ἐπιβῆναι: 37–39). Themis is associated with Aphrodite, who presides over the *thesmos* of marriage.[112] That her will is the will of Zeus Hikesios is indicated by the fact that Hikesia Themis is his agent or daughter (Ἱκεσία Θέμις, Διὸς Κλαρίου: 360).

For their part, however, the Danaïds also fail to act properly as suppliants and brides. Their threats to Danaos and to Zeus himself show that they are capable of the violent acts they will later commit against their husbands. The "suppliants' daggers" (21) they carry are not appropriate to the suppliant bride. Neither side, then, represents an ideal marriage partner.[113]

The *Suppliants*, then, contrasts two kinds of marriage. One, associated with Argive Hera, whom the Aigyptiad suitors resemble, is a kind of slavery for the wife, in which the male, who is motivated solely by lust, treats her with *hybris*. The other kind of marriage, associated with Aphrodite, Zeus Hikesios, and Themis, treats the wife as suppliant and *xenê*. In this marriage, male and female have *aidôs* for one another, just as do the two parties in supplication. This interpretation has implications for the trilogy as a whole.

7. The *Suppliants* and the Trilogy

It is generally agreed that the lost plays of the trilogy, *Aegyptii* and *Danaïdes*, dramatized the well-known myth in which all of the Danaïds except Hypermestra murder the sons of Aigyptos on their wedding night. On the other hand, we do not know how the marriages were brought about, why Hypermestra spared her husband, or what else happened in the plays.[114] Winnington-Ingram suggests that the second play may have focused on Zeus Xenios, just as the extant play is centered on Zeus Hikesios.[115] It is also possible that two kinds of reconciliations occurred in the lost plays: that of at least one of the Danaïds with marriage and Aphrodite, and that of Zeus with Hera. These two reconciliations would be closely linked, for the quarrel of Zeus and Hera begins with Io and continues as Hera pursues Io's descendants. Since Hera is goddess of marriage, a reconciliation of the Danaïds with marriage is also a reconciliation with Hera, and the reconciliation of the Danaïds and Hera in turn implies the reconciliation of Zeus and Hera. If the trilogy ended with a divine reconciliation in the form of a renewed marriage of Zeus Hikesios and Argive Hera, goddess of marriage, it would provide a divine prototype for a new kind of mortal marriage, anticipated in the Io myth, in which the bride is respected as willing suppliant and *xenê*. Several considerations support the view that the two reconciliations figured in the lost plays.[116]

At the end of the *Suppliants*, the Danaïds appear to be irrevocably opposed to marriage, at least with their present suitors (1030–33, 1052–53, 1062–64). Nevertheless, the Chorus of Argive men[117] sing (1034–42) of the power of Aphrodite, aided by Desire, "enchanting Persuasion" (θέλκτορι Πειθοῖ: 1040), and Harmony. That Θέλκτωρ and its cognates have erotic connotations is suggested by the fact that Danaos expresses fears that his daughters will be corrupted by the "enchanting arrow" (θελκτήριον τόξευμα: 1004–5) of men's eyes. When the Danaïds say that they are "unenchantable" (ἄθελκτον: 1055) but pray to Zeus for a release from pains like that of Io (1064–67), we should remember that Zeus enchanted (θέλξας: 571) Io before he impregnated her. In *Prometheus Bound*, it is Hypermestra who is enchanted: "But the desire for children will enchant one woman, so that she will not kill her bedfellow" (μίαν δὲ παίδων ἵμερος θέλξει τὸ μὴ κτεῖναι ξύνευνον: 865–66).[118]

Because of this desire, Hypermestra will be the only Danaïd to spare her husband so as to bear "a race of kings" (869). It is possible that the desire for children was also Hypermestra's motivation in the two plays that followed the
Suppliants; this would certainly be consistent with the emphasis on Zeus's
role as fertility god in the extant play.

Another hint of a reconciliation at the end of the trilogy is given by lines
1043–44, spoken by a chorus of Argive men. Although the text is unfortunately
corrupt, Martin West's reading is attractive: φυγάδεσ‹σιν› δ᾽ ἐπιπνοίας κακά
τ᾽ ἄλγη / πολέμους θ᾽αἱματόεντας προφοβοῦμαι. Following West, who comments in his apparatus, "sin autem Veneris afflatum fugietis," the lines may be
translated: "But I fear evil pains and bloody wars for those fleeing the breath
[of Aphrodite]." According to this reading, a marriage of the Danaïds, in which
they accept the fertilizing breath of Aphrodite, is presented as an alternative
to war. West's interpretation is especially attractive in view of the use of ἐπι-
πνοία to refer to the breath of Zeus that fertilized Io, the mythological
antecedent of the Danaïds (see above, section 5).

There are also suggestions that a divine reconciliation may have con-
cluded the trilogy. Just before speaking of "enchanting Persuasion," the
Chorus of Argive men tell the Danaïds:

Κύπριδος ‹δ᾽› οὐκ ἀμελεῖ‹ν›, θεσμὸς ὅδ᾽ εὔφρων·
δύναται γὰρ Διὸς ἄγχιστα σὺν ῞Ηραι. (1034–35: West)

Do not neglect Kypris, this gracious ordinance,
for she is mighty, nearest to Zeus with Hera.[119]

Zeus and Hera quarreled over Io (298), and the dispute continues into the present, for the Danaïds fear that Hera will persecute them as Io's descendants
(162–67). The passage just quoted may be a hint that the divine quarrel will
eventually be brought to an end by Aphrodite.

A rupture followed by a reconciliation of Zeus and Hera would follow the
pattern of separation and reunion, or departure and return, that is important
in other ways in the *Suppliants,* in the trilogy, and in myth and cult associated
with Hera or with marriage. In the *Suppliants,* Io, priestess of Argive Hera,
leaves Argos and does not return; her descendants, however, return to her old
tracks in Argos (538–39). According to a tradition that Aiskhylos may have followed in the other two plays of the trilogy, one of the Danaïds, Hypermestra,
becomes a priestess of Hera, thus effecting a reunion with the goddess who
persecuted Io.[120] Io's relationship with Zeus also follows the pattern of separation and return, since she is separated from Zeus in Argos and then reunited
with him in Egypt. Another pattern of sexual separation and reunion may have
been represented in the lost plays of the trilogy, if the Danaïds remarried after
killing their first husbands.[121]

Myth and cult surrounding Hera also reflect the pattern of separation and
reunion. The fact that the priestess of Hera was escorted in a procession to the
temple at the Argive festival of the Heraia indicates that she first departed from
the shrine.[122] A remarriage of Hera and Zeus may also have taken place at this

festival.[123] In Samos, Hera's image was said to have been stolen and then brought back to the temple, and in the cult commemorating this event the goddess's image was given a ritual bath, which was said by some to renew her virginity prior to her remarriage with Zeus.[124] In the *Iliad* also, Hera is associated with the rupture and reconciliation of husband and wife. At the end of Book 1, Hera quarrels with Zeus over his promise to Thetis to give honor to Akhilleus, but is then persuaded by Hephaistos to make it up with her husband. The book ends with the divine pair in bed. In Book 14, Hera asks Aphrodite for her girdle on pretense of wanting to effect a reconciliation between her parents, who, she says, have kept away from their bed for a long time (14.197–210). Hera actually uses the girdle to seduce and trick Zeus, who is angry after he discovers that he has been deceived (15.13–33). This brief rupture is quickly over, however, as Zeus smiles at Hera (15.47) just as she smiled after their previous quarrel (1.595–6).

Separation and reunion in human marriage were enacted in the festival of the Thesmophoria. According to Hesiod and Herodotos, this festival was instituted by the Danaïds, and some scholars suggest that the trilogy ended with its foundation.[125] Although Hera had no definite part in the Thesmophoria, as far as we know, the festival was relevant to her role as goddess of marriage, and it reflected the same pattern of separation and reunion that is found in Hera myths and rituals. In the Thesmophoria married women temporarily left their homes and husbands to live apart from men. The festival was marked by sexual abstinence and verbal obscenities (*aischrologia*), while the antimale character of the festival was reflected in stories of attacks on men. The true purpose of the festival, however, was revealed in the invocation, on the last day, of Kalligeneia, goddess of beautiful birth: temporary separation and abstinence ensured fertility after the women returned to their husbands.[126]

The pattern of separation and reunion after marriage has obvious affinities with the pattern of departure and return of the young girl before marriage, with which Hera is also associated. In one myth, Hera drives the daughters of Proteus mad, because they have offended her, and she causes them to wander for a time before they return and marry.[127] The pattern of premarital departure and return is particularly appropriate to Hera's role as cow goddess, for the young girl before marriage is compared to a horse or a heifer that has to be tamed and yoked, and it is Hera βοῶπις who "yokes" untamed girls in marriage.[128]

Premarital reluctance or separation is certainly relevant to the story of the Danaïds in the *Suppliants*.[129] However, the Io story in the extant play and, if my interpretation is correct, the trilogy as a whole reflect instead the pattern of separation and reunion after marriage. Unlike Io in the *Prometheus Bound*, who is a virgin until she arrives in Egypt (739–40, 834–35), Io in *Suppliants* is first sexually united with Zeus (295, 300), then parted from him in a long and painful separation, and at last reunited with her divine lover in Egypt. This feature of the *Suppliants* version is crucial to an understanding of the trilogy. If

Io's story is paradigmatic, the primary focus is not on premarital reluctance but on a renewal of marriage.

Further evidence for a divine reconciliation at the end of the trilogy is provided by a fragment thought to belong to the end of the *Danaïdes*, the last play of the trilogy. It is spoken by Aphrodite, in an uncertain context:

ἐρᾷ μὲν ἁγνὸς <u>οὐρανὸς</u> τρῶσαι χθόνα,
ἔρως δέ <u>γαῖαν</u> λανβάνει <u>γάμου</u> τυχεῖν·
ὄμβρος δ' ἀπ' εὐνάεντος <u>οὐρανοῦ</u> πεσὼν
ἔκυσε γαῖαν· ἡ δὲ τίκτεται <u>βροτοῖς</u>
<u>μήλων</u> τε βοσκὰς καὶ βίον Δημήτριον
δένδρων τ' <u>ὀπώραν</u>· ἐκ νοτίζοντος <u>γάμου</u>
<u>τελεῖθ</u>' ὅσ' ἔστι· τῶν δ' ἐγὼ παραίτιος. (frag. 44 Radt)

Holy sky desires to pierce the earth,
and desire for marriage seizes the land.
Rain falling from fair-flowing sky
fertilizes the land, and she bears for mortals
pasturage for herds, life-giving grain of Demeter,
and the fruit of trees in season. By the moistening marriage
all that exists is perfected.
These things I help to cause.[130]

This passage contains a mythological version of the theory of generation discussed in section 5. Here, as in Aristotle, the male principle, moist and heavenly, fertilizes the female, earthy material, and thus "perfects" generation. Sky in the fragment plays a role very similar to that of Zeus in *Suppliants* in his role as fertility god:

καρπο<u>τελῆ</u> δέ τοι
<u>Ζεὺς</u> ἐπικραινέτω
φέρματι <u>γᾶν πανώρῳ</u>·
πρόνομα δὲ <u>βοτὰ τοῖς</u>
πολυγόνα <u>τελέθοι</u>,
τὸ πᾶν τ' ἐκ δαιμόνων θάλοιεν· (*Supp.* 688–93)

May Zeus fulfill the fruit-perfecting earth,
so that she bears crops in every season.
For them [sc. Argives] also, may forward-grazing herds be perfected
having many offspring,
and may they flourish in all things by the will of the divinities.

The words underlined in the Greek text show that the two passages use similar vocabulary to express the earth's fertility. Earth (γαῖαν, γᾶν), through the agency of the sky god (οὐρανὸς, Ζεὺς), is said to give to mortals (βροτοῖς, τοῖς) fruits in season (ὀπώραν, πανώρῳ). Herds of animals (μήλων, βοτά) are also among the blessings mentioned. In both passages, fruit and animals are said to be the result of a process of perfecting or completing (τελεῖθ', καρποτελῆ, τελέθοι) through the agency of the fertilizing sky god, and in fragment 44, this perfecting is part of the *telos* (fulfillment) of marriage (γάμου). Since sky in the fragment plays the same role as Zeus the fertilizer in *Suppliants*, the *hieros gamos* (sacred marriage) of the fragment may well be associated with a reconciliation of Zeus and Hera and with a renewal of their marriage.[131]

In the *Suppliants*, then, and in the trilogy as a whole, *philia* relationships are of primary importance. Suppliants claim protection from blood kin on the basis of kinship, and they explicitly threaten the kin they supplicate. One kind of harm to kin is averted when the suppliants are accepted as *xenoi*, but when the play ends they are still in danger from their pursuing cousins. In the lost plays, harm to *philoi* actually occurred when the Danaïds murdered their cousin-husbands. Marriage relationships are important in other ways also. The Io story can be seen as a mythological prototype of the ideal Greek marriage in which the bride is a suppliant and *xenê* of her husband. Moreover, the pattern of marital rupture followed by reconciliation is repeated among both gods and mortals. In the *Suppliants*, proper treatment of *philoi*—kin by blood and marriage, suppliants, and *xenoi*—is associated with fertility, peace, and good government, for the Danaïds pray for these blessings upon those who have honored kin and suppliants (ἅζονται γὰρ ὁμαίμους Ζηνὸς ἵκτορας ἁγνοῦ: 652–53). Attention to *philia* relationships in this play, then, shows that *Suppliants* is not a study in the pathological psychology of individuals, but is instead concerned with profound social and religious issues affecting the entire community.

A Token of Pain: Betrayal of *Xenia* in Sophokles' *Philoktetes*

Philia and its betrayals are among the central issues of Sophokles' *Philoktetes*. Deserted by his Greek friends, Philoktetes has been left on Lemnos with only his powerful bow, the gift of his friend Herakles, to save him from starvation. When a prophecy reveals that Philoktetes or his bow — or both — are necessary to the conquest of Troy, Odysseus is determined to persuade or trick Philoktetes, who now hates his former friends, into rejoining the Greek army.[1] Odysseus persuades Neoptolemos, the son of Philoktetes' friend Akhilleus, to gain Philoktetes' confidence (70–71) by pretending to hate the Greeks as much as Philoktetes does (59). After gaining control of the bow by pretending to be Philoktetes' friend, Neoptolemos is overcome with disgust at his role of false friend. He returns the bow to Philoktetes and proves himself to be a true friend. Although he is unable to persuade Philoktetes to go to Troy, Neoptolemos is willing to sacrifice glory for friendship. The play ends with the appearance ex machina of the deified Herakles, who orders his friend Philoktetes to go to Troy and ratifies the bond of friendship between Neoptolemos and Philoktetes, who will take Troy together, guarding one another like two lions (1436–37).

Much has been written about the different kinds of friendship with which this play is concerned: friendship between fellow Greeks, between military or political allies, between gods and mortals, between people who share the same ideals and have the same natures; friendship based on hate for the same people, friendship founded upon sympathy and pity, even friendship of humans with inanimate objects.[2] Little attention, however, has been paid to one important kind of *philia* relationship to which Sophokles repeatedly alludes: *xenia*.[3]

I argue in this chapter that the formal *xenia* relationship between host and guest has an essential role in the interactions of Neoptolemos and Philoktetes.

The two men not only become *philoi* who like and respect one another, they also establish a *xenia* relationship, initiated by definite prescribed acts and sanctioned by the gods, that obligates each of them to carry out certain responsibilities toward the other. Although blood kinship is not an issue in this play, the *xenia* relationship has a similar dramatic function. This reciprocal relationship resembles blood kinship in many ways, and the *xenia* relationship is particularly close in this case because Philoktetes treats Neoptolemos as a son. For these reasons, when Neoptolemos is about to betray Philoktetes, his act is emotionally and dramatically similar to imminent harm to blood kin, and his subsequent acknowledgment of Philoktetes as a *xenos* is like a recognition between blood kin that averts a *pathos*.

The formal initiation of *xenia* is preceded by a number of preliminary steps that create only a temporary bond. Among these preliminaries are *euergesia* (doing of good services), supplication, and the exchange of *pista* (pledges).[4] *Euergesia* consists in such good service as gift giving or saving someone's life. *Xenia* may also be initiated by supplication; indeed, Gabriel Herman classifies supplication as a kind of "solicited *euergesia*."[5] The initiation of *xenia* may also be preceded by the exchange of *pista*, said by Herman to be objects "of immense symbolic significance. Being imbued with the personality of the giver, they are thought to exercise a binding force upon the personality of the recipient." The *pista* are also called *dexia*, and the initial bond is typically sealed by a ritual handclasp (*dexiôsis*). The gods are called upon to be present as witnesses by means of oaths and libations.[6]

After peaceful relations are established by these preliminaries, a formal ritual is required to initiate *xenia*. The essential elements of *xenia* initiation are a declaration of friendship and an exchange of objects; feasting and oath taking are optional. The ritual may be sealed by the exchange of *symbola* (two halves of a single object, each of which is kept by one partner as a token of their *xenia* relationship).[7] The exchange of gifts in *xenia* initiation differs in several respects from other kinds of gift exchanges that may precede or follow the formal initiation. The initiatory gifts are called *xénia*[8] or *dora*, in distinction from the *pista* that may be exchanged before the initiation and from the *symbola* that may be exchanged after the establishment of *xenia* relations. In literature, the distinctions between *pista* and *xénia* and between a temporary bond and the more permanent *xenia* relationship can be somewhat fluid. Herman notes that Hektor and Aias exchange gifts in *Iliad* 7.287 ff. "not in order to establish *xenia* but in token of temporary cessation of fighting," but that Sophokles represents the exchange as an initiation of *xenia*, since Aias refers to Hektor as his *xenos* (*Aias* 817 ff.).[9] In the exchange of *xénia*, gift is promptly followed by countergift of commensurate worth. A refusal to reciprocate amounts to a declaration of hostilities, and acceptance of the gifts marks the beginning of the *xenia* relationship. Because *xénia* have symbolic as well as functional value, they are unusual objects, each with its own history.[10] This combined symbolic and functional value makes it understandable that weapons are frequently exchanged in Greek warrior societies.[11] Weapons may also be exchanged at an earlier stage as *pista*.[12]

I argue that in the *Philoktetes*, Sophokles alludes to and adapts many features of the *xenia* relationship and its initiation. Like Aias's sword in the *Aias*, Philoktetes' bow is a powerful visual symbol of the instability of friendship, in large part because of its associations with *xenia* ritual. Philoktetes entrusts his bow to Neoptolemos in a way that strongly recalls *xenia* rituals, and Neoptolemos's initial failure to return the bow has connotations of violation of *xenia*. His decision about whether or not to return the bow is in part a decision about whether or not to fulfill the ethical and religious obligations he has incurred toward someone who is much like a *xenos*. When Neoptolemos does return the bow, he completes the initiation of *xenia* and thereafter acts as a *xenos* toward Philoktetes. Sophokles uses language as well as actions to express the instability of friendship. The word *xenos* can vary in meaning and connotation to refer to an enemy stranger, a friendly stranger, a guest, or a ritual friend, and it is often impossible to tell which sense is appropriate in a given passage. The poet skillfully exploits the ambiguities of this word and its cognates in his portrayal of the ambiguous relationship between Neoptolemos and Philoktetes.

After discussing these points in sections 1 and 2, I argue, in section 3, that indirect allusions to violation of *xenia* in the mythological past are also relevant to an understanding of the ambiguities of the dramatic present. In the mythological tradition, Akhilleus begot Neoptolemos on the island of Skyros by means of a deceitful act that violated his *xenia* relationship with Lykomedes. Allusions to Skyros in *Philoktetes* indirectly allude to this less-than-heroic beginning of "the son of Akhilleus," who will, like his father, abuse *xenia* relationships. The emphasis on *xenia* within the play is reinforced by allusions to this mythical background.

1. Initiation of *Xenia*

The importance of the concept of *xenia* in the *Philoktetes* is indicated by the prominence of *xen-* words in the first part of the play. These words occur twice in the first line spoken by the Chorus of Neoptolemos's sailors: "What, oh what, master, should I, a stranger in a strange land [ἐν ξένᾳ ξένον], conceal, or what should I say to the stranger-shy man?" (135–36).[13] Here, *xenos* means primarily "stranger," but the dramatic situation gives the word other connotations as well. These strangers have come in order to gain Philoktetes' trust, and in so doing they will have to become, to some extent, guests of their host Philoktetes. They are in the position of Odysseus and his men arriving at the island of the Kyklopes, who want to know "whether they are savage and violent, and without justice, or hospitable to strangers and with minds that are godly" (*Od.* 9.175–76).[14] The Chorus evidently fear that the man will be as inhospitable as the harborless land of Lemnos (ἄξενον . . . ὅρμον: 217–18) when they hear cries of pain from far off. The sick man then enters on the cue, "He cries aloud something terrible!" (218). Philoktetes' first words, "O, *xenoi!*" (219), recall the Chorus's own first words. The powerful emotional effects of this short line *extra metrum* are enhanced by the rich overtones of the word *xenos*.[15] It rings out like the cries of pain heard by the Chorus, and it echoes *axenon* (inhospitable) in the previous line. At the same time, the word has warmer connotations than "strangers," for the lonely man hopes that these strangers will become friends. He refers to himself as "friendless" (ἄφιλον) and asks Neoptolemos and the sailors to pity him, if they have come as *philoi* (227–29). He also uses *phil-* words of Greek dress (224), Greek speech (234), the wind that brought Neoptolemos (237), and Neoptolemos's native land of Skyros (242).

Philoktetes' friendly feelings toward Neoptolemos are in large part due to his previous friendship with Akhilleus. Although we are not told in this play that Akhilleus and Philoktetes were *xenoi*, this is certainly possible, especially since Philoktetes acts like a *xenos* in treating Akhilleus's son as his own child. He calls the young man "son [παῖ] of the dearest father" (242) and addresses him as though he were his own son: "O child, O son [ὦ τέκνον, ὦ παῖ] of your father Akhilleus" (260). In these passages and others, he frequently uses two words for "child": *teknon* and *pais*.[16] The fact that Philoktetes treats Neoptolemos like a son makes the young man's threatened betrayal all the more pitiable and terrible.

Neoptolemos and the Chorus respond to the lonely man's straightforward appeals for friendship with a reserve that may reflect Neoptolemos's embarrassment at being in a false situation. Neoptolemos uses no *phil-* words or other expressions of friendship or pity, and he even pretends not to have heard of Philoktetes.[17] When he addresses Philoktetes as *xenos* at 232, the word means simply "stranger." Philoktetes now tells the story of his life on Lemnos, complaining that the island has no harbor to receive ships as guests (ξενώσε-ται: 303) and that those who happened to arrive offered him pity only in words (305–13). In a response, the irony of which cannot be missed by the audience, the Chorus state that they pity Philoktetes just as much as those "strangers who had arrived" (ἀφιγμένοις . . . ξένοις: 317–18).[18] In answer to Philoktetes' questions, Neoptolemos now tells a story about his own maltreatment by Odysseus and the sons of Atreus. He addresses Philoktetes as *xenos*, again using the word in the sense of "stranger" (348). Neoptolemos uses the word *philos* for the first time at the end of the story (390). It is important to note, however, that he does not directly address Philoktetes as "friend," but makes the general statement that whoever hates the Atreidai is a friend of his (cf. 585–86). It is Philoktetes who applies this general principle to himself, for, as he thinks (405–6), he and Neoptolemos have both suffered at the hands of the Atreidai and Odysseus.[19] Philoktetes answers, "Having, as it seems, a clear *symbolon* of pain, you have sailed to us, O *xenoi*" (403–4). The prominent position of these words, coming immediately after a brief choral interlude, emphasizes the importance of the new concept they express. These *xenoi*, Philoktetes suggests, do not pity only in words, like the strangers who arrived in the past, but can be compared to ritual friends who carry half of a token (*symbolon*). The comparison suggests not only warm emotion but also the hope and expectation that Neoptolemos will act like a *xenos*. The young man, however, still does not directly express pity or sympathy for Philoktetes.[20] When he again addresses Philoktetes as *xenos* (412), we cannot tell whether this ambiguous word means "friend" or "stranger."

Increased friendly feelings for Neoptolemos lead Philoktetes to take the first steps toward a more formal *philia* relationship. He crouches in the suppliant position (ἱκέτης ἱκνοῦμαι), beseeching Neoptolemos by his parents and dear ones (468–70) and by Zeus of suppliants (484), asking Neoptolemos to pity him (501) and to take him home. He grasps Neoptolemos's knees (προσπίτνω σε γόνασι: 485) in the gesture of supplication and remains in this position until his request is granted. The Chorus ask Neoptolemos to pity Philoktetes, who has experienced things they hope no friend of theirs may suffer (507–9), and they remind their leader that if he rejects this suppliant he will have to fear retribution from the gods (517–18). Neoptolemos, in his deceptive role, pretends to yield to their entreaties when he says, "If it seems good to you, let us sail" (526). At this point, he surely takes Philoktetes by the hand and raises him from his kneeling position, in acknowledgment that he accepts him as suppliant.[21] This gesture, as John Gould notes (see above, chapter 3, section 1), is an integral part of the ritual of supplication, and it is reasonable to believe that it would have been represented on stage. In fact, shortly after 526 Philoktetes explicitly states that Neoptolemos has "raised" him (ἀνέστησας: 666). Now at last when he calls Philoktetes *xenos* (525), the young man's friendly actions appear to Philoktetes to give the word the warmer connotations that it had previously lacked. In accepting Philoktetes as suppliant, Neoptolemos has made him a friend. Philoktetes responds warmly. Although he had frequently called Neoptolemos "child" (*teknon*) up to this point,[22] he had not directly addressed either Neoptolemos or the sailors as *philoi*. Now, however, Philoktetes greets the Chorus, who had asked Neoptolemos to pity him, as *philoi* (531). Although he calls Neoptolemos "the sweetest man" (530), he will not address him as *philos* until 1301, after the young man returns the bow.[23] For his part, Neoptolemos does not reply with any expression of friendship until the next scene, after the entrance of the Merchant. Even then he does so only indirectly, referring to Philoktetes in the third person. He tells the Merchant that Philoktetes is his "greatest friend" (586), a man who shares his hatred of the sons of Atreus. In the absence of direct address, as well as in the sentiment, this passage recalls 389–90, where Neoptolemos expressed his hatred of the Atreidai at the end of his story.

Philoktetes collects his possessions in preparation for departure, giving Neoptolemos an opportunity to remark on the bow he carries: "Is this the famous bow which you now hold?" (654). Neoptolemos then asks to be allowed to touch Herakles' bow, and Philoktetes agrees (656–73), in a scene that contains many allusions to a traditional *xenia* ritual. We have been well prepared for these allusions. Closer friendship ties have been preceded by good service and establishment of *philia* between suppliant and supplicated, as was frequently the case in *xenia* relationships. Philoktetes acts like a *xenos* of Akhilleus in treating his dead friend's son as his own child. Moreover, Philoktetes had explicitly compared the young man to a *xenos* when he mentioned a *symbolon* of pain (403–4). Now, like *xenoi*, the two men make a reciprocal declaration of friendship. Philoktetes' words at 662–70, when he agrees that Neoptolemos will be allowed to touch the bow because of his good deeds, are an implicit declaration of friendship. Neoptolemos makes an explicit statement that he takes Philoktetes as friend (λαβὼν φίλον: 671).[24] No oaths to the gods are given, as sometimes happens in *xenia* initiation, but the bow itself has divine qualities: Neoptolemos asks to be allowed to "do reverence to it as to a god" (657).

It is this bow that gives the scene its most significant resemblances to a *xenia* initiation. The bow is a weapon, and weapons were often exchanged by *xenoi*. Like *xénia*, the bow has functional value, as Philoktetes' means of acquiring food and as the weapon that will capture Troy. The sacred bow also has the immense symbolic value of *xénia*, because it represents Philoktetes' friend Herakles and has the divine qualities of the hero. Later in the play, Philoktetes will personify the bow itself as the friend that pities him (ὦ τόξον φίλον: 1128–31). Philoktetes received the bow from Herakles for *euergesia* (good service: 670), and he in turn says that he will allow Neoptolemos "alone of mortals to touch it, because of your excellence" (668–69).[25] As David Seale notes, this statement indicates that the bow has never before left Philoktetes' hands; it is untouchable as well as sacred.[26] Philoktetes' own identity is defined in terms of his bow. When he tells Neoptolemos who he is, Philoktetes first states that he is the owner of Herakles' bow, only after this giving his own name and that of his father (262–63).[27] In Philoktetes' view, which Neoptolemos implicitly accepts when he agrees to the exchange, the bow symbolically unites Herakles, Philoktetes, and Neoptolemos as friends, for Philoktetes has received it for being "another Herakles, another self," and, in turn, Neoptolemos will receive it for being "another self" to Philoktetes.[28]

Although the symbolic significance of the bow and of the promised exchange mark this scene as much closer to a *xenia* ritual than to the ritual establishment of a temporary bond for a limited purpose by means of declarations and exchange of *pista*, a full and unequivocal *xenia* initiation does not take place here. The two men declare friendship rather than *xenia*, and Neoptolemos does not actually touch the bow at this point, as the future tenses at 659 and 667 indicate. For him to do so now would undercut the dramatic force of the next scene, in which Philoktetes actually gives the bow to the young man.[29] Another departure from the usual pattern of *xenia* initiation is that Neoptolemos will not immediately give another gift to Philoktetes in exchange. Because nothing can be commensurate with Herakles' bow, the

young man's return of the same object to the giver (δόντι δοῦναι: 668) will constitute the traditional gift given in exchange. Even these peculiarities of the
exchange, however, acquire most significance when seen as variations on an
underlying *xenia* pattern. Here, as often in tragedy, the poet adapts ritual patterns for dramatic purposes.[30]

When Philoktetes actually gives the bow to Neoptolemos in the following scene, the previous allusions to *xenia* initiation contribute to the dramatic
power of the gesture. Philoktetes, sensing an attack of his illness coming on,
asks Neoptolemos to keep and guard his weapon, "holding this bow, just as you
asked me a moment ago" (762–66). In this way, he reminds Neoptolemos of
their previous conversation, in which the promised exchange was given many
of the ritual qualities of *xenia* initiation. Next, Philoktetes asks Neoptolemos
not to give the bow up to the Greeks, reminding the young man that he is a
suppliant (πρόστροπον) whose betrayal will lead to Neoptolemos's own punishment by the gods (769–73).[31] Neoptolemos states that the bow "will only
be given to you or to me" (774–75), words that recall the reciprocity of 668
(δόντι δοῦναι).[32] Philoktetes then holds the bow out to Neoptolemos, saying,
"Here, take it" (ἰδού, δέχου: 776). At this point, Neoptolemos stretches out his
right hand and takes the bow from Philoktetes' right hand in a gesture recalling the handclasp of friendship as well as the exchange of *xénia*.[33] In this context, however, the gesture also has overtones of betrayal, because Neoptolemos
has been persuaded by Odysseus to steal the bow from Philoktetes. Mad with
pain, Philoktetes now asks the young man to end his torment by burning him,
as he himself mercifully ended Herakles' life: "Indeed I also once thought it
right to do this service for the son of Zeus, in return for these weapons, which
you now guard" (801–3). This request does not appear to be meant literally,
but it serves to remind Neoptolemos yet again of the scene at 656–73, in which
the divine and symbolic qualities of the bow were so strongly felt. Next
(809–13), Philoktetes says that he does not require Neoptolemos to swear an
oath that he will not abandon him, but he asks instead for a handclasp. As he
grants this, Neoptolemos switches the bow from his right to his left hand, and
the two men engage in the ritual handclasp so often represented in the visual
arts.[34] In giving his hand, Neoptolemos promises only to remain (ἐμβάλλω
μενεῖν: 813) with Philoktetes. The handclasp is also, however, the culmination
of a series of promises, explicit and implicit, by means of which Neoptolemos
has incurred ethical and religious obligations to return the bow and to take
Philoktetes home.[35] Neoptolemos has accepted Philoktetes as suppliant, the
two men have declared their friendship in the presence of the divine bow,
Neoptolemos has said that he will give the bow back only to Philoktetes, and
he has promised to remain. The two men have clasped hands and the bow has
changed hands, in a context giving the exchange connotations of *xenia* initiation. We are made to feel that Neoptolemos's return of the bow will be a com-
pletion of the *xenia* ritual, but that his failure to do so will be a failure to
reciprocate in the exchange of *xénia* and a declaration of hostility.

2. Betrayal and Repentance

These obligations help to create the dilemma Neoptolemos now faces. The Chorus urge him to take advantage of his present opportunity, but Neoptolemos refuses to leave without Philoktetes, saying that the man himself must go to Troy (839–42). In the following episode, Neoptolemos is at a loss (895, 969, 974), torn between conflicting loyalties to military superiors (925–26) and to the man whom he has come to pity (759, 965), and toward whom he has incurred *xenia* obligations. In representing this dilemma, Sophokles continues to allude to *xenia* rituals and to exploit the ambiguities of the word *xenos*.

In his first words after his illness has passed, Philoktetes rejoices that his *xenoi* have kept watch (867–68), using the word to mean something between "friendly strangers" and "ritual friends." Philoktetes believes that Neoptolemos, and the sailors whom he had previously addressed as *philoi* (531), are true friends, who have done good service to him. He also believes that Neoptolemos has acted like a ritual friend in protecting a helpless stranger who has given him a gift. On the other hand, the word also has ironic connotations for Neoptolemos and the audience, who know that this "friend" has acted falsely, as a stranger and an enemy. As he is about to lead Philoktetes to the ship, Neoptolemos is overcome with disgust at his role of false friend (902–3), and he confesses that he has deceived Philoktetes (915–16). Philoktetes says that he has been betrayed and asks Neoptolemos to return the bow, calling the young man *xenos* (923–24). Ivan Linforth takes this word to mean "'stranger'. . . one with whom he had no bond of friendship."[36] This does not, however, capture the rich nuances of the word, used here to allude to Neoptolemos's betrayal of someone toward whom he has incurred the obligations of a *xenos*. Philoktetes is angry and calls Neoptolemos "most hated" (928) precisely because a bond of friendship exists and is on the point of being violated. He begins to curse him but waits to see if Neoptolemos will repent (ὄλοιο—μή πω: 961), believing that the young man's essential nature is good.

In his speech at 932–62, Philoktetes appeals to Neoptolemos as a *xenos*. He supplicates the young man, whom he calls "child" (*teknon*: 932), and he reminds him of his promise, the handclasp, and the gift of the bow:

> ὀμόσας ἀπάξειν οἴκαδ᾽, ἐς Τροίαν μ᾽ ἄγει·
> προσθείς τε χεῖρα δεξιάν, τὰ τόξα μου
> ἱερὰ λαβὼν τοῦ Ζηνὸς Ἡρακλέους ἔχει. (941–43)

> Having sworn to take me home, he leads me to Troy;
> And giving his right hand, taking from me the sacred bow
> of Herakles, the son of Zeus, he keeps it.[37]

Most editors and translators take the phrase προσθείς τε χεῖρα δεξιάν ("giving his right hand") to refer to the handclasp confirming the oath that was given at 813 and mentioned in 941: "having *added* the pledge of his hand to his word."[38] The phrase is ambiguous, however, and can also be taken closely with what follows: "taking from me the sacred bow of Herakles" (942–43). In that case, "giving his right hand" refers not to the handclasp but to Neoptolemos's act of grasping the bow in his right hand (776).[39] Nearly identical language is used when Neoptolemos gives the bow back: "Stretch out your right hand" (δεξιὰν πρότεινε χεῖρα: 1291–92). By accepting this gift, Philoktetes means to suggest in his speech at 941–43, Neoptolemos has pledged himself to return the bow, just as the acceptance of *xénia* obligates the recipient to give a gift in return.

Philoktetes' appeal to Neoptolemos's sense of shame (929) and better nature (940, 950) have a powerful effect, in large part because of these allusions to *xenia* rituals and obligations. They cause the young man to be silent and avert his eyes (934–35, 951),[40] to express his "terrible pity" (965), and to ask, "What shall we do?" (974). The sudden appearance of Odysseus prevents Neoptolemos from acting on any impulse he may have had to return the bow and makes Philoktetes more adamant than ever in his refusal to accompany the Greeks to Troy. Philoktetes continues to appeal to *xenia* obligations when he addresses the Chorus as *xenoi* at 1070, 1190, 1203, and 1184, when he supplicates them and Neoptolemos, calling on "Zeus of the curses" (1181), that is, Zeus who punishes those who harm suppliants and *xenoi*.[41] The confusion of Neoptolemos and his followers is reflected in the Chorus's use of the word *xenos* in two different senses. At 1045–46, they refer to Philoktetes as a "burdensome stranger" (βάρυς . . . ξένος) who cannot yield to his misfortunes, using the same word that Neoptolemos later uses of Philoktetes' "burdensome sickness" (νόσου βαρείας: 1330). Shortly afterwards, they again blame Philoktetes for not yielding (1165–68) but now show much more sympathy in their address to him, as they continue to urge him to go to Troy:

πρὸς θεῶν, εἴ τι σέβῃ ξένον, πέλασσον,
εὐνοίᾳ πάσᾳ πελάταν. (1163–64)

By the gods, if you have any reverence for a *xenos* who approaches in all good will, approach.[42]

Here, the *xenos* who is an object of reverence can only be a ritual friend, as commentators have suggested.[43]

Neoptolemos actually completes the initiation of a *xenia* relationship with Philoktetes when he returns the bow at 1287–92. Philoktetes has retreated into his cave, having given up all hope that Neoptolemos will keep his promise. When Neoptolemos calls him out, Philoktetes addresses him and the Chorus as *xenoi*, using the word in the sense of "enemy strangers" who have come to do further evil to him (1264–66). He calls Neoptolemos "most hated" (1284) and curses him, this time without his previous hesitation (ὄλοισθ': 1285; contrast 961). In response, Neoptolemos tells Philoktetes to take the weapons from his hand, and he swears by Zeus that he is no longer "enslaving" Philoktetes, words the older man calls φίλτατ', "most friendly" (1287–90). Neoptolemos then tells Philoktetes to stretch out his right hand and take the bow: δεξιὰν πρότεινε χεῖρα (1291–92). The gesture recalls that by means of which Philoktetes gave the bow to Neoptolemos, and the language reminds us of that used by Philoktetes to allude to this act in his earlier pleading: προσθείς τε χεῖρα δεξιάν ("giving his right hand": 942). The parallels serve both to stress the reciprocity of the exchange and to contrast Neoptolemos's present act of true friendship with his previous deceptive practices. The stage action heightens the symbolism. Visually, the two men are united in a symbolic handclasp, mediated by the bow, in a ratification of *xenia*, confirmed by oath.

The language used by the two men reflects their changed relationship. The word *xenos*, so charged with ambiguity throughout most of the play, does not recur after 1264, where Philoktetes used it in the sense of "enemy stranger." After the return of the bow, *phil-* words are used of the friendship between Neoptolemos and Philoktetes. Philoktetes now uses a *phil-* word of Neoptolemos for the first time, addressing him as "dearest child" (φίλτατον τέκνον: 1301). Neoptolemos in turn refers to himself as the older man's *philos* (1375, 1385), using the word in a nondeceptive context for the first time.

Xenia is now expressed in acts rather than words. In contrast to the strangers arriving in Lemnos who had pitied only in words (307–8), Neoptolemos acts as a *xenos* toward Philoktetes, who reciprocates. Although Neoptolemos tries to persuade Philoktetes to go to Troy, the older man reminds Neoptolemos of his oath to take him home (1367–68) and asks the young man to keep this promise, made while touching Philoktetes' right hand (1398–99).[44] Neoptolemos yields, in words that recall his earlier deceptive pretense of yielding to similar requests ("If it seems good to you, let us walk": εἰ δοκεῖ, στείχωμεν: 1402; cf. "If it seems good to you, let us sail": εἰ δοκεῖ, πλέωμεν: 526, and "If it seems good to you, let us go": εἰ δοκεῖ, χωρῶμεν: 645).[45] He is prepared to keep his promise to a *xenos* at the price not only of glory, but also of enmity with his friends the Greeks, who, he fears, will attack his land (1404–5). In return, Philoktetes says that he will defend Neoptolemos with the bow of Herakles (1406–7). Philoktetes' willingness to use Herakles' bow, the symbol of *euergesia*, against fellow Greeks has often disturbed commentators.[46] His offer to use the bow in this way gains more intelligibility when seen within the context of the *xenia* relationship. One of the primary obligations *xenoi* had was to defend one another against enemies, and in offering to do this, Philoktetes proves his loyalty to a *xenos*.[47]

The appearance of Herakles adds new dimensions to the friendship between the two men, showing us this relationship from a divine point of view. Herakles arrives to do his mortal friend a favor (τὴν σὴν δ' ἥκω χάριν: 1413) and to give the "advice of friends" (γνώμη φίλων: 1467) that will send Philoktetes to Troy.[48] The god also represents the friendship between the two men that has been brought about by means of his bow. In addition, Herakles is the representative of his father Zeus (1415), to whom Philoktetes prayed when he called on "Zeus of suppliants" (484) and "Zeus of the curses" (1181). Herakles represents Zeus Xenios and Philios, who protects and rewards friendship, for it is his will that Philoktetes and Neoptolemos take Troy as friends fighting together. However, Herakles' words also contain a veiled allusion to "Zeus of the curses," for he warns Neoptolemos to act piously after the sack of Troy: Zeus, he states, values piety toward the gods above all else (1440–44). These words remind Neoptolemos that just as Zeus rewards those who act reverently toward friends, suppliants, and *xenoi*, so he punishes those who violate these relationships. Herakles' statement also reminds the audience that the Neoptolemos of myth in fact did violence to a suppliant, impiously killing Priam at an altar after the sack of Troy.[49]

3. Violation of *Xenia* at Skyros

This allusion, at the end of the play, to the less-than-heroic future of Akhilleus's son deepens the impression, created throughout the *Philoktetes*, that Neoptolemos is characterized ambiguously, as having a mixture of positive and negative qualities. The man who comes close to violating a *xenos* and suppliant in the stage action will actually kill a suppliant in the mythological future. It has not been recognized, however, that these two violations are connected with a third impious act in the mythological past that is also alluded to indirectly in this play. Akhilleus himself violated *xenia* by sleeping with his host's daughter, and this unheroic and treacherous union resulted in the birth of Neoptolemos. His irregular birth created a social ambiguity that helps to explain the young man's insecurity and that is closely connected with the ethical ambiguities that surround Neoptolemos. In this section, a study of the mythological background concerning Neoptolemos's birth shows that the play's emphasis on *xenia* and its violation is reinforced by allusions to Skyros.

In the mythical tradition, Thetis, fearing that her son would be killed at Troy, disguised Akhilleus as a girl and sent him to the court of Lykomedes, king of Skyros, who brought him up with his own daughter Deidameia. Akhilleus, however, abused Lykomedes' hospitality by sleeping with Deidameia in secret and thus begetting Neoptolemos. The Greeks then came to take Akhilleus to Troy. This is the subject of Euripides' *Skyrioi* and may also have been the subject of Sophokles' play of the same title.[50] This Skyrian Akhilleus has much in common with Odysseus, who tried to avoid military service by pretending to be insane, an incident twice alluded to in the *Philoktetes* (lines 73, 1025–26), and with Paris, who also treacherously violated the *xenia* relationship.

Although Sophokles does not allude to any details of this Skyrian episode in the *Philoktetes*, the play contains a number of allusions to Skyros, most of which have negative overtones. When Neoptolemos introduces himself to Philoktetes, he first says that his race (γένος) is from Skyros, and only afterwards states that he is the son of Akhilleus (239–41). Philoktetes' reply (242–43) also alludes to Skyros, although he reverses Neoptolemos's order, addressing the young man as "the son of the dearest father, and of a dear land," and his statement that Neoptolemos is the "foster child" (θρέμμα) of Lykomedes unmistakably alludes to the story of Akhilleus's union with Deidameia. Neoptolemos again mentions Skyros at 325–26: "So that Mykenai and Sparta may know that Skyros also is the mother of brave men." In the context of the mythological tradition, this statement surely has ironic overtones, reminding the audience of Neoptolemos's mother and of Akhilleus's cowardly and deceptive disguise. Skyros is mentioned or alluded to on a number of other occasions in the play, each time in unheroic contexts. According to the story Neoptolemos tells Philoktetes, Odysseus says that Neoptolemos will never carry Akhilleus's arms back to Skyros (381); at 459 Neoptolemos pretends to have given up heroic exploits and to be returning home to Skyros, and at 488 Philoktetes begs Neoptolemos to take him at least as far as Skyros toward his own home and away from Troy. Moreover, when Neoptolemos is in doubt about whether or not to carry on the deception, he wishes that he had never left Skyros (969–70), and Philoktetes begs Neoptolemos to keep his promise by returning home to Skyros and sending Philoktetes home (1367–69), thereby giving up the heroic capture of Troy. Finally, at 1405, Neoptolemos asks Philoktetes what will happen if the Greeks sack "my land," thereby evoking the unheroic scene of Neoptolemos and Philoktetes fighting against fellow Greeks at Skyros.

In *Philoktetes*, then, Skyros is the unheroic antithesis of Troy, and allusions to Skyros serve to characterize Neoptolemos as the child of the unheroic, Skyrian Akhilleus, begotten as a result of violation of *xenia*. The allusions to Skyros and to Lykomedes and the constant concern with the young man's status as Akhilleus's son could not fail to raise questions about his birth in an Athenian audience at the end of the fifth century.[51] That Sophokles was preoccupied with questions of legitimacy is also apparent in his characterization of Teukros in the *Aias* (especially 1008–20). Why, then, is Neoptolemos never explicitly called a *nothos* (bastard) in this play? Allusions to Skyros raise the issue of Neoptolemos's birth without labeling him as a *nothos* and thereby clearly settling the matter. The play thus suggests that Neoptolemos's status as a legitimate son is uncertain and ambiguous. Such as interpretation is in accord with the mythological tradition. Although the fact that Neoptolemos was begotten by an act of treachery to a host appears to have been essential to the myth, Akhilleus may later have married Deidameia.[52] This marriage might have been thought to confer a kind of retroactive legitimacy on Neoptolemos. However this may be, it is clear in *Philoktetes* that Neoptolemos is insecure about his status as Akhilleus's son and that he is portrayed as having an ambiguous nature, well suited to the irregularly begotten son of the Skyrian Akhilleus who violated *xenia* in begetting him.

Neoptolemos's concerns with his birth are reflected most clearly in the story he tells Philoktetes in order to persuade him that they have a common enemy in Odysseus (343–90). Although it is debatable to what extent this story is true, it certainly reveals the young man's preoccupations and desires. After Akhilleus's death, Neoptolemos says, Odysseus and Phoinix took him to Troy on the pretext that he alone could capture the city. Neoptolemos, however, states that his first desire was to see his father while he was still unburied (350–51). Although such a desire would be natural in any son, its expression by a son of doubtful birth reflects particular concern with asserting the rights a legitimate heir would have to participate in the burial of his father. Other events recounted in the story confirm the view that Neoptolemos is preoccupied with his social status. After mourning his father, Neoptolemos says, his first act was to assert his rights as heir, asking the Atreidai "as was right" (ὡς εἰκὸς ἦν) for his father's weapons and other possessions (360–62). The extreme fury Neoptolemos claims to have felt when he learned that they had given the arms to Odysseus (367–70) also reflects his social insecurity, for to deprive a son of his father's weapons is to deny that he has a right to them, as a true-born son without question does. This interpretation is supported by the explanation for taking the arms that Neoptolemos's story attributes to Odysseus:

οὐκ ἦσθ' ἵν' ἡμεῖς, ἀλλ' ἀπῆσθ' ἵν' οὔ σ' ἔδει.
καὶ ταῦτ', ἐπειδὴ καὶ λέγεις θρασυστομῶν,
οὐ μή ποτ' ἐς τὴν Σκῦρον ἐκπλεύσῃς ἔχων. (379–81)

You were not where we were, but were absent [in a place] where
     you should not have been.
Since you speak so boldly,
You will never sail back to Skyros having these [arms].

These words would have been especially bitter to Neoptolemos because they would have reminded him of his birth at Skyros, a place where he should not have been born, and of the doubtful social status that allowed him to be insulted and robbed (383–84) with impunity. Significantly, Neoptolemos suggests that Odysseus is himself a bastard when he says that his pretended enemy was born from "base men," that is, Sisyphos (384). Shortly afterwards, Philoktetes also calls Odysseus a bastard when he refers to him as "the man bought by Laertes, the son of Sisyphos" (417).[53]

Indeed, it is as hard to determine the truth about the story as it is about Helenos's prophecy.[54] Some evidence for the story's falsehood is provided by the fact that Odysseus tells Neoptolemos in the Prologue that he must deceive Philoktetes with words (55), telling the older man that he, Neoptolemos, is sailing home after being deprived of Akhilleus's arms (58–64). Odysseus's speech appears to single out the fact that Neoptolemos is the son of Akhilleus as the only true part of the tale (57: τόδ' οὐχὶ κλεπτέον). It would seem, then, that Odysseus proposes a false "plot," and that everything else, the "episodes," are invented by Neoptolemos (64–65).[55] According to this interpretation, all of the events of the story are completely false. On the other hand, there are reasons to question this view. Neoptolemos does not acknowledge that the story is false when Philoktetes says later on that Odysseus's taking of the arms was theft and *hybris* (1364–65). Moreover, according to the mythological tradition followed by Sophokles himself in the *Aias*, Odysseus did take Akhilleus's arms. Another possible interpretation of the story in the *Philok-*

tetes, then, is that Odysseus really did take the arms and that Neoptolemos resented this, either when it first occurred or later on, during the course of the stage action. It is also possible that, in inventing the story of his anger about the arms, Neoptolemos has come to be resentful in earnest. Perhaps when Philoktetes says later in the play that the Greeks have outraged Neoptolemos in stealing the arms from him, Neoptolemos sees that this is true and acknowledges as much in responding, "You speak rightly" (λέγεις μὲν εἰκότ᾽: 1373; cf., in the story narrative, ὡς εἰκὸς ἦν: 361). The text of the play simply does not give us enough information to allow for a decision about the story's veracity.

The fact that Neoptolemos's story is ambiguous, admitting of very different interpretations, accords well with the doubtful circumstances of his birth, for the ambiguous social status of bastards was often thought to be reflected in their words and characters. That bastards were associated with falsehood of all kinds is apparent from the fact that *nothos* can mean "spurious, counterfeit, supposititious" as well as "bastard" (LSJ s.v. νόθος). In Sophokles' time, as in later periods, words denoting illegitimacy were terms of general abuse, and bastardy was associated with such negative qualities as slavery, sterility, disease, and physical deformity.[56]

4. The Son of Akhilleus

Against the background of Skyros and Neoptolemos's irregular birth, Sophokles' ambiguous characterization of Neoptolemos in the story and elsewhere in the play appears less puzzling. Many scholars hold that at the end of the *Philoktetes*, the young man shows that his true *physis* (nature) is the same as that of the Akhilleus who emerges at the end of the *Iliad*: courageous, honest, loyal to friends, compassionate to the weak, ruled by shame, and entirely opposed to deceit. According to this interpretation, "Neoptolemos derives his *phusis* from Achilles, betrays it and then redeems himself: acting in accordance with his *phusis*."[57] It is undeniable that Neoptolemos is characterized as having many noble qualities. The young man's noble *physis* is shown, first, by his reluctance to obey Odysseus, saying that he would rather fail while doing good than win victory by doing evil (94–95). Odysseus admits that it is contrary to Neoptolemos's nature to speak or contrive evil things (79–80). When Odysseus tries to persuade Neoptolemos to give himself to Odysseus "for shamelessness, for one brief part of a day" (83–84), Neoptolemos asks whether it is not shameful to speak falsehoods (108). Neoptolemos's noble *physis* is also shown by his natural pity for Philoktetes (ἔφυν οἴκτου πλέως: 1074), by his natural disgust with deceit ("All is disgusting, when one leaves one's own nature": 902–3), and by his decision to return the bow, at which Philoktetes exclaims, "You have shown the nature, son, from which you sprang" (τὴν φύσιν δ᾽ ἔδειξας, ὦ τέκνον, / ἐξ ἧς ἔβλαστες: 1310–11). It is shown, finally, in his decision at the end of the play to keep his promise to Philoktetes at the price of glory, victory, friendship with the other Greeks, and perhaps even his life if his former friends attack him.

On the other hand, William Calder believes that Neoptolemos is portrayed as an arch-deceiver throughout the *Philoktetes*.[58] Although this assessment goes too far, Calder's point that a noble Neoptolemos is contrary to the Greek tradition deserves serious consideration. In the *Little Iliad*, Neoptolemos killed Priam and the child Astyanax after the fall of Troy. According to Pindar (*Paean* 6, 112–21), Neoptolemos killed Priam at an altar, for which Apollo caused him to be killed at Delphi. Neoptolemos prevents Andromakhe from burying Astyanax in Euripides' *Trojan Women* (1155–1206), and he kills Polyxena in the *Hekabe* (518–82).[59] In Euripides' *Andromakhe*, Neoptolemos offends Apollo and outrages human decency in his own house by forcing his wife to live with his slave concubine. Sophokles' *Hermione* was about the same story (see appendix B) and may also have contained a negative portrayal of Neoptolemos.

In addition to those already noted, there are many other indications in the *Philoktetes* that Sophokles followed the mythological tradition in characterizing Neoptolemos not simply as a young man with a noble nature who has been corrupted by the education in deceit he has received from Odysseus,[60] but as someone whose very nature is flawed, having inherent, Odyssean aspects.

In the Prologue, Neoptolemos differs strikingly from the Akhilleus of *Iliad* 9 in being so quickly persuaded by Odysseus. Neoptolemos asks if it is not shameful to tell lies (108), but after Odysseus states that only by deceiving Philoktetes can Neoptolemos get the profit (κέρδος: 111, 112) of taking Troy, Neoptolemos immediately yields: "If that's the way it is, it [the bow] must be hunted down" (116). He is now ready to cast off all shame (120) for personal gain. In contrast, the Akhilleus of *Iliad* 9 stubbornly resists Odysseus, Phoinix, and Aias, scorning the gifts and the promise of glory offered him by the Greeks. This contrast between father and son is highlighted at 343–44, where, according to the story Neoptolemos tells Philoktetes, two members of the embassy to Akhilleus, Odysseus and Phoinix, go to Skyros to persuade Neoptolemos to go to Troy and easily succeed.[61]

Neoptolemos's manner of telling the story about the arms to Philoktetes also suggests that he is by nature in some ways more like Odysseus than like Akhilleus.[62] Akhilleus states (*Il.* 9.312–13) that he hates a liar like death. Neoptolemos, however, shows no sign at all of shame as he tells what we have been led to believe are the lies invented by Odysseus. He adds vivid details and dramatic dialogue to the story Odysseus told him to tell, and his story is as good as any Odysseus himself tells in the *Odyssey*. It is a masterpiece of persuasion, exactly calculated to arouse Philoktetes' sympathy.[63] Neoptolemos's ability to speak and persuade is especially remarkable in so young a man, and his lack of embarrassment at speaking at such length before an older man is in itself evidence of the fact that he has cast off shame. In contrast, Odysseus's son Telemakhos hesitates to question Nestor, remarking that a younger man is ashamed to speak before an older man (*Od.* 3.24).

There are other disturbing elements in Neoptolemos's words and actions. He yields to Odysseus after fewer than seventy lines, but does not "return to himself" for 1,000 lines after meeting Philoktetes.[64] Moreover, Neoptolemos's attitude toward Philoktetes during this period is portrayed as ambiguous. What we are presented with is not a noble young man playing the part of a villain, but someone playing a double role. His words and actions admit of two opposite interpretations; they may be viewed as either sincere or deceitful, and Sophokles does not allow us to decide the issue definitively.[65] Even after Neoptolemos returns the bow, his conduct is open to question in some respects. As noted above, he fails to confess, when Philoktetes mentions the theft at 1364–65, that his story about the arms of Akhilleus was inspired by Odysseus. Yet this story was one of the foundations for the *philia* between Neoptolemos and Philoktetes. It was the "token of pain" (403) that led Philoktetes to befriend Neoptolemos, and it remains, for Philoktetes, an important basis for this friendship.[66] In addition, Neoptolemos shows an Odyssean concern with profit, even at the end of the play, asking, "How could one be ashamed of profiting?" (1383).[67]

Sophokles' negative portrayals of Neoptolemos are reinforced by ironies and ambiguities in the Prologue, where the young man states:

ἔφυν γὰρ οὐδὲν ἐκ τέχνης πράσσειν κακῆς,
οὔτ' αὐτὸς οὔθ', ὥς φασιν, οὑκφύσας ἐμέ.
ἀλλ' εἴμ' ἑτοῖμος πρὸς βίαν τὸν ἄνδρ' ἄγειν
καὶ μὴ δόλοισιν. (88–91)

It is my nature to do nothing by evil craft,
nor was it, so they say, his who begot me.
But I am ready to lead the man off by force
and not with deceit.

This statement is ironic in view of the fact that Akhilleus used deceit precisely in the act of begetting Neoptolemos. Moreover, it admits of two interpretations. Neoptolemos might be claiming that it is his nature, as it was Akhilleus's, to do brave deeds by force (*bia*), while the use of deceit to do evil is contrary to his nature. However, Neoptolemos's words can also mean that although doing evil by craft is contrary to his nature, doing evil by force is not. Neoptolemos's next words support the latter interpretation: "with only one foot he will not by force defeat us, who are so many" (91–92). This readiness to use force *because* (γάρ) he is one of many against a single, one-footed man shows Neoptolemos to be undisturbed by a cowardly, ignoble use of violence that is far removed from bravery.[68] It is noteworthy that Neoptolemos is prepared to do this even though he is still resisting Odysseus. The young man does not yield, "casting off all shame," until line 120. Sophokles again represents Neoptolemos as willing to use ignoble violence when Philoktetes reproaches the "son of Akhilleus" (940) for leading him off by force as though he had captured a strong man, although in fact Philoktetes is a corpse, the shadow of smoke, a phantom (945–47).

In representing Neoptolemos as being prepared to use force in a cowardly way, even before he has been persuaded by Odysseus, Sophokles characterizes him as being in some respects Odyssean by nature. Violence against a defenseless person is also employed or threatened by Odysseus (983, 988, 1003, 1297), who is a coward, running ignominiously and threatening to call in the Greek army when Neoptolemos is about to draw his sword (1257–58) and again after Philoktetes regains his bow and threatens him with it at 1299.[69] In associating cowardly violence with Odysseus in this way, Sophokles is using and adapting the epic tradition according to which Akhilleus represents *bia* while Odysseus represents artifice (*mêtis*).[70] Sophokles' Odysseus, like Homer's, is a man primarily of words, not deeds. He says that he has learned that the tongue is supreme, not deeds (99), and he tells Neoptolemos that *bia* will not succeed against Philoktetes, although deception will (101–3). However, Sophokles' Odysseus differs from the epic Odysseus in also being Ὀδυσσέως βία ("the force of Odysseus"), a man who employs a violence that is the opposite of courageous force.[71] This cowardly, Odyssean nature, of course, also belongs to the Skyrian Akhilleus, draft dodger and host deceiver. Against the Skyrian background, Philoktetes' words to Neoptolemos have a certain irony: "You have given proof of the nature, child, from which you sprang: not from Sisyphos as father, but from Akhilleus" (1310–12).

Herakles' allusions at the end of the *Philoktetes* to Neoptolemos's actions at Troy also forcibly remind us that the Neoptolemos of tradition will eventually turn out to be the opposite of the admirable Akhilleus of the end of *Il.* 24. At the beginning of this book, Akhilleus is characterized by Apollo as someone who is like a savage lion in his *bia*, without pity or shame (39–45). In the course of this book, however, Akhilleus acquires both of these traits. His pity for Priam and *aidôs* for the gods (503) are shown by his act of giving back Hektor's corpse. Neoptolemos, however, will undergo the opposite transformation. When he sets out for Troy at the end of the *Philoktetes*, Neoptolemos resembles the Akhilleus of the end of *Il.* 24, for he has come to pity Philoktetes and to be governed by the shame he cast off in the Prologue. After the fall of Troy, however, the Neoptolemos of tradition will prove to be more like Akhilleus as he is portrayed earlier in this book. Instead of giving back the body of Priam's son, Neoptolemos will kill Polites before his father Priam's eyes, and instead of pitying Priam the suppliant, as Akhilleus did, Neoptolemos will kill the old man at an altar. The obvious contrast, together with aspersions on Neoptolemos's legitimacy, is made by Virgil's Priam, in his address to Neoptolemos just before his death:

> at non ille, satum quo te mentiris, Achilles
> talis in hoste fuit Priamo; sed iura fidemque
> supplicis erubuit corpusque exsangue sepulcro
> reddidit Hectoreum meque in mea regna remisit.

> Achilles—
> you lie to call him father—never dealt
> with Priam so—and I, his enemy;

> for he had shame before the claims and trust
> that are a suppliant's. He handed back
> for burial the bloodless corpse of Hector
> and sent me off in safety to my kingdom. (*Aeneid* 2.540–43: Mandelbaum)

In all of these ways, Sophokles portrays Neoptolemos as an ambiguous figure, whose doubtful status as a son irregularly begotten by the deceitful Skyrian Akhilleus is reflected in his ambiguous words and in the constant tension between heroic and antiheroic traits in his characterization. It is significant that the figure who resolves the dramatic impasse at the end of the play, in a way that many modern readers find troubling and ambiguous, is Herakles, himself a bastard and the patron of bastards in Athens.[72]

This chapter has shown that the closing scene of the *Philoktetes* is a fitting conclusion to a play in which the ambiguities of friendship and *xenia* relationships have had so important a role. It leaves us with the final image of a god uniting in friendship two men who have been *xenoi* in all its different senses: enemy strangers, friendly strangers, host and guest, ritual friends. The ambiguities of their relationship are reflected in the ambiguities associated with Herakles, bastard and deified mortal, and they are well symbolized by Herakles' bow, now carried by Philoktetes. The bow, like the relationship between the two men, has both positive and negative aspects. It represents past good service of Philoktetes to Herakles (670), present *xenia* between Philoktetes and Neoptolemos, and future friendship and good fortune, since it will be used by the two men to take Troy. On the other hand, the bow is also associated with bad fortune and betrayal.[73] It brought "much pain and labor" (πολύπον') to Herakles and Philoktetes (776–78), and Neoptolemos originally obtained it from Philoktetes in a deceptive pretense of friendship and *xenia*. As the god's bow and the instrument that will take Troy, the bow also reminds us of the last words of the gods, promising good fortune but containing a warning as well. Neoptolemos will be a "stranger in a strange land" (ἐν ξένᾳ ξένον: 135–36) in Troy, just as he has been on Lemnos, and there also he will need to act reverently toward suppliants in order to avoid the wrath of the gods. For the moment, the bow symbolizes the ties of friendship that unite men and gods and the story appears to have a happy ending. We know, however, that the story is not finished.[74]

Sleeping With the Enemy: Euripides' *Andromakhe*

The *Andromakhe* is one of six exceptional plays (see chapter 1, section 3) in which harm to *philoi* at first appears to be less central than in most other plays. Menelaos and Hermione threaten Andromakhe and Molossos, who are not blood kin to them, and Orestes is implicated in the murder of Neoptolemos, who is not his kin. Although threats to a suppliant occur in the first part of the play, suppliancy is not the main concern of the play as whole. *Xenia* does not figure in *Andromakhe*, nor does spouse murder spouse, as happens in Aiskhylos's *Agamemnon* and Sophokles' *Women of Trakhis*. Nevertheless, this play, focusing as it does on conflict between the wife and concubine of Neoptolemos, is centrally concerned with violations of *philia* within the marriage relationship. In the Greek view, the acts it represents are just as dreadful as kin murder and incest.

This play is concerned with events in the troubled household of Neoptolemos, son of Akhilleus and grandson of Thetis and Peleus. After Akhilleus kills Hektor in the Trojan War, his son Neoptolemos takes Hektor's wife Andromakhe as a slave and has a son by her, unnamed in this play, but called Molossos in the later tradition. Neoptolemos has also married the daughter of Menelaos, Hermione, who is still childless when the stage action begins. When Neoptolemos goes to Delphi to make amends for his previous impiety in demanding that Apollo pay the penalty for killing Akhilleus, Hermione takes advantage of his absence to threaten the lives of Andromakhe and Molossos. Andromakhe sends her son away to save him and flees for protection to Thetis's shrine. Andromakhe resists Hermione's attempts to dislodge her from the sanctuary, but when Menelaos arrives with Molossos, whom he threatens to kill unless Andromakhe yields, the mother is forced to leave the altar. Menelaos then goes back on his agreement to save Molossos and seizes both mother and son. Peleus arrives at the last minute and succeeds in freeing the prisoners and forcing Menelaos to retreat to Sparta. Left behind by her father, Hermione attempts suicide and expresses great fear of Neoptolemos's anger. She is saved from her plight by the arrival of Orestes, to whom she had previously been betrothed. He offers her protection and marriage and reveals that he has contrived a plot against Neoptolemos. After they leave together, a messenger reports the death of Neoptolemos at Delphi. The young man's body is then brought in and Peleus mourns the death of his grandson and heir. The play ends with the appearance of Thetis ex machina, revealing that Peleus is to live with her as an immortal, that they are to be reunited with their son Akhilleus, who now lives in the Blessed Isles, that Andromakhe is to marry the ruler of the Molossians, and that Molossos will be the father of Molossian kings.

In this tangled plot, Neoptolemos's *philoi* injure or attempt to injure one another in a series of actions that leads to the destruction of his house. Relationships in this play are so twisted and perverted that not only do *philoi* treat one another as enemies, but enemies also treat one another as close *philoi*. Andromakhe, the wife of Hektor, is the natural enemy of the family of Akhilleus, who killed Hektor. Yet, she is treated as a close *philê*, who lives in Neoptolemos's house and has a child by him. In treating this enemy as a friend, Neoptolemos also thereby treats his *philoi* as enemies. In *Andromakhe,* inappropriate relationships with enemies play the same role that kin murder does in other tragedies.

1. The *Authentês* Relationship

When *philos* harms *philos*, as happens in many tragedies, the distinctions between friends and enemies are confused and perverted. In committing patricide and incest, Oidipous not only mixes up the roles of father and son, wife and mother,[1] he also blurs the distinctions between friend and enemy by treating his *philoi* as enemies. In all three dramatizations of Orestes' matricide, son becomes enemy of his mother, his natural *philê*, and his relations with other kin also become problematic. Euripides exploits these possibilities in the *Orestes,* in which Orestes' matricide involves him in a complex network of ambiguous relationships with his other kin: Menelaos, Tyndareos, Helen, and Hermione. In the *Andromakhe,* on the other hand, Euripides shows that treating an enemy like a friend results in a confusion of the categories of friend and enemy similar to that caused by kin murder and incest. Hermione makes this explicit:

> You are so ignorant, wretched woman, that you dare to sleep with the son of the man who killed your husband, and to bear children to a murderer of your family.[2] All the barbarian race is like this. Father has intercourse with daughter, son with mother, sister with brother; they murder their closest kin, and law does not prevent them from doing any of this. Do not bring these things

to us. It is not good for one man to hold the reins of two women, but he is content to look to one marriage bed, whoever does not wish to live badly in his house.[3] (170–80)

It is reasonable to see a parallel between kin murder and incest on the one hand and sleeping with one's enemy on the other, for, according to Greek thought, helping enemies is just as wrong as harming friends.[4] To help enemies is in fact equivalent to harming friends, because one's enemy is also the enemy of one's friends and may be expected to use any advantage to harm them.

In Hermione's speech, Andromakhe is said to be guilty of treating as a *philos* a specific kind of enemy: an *authentês*. In some instances the term *authentês* refers to a person who kills his or her own kin, but the term is most commonly used to refer to the murderer of someone else's kin.[5] That is, X is *authentês* to Y if X has killed a relative of Y. This relationship, like *xenia* and suppliancy, is one between families, so that the relatives of X are also *authentai* to the relatives of Y. Thus, not only Akhilleus but also Neoptolemos, the son of the man who killed Hektor, is *authentês* to Hektor and his family. That Andromakhe is just as much aware of this relationship between families as is Hermione is shown by her use of the plural in stating, "I was married to the murderers of Hektor" (403). The idea that the *authentês* relationship is one between families has a basis in Greek law, according to which the relatives of a murdered person have the right and the duty to avenge his or her death on the family of the murderer. On the other hand, to fail to punish an *authentês* is to fail in important obligations to *philoi*. This helps explain why pollution is created by association with an unrelated murderer of one's own kin as well as by association with someone who has committed kin murder. According to Antiphon, murder trials were held in the open air so that the murdered person's *philoi* would not have to incur the pollution of being under the same roof with those who were *authentai* to them.[6] For an *authentês* to sleep with the wife of the man he has killed is the worst of pollutions for her and the ultimate insult to other kin of the dead.[7] Sophokles' *Elektra* says that the ultimate *hybris* is for Aigisthos, an *authentês*[8] to her family, to share Klytaimestra's bed (271–74), and Andromakhe in Euripides' *Trojan Women* shudders at the idea of being the concubine of Neoptolemos and a slave in the house of those who are *authentai* to her (659–60).[9]

The *authentês* relationship plays an important role in *Andromakhe*. Not only is Neoptolemos *authentês* to Andromakhe, she is *authentês* to him. Menelaos says that Andromakhe is a sharer in the murder of Akhilleus, since she was the sister-in-law of Paris, who killed Akhilleus (654–56). He blames Peleus for not only living in the same house with the woman who is *authentês* to him, an act which would in itself cause pollution, but for actually sharing his table with her and allowing her to bear enemy children in his house (657–59). In Homer, Andromakhe's enmity with Akhilleus and his *philoi* has even deeper roots, for Akhilleus, who killed her father and brothers (*Il.*

6.414–24), was *authentês* to Andromakhe even before killing Hektor. Although this is not mentioned in Euripides' play, it is reasonable to suppose that the audience would have remembered the story, which is recounted in one of the most famous passages in Homer, the farewell scene between Hektor and Andromakhe. In some versions of the myth, Neoptolemos killed Priam and had a role in the murder of Astyanax. These events, however, do not seem to be consistent with the version given in the *Andromakhe*, in which Astyanax and Priam are mentioned but no hint is given of Neoptolemos's role in their deaths. Dramatic emotion in this play is concentrated on the central horror of Andromakhe's marriage to the son of a murderer of her husband.[10] Menelaos's statement that Andromakhe shares in Akhilleus's murder is a response to Peleus's accusation that Menelaos himself, the instigator of the Trojan War, is *authentês* to Akhilleus (614–15). Here, the word means simply "murderer," but because of its connotations, Peleus is also suggesting that Menelaos is *authentês* to Peleus.[11] If Menelaos is *authentês* to Peleus and Neoptolemos, so is his daughter Hermione. It is not surprising, then, that Andromakhe and Hermione also accuse each other of being involved in the murder of Akhilleus. Hermione says that Thetis hates Andromakhe's country for the murder of Akhilleus, to which Andromakhe retorts that Helen, Hermione's mother, is really his killer (246–48). In attempting to kill Andromakhe and her son by Neoptolemos, Menelaos and Hermione actually act as *authentai* to their relation by marriage. Finally, in demanding justice from Apollo for the death of his father Akhilleus (53, 1106–8, and 1194–96), Neoptolemos treats a god as though he were a human *authentês*.[12]

In *Andromakhe* these inappropriate relationships between murderers and victims lead, as does kin murder in other tragedies, to a confusion of the roles of friend and enemy and to the confounding of houses (σύγχυσιν δόμων: 959). Central to this play are the disastrous consequences that result from the union of Neoptolemos and Andromakhe, a woman to whom he is *authentês* and a foreign slave whom he treats as a wife. It is Andromakhe, not Hermione, whose relationship with Neoptolemos is ambiguous and problematic.[13] Hermione has many defects as a wife, but in this play, her marriage to Neoptolemos leads to ruin only because of the presence of Andromakhe and Molossos. The union of Neoptolemos with Hektor's widow would be problematic even in the absence of Hermione or any other legitimate wife; it is especially disastrous in this case because it results in the birth of a son, while Neoptolemos's legitimate wife remains barren. Andromakhe's introduction to Neoptolemos's household even leads to a confusion of roles on the divine level, for she is both the widow of the enemy of Thetis's son Akhilleus and the mother of the goddess's great-grandson. As Thetis's speech at 1242–52 makes clear, divine intervention alone can resolve the resulting difficulties. In bringing Andromakhe into his house, Neoptolemos, like Paris, contracts a marriage that is no marriage, but ruin (*atê*: 103). Just as Paris's relationship with Helen destroyed both Troy and himself, so Neoptolemos's "marriage" to Andromakhe destroys his house.

The view that it is Neoptolemos's relationship with Andromakhe that is problematic is supported by a passage in Andokides comparing Alkibiades' relationship with a slave woman to events that take place in tragedy. There can be little doubt that the author had Euripides' *Andromakhe* in mind:

> [Alkibiades,] who goes so far in excessive villainy that, after giving his opinion that the Melians should be enslaved, he bought one of the captive women and begot a son from her. This child came into being so much more lawlessly than did Aigisthos[14] that he was born from those who were the greatest enemies to each other; moreover, of those who are his closest relatives, some have done the greatest wrongs, and others have suffered them. It is right to make his recklessness still more obvious. He begot a son from this woman whom he made a slave instead of free, and whose father and relatives he killed, and whose city he devastated, so that he might make his son the greatest enemy to himself and his city; by such great necessities is he compelled to hate. When you see these kinds of things in tragedies, you think them terrible, but when you see them happening in the city you think nothing of them.[15]

2. Ambiguities

Neoptolemos's union with Andromakhe has created a situation in which they themselves and the other dramatic figures are both *philoi* and enemies to one another. When they are forced to act in these circumstances, their actions are ambiguous, since they help or harm someone who is both *philos* and enemy.[16] All of those connected by blood or marriage with the house of Peleus— Neoptolemos, Andromakhe, Molossos, Peleus, Hermione, Menelaos, Orestes, and Thetis—are involved in ambiguous situations.

2.1. *Neoptolemos*

Although Neoptolemos is absent throughout the play, appearing only as a corpse, he is at the center of the web of relationships from which the dramatic action springs.[17] He is related to every other major figure in the play either by birth (Thetis, Peleus, and Molossos) or by marriage (Andromakhe, Hermione, Menelaos, and Orestes). Moreover, because we see him only through the eyes of others, Neoptolemos is defined by his relationships with them, by his roles as husband, master, father, grandson, and son-in-law.

To each of these dramatic figures Neoptolemos is both friend and enemy, the sum of the perverted relationships he has created. Neoptolemos is Andromakhe's enemy, as a Greek and the son of her husband's murderer. Yet in taking her into his household, he treats her as a *philê*, becoming her "husband" and the father of her son, Molossos. Neoptolemos, however, has not acted as a *philos* to Andromakhe and her son. He thrust her aside after marrying Hermione (30, 37), and he left Phthia without providing for her protection or clarifying her position in his household. Andromakhe comments on his absence in time of need and complains that he does not act as a father to Molossos (49–50, 75–76). By failing to protect Andromakhe, Neoptolemos violates the obligations of *philia* he has incurred toward her and Molossos.

On the other hand, in keeping Andromakhe and her son in his household, Neoptolemos injures Hermione, his legitimate wife.[18] Greek custom held that while a man might keep a concubine in a separate establishment, he should never bring her into contact with his legitimate wife, much less allow the two to live in the same house. It was also held to be shameful for a concubine to usurp the wife's place by bearing and rearing children; only legitimate children should be reared in a man's house. Menelaos calls attention to this violation of custom when he complains that Neoptolemos, by allowing Andromakhe "to bear children in his house" (τίκτειν δ' ἐν οἴκοις παῖδας: 659), wrongs both his Greek subjects and Hermione (660–77).[19] By acting in this way, Neoptolemos has produced an explosive situation, highly conducive to the amphimetric strife condemned by the Chorus: "Two beds . . . amphimetric children . . . strife in houses" (δίδυμα λέκτρ' . . . ἀμφιμάτορας κόρους, ἔριδας οἴκων: 465–67).[20] Andromakhe is said to be Hermione's "sharer in marriage" (συγγάμῳ: 836), a word that more often refers to spouses. Unlike that of spouses, however, the union of the two women is an involuntary association that leads to enmity between them and between Andromakhe and Hermione's father, Menelaos. Andromakhe and Hermione are also united by another unfortunate marriage, that of Paris and Helen, for Andromakhe is Paris's sister-in-law by her first marriage (655–56), and Hermione is Helen's daughter.

Neoptolemos also acts wrongly in other ways with regard to Hermione. He marries her against Peleus's will and advice (619–21); he marries a woman who had been promised to Orestes, her relative; and, moreover, he insults his rival (966–81). Neoptolemos also acts wrongly in leaving Hermione in his house during his absence, just as Menelaos did when he left Hermione's mother Helen alone (592–95).

Neoptolemos wrongs other *philoi* as well. He acts offensively toward his father-in-law, Menelaos, in keeping, in the same house as his daughter, a concubine who is, moreover, the widow of Hektor, the brother of Paris (655–56), who committed adultery with Menelaos's wife. Although the play does not explicitly mention Neoptolemos's injuries to Peleus and Thetis, we may infer that he also wrongs his grandparents when he brings into his household the wife of their son's enemy. In addition, Neoptolemos fails to protect their only great-grandson and deserts his aged grandfather, leaving him without protection in the midst of disorder. Neoptolemos not only acts badly toward Thetis and all of the major mortal dramatic figures, he also insults Apollo, treating a god who should be honored as the enemy who killed his father (53, 1106–8, 1194–96).

2.2. *Andromakhe*

Andromakhe, the former queen of Troy, is an enemy of all the Greeks (203–4, 515–16, 520, 652–54), but as a member of Neoptolemos's household, she is also their friend. To Neoptolemos she is both friend, as his "wife" and the mother of his son, and enemy, as the wife of Hektor, killed by Neoptolemos's father Akhilleus. Because her two "husbands" are enemies, she cannot be friend to both. Andromakhe states the resulting dilemma in *Trojan Women* 661–64: "If I thrust away dear Hektor and open my heart to my present husband, I will prove false to the dead. But if I love my former husband, I will be hated by my masters." She must either be false to her first husband in order to be loved by her second, or be loyal to her first and hated by her second. Andromakhe's objective position as friend and enemy of Neoptolemos thus has an important psychological counterpart. Andromakhe also has ambiguous relationships with the other dramatic figures. Peleus and Thetis are her grandparents by marriage, the great-grandparents of her child, and the protectors to whom she naturally appeals, but they are also the parents of Akhilleus, who is *authentês* to her. Molossos, Andromakhe's son, is her closest *philos*, but he is also the grandchild of her husband Hektor's murderer.[21]

Andromakhe is placed in these ambiguous relationships against her will, and she does not act as enemy to any of the other dramatic figures. Hermione's charge that she has used drugs to make her rival sterile (32–33, 157–58) is clearly false. On the other hand, Andromakhe errs by being too ready to treat enemies as *philoi*. She is portrayed as attempting to remain loyal to Hektor while sleeping with his enemy, without having resolved the psychological dilemma in which her position places her. Andromakhe refers to Hektor, not Neoptolemos, as her husband (4, 8–9, 107, 112, 227, 456, 523) and her dearest one (222), and she broods over her past life as his wife.[22] She says that she sleeps with Neoptolemos against her will (38), but her own words indicate that she has done her best to comply with and please him. When Andromakhe tells Hermione that being complaisant (ἐπιτηδεία) is a love charm and equates this quality with virtue (206–8), she implies that she has this charm in her relations with Neoptolemos while Hermione does not. As an example of the kind of virtue (226) that attaches a husband to a wife, Andromakhe cites her own frequent (πολλάκις: 224) suckling of Hektor's bastards. This kind of complaisance is *philia* carried to harmful extremes.[23] It is not only contrary to all Greek custom, but was also harmful to her own son Astyanax, Hektor's legitimate heir, whose bastard siblings her acceptance would have helped to legitimate. Indeed, in holding up this kind of wifely virtue as an example to Hermione, Andromakhe implicitly urges her not only to spare Molossos,[24] but also to accept him as heir of the house of Peleus. That Andromakhe's complaisance leads to confusion about who her friends and enemies are is particularly evident in her scenes with Menelaos. Although she says that the Spartans are the greatest enemies (445–46) and that she scorns to fawn on Menelaos (459–60), a change of attitude is suggested by her speech urging her son to supplicate him (528–30). Moreover, instead of calling on Neoptolemos, the father of Molossos, for help, Andromakhe says that she wishes she had Hektor, the son of Priam, as an ally (523–25), apparently forgetting that her late husband would not be eager to give aid to the grandson of his own murderer.

2.3. *Molossos*

Molossos is the embodiment of the contradictions inherent in his parents' relationship. The boy is Neoptolemos's *philos*, as his son, but he is also the son of the wife of a Trojan enemy to whom Neoptolemos is *authentês*. His status as Neoptolemos's only son makes him the enemy of Hermione, his father's legitimate wife, and of Menelaos. Other circumstances of Molossos's birth also put him in an ambiguous position in his father's household. Although he is Neoptolemos's only son, he is a bastard[25] and the son of a barbarian slave mother. The ambiguities are reflected in the conflicting evidence in the play about Molossos's status. He sometimes seems to be a possible heir to Neoptolemos. Menelaos asks whether Andromakhe's children will rule over Greeks (663–66), and Peleus seems to confirm these fears when he says that he will raise the boy in Phthia as an enemy to Menelaos (723–24), using words that suggest that he is planning to adopt the boy as his heir.[26] This suggests that the boy's status is parallel to that of Euripides' Hippolytos, oldest son of Theseus by a barbarian queen he had conquered in war.[27] The Nurse tells Theseus's legitimate wife, Phaidra (*Hipp.* 304–10), that if she dies she will deprive her children of their inheritance. The Nurse further warns Phaidra against Hippolytos, a bastard who aspires to the position of a legitimate son (νόθον φρονοῦντα γνήσι': 309).[28] If Hippolytos could aspire to inheritance, it is reasonable to infer that Molossos could also. On the other hand, Peleus does not appear to take Molossos into account, as he might be expected to do if the boy were his heir, when he laments, after Neoptolemos's death, that his house is empty and that he is childless (1205, 1207, 1216).

According to some scholars, the ambiguities in the status of Molossos as son and Andromakhe as wife result from a tension between heroic and fifth-century values.[29] Although there is much truth to this, it is important to remember that there is no simple dichotomy between heroic and fifth-century values concerning legitimacy. The evidence for the heroic period is hard to evaluate. Homeric bastards seem to have been better off than those of later periods, but they were certainly not on a par with legitimate children. Daniel Ogden notes that the name of Priam's bastard son Isos ("Equal") "salutes both the status to which a bastard might aspire, and the difficulty in achieving it."[30] Even in the fifth century there were significant tensions among competing standards for legitimacy. In the period from the enactment of Perikles' citizenship law of 451/450 until sometime before 403, Athenian citizens were defined as the sons of citizen fathers and of mothers who were the daughters of citizen fathers. They were born from mothers married by *enguê* (betrothal) or *epidikasia* (legal judgment), and were accepted by their father's phratry and deme.[31] Yet even in this period, the system was controversial, under constant pressure, and subject to numerous challenges.[32] Exceptions were made for groups and individuals, including Perikles himself, whose phratry's acceptance of his son by the non-Athenian concubine Aspasia constituted an effective legitimation.[33] Further complications resulted from a law allowing bigamy. For a short time beginning around 413, after the loss of manpower in the Sicilian Expedition, the law allowed a man to marry two citizen women at the same time. Both Sokrates and Euripides took advantage of this bigamy concession, with unhappy consequences.[34]

These complexities mean that there is no firm historical basis for determining the status of Molossos. The children of an irregular or bigamous marriage were not necessarily illegitimate. Nor is Andromakhe's foreign origin decisive. Her son, like the children of Medeia, would, in fifth-century society, fall into the category of the *metroxenoi*, children of a citizen father and a non-citizen mother.[35] Although these children were excluded from citizenship by Perikles' law of 451/450 and discriminated against even before this period, we have just seen that exceptions to Perikles' law were made. Not even Andromakhe's slavery settles the issue of her son's status, for the children of slaves had different expectations in different historical periods. In Homer, slaves could bear free children and perhaps even inherit in the absence of legitimate children.[36] Beginning in the Solonian period in Athens, however, the children of slave concubines, like other *nothoi*, were excluded from the right of succession, from the duty of caring for parents, and from citizenship,[37] and they were probably slaves themselves.[38] The children of slaves could not be legitimized by adoption, or by freeing the mother.[39] In any case, even if there were clear and unambiguous criteria for legitimacy in the heroic age and in the fifth century, neither the play as a whole nor separate elements in it can be assumed to be accurate reflections of any particular historical period.

Further uncertainty about the status of Molossos is created by the fact that Andromakhe's position in Neoptolemos's household is just as ambiguous as that of her son. She sometimes appears to be a slave, but at other times her position seems to be closer to that of a secondary wife. Andromakhe is often called a slave (12, 30, 401, 933, 1243), and she refers in particular to her slavery to Hermione (114). Yet she often behaves more as mistress of the house than slave,[40] and Hermione's threat that she will force Andromakhe to perform the slave's tasks of sweeping and sprinkling the floor (163–68) is an indication that Andromakhe has not yet had to do these things. Moreover, when Menelaos accuses Peleus of allowing her to share a table with him and to bear children in his house (καὶ ξυντράπεζον ἀξιοῖς ἔχειν βίον, / τίκτειν δ' ἐν οἴκοις παῖδας ἐχθίστους ἐᾷς: 658–59), he implies that she is more than a slave. Slaves do not share tables with their masters,[41] and it is wives, not slaves, who live with men and produce children for them.[42] Furthermore, Andromakhe is called a "bride" (νύμφα: 140) by the Chorus, and she herself says that she "married" (νυμφεύομαι: 403) Neoptolemos, using a cognate of the word that refers to

Thetis's marriage to Peleus (20, 1231) and to Hermione's legitimate marriage (193, cf. 987).[43]

All of this conflicting evidence indicates that neither the text of the play nor historical evidence can resolve the ambiguities in the status of Molossos or that of his mother. The boy is represented as having no clear position in the society into which he was born; he must await a divine dispensation to receive his proper heritage.

2.4. *Peleus*

Neoptolemos's marriage to Andromakhe places Peleus in a difficult position as an aged head of household (21–23) concerned about leaving an heir. Peleus's only son is dead, and the only son of that son also has an only son (see 1083) by a woman who is a foreign slave and to whom Peleus is *authentês* as the father of Akhilleus. The ambiguous status of Molossos, who is the eldest son, would be a threat to any future legitimate offspring Neoptolemos might have, just as Hippolytos is a threat to Phaidra's children (Eur. *Hipp.* 304–10). To make matters worse, Peleus dislikes Neoptolemos's legitimate wife, who is the daughter of a vicious woman (619–22). When he is forced to choose between his grandson's legitimate but barren wife and the concubine mother of his great-grandson, Peleus chooses the latter,[44] defending Andromakhe and her son against Menelaos and escorting them to his own home. This act makes him an enemy of his relation by marriage, Menelaos. In protecting Andromakhe and Molossos as *philoi* and quarreling with Hermione and Menelaos as enemies, Peleus seems to Menelaos to be confusing *philoi* and enemies. Menelaos claims that Andromakhe is *authentês* to Peleus as a relation by marriage of Paris, who killed Akhilleus (654–56), and that her offspring are "enemy children" (659), while Menelaos himself and his daughter Hermione are Neoptolemos's "necessary *philoi*" (671). Indeed, Menelaos suggests, mistreatment of *philoi* is in character for Peleus, who killed his brother Phokos (687). Peleus alone, however, is not strong enough successfully to defend Molossos as his heir. After Neoptolemos's death, Peleus appears to recognize that the boy could not have hoped to become king of Phthia when he laments the destruction of his house (1186–87, 1205) and the loss of his rule (1223).

2.5. *Hermione*

Hermione is a worthy child of parents who treated their *philoi* as enemies. Her mother is Helen, a woman whose faithlessness made her the enemy of her husband (592–604), and her father is Menelaos, who ordered his brother Agamemnon to kill Iphigeneia, his own daughter (624–25). As the daughter of Helen, Hermione is an enemy of her fellow Greeks just as much as Andromakhe is,[45] a point made by Andromakhe when she tells her rival that it was Helen who killed Akhilleus (248), thus implying that Hermione is *authentês* to Akhilleus's family. Hermione is also both friend and enemy to her husband, who has married her but has also made her share a house with her rival, thus failing to give her the honors due a wife. Although the play does not explicitly make this point, it would have been obvious to the original audience that, as a barren wife, she is also a threat to his lineage. Placed in this position, Hermione acts as an enemy to her husband and his house, including Peleus and Thetis, in seeking to kill Neoptolemos's son and the mother of his son, an act the Chorus call "godless, lawless, showing no gratitude [ἄχαρις]" (491). These murders would make Hermione *authentês* to her husband and call down his vengeance, as Andromakhe reminds her (338–44). When the attempt fails, Hermione rightly fears that her husband will kill her or drive her from his house (808–10). Although some scholars do not take seriously the idea that Hermione could be in danger of being killed by Neoptolemos,[46] her fear is justified by the Greek view that vengeance was the duty of the kin of murder victims. In seeking to kill Neoptolemos's slave-wife and the son he has allowed to be reared in his house, Hermione acts as *authentês* to him and his family and can expect to be treated as such. As she says to Orestes, Neoptolemos "will justly destroy me" (920). Hermione also acts as an enemy to Thetis when she threatens to violate Andromakhe, a suppliant at her altar.[47] The culmination of Hermione's acts of enmity against Neoptolemos and his house is her running off with Orestes, who has plotted Neoptolemos's murder. She, like Andromakhe, sleeps with an *authentês*.[48]

2.6. *Menelaos*

Menelaos's relationship to Neoptolemos shares in the ambiguities of his daughter's marriage. As Neoptolemos's father-in-law, Menelaos is the friend of Neoptolemos and his house, but he is also an enemy, because of Neoptolemos's relationship to Andromakhe and consequent mistreatment of Hermione. The antithesis of Andromakhe, who tries to be friends with everyone, Menelaos treats everyone as an enemy.[49] He attempts to kill his son-in-law's concubine and son, and he quarrels violently with Peleus, his relation by marriage, who attempts to protect them. He refers to Molossos as the child of an enemy (659), forgetting that the boy is also the child of his own son-in-law.[50] Although Menelaos is the natural friend of his daughter, he does not act as her friend but returns to Sparta without her, thus deserting her in her time of need (805, 854–55). He also acts badly toward Thetis in luring a suppliant away from her altar by a trick. According to Peleus, Menelaos acted as an enemy to all the Greeks in instigating the Trojan War (605–15) and was complicit in the murder of his brother's daughter (624–25).

2.7. *Orestes*

Orestes is both friend and enemy to Neoptolemos. As Hermione's cousin, he is related to him by marriage, but as kin of a wronged wife and insulted rival suitor (977, 994) for that same wife, he is an enemy (1006). Neoptolemos's absence and the quarrel between Andromakhe and Hermione give Orestes the opportunity to assert his claim to Hermione as both kin (887–88, 985–86) and former betrothed (966–69). In killing Neoptolemos with the knowledge of Hermione and taking Hermione as wife, Orestes acts exactly like Aigisthos: both are *authentai* who sleep with the wives of their victims.[51] Orestes is also *authentês* to his blood kin, having killed his mother (an act of which he appears to boast: 999–1001) because she in turn had killed her husband (1028–36). This made it difficult for Orestes to marry outside his own family and contributed to his quarrel with Neoptolemos (974–78). Orestes' matricide gives an ironic twist to Hermione's appeal to Zeus of Kindred (921) when she asks Orestes to save her, to Orestes' statement that he has to marry within his family (974–75), and to his praise of kinship:

τὸ συγγενὲς γὰρ δεινόν, ἔν τε τοῖς κακοῖς
οὐκ ἔστιν οὐδὲν κρεῖσσον οἰκείου φίλου. (985–86)

Kinship is a wonderful thing, and in the midst of evils
nothing is better than one's own family.[52]

Kinship is indeed wonderful. Orestes, *authentês* of his own mother, marries his cousin, to whom, after he kills her husband, he is doubly *authentês*.

2.8. *Thetis*

Thetis is in a position of both friendship and enmity to Andromakhe and Molossos, just as Peleus is. Her marriage to Peleus, moreover, is both cause and paradigm of the troubled relationships in Neoptolemos's household. This topic requires a separate discussion.

3. Thetis and Peleus

Thetis plays an essential role in the mythological background of the play, in the stage setting (dominated by her shrine), and in the resolution. Like her grandson Neoptolemos, Thetis is absent for most of the play but nevertheless central to the dramatic action. Like him, she is visible on stage only at the end of the play, and in an unusual form: he is a corpse, and she appears ex machina. And just as the grandson is defined in terms of his relationships with others, so the grandmother is characterized by her roles as wife and mother.

Thetis figures throughout the play as the bride of Peleus. In the Prologue (16–20), Andromakhe explains that she is in Thessaly, the land where Thetis "used to live with Peleus, apart from people." The goddess has given her name to the place, called "Thetideion"[53] by the natives, "for the sake of the marriage of the goddess" (θεᾶς χάριν νυμφευμάτων). In her appearance ex machina Thetis echoes these words, telling Peleus that she has come "for the sake of our former marriage" (χάριν σοι τῶν πάρος νυμφευμάτων: 1231; cf. 1253: τῆς ἐμῆς εὐνῆς χάριν, "for the sake of my bed"). Visible on stage throughout the play is the shrine of Thetis, reverenced by Peleus and his descendants as a "memorial of the marriage of the daughter of Nereus" (ἑρμήνευμα Νηρῆδος γάμων: 46). This shrine, the representation in stone of Thetis's marriage,[54] is the focal point of the suppliant action in the first part of the play and a silent audience throughout, as it continues to dominate the stage. Andromakhe calls attention to these functions of the shrine when she asks Hermione, "Do you see this image of Thetis watching you?" (246).

Thetis, her marriage, and its visible symbol play ambiguous roles in the play. Thetis is Andromakhe's natural protector, as the great-grandmother of her son and the wife of this son's great-grandfather Peleus, and her shrine is Andromakhe's natural refuge. The woman throws her arms around the goddess's image as suppliant (115) and appeals to Thetis's image when Hermione threatens her with death (246). Yet the shrine and its goddess do not help her. The Chorus imply that the shrine is useless when they repeatedly urge Andromakhe to leave it (129–30, 135), and Hermione explicitly denies that the shrine will help her rival (161), arguing that Thetis hates Troy because of the death of Akhilleus (247). These judgments about the shrine turn out to be correct, for Hermione threatens to attack Andromakhe even at her place of refuge, and Menelaos succeeds in luring her away by a trick. It is not Thetis but the goddess's mortal husband Peleus who saves Andromakhe and Molossos. Not only do Thetis and her shrine fail to save Andromakhe, they also represent the cause of all of her troubles, for Thetis's marriage to Peleus led to the birth of Akhilleus. It was the "son of Thetis of the sea," who killed Hektor and dragged him around Troy (107–8), a murder that led to the fall of Troy, to Andromakhe's enslavement (109–10), and to her present troubles as "most wretched bride" (παντάλαινα νύμφα: 140) of Akhilleus's son. The very goddess whom Andromakhe supplicates is the mother of Akhilleus and thus *authentês* to her.

Thetis's marriage not only had negative consequences for Troy and Andromakhe, it is a divine paradigm of Andromakhe's unfortunate "marriage" to Neoptolemos. Andromakhe says that she, like Thetis, has borne a son to the house of Peleus (24), and just as Thetis has left Peleus (ξυνῴκει: 18, πάρος νυμ-φευμάτων: 1231), so Andromakhe no longer shares Neoptolemos's bed (30). The marriages of both goddess and woman are unnatural and unequal, and Thetis's marriage to Peleus caused her grief, just as Andromakhe's union with Neoptolemos is a source of grief.[55] Andromakhe, a former barbarian queen, is enslaved and bears a child to the Greek son of her Trojan husband's murderer. For her part, Thetis, a goddess (1254), who should have borne immortal children who give no cause for tears (1235), is joined to a man and bears him a mortal son, whose death gives her pain. Like Molossos, Akhilleus is a kind of bastard, the child of an unequal union.[56]

Other aspects of the mythological tradition, to which Euripides alludes more indirectly, suggest that Thetis's marriage is cause and paradigm of the human sufferings represented in the play. As Kirk Ormand notes, the marriage of Peleus and Thetis "is one of the myths that most strongly indicates the bride's dismay at being married, and her disgust at her (lower-class) husband."[57] Many literary sources give accounts, some of which differ significantly from others in the details, of the marriage of Peleus and Thetis and its causes and consequences.[58] Seven passages may serve to represent those aspects of the mythological tradition that are most relevant to the *Andromakhe*. These sources contain important information about a tradition that influenced Euripides, a tradition according to which the marriage is associated with war and disagreement.

Homer's Thetis laments that she has more sorrows than any other goddess, for Zeus forced her to marry Peleus against her will:

1. ἐκ μέν μ' ἀλλάων ἁλιάων ἀνδρὶ δάμασσεν,
   Αἰακίδῃ Πηλῆϊ, καὶ ἔτλην ἀνέρος εὐνὴν
   πολλὰ μάλ' οὐκ ἐθέλουσα.

   Of all the other sisters of the sea he gave me to a mortal,
   to Peleus, Aiakos's son, and I had to endure mortal marriage
   though much against my will.[59]

Homer does not explain why Zeus married Thetis to a mortal, but other sources give two different accounts of his reasons.[60] In the Pindaric version (*Isth.* 8.29–52), Zeus and Poseidon, who are both in love with Thetis, learn from Themis that the goddess is destined to bear a son greater than his father. Since each god fears that he will be overthrown if Thetis marries an Olympian, the gods marry her to a mortal. According to the *Kypria*, on the other hand, Thetis refuses to sleep with Zeus out of gratitude to her foster mother Hera. Zeus then marries her to a mortal because he is angry:

2. [ὁ δὲ τ]ὰ Κύπ[ρια ποίησας "Η]ραι χαρ[ιζομένη]ν φεύγειν αὐ[τοῦ τὸ]ν γάμον, Δ[ία δὲ ὀμ]όσαι χολω[θέντ]α διότι θην[τῶι συ]νοικίσει.

   The author of the *Kypria* [says that Thetis,] in gratitude to Hera, avoided marriage with him [sc. Zeus], and that Zeus in anger swore that he would marry her to a mortal.[61]

According to some accounts, the first union of Peleus and Thetis was a rape. Peleus wrestled with Thetis, who kept changing shape, until he subdued her. After this initial violent encounter, their wedding was celebrated by the gods:

3. Χίρωνος οὖν ὑποθεμένου Πηλεῖ συλλαβεῖν καὶ κατασχεῖν αὐτὴν μετα-
   μορφουμένην, ἐπιτηρήσας συναρπάζει, γινομένην δὲ ὁτὲ μὲν πῦρ ὁτὲ δὲ
   ὕδωρ ὁτὲ δὲ θηρίον οὐ πρότερον ἀνῆκε, πρὶν ἢ τὴν ἀρχαίαν μορφὴν εἶδεν
   ἀπολαβοῦσαν. γαμεῖ δὲ ἐν τῷ Πηλίῳ, κἀκεῖ θεοὶ τὸν γάμον εὐωχούμενοι
   καθύμνησαν.

   Khiron advised Peleus to catch and hold her [sc. Thetis] while she changed shape. Keeping watch he seized her while she became fire, then water, then beast, and did not let go until he saw that she had regained her former shape. He married her on Pelion and there the gods sang, feasting at the wedding.[62]

Not only did the marriage of Peleus and Thetis begin in strife between them, the wedding celebration itself was, according to the *Kypria*, a source of the strife among three goddesses that led to the Judgment of Paris and the Trojan War:

4. Ζεὺς βουλεύεται μετὰ τῆς Θέμιδος[63] περὶ τοῦ Τρωϊκοῦ πολέμου. παρα-
γενομένη δέ Ἔρις εὐωχουμένων τῶν θεῶν ἐν τοῖς Πηλέως γάμοις νεῖκος
περὶ κάλλους ἐνίστησιν Ἀθηνᾷ, Ἥρᾳ καὶ Ἀφροδίτῃ, αἳ πρὸς Ἀλέξανδρον
ἐν Ἴδῃ κατὰ Διὸς προσταγὴν ὑφ' Ἑρμοῦ πρὸς τὴν κρίσιν ἄγονται· καὶ
προκρίνε τὴν Ἀφροδίτην ἐπαρθεὶς τοῖς Ἑλένης γάμοις Ἀλέξανδρος.

Zeus takes council with Themis about the Trojan War. Strife, arriving when the gods are feasting at the marriage of Peleus, begins a quarrel about beauty among Athena, Hera, and Aphrodite. The goddesses, at the command of Zeus, are led by Hermes for judgment to Alexandros on Ida. Alexandros judges in favor of Aphrodite, persuaded to do so by [promise of] marriage with Helen.[64]

Another passage in the *Kypria* also connects the marriage of Peleus and Thetis with the origin of the Trojan War and gives more information about Zeus's reasons for provoking the war in the first place:

5. φασὶ γὰρ τὴν Γῆν βαρουμένην ὑπὸ ἀνθρώπων πολυπληθίας, μηδεμᾶς ἀνθρώπων οὔσης εὐσεβείας, αἰτῆσαι τόν Δία κουφισθῆναι τοῦ ἄχθους· τόν
δέ Δία πρῶτον μὲν εὐθὺς ποιῆσαι τὸν Θηβαϊκὸν πόλεμον, δι' οὗ πολλοὺς
πάνυ ἀπώλεσεν. ὕστερον δέ . . . [ἐποίησεν] τὴν Θέτιδος θνητογαμίαν καὶ
θυγατρὸς καλὴν γένναν, ἐξ ὧν ἀμφοτέρων πόλεμος Ἕλλησί τε καὶ βαρ-
βάροις ἐγένετο.

They say that Earth, burdened by an excess of humans, who lacked all piety, asked Zeus to lighten her burden. Zeus first at once caused the Theban war, by means of which he destroyed very many. Then . . . [he caused] the mortal marriage of Thetis and the fair birth of a daughter [sc. Helen], from both of which [causes] a war came about between the Greeks and the barbarians.[65]

A similar account of Zeus's reasons for provoking the war is given by Hesiod. After the birth of Helen's daughter Hermione, the gods were divided by strife (*eris*) as Zeus was planning the destruction of humans:

6. ἤδη δὲ γένος μερόπων ἀνθρώπων
πολλὸν ἀϊστῶσαι σπεῦδε, πρ[ό]φασιν μὲν ὀλέσθαι
ψυχὰς ἡμιθέω[ν . . .] οισι βροτοῖσι
τέκνα θεῶν μι[. . .] ο [ὀφ]θαλμοῖσιν ὁρῶντα,
ἀλλ' οἳ μ[ὲ]ν μάκ[α]ρες κ[. . .]ν ὡς τὸ πάρος περ
χωρὶς ἀπ' ἀν[θ]ρώπων[βίοτον κα]ὶ ἤθε' ἔχωσιν.

> Already he was hastening to cause great destruction of
> the race of mortal humans, with the purpose of destroying
> the lives of the demigods [. . .] with mortals
> the children of the gods [. . .] seeing with their eyes,
> but the blessed ones [. . .] as in former times
> apart from humans might have their life and dwelling places.[66]

Although the fragmentary nature of the text leaves some of the meaning unclear, the general idea is that Zeus intends to kill mortals, to destroy the race of the demigods, and to separate gods and mortals.[67] This interpretation is supported by a passage in Hesiod.

> 7. According to Hesiod, after the Race of Bronze perished, Zeus made a fourth race, "the divine race of hero men, who are called the demigods [ἀνδρῶν ἡρώων θεῖον γένος, οἳ κελέονται ἡμίθεοι]." Of these, some perished at Thebes, others at Troy, while still others were taken to live on the Blessed Isles by Zeus: "giving to others a life and dwellings apart from humans [τοῖς δὲ δίχ' ἀνθρώπων βίοτον καὶ ἦθε' ὀπάσσας], Zeus, son of Kronos, settled them on the bounds of the earth."[68]

From these sources collectively, an account can be derived according to which Thetis's marriage both begins with and results in strife. The marriage of Peleus and Thetis is brought about by Zeus (passages no. 1 and no. 2) as part of his plan to cause the Trojan War (no. 4 and no. 5). She marries Peleus against her will (no. 1) following a violent struggle with her future husband (no. 3). At the wedding celebration, Eris (Strife) provokes a dispute among three goddesses that leads, by way of the Judgment of Paris, to the Trojan War (no. 4 and no. 5). As a result of this war, human impiety is punished (no. 5), Troy is destroyed, the demigods are either destroyed or settled in the Blessed Isles, and mortals and gods are separated (no. 6 and no. 7). In *Andromakhe*, Euripides seems to have followed just such an account.

Euripides never explicitly alludes to the presence of Eris at the wedding of Peleus and Thetis in any of his extant works. However, his frequent use of the word *eris* in connection with this marriage, in *Andromakhe* and in other plays, suggests that he expected his audience to be aware of this tradition.[69] In the first stasimon of the *Andromakhe* (274–308), the story of the "hateful *eris*" (279) of the three goddesses begins not on Olympos but on Ida. In the previous scene, however, Thetis's shrine, the memorial to her marriage, has just been the site of a quarrel between two women over a marriage, a dispute that is called *eris* at 563 and 960. The audience could not fail to be reminded of the well-known story of Eris's presence at Thetis's marriage.

Euripides does not explicitly say that Thetis married Peleus against her will, but the idea is suggested by the fact that Thetis no longer lives with Peleus (18, 1231) and by her statement that she ought to have borne children who are not the objects of lamentation (1235), that is, immortal children fathered by a god. When Thetis tells Peleus to wait for her at Sepias (1265–66), a cape near

Pelion that is the traditional site of the wrestling match of Peleus and Thetis (passage no. 3), it is probable that Euripides alludes to this incident, especially since there is evidence that Thetis's metamorphosis figured in a lost play of his.[70] It is also possible to see an allusion to Peleus's struggle with Thetis in his words at 1277–78: "I will go to the glens of Pelion, where I seized with my hands [εἷλον χεροί] our most beautiful body."[71] Even the first line of the "tail-piece," "Many are the forms of divinities" (1284), is appropriate to the story of Thetis's metamorphosis.[72] Although Euripides alludes in other plays to the Kyprian account (passage no. 5) of Zeus's reason for provoking the Trojan War—the desire to relieve earth of her burden of excessive numbers of humans[73]—the *Andromakhe* says nothing explicit about this. On the other hand, the play represents the accomplishment of the goals of this war mentioned in our sources (nos. 5, 6, and 7). Many mortals have perished at Troy, and human impiety is punished when Neoptolemos, who had charged Apollo with Akhilleus's murder, is killed at Delphi. The demigods, the heroes who fought at Troy,[74] are either killed at Troy or, like Akhilleus (1260–62), settled in the Blessed Isles. Finally, the reunion of Thetis with Peleus, now to be deified (1258), itself marks the separation of gods and mortals, just as their first union was an intermingling of the two races.

Thetis's marriage, then, is of primary importance in this play, and it is represented in overwhelmingly negative terms, both in itself and for its consequences. Just as the play begins and ends with Thetis's marriage, so this marriage begins and ends the whole terrible chain of events represented or alluded to in *Andromakhe*.[75] If Peleus married Thetis against her will, as the end of the play seems to suggest, their union began with a rape. Moreover, a marriage between a goddess and a mortal is as incongruous as the marriage of mortal enemies and has equally disastrous consequences. The marriage of Thetis and Peleus began in *eris* between goddess and mortal, led to *eris* among three goddesses, to the union of Trojan Paris and Greek Helen that was "no marriage but ruin" (103), and to the *eris* over a woman that destroyed Troy (γυναικείαν ἔριν: 362). The war also led to Agamemnon's murder by his wife, to Orestes' matricide, to the marriage of Hermione to Neoptolemos (a direct consequence of the war: 968–70), to Akhilleus's murder of Hektor, and to the union of Andromakhe with the son of Hektor's murderer. The marriage of Peleus and Thetis led, finally, to the *eris* within Neoptolemos's household that destroyed his house (ἔριν τε τὴν σὴν καὶ γυναικὸς Ἕκτορος: 960).[76] Peleus laments, "O marriage, marriage, that destroyed this house" (1186–87), using words appropriate not only to the marriage of Hermione and Neoptolemos,[77] but also to the other three marriages that have helped to bring about the catastrophe: that of Neoptolemos and Andromakhe, that of Paris and Helen, and, not least, his own union with Thetis that was the beginning of strife. In vain, as the Chorus state, did the gods bless him in marriage (1218). However, just as strife began with the first union of Peleus and Thetis, so will it end with their reunion. This resolution is announced by Thetis.

4. The Final Solution

At the end of the play, Thetis seems to set everything right. She herself is to be reunited with her deified husband, and both parents look forward to flying over the sea to visit their son, now also immortal (1253–62). On the human level also, a happy ending seems assured. Neoptolemos, the villain of the piece, is punished, while Andromakhe and her son live happily ever after. It would be naïve, however, to conclude that all is well, for these apparently happy endings have a dark side, closely connected with Thetis's disastrous marriage.

On the divine level, the unequal marriage between goddess and mortal is replaced by a new marriage between goddess and god: Peleus will become a god and live happily ever after with Thetis. This divine favor (χάριν: 1253), however, gives Peleus a happy future as a god at the cost of losing human glory, for immortalization is the antithesis of heroic death.[78] Moreover, Thetis bids him cease mourning for Neoptolemos, because the young man is a mortal, and the gods have decreed that all mortals must die (1270–72). Although Peleus had been deeply sorrowful just before his wife's appearance (1186–1225), he at once adopts the divine perspective, agreeing, in one line (1276), to cease mourning[79] and looking joyfully forward to his apotheosis. As a god, he ceases to care for mortals, even those of his own family. Like Apollo, who helped to build Troy but did not save it (1010–18), the gods in this play are indifferent to human suffering, caring only for their own affairs.

As for Neoptolemos, who offended both Apollo and mortals, he has paid a debt, but his punishment, at least within the action of the play, is extreme: the denial of *kleos* (glory). He will not join his father and grandfather in immortality, nor is there any suggestion that he will be honored as an ancestor, for his tomb is at Delphi, far from Phthia, Molossia, and Troy. Although the circumstances of his death are those of the hero of cult, and he did historically have a cult at Delphi,[80] Thetis's brief command to Peleus to bury Neoptolemos and erect a tomb announcing his death at the hand of Orestes (1239–42) does not encourage the audience to think that a hero cult is initiated within the action of the play. At the end of the play, neither grandparent refers to him by name, Thetis speaking only of "the dead son of Akhilleus" (1239) and Peleus merely calling his grandson "him" (τόνδε: 1277). Neoptolemos has no further effect on the lives of the mortals in the play. He is no longer mourned by his soon-to-be-immortalized grandfather, and there is no suggestion that Molossos—now the heir of Helenos, king of Molossia, rather than of the house of Peleus—will avenge his father's murder. Since Hermione has not had a child by Neoptolemos, his marriage with her is as though it had never been. With Neoptolemos's death, the other ambiguous relationships are also dissolved, and Menelaos, Peleus, Hermione, and Andromakhe go their separate ways.[81] Neoptolemos suffers the fate that Hippolytos calls down on himself if he should break his oath: "May I perish without fame, without name."[82]

Not only does the death of Neoptolemos fail to bring *kleos* to himself, it also fails to provide benefits for his race or city. Thetis tells Peleus that Neoptolemos's son Molossos, the future ancestor of the kings of Molossia, will save from destruction the races of both Troy and Peleus: "Your race and mine, old man, and that of Troy, must not be thus ruined" (οὐ γὰρ ὧδ᾽ ἀνάστατον/ γένος γενέσθαι δεῖ τὸ σὸν κἀμόν, γέρον, / Τραίας τε: 1249–51). From the mortal perspective, however, the two races are not saved from ruin by the hybrid Molossos, but instead lose their identity. Troy has been annihilated, and in any case, Andromakhe's son is not really a Trojan at all, since Andromakhe was a Kilikian by birth (*Il.* 6.414–16) and a Trojan only by marriage. The bastard son of a foreign slave, left without the protection of his father, Molossos is a very dubious representative of the house of Peleus. Peleus himself does not count the boy as a descendant when he mourns the death of Neoptolemos and says, "There are no children left in my house" (1177; cf. 1207, 1216). Molossos, indeed, will have no further share in Peleus's house or in Phthia, but will become the heir of Helenos, the Trojan ruler of a non-Trojan, barbarian city.[83] Peleus's bloodline may continue in Molossos, but his house will not, since the boy will not perform the essential duties of a legitimate descendant: inheriting property, keeping the household cults, avenging his father's death, caring for Peleus in old age, and burying his father and great-grandfather.[84] Thus, what Thetis counts as saving the two races from ruin (οὐ . . . ἀνάστατον) is, from the human perspective, a driving away from one's home, an exile worse than death.[85]

For the mortals in the play, then, the resolution announced by Thetis and sanctioned by Zeus is a final solution, in which the ambiguous relationships between Trojans and Greeks, Phthians and Spartans are resolved by means of a genocidal destruction that appears to include cities (σύγχυσιν βίου Φρυγῶν πόλει: 291) as well as families (σύγχυσιν δόμων: 959).[86] In tragedy, the destruction of the royal house by means of kin murder usually results in salvation for the city.[87] In Euripides' *Herakles*, for example, Lyssa says that she brings harm not to the city but to the house of one man (824–25). Troy, a non-Greek city that is utterly destroyed, is an exception to this rule. In the *Andromakhe*, however, Euripides underlines the exceptional fate of Troy and assimilates the destiny of Phthia to this fate. Troy's destruction could have been averted by a single act of kin murder in the royal family. Paris, the cause of the destruction of Troy, should have been killed by his own mother, and his sister Kassandra repeatedly tried to persuade her countrymen to kill him (293–300). Instead, Paris lived to bring a foreign woman into his household, treating as a *philê* the ruin that destroyed his house and city (103–6). Similarly, kin murder is avoided in Phthia, but house and city are devastated by Neoptolemos's introduction into his household of a foreign enemy whom he treats as a *philê*. The parallel is underscored by Andromakhe's comparison of her own quarrel with Hermione to the quarrel over a woman that began the Trojan War (362–63).[88] Although Phthia survives, Euripides' silence about its future suggests that it might as well be as dead as Troy,[89] and there is no hint that it benefits from the destruction of the royal house. Neoptolemos is buried in Delphi, not Phthia, and Peleus laments the loss of his city as well as that of his house and race (1186–87, 1222).[90] Nor does Thetis say anything about a cult at her own shrine in Phthia, which she might be expected to do, especially since this shrine has been so important in the stage action. The focus shifts from Phthia to the gods, to Panhellenic Delphi, and to barbarian Molossia. Thus, instead of benefiting Phthia, the destruction of the royal house will benefit a new, non-Greek community, about which we are given no information. The impression that the fate of Phthia is like that of Troy is strengthened by the fact that all that remains in Phthia, as far as we are shown, is the Chorus of women, just as all that remained of conquered Troy were Andromakhe and the other enslaved and exiled women.

Of course, this is only an impression, and the fates of Troy and Phthia are in fact very different. Phthia is not destroyed, nor are her women enslaved and exiled, and a new ruling family will presumably replace that of Peleus. When Peleus laments the loss of this city, he does not mean that Phthia is destroyed, but only that his own rule is over.[91] Emphasis on the similarities rather than the differences, however, serves an important dramatic purpose. In implicitly following the Kyprian and Hesiodic accounts (nos. 5 and 6), according to which Zeus brought about the Trojan War as a means of mass destruction for the demigods and for impious mortals, both Greeks and Trojans, Euripides links the end of the play to traditional stories about Thetis, *eris*, and the Trojan War. In locating away from Greek Phthia the closure provided by the institution of a cult within the *polis* after the destruction of the royal family, he emphasizes the failure of Greek society.

The solution of Zeus (1269), announced by Thetis, in which friends and enemies, mortals and gods are separated and confusion ceases, cannot, then, be said to be a happy ending. Euripides leaves us with the impression that Greece, as well as Troy, has failed to create a civilized society, based on the principles of piety, law, and positive reciprocity (*kharis*). A civilized society requires *kharis* for *philoi*, in which Hermione is lacking when she attempts the *akharis* ("lacking in *kharis*") murder of her husband's *philoi* (491). It also requires one to take vengeance on enemies, the negative counterpart of *kharis*,[92] a Greek virtue in which Neoptolemos shows himself to be deficient when he takes into his house a woman to whom his father is *authentês*. Treating enemies as *philoi*, Euripides shows, has consequences as disastrous as those resulting from treating *philoi* as enemies. The achievement of a just and pious society, in which friends are benefited and enemies harmed, is left to a new community, neither Greek nor Trojan, but, it is to be hoped, heir to the best of both.

Killing One's Closest
Philos: Self-Slaughter
in Sophokles' *Aias*

The last play analyzed in detail here is another tragedy, one that is exceptional in its apparent lack of emphasis on harm to blood kin or to those in formal reciprocal relationships. A minor act of suppliancy takes place at Aias's corpse, but the play is certainly not a suppliant drama. Aias tries to harm his unrelated companions in the Greek army, but his attempt fails ludicrously, and the only person he actually kills is himself. The suicide itself, however, is best interpreted as an instance of harm to *philos*. Just as the *philos* is another self, in Greek thought, so the self is a person's closest *philos*. This view of Aias's self-killing is supported by evidence in the text, and it helps to illuminate a paradox connected with the suicide.

The *Aias* concerns the events that take place after the arms of Akhilleus are awarded by the Greek army to Odysseus rather than to Aias. Enraged by this judgment, Aias attempts to kill those responsible, Agamemnon, Menelaos, and Odysseus, as well as others in the army, but is instead maddened by Athena so as to attack cattle under the impression that they are men. The play opens on the morning after these events. Athena calls to her favorite, Odysseus, and shows him the mad Aias, who boasts of his exploits. Odysseus, however, pities his former companion and draws the conclusion that all mortals are weak. Athena states that one day lowers and raises mortal affairs, but that the gods love those who are of sound mind (σώφρονας) and hate evil people (131–33).

After Aias's concubine Tekmessa tells the Chorus of his Salaminian followers about the events of the past night, Aias himself emerges from his tent. Now that he fully understands the evils he has done and the disgrace he has incurred, he searches for a way to either nobly live or nobly die (479–80). Tekmessa pleads with him to pity and protect her and their son, Eurysakes, instead of leaving them as prey to his enemies after his death. Instead of responding directly, Aias makes provisions for his dependents, entrusting his son to the care of his brother Teukros and telling the Chorus to take mother and child home to his father Telamon. He bequeaths his shield to Eurysakes and orders that the rest of his armor be buried with him. After this speech, Tekmessa and the Chorus fear the worst and plead with him to soften his thoughts.

In his next speech (646–92), Aias states that Tekmessa's words have made him womanlike, and that he pities her and his son. He says that he is going to perform ritual purification to appease Athena, hide in the earth the sword given him by Hektor, yield to the gods, and respect the sons of Atreus, thus showing that he has learned soundness of mind (σωφρονεῖν). The Chorus express relief that Aias has changed his mind, but their rejoicings are cut short by the arrival of a messenger. Teukros, he reports, has barely escaped stoning by the Greek army, and Kalkhas has revealed that Athena is angry with Aias for boasting that he did not need the gods' help. The man must be closely watched until this one day is over and her wrath ceases. Alarmed, the Chorus and Tekmessa leave the stage to search for their missing friend. Aias then enters the empty stage, and in his "suicide speech" (815–65) calls on Zeus to send Teukros to give him honorable burial, on Hermes to give him a swift death, on the Erinyes to punish the Atreidai, and on the Sun to report his death to his parents. He then falls on Hektor's sword.

The Chorus and Tekmessa return, and she discovers the body. Teukros also arrives and quarrels with Menelaos, who forbids burial. When Menelaos leaves, Teukros orders Tekmessa and Eurysakes to sit as suppliants beside the corpse while he goes to arrange for burial. Teukros quickly returns, however, having seen Agamemnon approaching. The two men quarrel until Odysseus arrives and persuades Agamemnon to allow burial. The play ends with Teukros giving orders for the funeral.

In this play, then, after suffering the depths of disgrace before friends and enemies, Sophokles' Aias searches for a way to regain his lost honor: "The well-born must either nobly live or nobly die" (ἢ καλῶς ζῆν ἢ καλῶς τεθνηκέ-ναι / τὸν εὐγενῆ χρή: 479–80). He then commits suicide. In the view of many scholars, Aias's suicide is itself the "noble death" he seeks, a way of wiping out shame and regaining lost honor. According to Ivan Linforth, "a continuance of life would be a continuance of intolerable disgrace." Aias therefore has a "lofty motive for putting an end to his life," knowing, as line 479 states, that "death with honor is better than life with dishonor." By means of suicide, "from the depths of shame and dishonor, from which there seemed to be no tolerable issue, he has rescued himself by sheer greatness of spirit."[1] One problem with Linforth's view is the unstated premise that if life involves "intolerable disgrace," suicide is *therefore* "death with honor."[2] Suicide is undeniably a means of escape from a life of pain and humiliation, but it does not necessarily follow that it can also restore lost honor and wipe out shame. In Aristotle's view, to die in order to escape poverty, love, or pain is not courageous but cowardly (*NE* 1116a12–15). Plato's Sokrates also condemns suicide, which he holds to be theft of the gods' property and a desertion of one's post.[3] Negative attitudes toward suicide are not restricted to the philosophers. Nicole Loraux argues convincingly that in Greek tragedy suicide "was a woman's solution and not, as has sometimes been claimed, a heroic act." In the heroic code, "the death of a man could only be that of a warrior on the field of battle."[4]

These considerations suggest that the idea of suicide as a noble death is problematic and deserves more critical attention than it has usually received in studies of the *Aias*. Although Aias's suicide speech seems to indicate that he has found the noble death he sought, and his subsequent honorable burial suggests that he is right, male suicide was not usually considered by the Greeks to be honorable. How can this paradox be explained? How can Aias's suicide be the kind of noble death that usually results only from heroic combat with enemies? I argue that the paradox is the result of Aias's paradoxical relationships to himself and others. His disgrace has entailed the destruction of his normal reciprocal relationships with friends and enemies and has made him an enemy to himself. As an enemy to friends and enemies alike, Aias can no longer either help his friends or harm his enemies. His suicide is a noble death because it allows him to repay his debts of *kharis* (positive reciprocity) to friends and vengeance to enemies, thus returning to proper reciprocal relationships with all.

1. Greek Attitudes Toward Suicide

Before turning to a detailed analysis of Sophokles' play, I begin with a brief examination of the evidence for Greek attitudes toward suicide. Elise Garrison's comprehensive studies of available data provide a valuable starting point for a study of this subject.[5] Garrison's conclusions, however, like those of many scholars in this field, are too general to account for many distinctions apparent in the evidence she herself cites: "Suicidal obedience to orders in battle is praised. Institutional suicide carries no stigma. Suicide out of shame or guilt or fear of dishonor is commendable. . . . Suicide to restore one's honor is embraced approvingly."[6] Garrison's generalizations result in part from an excessive reliance on Emile Durkheim, who gives a very broad definition of suicide: "The term suicide is applied to all cases of death resulting directly or indirectly from a positive or negative act of the victim himself, which he knows will produce this result." Durkheim insists that self-sacrifice (martyrdom, for example) is a form of suicide: "All those . . . who without killing themselves, voluntarily allowed their own slaughter, are really suicides. Though they did not kill themselves, they sought death with all their power and behaved so as to make it inevitable. To be suicide, the act from which death must necessarily result need only have been performed by the victim with full knowledge of the facts."[7] Garrison does not see that Durkheim's theories are vitiated by blatant sexism and chauvinism[8] and that his broad definition of suicide obscures important distinctions made by the Greeks among different forms of self-caused death. The evidence indicates that the Greeks have a particular horror of suicide directly caused by one's own hand (αὐτόχειρ) and that they place institutional suicide (execution by means of state-ordered suicide) in a different category from freely chosen suicide. They consider self-sacrifice (dying for a greater good) to be praiseworthy, but they call it "self-killing" only in exceptional cases. Suicide to avoid future dishonor is justifiable, although it is not thought to be capable of restoring lost honor. On the other hand, suicide to escape present pain or dishonor is not positively commended. It is at best excused, and at worst condemned as cowardice. Vengeance suicide is in a category of its own.

One important distinction made by the Greeks is that between more and less direct forms of self-caused death. David Daube notes that the Greek term αὐτόχειρ, "own-handed," reflects the particular horror felt in response to death inflicted directly by a murderer's own hand, and to suicide committed in this way. This term is not applied to more indirect forms of suicide, by starvation, for example. Even today, Daube notes, we would hesitate to call death as a result of a hunger strike "death by one's own hand."[9] Plato distinguishes between the αὐτόχειρ and the instigator of murder who does not actually commit the deed (*Laws* 9. 871a3: αὐτόχειρ; 872a1: αὐτόχειρ μὲν μή, βουλεύσῃ δε θάνατον). The practice of burying the hand of a suicide apart from the rest of the body is perhaps connected with the revulsion felt toward the murdering hand.[10] One important kind of self-caused death occurs when an external force, especially the law, compels someone to commit suicide. Although institutional suicide is called "self-killing," it is placed in a category of its own.[11] This is the only kind of suicide condoned by Plato as a "necessity" sent by the god (*Phaedo* 62c7–8; cf. *Laws* 873c5).

Another indirect kind of self-caused death is self-sacrifice. In one sense this is voluntary death, since the agent could have chosen to live instead. In another sense, however, it is not voluntary, because death is not the agent's goal, even if he or she knows that it is an inevitable consequence of a voluntary action. Modern scholars have often objected to categorizing self-sacrifice as suicide.[12] Just as we distinguish the two, so the Greeks have special terms for the act of sacrificing one's life for another, which they do not usually think of as suicide.[13] Although he condemns suicide, Sokrates praises, as a heroic choice of danger over dishonor, Akhilleus's decision to fight Hektor even though he knows that Hektor's death will lead to his own (*Apol.* 28c-d, on *Il.* 18.94–126). In Euripides' play, Alkestis, whose choice to die for her husband provides the paradigmatic example of self-sacrifice, is never said to kill herself, even though Pheres accuses his son Admetos of murdering her (*Alc.* 696, 730). Only in very special cases can self-sacrifice be called suicide. When Menoikeus dies to save his country after hearing Teiresias's prophecy, he commits suicide by cutting his throat (σφάξας ἐμαυτόν: Eur. *Phoen.* 1010), but he also sacrifices himself for his country (ὑπερθανεῖν χθονός: 998). This direct form of self-sacrifice by killing oneself with one's own hand is clearly exceptional and is very different from the usual cases in which one merely behaves "so as to make [death] inevitable."[14]

The Greeks also make important ethical distinctions among kinds of self-caused death. Self-sacrifice is most noble. Alkestis shows exceptional excellence in sacrificing herself for her husband, even though she has no obligation to do so.[15] In other cases, a contributing motive for self-sacrifice may be the desire to avoid disgrace. Menoikeus says that he will be a coward if he fails to sacrifice himself (Eur. *Phoen.* 1004–5), and Admetos accuses Pheres of cowardice in failing to die for his son (*Alc.* 642). Less noble than self-sacrifice is suicide committed to avoid such future disgrace as shameful punishment by enemies. This kind of suicide is justifiable, since it avoids future dishonor, but it is not a way to regain lost honor. Nitokris, who throws herself into a house filled with ashes to avoid being punished by her enemies (ὅκως ἀτιμώρητος γένηται: Herod. 2.100), and the Athenians, who fling themselves from the Acropolis to avoid capture by the Persians (Herod. 8.53), are neither praised nor blamed by Herodotos. A special category is vengeance suicide, in which people in hopeless situations use their own deaths as powerful curses and causes of pollution.[16] This is a weapon frequently used or threatened by suppliants (in Ais. *Supp.*, for example) and others as a way of punishing those who have caused them injury (for instance, Antigone, Haimon, and Eurydike in Soph. *Ant.*, on which see appendix A). This kind of suicide avoids dishonor in that it punishes enemies, but it is also dishonorable in that it is an admission of powerlessness. Least honorable is suicide due to an inability to face the misfortune or disgrace one is already in. Opinions about this kind of death differ. Some, Aristotle, for example (*NE* 1116a12–15), condemn it, although others find it to be understandable and excusable.[17] I find no indication that it is considered by any Greek to be positively honorable and noble. Plato (*Laws* 9.873c–d) writes that suicide should not be punished in three circumstances: when it is ordered by the state, when it is compelled by inescapable pain, and when a person has acquired some shame from which there is no way out and which makes life unlivable (αἰσχύνης τινὸς ἀπόρου καὶ ἀβίου). It is important to note that he does not say or imply, as scholars sometimes suggest, that suicide in this last circumstance is honorable.[18]

These distinctions among direct and indirect forms of self-caused death and among more and less honorable forms of self-caused death can help us to recognize significant differences in the examples Garrison classifies simply as cases of "honorable release" by suicide.[19] When Leonidas chooses to stay and die fighting for his country at Thermopylai rather than leaving (Herod. 7.220–21), the Spartan leader is said not to have killed himself but to have gotten great glory by remaining (220.2). The fact that he has no chance of winning makes no difference to the fact that flight would have been disgraceful, as the case of Pantites (discussed below) makes clear. Anaxibios, like Leonidas, chooses to face certain death in battle rather than fleeing, saying, "It is noble for me to die here" (Xen. *Hell.* 4.8.39). These are acts of self-sacrifice for a greater good—country and glory—rather than suicide. Examples of suicides committed to avoid future disgrace are the suicides of Nitokris and of the Athenians, mentioned above (Herod. 2.100, 8.53), and those of the Messenian prisoners who refused to be tried by their captors (Thuc. 3.81). A suicide explicitly praised by Herodotos is that of Boges, who, after refusing to abandon his city when it was certain to fall, throws himself into fire to avoid capture by his enemies (Herod. 7.107). This death combines self-sacrifice for his country with suicide to avoid future disgrace. Very different is the case of Adrastos, who commits suicide after involuntarily killing the son of his host Kroisos (Herod. 1.45). The suicide of this man, who is "most unfortunate" and deserving of Kroisos's pity (κατοικτίρει), is excusable, but there is no indication that it is noble. A similar case is that of Pantites, who suffers disgrace because, through no fault of his own, he avoided death at Thermopylai. This man hangs himself "because he had been dishonored" (Herod. 7.232). Pantites avoids present disgrace, but there is no suggestion that he gains honor. In unusual cases, ethical opinions may differ. After suffering disgrace because an eye infection prevented him from fighting at Thermopylai (Herod. 7.229–31), Aristodemos eventually dies in battle at Plataia. He is called "most excellent" (ἄριστος) by Herodotos (9.71), in whose opinion Aristodemos's final bravery in battle removed his former disgrace (7.231–32), but he is denied honor by the more severe Spartans, who say that he wanted to die only because of his previous fault (βουλόμενος ἀποθανεῖν διὰ τὴν προειρημένην αἰτίην οὐκ ἐτιμήθη: 9.71). Even death in battle, heroic under ordinary circumstances, could not, in the opinion of the Spartans, wipe out Aristodemos's disgrace; suicide certainly could not have done so.

The distinctions among kinds of self-caused deaths—self-sacrifice, suicide to avoid future disgrace, and suicide to escape present pain or disgrace—are also useful for an evaluation of literary and rhetorical examples. In epic, suicide is clearly antiheroic. Odysseus contemplates suicide after he discovers that his companions have released the winds of Aiolos. When he instead decides to endure and remain (ἔτλην καὶ ἔμεινα: *Od.* 10.53), he shows his nature as the "much-enduring" (πολύτλας) hero. Akhilleus also wants to die after Patroklos's death and is forcibly restrained so that he will not cut his throat (*Il.* 18.32–34). Akhilleus, like Odysseus, shows his heroic nature by rejecting suicide, deciding instead to win glory by killing Trojans before his own fated death (121).[20] This heroic self-sacrifice is obviously opposed to his earlier suicidal impulses. Although Demosthenes 60.31 is sometimes cited as evidence that the Greeks consider Aias's suicide to be a noble death,[21] this passage is open to another interpretation. Demosthenes writes: "It did not escape the notice of the Aiantidai that Aias, deprived of the reward for valor, thought his own life to be not worth living. So, when the god was giving to another the reward for valor, they thought they should die while defending themselves against their enemies, so as to suffer nothing unworthy of themselves." Aias is said to be an example to the Aiantidai of someone who died because of loss of honor, but Demosthenes does not state that his suicide was heroic. Only the Aiantidai, who died in battle, are said to "suffer nothing unworthy of themselves."

Tragedy offers little support for the view that male suicide is considered to be a way of restoring lost honor. As Loraux notes, suicide is a woman's act rather than the heroic act of a male.[22] Although suicide is frequently contemplated or threatened in the extant tragedies, the act itself is much rarer. It never occurs in Aiskhylos. In Sophokles, Iokaste in *Oedipus the King*, Deianeira in *Women of Trakhis*, and Antigone, Eurydike, and Haimon in *Antigone* all, like Aias, kill themselves with their own hands. In Euripides, Phaidra in *Hippolytos*, Iokaste and Menoikeus in *Phoenician Women*, and Evadne in *Suppliants* do so.[23] Thus, aside from Aias, only two males, Menoikeus and Haimon, commit suicide in extant tragedy. Menoikeus's suicide is undeniably heroic, committed in order to save his country in war. Menoikeus compares this suicide to death in battle and avoidance of it to fleeing battle in cowardice (*Phoen.* 991–1018). Aias's suicide is very different. In some respects it resembles death in battle, yet it certainly does not help to protect his country from an enemy. Aias's suicide more closely resembles that of Haimon, who kills himself after he attacks his father with his sword and misses. Haimon, far from dying a noble death, is a failed patricide (Aristotle calls his attack on Kreon *miaron*, "polluted": *Po.* 14.1453b39), and there is no suggestion in the play that suicide wipes out this shame. On the contrary, his act is a vengeance suicide, in which patricide is attempted more indirectly.[24] Although it has been argued that Aias's suicide is honorable because it is an act of atonement for his offenses against Athena, no parallels in tragedy support this view.[25] The idea that suicide is commonly thought to be a way of wiping out shame is best refuted by Sophokles' Oidipous, who notably fails to commit suicide even under the pressure of intolerable shame. When the Chorus ask Oidipous whether death would not have been preferable to self-blinding, he replies, "I do not know with what eyes I could have looked on my father, or my wretched mother, when I went to Hades, two people to whom I have done deeds too terrible for hanging" (*OT* 1371–74). The shame of patricide and incest will cling to Oidipous even in the underworld and cannot be removed merely by suicide.

Euripides' *Herakles* provides some of the most useful information in tragedy on Greek attitudes toward suicide. One passage may possibly suggest that male suicide can remove disgrace: Herakles considers burning his flesh to remove dishonor (1151–52). Even if this passage, unique in tragedy, did express a common view, however, it would still not provide evidence that other methods of suicide are also thought to purify.[26] Moreover, this play provides some of the clearest evidence in Greek literature that male suicide is considered cowardly. Herakles, having killed his own family in a fit of madness, suffers even greater disgrace than that incurred by Aias. Nevertheless, Herakles, unlike Aias, decides to live, arguing that suicide is cowardice (1348). The view of some scholars that Aias represents the old, heroic code, according to which suicide is preferable to dishonor, while Herakles represents a new, more negative attitude toward suicide, ignores some fundamental differences in the positions of the two heroes.[27] Aias can neither stay in Troy nor go home; he is friendless and has no way of regaining honor while he lives. On the other hand, Theseus offers Herakles friendship, purification, a home, wealth, and honor from the Athenians (1324–37). In Herakles' position, Aias might well have chosen to live, while Herakles, in Aias's place, might have killed himself. Moreover, even if it could be shown that the argument that suicide is cowardice is new to Euripides,[28] this would still not prove that prior to the *Herakles*, suicide was seen as a way of regaining lost honor. On the contrary, the evidence considered above suggests that male suicide, from Homer on, is not usually thought to be heroic.

Linguistic parallels give indirect support to the view that male suicide is not usually considered to be a noble death. Variants on Aias's words at 479–80, "to live nobly or die nobly" (καλῶς ζῆν ἢ καλῶς τεθνηκέναι), occur frequently in Greek drama in contexts where a noble death is one that takes place during combat with one's enemies. Sophokles' Elektra, believing Orestes to be dead, expresses her intention of attacking her enemies with her own hand, thereby either gaining salvation or dying nobly (καλῶς ἔσωσ' ἐμαυτήν, ἢ καλῶς ἀπωλόμην: *El.* 1320–21). In Euripides' *Orestes*, the attempt to kill one's enemies is also said to lead either to a noble death or to a noble salvation (καλῶς θανόντες ἢ καλῶς σεσωσμένοι: 1152). Odysseus in Euripides' *Kyklops* (201–2) states that if they confront the monster, he and the satyrs will die nobly or live in safety (κατθανούμεθ' εὐγενῶς ἢ ζῶντες . . . συσσώσομεν).[29] In all of these cases, a noble death involves active aggression against an enemy.

2. Suicide as Noble Death

So little evidence supports the idea that suicide is a way to regain honor that some scholars frankly assert that Aias's suicide is humiliation, or, at most, a way to avoid continuing or increasing dishonor.[30] There is certainly some evidence in favor of this view, especially since Aias is in danger of being killed by the Greek army (229–32, with 254–55 and 408–9). On the other hand, there are many indications that when he actually kills himself, Aias does not view his suicide negatively or neutrally, as humiliation or avoidance of further dishonor, but in a very positive way, as a means of regaining lost honor. Aias seeks a way to show his father, whom he cannot bear to meet in his present disgrace (460–65), that he is not "by nature without guts" (470–72), and he concludes his deliberations by stating that the nobly born must either "nobly live or nobly die" (479–80). It is important to note that Aias does not say that when a man cannot live nobly, he must die — he says that he must "*nobly* die." Aias's actions and statements throughout the play express a belief that his suicide accomplishes this goal.

After his mad attack on the cattle, Aias is dishonored and overcome by shame.[31] All of the dramatic figures agree that his disgrace is worse than death. According to the Chorus, he is ill-famed throughout the Greek army (143) and would be better off dead (635). Tekmessa says that he has suffered a disaster like death (215) and recounts the uncharacteristic behavior of Aias on first learning what he has done. Although he used to blame as cowardly the groans of others, Aias gave shrill cries after falling on the ground among the animals he had killed, like a corpse among corpses (317–25).[32] Aias himself also equates dishonor with death (ἄτιμος ὧδε πρόκειμαι: 426–27; ἄτιμος ... ὧδ' ἀπόλλυμαι: 440) and grieves that he is laughed at by his enemies (367, 382, 454).[33]

Aias's actions are shameful, in large part, because he has acted as an enemy to his *philoi*, whose fortunes depend on him and whose disgrace is entailed by his.[34] The Salaminians speak of their leader's disgrace as their own (αἰσχύνας ἐμᾶς: 174), and Tekmessa addresses them as participants in his deeds (κοινωνὸς ὤν: 284). The Salaminians say that Aias has killed them (κατέπεφνες: 901), and they fear that they will be stoned to death along with their leader (254–55).[35] Teukros in fact narrowly escapes stoning as the brother of a madman (723–28). Tekmessa, like the Chorus, says that she has been destroyed by Aias (ὀλώλαμεν: 791) and laments that she and her son Eurysakes will become slaves of Aias's enemies (496–99). His disgrace is also a taint on his parents, and Aias laments that his own father will no longer look kindly on the son who has lost good fame (460–66). Having acted as an enemy to his own dependents, Aias is no longer a friend to anyone. He laments that he is hated by the gods, the Greek army, and even the plain of Troy (457–59). The Chorus say (615–20) that he is a great cause of mourning (πένθος) to his *philoi*, that is, his dependents,[36] and that his former deeds of *aretê* ("excellence") are now "friendless among the Atreidai, who are no friends" (ἄφιλα παρ' ἀφίλοις).

Aias has also acted as an enemy to himself, for his own hands have brought about his disgrace. It is this aspect of Aias's situation that Tekmessa first emphasizes in her account to the Chorus: "To see his own sufferings [οἰκεῖα πάθη], brought about with no accomplice, gives him great pains" (260–62). Athena says that Aias thought he was killing the Atreidai "with his own hand" (αὐτόχειρ: 57), using a word that often refers to kin murder or suicide.[37] Aias, in fact, has acted like a kin killer in committing, with his own hand, bloody acts that harm himself.

In this living death of dishonor, in which he can look to no god or human for any benefit, Aias expresses a desire for physical death, calling on the darkness as his only light and asking Erebos to carry him away (394–400). His statement that Troy will no longer see him (416–22) is a clear indication that he expects to die. However, none of the possible deaths he at first mentions would allow him to regain his honor. He first asks the Chorus to help him kill himself (με συνδάιξον: 361),[38] seeking a mercy killing by friends that would be pitiable rather than glorious. Next, he asks Zeus how he might destroy his enemies and afterwards die himself (τέλος θάνοιμι καὐτός: 387–91). These words express a wish unattainable in present circumstances, and Aias does not return to it when he again weighs the possibilities at 460–69. Finally, Aias expresses the fear that the entire Greek army will kill him (408–9). This traitor's death is the most disgraceful of all.

In his speech at 646–92, however, Aias expresses a radically different point of view, stating that he will no longer be "unfortunate" but "saved" (κεἰ νῦν

δυστυχῶ, σεσωμένον: 692).[39] The same positive attitude is evident in his suicide speech, in which Aias expresses no sense of dishonor.[40] Instead of seeking to hide in the darkness, he dies in the open, in the sunlight.[41] Far from
feeling shame before his father, Aias now asks Helios to tell his parents about
his death (845–51), and unlike the silent Aias of *Odyssey* 11 (563), Sophokles'
hero says that he will tell the rest to those in the underworld (865).[42] Aias's
proud death, upright, looking on the sun, and eager to have his fate revealed
to living and dead, contrasts vividly with his earlier shamed behavior, prone,
wailing, and seeking to hide from the gaze and voices of others. These changes
in Aias's behavior and speech suggest that he believes he has found the noble
death he sought, and his honorable burial at the end of the play vindicates
him. Aias's suicide, then, would seem to be portrayed not as humiliation or
escape from disgrace, but as a way of regaining lost honor. The problem, as the
previous discussion has shown, is that the Greeks usually considered male suicide to be dishonorable.

Scholars have called attention to two aspects of Aias's death that help to
mitigate its inherent dishonor. By stabbing himself with the sword of Hektor,
his greatest enemy, Aias chooses a suicide that resembles the death of a warrior in battle.[43] Aias also uses suicide to take vengeance on his enemies, calling down the Erinyes on the sons of Atreus.[44] These aspects of Aias's suicide,
however, are not in themselves sufficient to make it a noble death. Even
though "Aias is the model of the manly suicide," as Loraux notes, "his death
is only a poor imitation of a warrior's noble death."[45] Death in combat is honorable not merely because it punishes enemies, but also, and especially,
because it helps to protect friends from defeat or dishonor.[46] Menoikeus's suicide resembles heroic death in more than outward form because it is directed
toward the goal of helping friends (Eur. *Phoen.* 991–1018). Aias's suicide, on
the other hand, at first leads Tekmessa to believe that he has chosen to please
himself at the expense of his friends (966–68), a view with which the Chorus
(900–902), Teukros (1004–5), and many modern scholars agree.[47] If his suicide
does not help his friends, he not only lacks compassion but is also deficient in
aretê and honor. Aias needs, then, both to harm his enemies and to help his
friends, himself included, to whom he has acted as an enemy. How to regain
lost honor by benefiting his *philoi* is the greatest difficulty he faces after his disgrace.

Aias shows awareness of the dilemma in his speech at 430–80 as he wres-
tles with the problem of how to live nobly or die nobly in his present disgraceful situation. Because he is an enemy to friends and enemies alike, Aias
can neither go nor stay.[48] There is no way for him to remain in Troy without
incurring further disgrace. He cannot achieve glory as Akhilleus did, by killing
Trojans (466–69), because if he dies attacking the Trojans single-handed, he
will give joy to the Greeks, his enemies. Moreover, the Greek army will kill
him if he remains (409–10). On the other hand, he cannot leave Troy and
go home, being ashamed to face his father (462–66), disgraced (ἄτιμος: 426,
440) as he is. Neither of these alternatives would allow him to "nobly live or
nobly die."

3. *Kharis* and Retribution

Aias's speech at 646–92 indicates that he at last realizes how he can return to honorable reciprocal relationships with both friends and enemies.[49] He begins with cosmology, stating that time brings to birth unseen things and hides those that have appeared (646–47). The cosmology continues at 669–76, where Aias says that the strongest and most terrible things yield to the opposing authorities (τιμαί) in a cycle of alternation of opposites over time. Winter yields to summer, night to day, storm to calm, and sleep to waking. The opposites succeed one another in a continuous cycle, as night yields to day only to regain dominance in turn.[50] Aias's speech recalls the cosmology of Anaximander, in which opposites "pay penalty and retribution to each other for their injustice according to the assessment of Time" (διδόναι γὰρ αὐτὰ δίκην καὶ τίσιν ἀλλήλοις τῆς ἀδικίας κατὰ τὴν τοῦ κρόνου τάξιν).[51] Because Anaximander's opposites are equals, overall justice in the cosmos is maintained, paradoxically, by "the strict reciprocal nature of injustice." As Gregory Vlastos explains: "If . . . equality is maintained, justice is assured, for no opposite will be strong enough to dominate another. When encroachment occurs, it will be compensated by 'reparation,' as, e.g., in the seasonal cycle the hot prevails in the summer, only to suffer commensurate subjection to its rival in the winter."[52] Over time, each successive state of dominance is an "injustice" that receives "retribution," consisting in the dominance of the opposing authority.

Aias applies this cosmic principle of reciprocity to his own relationships with both gods and mortals. His former divine friends have now become enemies. In rejecting the help and advice of Athena, he has incurred a debt toward her, for which her wrath demands payment (770–77; cf. 112–13). Aias has angered Athena in particular, but he has also offended the other gods, for he is said, at 764–69, to have rejected divine help in general, and Athena speaks of "gods" in the plural at 118, 128, and 133. Aias recognized immediately that he was hated by the gods (447–48), but he did not at first see that he had to repay the debt he owed them by giving them honor. On the contrary, he told Tekmessa that he no longer owed service (ἀρκεῖν) to the gods (589–90). Now, however, Aias states that he will yield to the gods (666–67). He will make peace with Athena, and thus "escape the heavy wrath of the goddess," by performing purification rites before he kills himself (654–56).[53] By giving ritual acknowledgment and honor to the superiority of Athena as a goddess, Aias will repay the debt owed her because of his former lack of respect. He will thus become a friend of the gods once more and thereby secure their future aid in avenging his death and in protecting his dependents after his death. His suicide speech expresses a confidence in the friendship of the gods that was conspicuously lacking in his earlier speeches. Now, Aias calls on Hermes to give him a swift death, on the Erinyes to punish his enemies after his death, and most of all, on Zeus, his ancestor (387), to assist him, with full confidence in his own right to ask this favor (ἄρκεσον . . . καὶ γὰρ εἰκός: 824).

Aias also applies the principle of reciprocal alternation of opposites to the human world, stating that enemies should be treated as future friends and friends as future enemies (679–82). He is most explicitly concerned with his enemies among the Greeks, asserting that he, like the cosmological opposites, will learn to yield to the Atreidai, since they are his rulers (667–68). Aias will "revere" (σεβεῖν)[54] them not as individuals but as rulers who exemplify, on the human level, the divine principle of reciprocity. Aias yields to his enemies only so that they in turn may yield to him. Vengeance is the negative counterpart of the reciprocal exchange of *kharis* (favor) to which Tekmessa appeals (522). If *kharis* must repay *kharis*, retribution is also a debt that must be paid, in the course of time.[55] When Aias kills himself, he yields honor (τιμή) to the Atreidai, exacting with his own hand the retribution they are obligated to seek from him.[56] Aias in the *Iliad* (9.632–36) gives an eloquent statement of the principle of negative reciprocity, telling Akhilleus that acceptance of requital (ποινή) for a kinsman's death checks the injured man's anger and allows the murderer to remain in the land. Sophokles' Aias adheres to the same principle. However, in giving a life for murder that was merely attempted, he repays his debt to the Greeks with interest. Aias's enemies are now in his debt, owing him the honor that he can appropriately ask the Erinyes to exact in the form of retribution. Moreover, any further dishonor to Aias's corpse or to his dependents will be a new act of injustice, requiring retribution in its turn.

The principle of alternation of opposites is also applicable to Aias's own dependents. In the cases of Tekmessa and Teukros, friendship and enmity alternate in a particularly significant way. As Patricia Easterling notes, Tekmessa is a Trojan, and Teukros is the son of a Trojan mother.[57] Toward these and other *philoi* Aias has acted as an enemy in disgracing himself. Just as he will yield honor to his enemies in order to get honor from them in his turn, so he will give present pain to his dependents in order to benefit them in the future. This view of Aias's suicide is suggested by careful analysis of his speeches.

Aias expresses a great deal of concern for his *philoi*, although this is not always apparent either to them or to modern scholars. His words prior to his speech at 646–92 indicate that he cares greatly about his kin and other dependents, and he expresses a particular preoccupation with finding a way to remove the shame he has brought to his father (470–72). In providing his parents with a future protector in the form of his son Eurysakes (567–70), Aias also, in effect, recognizes the child as his heir. The same act also secures Tekmessa's future, as the mother of the child who will be a joy to her (559) in a very practical way.[58] Teukros is also given a secure place in Aias's "will" as a protector of Eurysakes during the boy's childhood (560–64). A concern for his dependents is also evident in Aias's speech at 646–92, which begins with words of pity for Tekmessa (650–52) and ends with a remarkable expression of human and divine solidarity. In the short space of six lines (684–89), Aias stresses the interconnections of all of his dependents, with each other, with himself, and with the gods. He addresses Tekmessa directly (σὺ δέ), asking her to pray to the very gods to whom he has just said that he will yield. He then addresses the Salaminians as "companions," asking them to join with Tekmessa in honoring what Aias himself honors. He also asks them to tell Teukros to take care of Aias and to be well disposed toward the Salaminians themselves. Word order and alliterations reinforce the sense of interconnectedness: ταὐτὰ τῇδέ μοι τάδε τιμᾶτε, Τεύκρῳ τ'. The future good fortunes of Aias, Tekmessa (and her son), Teukros, and the Salaminians are all interdependent and depend on the good will of the gods, who will now again be friendly.

Aias does not pity and care for his friends merely in words. In committing suicide, Aias will achieve salvation (σεσωμένον: 692) for himself and for the friends who are a part of himself.[59] Aias's death benefits his dependents in many ways.[60] Tekmessa fears slavery after Aias's disgrace (496–99) and after his death (944–45). In fact, however, his suicide will secure her the place in Telamon's house Aias allotted her earlier when he recognized her son as his legitimate heir. If he had gone on living, she would have shared his disgrace. Aias's suicide also benefits his son, for Eurysakes, who might have shared Tekmessa's slavery, will now have a secure position as Telamon's heir. Aias's suicide also removes from Eurysakes the obligation to avenge his father's death that the boy would have had if Aias had been killed by the Greeks. Moreover, by repaying his debt to the sons of Atreus, Aias prevents his son from being included in the vengeance they would have tried to exact on the living Aias. Teukros also benefits from Aias's death. As brother of the living Aias, Teukros is included in Aias's disgrace and is nearly stoned by the army (723–28). Once Aias is dead, however, this enmity becomes inappropriate. Teukros fears his father Telamon's wrath and according to another tradition was actually exiled by his father. Aias, however, has done much to help Teukros win his father's favor. By appointing him as guardian of his heir Eurysakes (562–70), a role Teukros begins to play at 1168–84, Aias gives his brother a way to prove that he is not plotting to usurp Aias's place. Finally, Aias's suicide helps the Salaminians. As Aias's dependents, they are included in his disgrace, and rightly fear being stoned by the army and losing their homecoming (254–55, 900). The suicide removes this danger. In all of these ways, Aias benefits the dependents he has injured and restores himself to a friendly relationship with them, returning *kharis* for *kharis*.

4. The Self as *Philos* and Enemy

The universal principle of alternation of opposites finds its most powerful application in Aias's relationship to himself. After his disgrace, Aias has become his own worst enemy. His suicide, however, restores him to a friendly relationship to himself.

Aias's paradoxical relationship to himself is symbolized by Hektor's sword. As a gift from Hektor, it is one of the "gifts of enemies that are not gifts" (665). It is "the most hated of weapons" (658), because it is the gift of the most hostile Hektor (662). Yet Hektor and his sword are friends as well as enemies. The Trojan enemy became a friend when he and Aias exchanged gifts, and he will become an enemy once more when his sword kills Aias. Aias calls him, appropriately, "the most hated of my *xenoi*" (817–18). Hektor's sword also exemplifies the principle of alternation of opposites. With this weapon of a friend-enemy, Aias has accomplished his own disgrace with his own hand, becoming his own enemy. Using the same sword, Aias will once again become his own friend through an act of enmity against himself. It is no wonder that Aias identifies this sword with himself. Holding Hektor's weapon (τόδ' ἔγχος: 658), he compares himself to a sword:

> ἀλλ' ἁλίσκεται
> χὠ δεινὸς ὅρκος χαἰ περισκελεῖς φρένες.
> κἀγὼ γάρ, ὃς τὰ δείν' ἐκαρτέρουν τότε,
> βαφῇ σίδηρος ὥς, ἐθηλύνθην στόμα
> πρὸς τῆσδε τῆς γυναικός. (648–52)

The dread oath is vanquished, and the stubborn will. Even I, once so wonderfully firm, like iron hardened in the dipping, have felt the keen edge of my temper softened by yonder woman's words.[61]

Aias's words must be understood within the context of ancient metalworking. An implement is given a hard edge (στόμα) by being first heated in fire and then plunged into cold water in a process called βαφή (dipping). Aias is like a sword that has lost this edge. He who was once as hard and strong (περισκελεῖς, ἐκαρτέρουν) as a sword that had received dipping, has now had his edge softened like a woman by pity for Tekmessa (649–53). Within this context, Aias's act of bathing in the sea is like the dipping that hardens iron. Just as the metal is given strength by alternate heating and cooling, so Aias's temper, now softened by pity, will be strengthened again by the ritual purification that prepares him for suicide (654–56). Both the heating and softening (pity) and the cooling (the ritual bath in preparation for suicide) are necessary to restore Aias's "temper." Because he himself has injured Tekmessa, his pity for her is a softening that contributes to a hardening of his resolve to take action against the enemy (himself) who has wronged her. He shows his pity in the epic fashion by acting against the man who has harmed a friend.[62] Thus, Aias returns *kharis* for *kharis*, just as Tekmessa asks (522), but in a way contrary to her expectation.[63]

In his suicide speech, both Aias and the sword have regained their edge. The sword is "most kindly" (822) because it is the instrument of a swift death. The weapon is "most cutting" (815) for four reasons, each of which involves paradox. It is the gift of a friend-enemy (817–18), and it is fixed firmly in the enemy land of Troy (819), which, like Aias's own mother, is also his nurse (849, 863).[64] Third, the sword is "newly sharpened" (νεηκονής: 820). In a literal sense, Aias himself has whetted the sword, but in a metaphorical sense, it has been newly whetted by his enemy the Erinys who forged it (1034) as retribution for the death of Hektor, caused, in Sophokles' version, by his being dragged by Aias's belt behind Akhilleus's chariot (1029–31).[65] Finally, the sword is "most cutting" because Aias himself has set it properly in the earth (821). As his own friend-enemy, Aias has prepared well for his own death by means of the sword of a friend-enemy, sharpened by a friend-enemy, and fixed in the earth that is a friend-enemy.

These ideas are reinforced by the words of Aias's curse, in which he uses the same word, *autosphagês* ("self-slain" or "slain by kin"), to refer both to his own suicide and to the murder by *philoi* he invokes on the Atreidai:

> ὥσπερ εἰσορῶσ' ἐμὲ
> αὐτοσφαγῆ πίπτοντα· τὼς αὐτοσφαγεῖς
> πρὸς τῶν φιλίστων ἐκνόμως ὀλοίατο. (840–42).

> Just as they see me fallen *autosphagê* ("self-slain"), so may they lawlessly perish, *autosphageis* ("slain by kin") by their closest *philoi*.[66]

Aias's self-slaughter becomes a curse on his enemies, leading to their slaughter by those who are friends turned enemies. In drawing a parallel between suicide and murder by one's "closest *philoi*" (Klytaimestra's husband murder and Orestes' matricide), this passage also recalls the Greek idea that the self is the closest *philos*. Plato expresses a common view when he equates suicide with parricide on the grounds that one is one's own "nearest and dearest friend" (πάντων οἰκειότατον καὶ . . . φίλτατον: *Laws* 9. 873c2). In Sophokles' *Oedipus the King*, Kreon tells his brother-in-law Oidipous: "I say that it is just the same to cast out an excellent *philos* as to throw away one's own life, which one loves most" (φίλον γὰρ ἐσθλὸν ἐκβαλεῖν ἴσον λέγω / καὶ τὸν παρ' αὐτῷ βίοτον, ὃν πλεῖστον φιλεῖ: 611–12). The idea that the self is a friend is the converse of the Greek commonplace that a friend is "another self" (Aristotle *EE* 1245a29–30, *NE* 1166a31–32, *MM* 1213a11–13), or a part of oneself (Aristotle *Rhet.* 1385b28–29).[67]

Aias's dependents, as he himself says, will understand only later, if at all, that his death is their salvation as well as his (τάχ' ἄν μ' ἴσως πύθοισθε . . . σεσωμένον: 691–92). In the play, they never see beyond the narrow mortal confines of the present day's sufferings. Aside from Aias, only Odysseus acquires the divine vision of the alternation of opposites, understanding that "a day lowers and again raises all human things" (131–32). The others merely act without understanding as they physically lift Aias's corpse and carry it out for burial.[68]

Events after Aias's death, however, show the audience that through suicide he has in fact returned to appropriate reciprocal relationships with friends and enemies, who give him honor in different ways. The solidarity Aias expressed in words at 684–89 is enacted in the ritual ending, as Teukros, Tekmessa, Eurysakes, and the Salaminians join in giving honor to Aias in the form of a funeral and "a tomb of eternal memory" (1166–67).[69] The community of friends, and consequently the honor, is even greater than Aias had expected, for it now includes Odysseus and the Greek army. Odysseus recognizes that Aias's death has canceled his debt to his enemies, who no longer have any right to dishonor him, and that to refuse the honor of burial to Aias is to offend the gods (1332–45). He is now as much a friend to Aias as he was once an enemy (1377) and is prepared to share in the burial. Odysseus calls Aias the best man of the Greeks, in word and deed giving his former enemy the very prize of honor (ἀριστεῖα) whose loss Aias mourned.[70] Teukros in turn forgives Odysseus, whom he now calls "best" (ἄριστ᾽: 1381), and although he cannot allow Aias's former enemy to touch the body, he does invite Odysseus and the army to attend the funeral procession (1396–97). Odysseus, who persuades Agamemnon to allow it, is instrumental in bringing about Aias's honorable burial. However, the text suggests that in so doing Odysseus also acts as an agent of the gods. Aias's prayer to Zeus in his suicide speech is answered when Teukros arrives and helps to give his brother burial,[71] and Odysseus is influenced to help his dead enemy by his encounter with Athena in the Prologue, who warns him against offending the gods and acting contrary to *sôphrosynê* ("soundness of mind:" 132–33). Odysseus shows that he has learned this lesson when he tells Agamemnon that to refuse burial to Aias would be contrary to the laws of the gods (1343). Thus, the burial is brought about by Odysseus among mortals, and, ultimately, by the gods, who are disposed to answer Aias's prayer because he has yielded to them and performed ritual purification.[72]

Aias will also receive honor from those who are still his enemies, in the negative form of the retribution they will have to pay. His dying curse on the Atreidai included "the whole army" (844), and especially, we may assume, Odysseus. Teukros, however, amends his brother's curse, restricting it to the Atreidai alone (1381–92). Agamemnon and Menelaos, who wanted to refuse honorable burial to Aias, are now excluded from the community of mortals and gods, as Aias himself once was.

Aias, then, succeeds in finding a way to "nobly die," a way that allows him to help his friends and harm his enemies. He achieves his goal, paradoxically, by means of the inherently shameful act of suicide, because his own relationship to friends, enemies, and self is highly paradoxical. Having injured himself and his friends with his own hand, Aias must perform against himself the act of an enemy in order to become once more his own friend and a friend of his own *philoi*. By returning evil for the evil he has done to friends and self, Aias also, paradoxically, reciprocates *kharis* for *kharis* and himself exemplifies the principle he states: "our enemy is to be hated but as one who will hereafter be a friend" (679–80).[73]

Conclusion

This book presents a great deal of evidence, based on close analysis of both extant and lost plays, that harm to *philoi* is a generic characteristic of ancient Greek tragedy. Chapter 1 surveyed the nature of biological and social *philia* relationships in Greek literature and society and showed that tragedy differs from epic in emphasizing incidents in which *philos* harms *philos*. Chapters 2–6 examined in detail five of the extant plays, in each of which harm to *philoi* is important in a different way. In *Iphigenia in Tauris*, killing of blood kin is first threatened and then avoided by recognition. Aiskhylos's *Suppliants*, Sophokles' *Philoktetes*, and Euripides' *Andromakhe* are concerned with relationships in which an outsider is brought into a group of *philoi*: suppliancy, *xenia*, and marriage, respectively. Sophokles' *Aias* focuses on the killing of the closest of *philoi*: the self. Appendix A presents evidence from the other twenty-seven extant tragedies indicating that twenty-one of them can readily be classified according to the various kinds of *philia* relationships—blood kinship, marriage, *xenia*, and suppliancy—with which their main *pathê* are concerned. From this material, some general conclusions may be drawn about all thirty-two extant plays. The statistics are summarized in chapter 1, section 3, and a table at the beginning of of appendix A.

In seventeen of the thirty-two extant plays, blood kin harm one another, and in fifteen, the *philoi* are either parent and child or siblings. These are the very relationships Aristotle mentions in *Poetics* 14: "When the *pathê* take place within *philia* relationships, for example, when brother kills or is about to kill brother, or does something else of this kind, or when son does this to father, or mother to son, or son to mother, these things are to be sought" (1453b19–22). Blood kinship also plays an important role in all four suppliant plays, in which either suppliant and pursuer or suppliant and supplicated, or both, are related. Chapters 1, 3, 4, and 5 provide evidence that the reciprocal relationships (marriage, suppliancy and *xenia*) with which nine of the extant plays are concerned are in many ways assimilated to blood kinship in Greek thought. The wife comes to her husband's home as a suppliant and *xenê*; she then becomes part of his household and after the birth of a child has indirect blood ties to her husband and his family. *Xenoi* have mutual obligations and rights that resemble those of kinship, while suppliants have the right to be treated with the respect (*aidôs*) due to kindred *philoi*, even before being accepted, and they may enter into formal *xenia* relationships after acceptance as suppliants. These interconnections among blood kinship and the various reciprocal relationships are apparent in Aiskhylos's *Suppliants* and Sophokles' *Philoktetes*, discussed in chapters 3 and 4, respectively, and in the seven other plays discussed in appendix A. All of the nine plays contain, in addition, numerous allusions to acts of harm to blood kin.

Six plays appear at first to be exceptions to the rule that tragedy is centrally concerned with harm to *philoi*. In *Persians*, *Trojan Women*, and *Rhesos*, enemy defeats enemy. The main *pathos* in *Aias* is Aias's suicide; in *Alkestis*, wife sacrifices herself for her husband; and in *Andromakhe*, wife attempts to kill concubine. Closer analysis, however, shows that three of these plays can be interpreted as variations on a pattern rather than as exceptions to the rule. Chapter 6 argues that Aias's suicide is a form of the killing of blood kin, inasmuch as the self is the closest *philos*. Because *Andromakhe*, as chapter 5 showed, is concerned with violations within the marriage relationship, it can be classified as a variant on the pattern of harm of spouse by spouse. Appendix A provides evidence that *Persians* is best interpreted as a play concerned with Xerxes' harm to his own kin and other *philoi*. In two other exceptional plays, *Alkestis* and *Trojan Women*, although harm to *philoi* does not occur in the main *pathos*, *philia* relationships play an important secondary role. This leaves only the *Rhesos*, of disputed date and authorship, in which harm to *philoi* does not have any significant role. Even in this play, however, the idea of violation of *philia* is much more important than it is in the Rhesos episode in the *Iliad*. These six plays, then, are less exceptional than they at first appear.

The little evidence we have indicates that harm to *philoi* was an important aspect of the lost tragedies of Aiskhylos, Sophokles, and Euripides, just as it is of the extant plays. Appendix B discusses 182 of the lost plays and concludes that harm within *philia* relationships occurred in 82 percent of those in which the *pathos* can be determined with some likelihood. In contrast, harm to *philoi* was unlikely in only 18 percent of the plays in which the *pathos* can be determined. The statistics are summarized in a table at the end of appendix B.

Of the lost plays in which harm was unlikely to have occurred within the *philia* relationships discussed, those focusing on three epic figures — Akhilleus, Odysseus, and Palamedes — are of particular interest because of their unusual qualities, which seem to place them somewhere between the epic and the tragic norms. These plays may provide some evidence for a development from the typical epic format, in which harm to *philoi* is downplayed, to the tragic norm, in which this element is stressed.

None of the lost plays about Akhilleus focused, as did the *Iliad*, on *pathê* among enemies. These plays also departed from the epic tradition in other ways. Aiskhylos's *Myrmidones* stressed an erotic relationship between Akhilleus and Patroklos, which helped to make harm to an unrelated companion seem more like harm to a relative. Euripides' *Skyrioi* focused on Akhilleus's violation of *xenia* in the home of Lykomedes. On the other hand, none of the plays about Akhilleus focused on harm to blood kin, as do many tragedies.

Most of the lost plays about Odysseus were exceptional tragedies in that they did not concern harm to *philoi*. Nevertheless, two of them (Soph. *Euryalos* and *Odysseus Akanthoplex*) departed significantly from the *Odyssey* in importing kin killing into the plot. In recounting Telegonos's killing of his father, Odysseus, *Akanthoplex* followed the *Telegony*, an epic that was exceptional in its representation of violence among kin.[1] Another play about Odysseus, Aiskhylos's *Psykhagagoi*, was a rare exception to the rule that kin killing takes place in tragedy but is avoided in epic. Although Odysseus was killed by his son in the epic, *Telegony*, in the tragedy, *Psykhagagoi*, he was killed by a fishbone dropped by a bird.

Finally, all five of the lost plays about Palamedes concerned active betrayal of a companion who was not, as far as the evidence indicates, included within any of the *philia* relationships discussed. These Palamedes stories, then, departed from both the epic and the tragic norms. In most tragedies betrayal takes place not between companions, but between blood kin, or within reciprocal relationships. In the *Iliad*, on the other hand, active betrayal even of unrelated companions is avoided. For example, although Akhilleus harms his companions by refusing to fight, the harm is indirect and passive.

The fact that so very little information of any kind has survived makes conclusions about the minor tragedians even more hypothetical than those about the fragmentary plays of Aiskhylos, Sophokles, and Euripides. Nevertheless, what evidence there is supports the view that tragedy as a genre was concerned with terrible events among *philoi*. Appendix C discusses or lists 139 plays by the minor playwrights, summarizing statistics about them in tables in section 4. In these plays, harm within *philia* relationships occurred within 79 percent of the plays in which the *pathos* can be determined with some likelihood. In contrast, in only 21 percent of the plays discussed or listed is harm to *philoi* unlikely to have occurred. These statistics are very similar to those for the fragmentary plays of Aiskhylos, Sophokles, and Euripides, a fact thst casts doubt on the claim made by some scholars that fourth-century tragedy was significantly different from that of the fifth century. Statistics for the plots of the minor tragedians in which violation of *philia* occurred also support the view that there is no significant difference between the plays of the fourth century and those of the fifth century and earlier.

From the scanty and fragmentary evidence surveyed in appendixes B and C only hypothetical conclusions can be drawn. However, all of the evidence that survives points in one direction: harm to *philoi* was just as prevalent in the lost plays as in those that are extant. It is highly unlikely that accidents of transmission alone could account for the large number of plays in which acts of harm to *philoi* appear to have occurred. Rather, these events seem to have been a defining characteristic of the genre as a whole.

Aristotle, then, has proved to be right about the importance of terrible events of a certain specific kind, those in which *philoi* harm *philoi*, in the tragedies of both the fifth and the fourth centuries. As far as can be determined from the evidence for both the extant and the lost plays, events in which blood kin harm or are about to harm one another are even more common than the *Poetics* indicates, taking place not only in a few of the "best" tragedies, but in more than half of all of the tragedies of Aiskhylos, Sophokles, and Euripides. When the concept of *philia* is extended, in accord with ordinary Greek usage, to include people within the formal reciprocal relationships of marriage, *xenia*, and suppliancy, then the evidence indicates that harm to *philoi* occurs or is about to occur in more than three-quarters of these plays. The same pattern appears to hold for the plays of the lesser dramatists. Moreover, *philia* relationships are also important in the less major events of the plays, in their imagery, in mythological allusions, and in the society represented. Whatever else tragedy is, however it originated, and whatever function it had within Greek society, tragedy is about violation of *philia*. In contrast, incidents of harm to *philoi* are either absent from epic or are given relatively little emphasis in this genre. For example, as was shown in chapter 1, the Klytaimestra of tragedy murders her husband and gloats over her deed, recounting it in vivid detail, but the Klytaimestra of epic merely helps Aigisthos plan the act.

In focusing on the generic characteristics of ancient Greek tragedy, this book contributes to the ongoing scholarly debate about its nature. A recent collection of essays contains many attempts to define tragedy and the qualities that make it "tragic."[2] Michael Silk writes that "the tragic" may refer to "some quality or qualities embodied in tragedy," for example, "something to do with catastrophic ends." Or, Silk continues, it may be defined as "a view of life, and even as a metaphysically defined view of life," as exemplified, for instance, in Nietzsche's summary of the "psychology of tragedy": "saying *yes* to life even in its strangest and hardest problems."[3] Rainer Friedrich surveys a range of views about Greek tragedy. For example, he writes that the "Cambridge ritualists . . . reconstructed . . . the ritual pattern of the slain and reborn god";[4] that according to Jean-Pierre Vernant, tragedy is connected with Dionysos as the god who "confuse(s) the boundaries between illusion and reality, who conjures up the beyond in the here, and who thus makes us lose our sense of self-assurance and identity";[5] and that Simon Goldhill holds that tragedy must be understood within the context of the Great Dionysia, which was "fundamentally and essentially a festival of the democratic *polis*."[6] According to Goldhill, Friedrich writes, "tragedy was made part of the civic discourse only in order to subvert it."[7] Friedrich himself maintains that Greek tragedy is "tragic . . . in an eminently political sense," in that "the *polis* and its *dikê*, its order of justice, were regarded as the manifestation of the divine and of divine *dikê* in the human world."[8] Richard Seaford defines Greek tragedy as "the dramatization of aetiological myth shaped by the vital need to create and sustain the *polis*."[9] Edith Hall writes of "the central defining features of the human condition explored in tragedy: that destiny is ultimately beyond human control, and that people die."[10] According to Emese Mogyoródi, "In Greek tragedy 'the tragic' is distinctively brought about in the mythical context of a doomed family."[11] Bernd Seidensticker bases his ideas on the definition of the tragic given by Peter Szondi: "a dialectical modality of impending or actual destruction."[12] Michael Ewans writes, "In the acknowledged masterpieces of Athenian drama, the dramatist creates the tragic effect . . . by shaping a serious story to conform with the same pattern as that of the *Iliad*; a *moira* [fate] gradually takes shape as the drama unfolds from beginning, through middle, to end, as a result of the actions of human beings who are perceived as choosing freely."[13] And George Steiner gives "one possible definition of 'tragedy' in its pure or absolute mode. 'Tragedy' is a dramatic representation, enactment, or generation of a highly specific world-view. This world-view is summarized in the adage preserved among the elegies ascribed to Theognis . . . : 'It is best not to be born, next best to die young.' "[14]

Scholars express such a bewildering variety of opinions partly because the question "What is Greek tragedy?" can itself be taken in so many different ways. It can be a historical question about the origin of Greek tragedy, or an anthropological question about the function of tragedy within the *polis*, or a religious question about the relationship of tragedy to the religious festivals at which it was performed and to the god Dionysos, who presided over these festivals. It can also be a literary question about the best ways of interpreting the tragedies so as to understand their emotional and intellectual power, or a philosophical question about the view of life contained in tragedy. The question might even be a purely personal one about an individual's response to tragedy.

Questions like these are easier to answer if we first understand more about what all or most tragedies have in common and what features characterize Greek tragedy as a genre and distinguish it from other genres. In attempting to provide an answer to these generic questions, this book has documented two frequently occurring tragic patterns. In many tragedies, as Aristotle writes, brother kills brother, son kills father, mother kills son, or son kills mother. As Polyneikes says, "How terrible . . . is the enmity of kindred *philoi*" (ὡς δεινὸν ἔχθρα . . . οἰκείων φίλων: Eur. *Phoen.* 374). On the other hand, these terrible events may be avoided by recognition. Orestes exclaims to his sister Iphigeneia, "If you had killed your brother, wretched woman" (εἰ σόν γ' ἀδελφόν, ὦ τάλαιν', ἀπώλεσας), and she in turn replies, "You escaped by little an unholy death, struck by my hands" (παρὰ δ' ὀλίγον ἀπέφυγες ὄλεθρον ἀνόσιον ἐξ ἐμᾶν δαϊχθεὶς χερῶν: Eur. *IT* 866–73). Whether harm to *philoi* actually occurs or is avoided, it appears that the function of tragedy is to arouse pity and fear by the representation of these events. The essence of "the tragic," for the ancient Greeks, is the representation of acts in which *philoi* harm or are about to harm *philoi*.

To approach Greek tragedy with this generic characteristic in mind greatly enhances our understanding of the plays, in large part because it leads us to pay attention to the role of biological and social relationships in tragedy. *Philia* is central to the plots of most of the tragedies and is an issue in nearly every scene. The dramatic figures define themselves in relation to their *philoi*, and they constantly speak and interact in terms of *philia*. *Philia* is not simply one "theme" or subject of tragedy, it constitutes the biological, social, religious, and emotional reality within which the action takes place. Only when we read or view the plays from this perspective can we fully appreciate the extent to which they are works whose meaning depends on the social structures that inform them.

Appendix A: Violation of *Philia* in the Extant Tragedies

Chapter 1 provided a typology of the thirty-two extant tragedies, grouping them according to various categories of *philia* relationships. Five of these plays (Aiskhylos's *Suppliants*, Sophokles' *Aias* and *Philoktetes*, and Euripides' *Iphigenia in Tauris* and *Andromakhe*) have been analyzed in detail in the preceding chapters. Appendix A provides a survey of the ways in which violation of *philia* figures in each of the remaining twenty-seven plays. I group the plays within the categories of relationships discussed in chapter 1. These categories are not intended to be rigid or exclusive; indeed, most of the tragedies represent or allude to harm to *philoi* in more than one category. Within each category the plays are grouped by author, in alphabetical order of the English titles. The study of each play begins with a short summary of the plot.

The table below summarizes the central *pathê* in all thirty-two of the extant tragedies according to the various kinds of relationships.

I. Blood kinship (17 plays)
   A. Parent harms child (7 plays)
      Aiskhylos: *Eumenides*
      Euripides: *Bacchae, Herakles, Hippolytos, Ion, Iphigenia in Aulis, Medea*
   B. Child harms parent (5 plays)
      Aiskhylos: *Libation Bearers*
      Sophokles: *Elektra, Oedipus the King*
      Euripides: *Elektra, Orestes*
   C. Sibling harms sibling (3 plays)
      Aiskhylos: *Seven Against Thebes*
      Euripides: *Iphigenia in Tauris, Phoenician Women*

    D. Harm to other blood kin (2 plays)
        Aiskhylos: *Prometheus Bound*
        Sophokles: *Antigone*
  II. Reciprocal relationships (9 plays)
    A. Marriage (2 plays)
        Aiskhylos: *Agamemnon*
        Sophokles: *Women of Trakhis*
    B. *Xenia* (3 plays)
        Sophokles: *Philoktetes*
        Euripides: *Hekabe, Helen*
    C. Suppliancy (4 plays)
        Aiskhylos: *Suppliants*
        Sophokles: *Oedipus at Kolonos*
        Euripides: *Children of Herakles, Suppliants*
  III. Exceptional Plays (6 plays)
        Aiskhylos: *Persians*
        Sophokles: *Aias*
        Euripides: *Alkestis, Andromakhe, Rhesos, Trojan Women*

I. Blood Kinship (17 Plays)

In seventeen plays, the central *pathos* is a violent act, whether actually occurring or only threatened, between *philoi* who are related by blood. The majority of these acts take place between parents and children.

I.A. *Parent Harms Child (7 Plays)*

■ Aiskhylos's *Eumenides*. In obedience to Apollo, Orestes has killed his mother, Klytaimestra, in punishment for her murder of his father, Agamemnon. Pursued by his mother's Furies, Orestes takes refuge in Apollo's sanctuary at Delphi. The god protects him and tells him to supplicate Athena, asking her to decide the case. When he does this, Athena says that her people must help in the decision. After presiding over a trial by jury, at which Orestes is acquitted, Athena persuades the Furies to be well disposed toward Athens.

    Eumenides has sometimes been categorized as a suppliant drama,[1] and its plot indeed follows the suppliant pattern in many respects.[2] Nevertheless, I group it with plays concerning harm to blood kin because the primary emphasis is on this *pathos*, and not on the suppliant action. Son has killed mother, and in turn she, in the guise of her Furies, attempts to harm him. In *Eumenides* the threat from suppliant to the agents supplicated is emphasized less than it is in the four suppliant plays (Ais. and Eur. *Supp.*, Soph. *OC*, Eur. *Heracl.*), in large part because those supplicated are divine. Moreover, the main issue in this last play of the trilogy is not supplication for its own sake, but the resolution of the problems resulting from a series of violent acts within the family.

In the primary *pathos* of this play, mother, in the form of her Furies, attempts with full knowledge to harm son, who has killed her. Because Klytaimestra's Furies are her curses (417), representing the anger of a *philos* who has been wronged, when they threaten to harm Orestes, they threaten him with harm by his mother. Klytaimestra herself urges on the Furies (94–139), and they threaten to kill Orestes by sucking his blood (264–75). Orestes' matricide plays a central role in this play as well as in *Libation Bearers*, and it is frequently alluded to (e.g., at 84, 100–102, 122, 202, 230, 256, 281, 425, 460, 463, 493, 595, 653).

Other violent acts against *philoi* also play a role. Orestes killed his mother in vengeance for her murder of her husband, an act that is alluded to in a number of passages (e.g., 211, 464, 602, 625–39, 740). Ixion, the first kin killer, is mentioned at 441 and 718 (πρωτοκτόνοισι προστροπαῖς Ἰξίονος). Among the gods, Zeus is said to have bound his father (640–41). More generally, the Furies are said to have the duty of punishing those who harm *philoi*: mothers (210), parents (513–14), *xenoi* and parents (270–71, 545–48), blood kin (604–5), and *philoi* within the house (354–59).

The main *pathos* takes place within the context of two supplications. Orestes is at first a suppliant of Apollo (41, 91–92, 151, 176, 205, 577–78), who fears the anger of a suppliant just as a human being does:

> ἐγὼ δ' ἀρήξω τὸν ἱκέτην τε ῥύσομαι·
> δεινὴ γὰρ ἐν βροτοῖσι κἀν θεοῖς πέλει
> τοῦ προστροπαίου μῆνις, εἰ προδῶ σφ' ἑκών. (232–34)

> I will aid and save the suppliant,
> for the wrath of a suppliant is terrible
> among mortals and gods, if I willingly betray you.

Apollo accepts Orestes as suppliant and thereby recognizes him as a *philos* when he says, "I will not betray you" (64, cf. 232). Pollution plays an important role in connection with this supplication. Orestes appears first as a polluted suppliant whose hands drip with blood (41–42), and according to the Furies, his presence pollutes the hearth of Apollo at which he is a suppliant (166–72). Apollo, like a human who gives refuge to a suppliant-exile, purifies Orestes of murder (φόνου δὲ τῷδ' ἐγὼ καθάρσιος: 578; cf. 280–83).[3] At Apollo's bidding, Orestes next supplicates Athena (79–80, 439–41, 474), whose role is similar to that of a human ruler in suppliant plays. Orestes supplicates the goddess, asking her to defend him, while his enemies, the Furies, argue that he should not be defended, threatening harm to both Orestes and Athens. After consulting her people by holding a formal trial, Athena decides in favor of the suppliant, recognizing his claim to be treated as a *philos*. Athena then defends Orestes against his enemies, not by going to war, as human rulers often do, but by persuasion.

■ Euripides' *Bacchae*. Agave and the other sisters of Dionysos's mother Semele have denied his divinity, as has Agave's son Pentheus, king of Thebes. The god punishes these unbelievers by causing mother and aunts to kill son and nephew in a Bacchic frenzy. Agave later realizes what she has done and goes into exile.

The central *pathos* of this play is the killing and tearing apart of son (Pentheus) by mother (Agave), who is maddened and does not know who he is. Pentheus's aunts also participate in the murder. Agave later recognizes her son and learns what she has done. This central event is recounted in gruesome detail by a messenger (1114–52), who describes Pentheus's supplication of Agave (1117–21). The aftermath is vividly represented on stage when Agave carries her son's head back to Thebes and invites her *philoi* to participate in a feast (1242).

Other instances of harm to *philoi* are less important in the play. The Theban women who deny the divinity of Dionysos are his aunts, his "mother's sisters, who ought least to do this" (26). The fact that Dionysos is Semele's son also means that Pentheus and Dionysos are cousins. However, this relationship is only indirectly alluded to. For example, Kadmos tells Pentheus that even if Dionysos is not a god, Pentheus should claim that he is so as to bring honor to the whole family (333–36). After the catastrophe, the old man states that Dionysos has destroyed his kin (βρόμιος ἄναξ ἀπώλεσ' οἰκεῖος γεγώς: 1250). The idea that Semele, who was killed by Zeus's lightning (3, 88–93, 598–99), was destroyed by her own "husband" may have figured in Aiskhylos's *Semele*, but this idea is not explicit in the *Bacchae*. An interesting side issue is the comparison of Pentheus's fate to that of his cousin Aktaion, who was torn apart by the dogs he himself had reared (ὃν ὠμόσιτοι σκύλακες ἃς ἐθρέψατο διεσπάσαντο: 338–39). This parallel is some evidence that the Greeks saw similarities between kin killing and the killing of masters by their own domestic animals, an event that is central to several fragmentary plays.[4]

■ Euripides' *Herakles*. Herakles has been away from home for a long time, persecuted by Hera and made to undergo many labors. At home, his city has been captured by an enemy, Lykos, and his family is about to be killed. He arrives home, is recognized by some, attacks, and is himself saved while he destroys his enemy.[5] Herakles is then driven mad by Hera. Intending to kill the children of his enemy, he instead kills his own wife and sons. Afterward, he recognizes what he has done. He is about to kill himself when Theseus arrives and, by offering him a refuge, prevents Herakles' suicide.

The main *pathos* is Herakles' murder, in ignorance, of his wife and children. The child-killing is in itself the more terrible act, since it involves the shedding of kindred blood, and its dramatic horror is increased in several ways. Even Madness is reluctant to cause Herakles to kill his family (858). In the Messenger's graphic report, Herakles does the deeds while about to perform purificatory sacrifice at the altar of Zeus, with the assistance of his family (922–30). Rejecting the supplications of his father (963–69) and son (984–94), he kills his wife and one son with a single arrow (1000) and is about to kill his father when Athena stops him (1001–6). The Messenger concludes with the statement that Herakles is now sleeping, "having killed children and wife. I know of no mortal who is more wretched" (1013–15). Herakles then appears on stage, surrounded by the corpses of those he has killed (1097). Herakles' pollution by kin murder is repeatedly stressed (1212, 1279–1300, 1324), and he veils his head and keeps silent in order to avoid polluting Theseus (1159–62, 1199–1201, 1219, 1234). He refers to himself as "child-killer" (παιδοκτονήσας: 1280), *authentês* of his own children (παίδων ὄντα μ' αὐθέντην ἐμῶν: 1359; cf. 839: αὐθέντῃ φόνῳ), and laments that he killed those he himself begot (1367–68; cf. 1183–84), and that he rewarded his wife's faithfulness with death (1371–73). Even his weapons are a source of pollution; Herakles imagines that they say to him, "With us you killed children and wife. In us you hold the killers of your children" ('Ημῖν τέκν' εἷλες καὶ δάμαρθ'· ἡμᾶς ἔχεις παιδο-κτόνους σούς: 1380–81).

Other acts of harm to kin also figure in the plot or are alluded to. Herakles tells Theseus that his life was unhappy from the beginning, for his father, Amphitryon, married his mother, Alkmene, while he was polluted with her father's murder (1258–62; cf. 16–17). The suicide Herakles is about to commit in order to avenge his children's murder (1150) is still another act of harm to kin—himself. The Chorus compare Herakles to others who harmed their *philoi*, to the Danaïds, who killed their husbands, and to Prokne, who killed one child; Herakles, however, who killed three children, has done deeds worse than these (1016–24). They fear that the sleeping Herakles will wake and go on to destroy his city, father, and house (1055–56). Amphitryon also fears that his son will wake and kill him (1068–75), acquiring still more pollution from kin murder (αἷμα σύγγονον: 1076–77). Zeus himself is accused of betraying his own grandchildren (339–47) and son (1087–88). Finally, Herakles compares his own fate to that of Ixion (1297–98), alluding to the first mortal to harm kin.[6]

Herakles is prevented from killing himself by the kindness of Theseus, his kin, friend, and *xenos* (συγγενὴς φίλος τ' ἐμός . . . φιλτάτῳ ξένων ἐμῶν: 1154–56; cf. φιλίαν ὁμόφυλον: 1200). In gratitude to Herakles for saving him from Hades, Theseus offers his friend purification, a refuge in Athens, and honors from the citizens in life and death (1322–1339). Dramatically and emotionally, these acts in which *philos* benefits *philos* are an inversion of the tragic *pathos* in the first part of the play, in which *philos* kills *philoi*.[7]

A subsidiary suppliant action takes place in the first part of the play when Lykos threatens to burn Herakles' suppliant family at the altar (238–46) and they in turn are about to commit suicide (289, 307, 451–53). The rescue of these suppliants by Herakles is reversed when Herakles himself kills them, after they have become his own suppliants (520–22, 963–69, 984–94).

■ Euripides' *Hippolytos*. Theseus has been away from home, leaving behind his wife, Phaidra, and a bastard son, Hippolytos, with whom Aphrodite has caused Phaidra to fall in love. When Phaidra's Nurse tells Hippolytos of her mistress's love for him, Hippolytos reacts with horror, and Phaidra kills herself. Theseus returns and finds a letter in which his dead wife accuses his son of rape. He curses his son, who is mortally injured as a result. Artemis then tells Theseus of his son's innocence, and the dying Hippolytos frees his father from blood guilt.

This plot has a pattern similar to that of *Oedipus the King*: Theseus kills Hippolytos, deceived by Phaidra into believing that his son is his enemy. He later recognizes that Hippolytos is a true *philos* (recognition leading to a state of *philia*). Theseus's ignorance is emphasized in a number of ways. Before his son's death, Theseus longs in vain for a token that will distinguish the true *philos* from the person who is not a *philos* (925–27). Not having such a token, he uses the curse given him by his father, Poseidon, to kill his son, when he might have used it against an enemy (1317). According to Artemis, Theseus kills his son involuntarily (ἄκων: 1433), and because of his ignorance, his *hamartia* (error) does not involve wickedness (τὴν δὲ σὴν ἁμαρτίαν τὸ μὴ εἰδέναι μὲν πρῶτον ἐκλύει κάκης: 1334–35). Compare Aristotle's characterization of the best plot as one that represents someone "changing [from good] to bad fortune, not because of vice and wickedness but because of some *hamartia*" (μήτε διὰ κακίαν καὶ μοχθηρίαν μεταβάλλων εἰς τὴν δυστυχίαν ἀλλὰ δι' ἁμαρτίαν τινά: Po. 1453a8–10). Theseus's *hamartia* is again mentioned at 1409 and 1434.

Even though Theseus acts in ignorance, the murder of his son is an act of impiety toward the gods, and in particular toward Artemis and Poseidon (παῖδ' οὐχ ὁσίως σὸν ἀποκτείνας, 1287, 1320), because he acted too quickly (1320–24). The horror of his deed is increased by the fact that Theseus uses a curse given by his own father, Poseidon, to destroy his own son (44–45, 1167–68), and by the fact that Hippolytos is killed by the horses he himself fed and reared: "Oh hateful chariot team," he says, "fed by my own hand, you have utterly destroyed me, you have utterly slain me."[8] On the other hand, the fact that Hippolytos lives to absolve his father (1442, 1448–51) helps to mitigate the evil consequences of this act of kin murder. The killing of son by father is powerfully represented on stage, as Theseus curses his son (887–90), then reviles and exiles him (936–80). A touch of irony is added when Hippolytos, who does not know that Theseus has already cursed him, tells his father that if he were in his place he would kill, not merely exile, a son who touched his wife (1041–44). The Messenger's speech recounts Hippolytos's accident in great detail (1198–1248), and the dying man himself appears on stage (1342–1466).

Harm to *philoi* also figures in other ways in the *Hippolytos*. Another act of kin murder is mentioned: Theseus killed the Pallantidai (35), who are his cousins in myth,[9] although the relationship is not alluded to in this play. In revealing Phaidra's secret, the Nurse betrays an unrelated *philos* (592–97, 682), and abuses an act of supplication by forcing (βιάζῃ: 325) her mistress to reveal her love.[10] Violation of the marriage relationship is of particular significance in the play. Phaidra's love for her stepson is never said to be incestuous, but

Hippolytos accuses her of betraying her husband's bed (590), just as Theseus accuses his son of committing an outrage against his father's wife (885–86; ὑβρίζειν: 1073) and says that Hippolytos's very presence before Theseus is pollution (*miasma*: 946). Phaidra's adulterous love leads directly to her suicide, which is also a means of destroying Hippolytos (728–29), her *philos* (319, 613). Amphimetric strife is not an issue here, although both the Nurse (305–10) and Theseus (962–63) think that it is. Several mythological exempla of violation of the marriage relationship are alluded to. Phaidra mentions her mother Pasiphaë, who loved the bull, and her sister Ariadne, wife of Dionysos (337–39), and the Chorus mention the "murderous bridals" (φονίοισι νυμφείοις: 552) of Iole and Herakles, who raped her after sacking her city, and the "bloody fate" (πότμῳ φονίῳ: 561–62) given Semele by her marriage to the thunder god.[11]

■ Euripides' *Ion*.   After Kreousa, daughter of the king of Athens, exposed the child she bore to Apollo, the god ordered it taken to Delphi to be reared. The child, Ion, grew up as a priest of Apollo, while Kreousa married Xouthos, with whom she has not yet had a child. When the play opens, husband and wife have come to Delphi to consult the oracle about their childlessness. Trusting in revelations by the oracle, Xouthos believes that Ion is his own son and tries to embrace him. Ion, after questioning him, acknowledges the older man as his father. Upon learning that her husband intends to make the young man the heir to her father's kingdom, Kreousa attempts to kill Ion, not knowing that he is her son. The attempt fails, and, her life threatened by her son, she takes refuge at an altar. Mother and son recognize each other by tokens. Kreousa tells Ion that he is the son of Apollo, but he does not believe this until Athena confirms it.

This play is concerned with violence between mother and son. Kreousa is about to kill her son Ion, in ignorance of the relationship, but her attempt fails. Then, after he discovers that Kreousa has attacked him, Ion, also in ignorance, attempts to kill his mother. In this case, recognition prevents the act from taking place. These two *pathê* occupy the entire second half of the play, from line 844, when the Old Man first suggests killing Ion. Of the two events, the mother's attack on her son is of greater dramatic importance, occupying more time and motivating Ion's retaliation. It is also more vividly presented, in a powerful messenger speech describing the death of a dove that drank poisoned wine meant for Ion (1196–1208).

Many other acts of violation of *philia* play a lesser role in the plot or are alluded to. Kreousa's family history is stained with kin murder, for her father Erekhtheus sacrificed his other daughters (277–78). She herself exposed her child, an act of injustice for which she blames herself (963). The mortals in the play, however, hold Apollo to be more blameworthy (252–54, 384–89, 960), since he raped Kreousa and then abandoned his son (881–922, 952). Although both Ion and Kreousa agree with Athena, at the end of the play, that "Apollo has done all things well" (1595), the god's violence to his "wife" causes her lasting pain, and his concealment of his son's identity leads to the enmity between mother and son that nearly results in kin murder. Kreousa attempts to kill Ion with poison from the Gorgon, son of Earth, which was given to Kreousa's ancestor Erikhthonios by Athena after she killed the Gorgon in the battle of gods and Giants (987–1019). Thus enmity between Kreousa, daughter of the earthborn Erekhtheus, and Ion, son of Apollo, is associated with the strife between the gods and their earthborn kin, the Giants, recounted in detail in the Parodos (184–218). Just as Kreousa's divine husband, Apollo, injures her, so her mortal husband, Xouthos, is about to do so when he plans to bring to Athens a man whom he believes to be his bastard (*nothos*: 592, 1105). Since Kreousa is an heiress (814) and Xouthos a foreigner, this is a betrayal and an act of enmity to Kreousa's house, which rules Athens (808–16, 864–80, 1090–1105). It also leads to a form of amphimetric strife, as Kreousa sees her supposed stepson as an enemy. Ion attempts to force Kreousa to leave the sanctuary, threatening violence to a suppliant (1275–76,[12] 1306), and she in turn threatens to injure Apollo if he does not protect the suppliant at his altar (1311).

The possibility of harm to other *philoi* is more briefly suggested. When Xouthos first tries to embrace Ion as his son, the young man threatens him with the bow, leading Xouthos to warn him not to become the murderer of his father (527). The Old Man suggests that Kreousa kill her mortal husband (845,[13] 976) and burn the oracle of her divine lover (974).

■ Euripides' *Iphigenia in Aulis*.   The text of this play, in which Euripidean lines are inextricably mixed with later additions, is very uncertain. The ending in particular (1532–1629, bracketed in the summary below) is spurious.

Agamemnon intends to sacrifice his daughter Iphigeneia to Artemis, in obedience to a prophecy, and he deceives his wife Klytaimestra in order to persuade her to bring the girl to him at Aulis. After mother and daughter arrive, they learn that Agamemnon intends to kill Iphigeneia. His wife and daughter supplicate Agamemnon, but he does not yield. The girl resolves to die voluntarily and goes to her death. [Artemis saves Iphigeneia, substituting a deer for her.]

The central *pathos* in this play is the murder of daughter by father, an act frequently alluded to in the text. For example, Klytaimestra tells Agamemnon that she will say to herself after the sacrifice: "The father who begot you, child, destroyed you, himself and no other killing you, with no other hand than his own" (Ἀπώλεσέν σ᾽, ὦ τέκνον, ὁ φυτεύσας πατήρ, / αὐτὸς κτανών, οὐκ ἄλλος οὐδ᾽ ἄλλη χερί: 1177–78; cf. 89–98, 364, 396, 399, 490, 511–12, 873, 935). This event is made more pitiable by Iphigeneia's lamentations on stage at 1080–84 and 1312–18, by Klytaimestra's representations to Agamemnon of the girl's laments (1098–1105) and of her own future mourning at home (1164–93), and especially by Iphigeneia's supplication of her father (1211–52).

Other acts of harm to *philos* by *philos* also figure in the play. Agamemnon and Menelaos quarrel (304–414) over the sacrifice, and the Chorus comment: "It is terrible when insults and fights take place between brothers, when they fall into strife" (376–77). Enmity between husband and wife is prominent in the fourth episode (1098–1275), where Klytaimestra not only blames Agamemnon for intending to sacrifice their daughter but also recalls earlier wrongs and hints at future crimes. Their marriage, she says, began when Agamemnon raped Klytaimestra after killing her husband, Tantalos, and their young child (1149–52).[14] He is thus *authentês* to her as the murderer of members of her family. If he kills Iphigeneia, Agamemnon will again be *authentês* (1190) to her, as well as to his other children, and he will deserve an evil homecoming (1180–93). There are also quarrels among unrelated companions. Both Agamemnon (531–35, 1267–68) and Akhilleus (1348–53) fear being killed by their own armies, and Akhilleus is angry that his *philos* (1019) Agamemnon has committed *hybris* against him (961). In representing these many kinds of harm to *philoi*, the play suggests that a single act of kin murder has broad implications, mirroring, as it does, similar past acts and leading to family quarrels in the present, to continued troubles in future generations, and to strife among the unrelated *philoi* of the Greek army.

■ Euripides' *Medea*.   Medeia betrayed her family and country in order to help her husband Iason, who has now betrayed her in order to marry another wife. To punish her husband, Medeia kills his new wife and father-in-law, then murders her own children. She escapes, taking refuge in Athens.

The central *pathos* in this play is the murder of children by mother, vividly represented to the audience by means of cries offstage (1270a–78) and the display of the bodies in the chariot (1317–1410). The child-murder is frequently mentioned, as when Medeia says, "I who bore them will kill them" (ἡμεῖς κτενοῦμεν οἵπερ ἐξεφύσαμεν: 1241; cf. 792–96, 816, 846–65, 976–1001, 1251–82, 1325–26, 1393, 1407, 1410–11). Aristotle cites this play in *Poetics* 14 as an example of the killing of *philoi* with knowledge, the second worst kind of plot (1453b27–29). That Medeia kills her children with knowledge is evident from her own statement in the play: "I know what evil I am about to do" (1078). As Gerald Else notes, a recognition leading to a state of enmity occurs when Iason realizes that Medeia has killed their children and calls her his "greatest enemy" (μέγιστον ἐχθίστη: 1323).[15]

Other acts of harm to blood kin are also alluded to. Medeia has made enemies of her *philoi* at home (τοῖς μὲν οἴκοθεν φίλοις ἐχθρὰ καθέστηχ': 506–7) by betraying her father and country (31–32, 483, 502–3) and by killing her brother (167, 1334). She has also killed Pelias, king of Iolkos, "in the way it is most painful to die, at the hands of his own children" (486–87; cf. 9–10, 504–5). Medeia's child murder is compared to the act of Ino, who, in madness, leapt into the sea with her children (1283–89).

Iason, in turn, has betrayed his wife and children, behaving badly to his *philoi* (κακός γ' ὢν ἐς φίλους: 84; cf. 470). As a result of his actions, *philoi* have become enemies (ἐχθρὰ πάντα καὶ νοσεῖ τὰ φίλτατα: 16; cf. 467). In betraying his wife, Iason has also violated suppliancy and *xenia*. He has not kept the pledge (δεξιᾶς πίστιν μεγίστην: 21–22) made during his supplication of

Medeia (φεῦ δεξιὰ χείρ . . . καὶ τῶνδε γονάτων: 496–97), and she calls him an "oath breaker and deceiver of *xenoi*" (ψευδόρκου καὶ ξειναπάτου: 1392).[16]

Amphimetric strife also plays a role in *Medea*. Iason's plan to advance the children of his first wife, Medeia, by giving them siblings by his second wife (547–65) fails to take this kind of rivalry into account. Medeia replies angrily when he explains this idea (579–87), and Iason's new wife is also angry at the sight of Medeia's children, only being persuaded to welcome them by the gifts they bring and by Iason's mollifying words (1147–55).[17]

I.B. *Child Harms Parent (5 Plays)*

In five plays, the main *pathos* involves harm to parent by child. As was shown above, this is also an important secondary *pathos* in Euripides' *Ion*. Four of the five plays are about the Orestes story. In three plays (Ais. *Cho.*, Soph. *El.*, and Eur. *El.*), the murder of Klytaimestra by her son is the main event in the stage action. Although each treats the subject differently, all three of these plays have a similar plot: Klytaimestra has killed her husband, King Agamemnon, and now rules in his stead, along with her lover, Aigisthos, who is implicated in the murder. Orestes, the son of Agamemnon and Klytaimestra, lives in exile, while their daughter Elektra lives at or near home and is at enmity with her mother. Orestes returns from exile and is recognized by his sister. He kills his mother's lover and with or without his sister's help puts his mother to death. In the fourth play about Orestes, Euripides' *Orestes*, the stage action begins after the matricide. Aiskhylos's *Eumenides* (see section I.A) focuses on the harm Klytaimestra and her Furies attempt to do Orestes. Euripides' play, however, is included in section I.B because the emphasis is on the matricide that has just taken place. Only one play in this group is about another family in which harm to parents takes place: Sophokles' *Oedipus the King*. This play is praised by Aristotle as having one of the best plots, one in which someone acts in ignorance and later recognizes *philia* (*Po.* 1453b29–31).

■ Aiskhylos's *Libation Bearers*.   See the plot summary at the beginning of section I.B.

In this play, son kills mother, with knowledge, but this act is made to appear less blameworthy because he does so in obedience to Apollo's oracle, telling him to avenge his father's murder and threatening him with his father's Furies if he disobeys (269–305). The divine command is stressed in Pylades' speech at 900–902, when Orestes hesitates as he is about to commit matricide: "Count all humans as enemies rather than the god." The matricide is vividly represented in the stage action by means of Klytaimestra's supplication of her son (896–930), the display of the bodies of Klytaimestra and Aigisthos at 973ff., and Orestes' pursuit by his mother's Furies (1048ff.). On the other hand, the play also emphasizes the horror of Klytaimestra's murder of her husband (306–509, 909, 930, 973–1015, 1070–71). As the killer of Orestes' father (πατρο-κτόνον: 1028; cf. 909, 974), she has become the enemy of her children. Orestes says: "I know that our nearest kin are bitter to us" (τοὺς φιλτάτους γὰρ οἶδα νῦν ὄντας πικρούς: 234), and he remarks that Klytaimestra's child "once dear is now an enemy" (φίλον τέως, νῦν δ' ἐχθρόν: 993). Other acts of harm to kin are briefly alluded to: the feast of Thyestes (1068–69); the sacrifice of Iphigeneia (242); Althaia's destruction of her son Meleagros (603–12); Skylla, who caused the death of her father Nisos (613–22); and the Lemnian women, who killed their male *philoi* (631–34).

The play has several recognitions. That of Orestes by Elektra, beginning at 212, involves much more than a realization on Elektra's part that the man before her is her brother. This recognition leading to a state of *philia* involves the acknowledgment of the mutual rights and obligations that are entailed by the *philia* relationship, as the siblings pledge loyalty to their father and enmity to their mother. In contrast, Orestes' recognition (16–18) that the woman he sees is his sister (recognition of *philia*) has relatively little emotional impact. Another recognition, that of Orestes by Klytaimestra (887–88), is a recognition leading to a state of enmity. The mother recognizes that her son is her enemy, because he has just killed Aigisthos, the man who is most *philos* to her (893).

In *Libation Bearers* there is a close connection between kinship on the one hand and suppliancy and *xenia* on the other. The bringing of offerings to Agamemnon's tomb is a supplication (προστροπῆς: 85, cf. 21); Orestes and Elektra are suppliants when they invoke their dead father (τάφος δ' ἱκέτας δέδεκται: 336, cf. 501: ἐφημένους τάφῳ); and Agamemnon himself is a suppliant to his kin for vengeance.[18] Klytaimestra supplicates Orestes when she bares her breast to him, asking for *aidôs* (896–98), and when she threatens him with the curses and Furies of a mother (912, 924). At the end of the play, Orestes leaves Argos, carrying suppliant branches, in order to seek purification at Apollo's shrine (1034–39, cf. 1059–60). Moreover, Orestes and Klytaimestra are in a false relationship of *xenia* to each other. In order to gain entrance to his mother's house, Orestes says that he will pose as a *xenos*, the friend of Pylades, who is the spear-friend (*doryxenos*) of the house of Agamemnon (560–62); he will be a *hiketês* at the gates of Aigisthos (569). Klytaimestra's first word to Orestes and Pylades is *xenoi* (668), and *xenos* (674) is the son's first word to his mother.[19] This false *xenia* relationship between mother and son foreshadows Apollo's theory in *Eumenides* (657–61) that the relationship between mother and child is not blood kinship but *xenia*. Ideally, the *xenia* relationship is a most kindly one (τί γὰρ ξένου ξένοισιν ἐστιν εὐμενέστερορον: 702–3), but this pretended *xenia* cloaks enmity.

■ Sophokles' *Elektra*.   See the plot summary at the beginning of section I.B.

In the central *pathos* of this play also, Orestes kills his mother, with knowledge of the relationship. However, unlike Aiskhylos's Orestes, who is reminded of the oracle as he hesitates at the crucial moment, Sophokles' matricide states (59–72) that he is moved by desire for glory, vengeance, and gain (κέρδει: 61). The oracle's role is limited to telling him how (ὅτῳ τρόπῳ: 33) he can accomplish his goal. The matricide is frequently alluded to, before, during, and after its occurrence. Orestes has been raised by the Pedagogue to be the avenger of the murder of his father (14), and Apollo's oracle has told Orestes how he might punish the murderers (τῶν φονευσάντων) of his father with "just slaughter" (34–37).[20] Elektra mentions the bloody ax that split her father's head (99), as do the Chorus (484–87); she prays for vengeance (115–16; cf. 248) and hopes that Orestes will come as the avenger of his father's murder (953, 1154–56). When she thinks that Orestes is dead, Elektra herself is about to undertake this vengeance, either with her sister (954–89) or alone (1019–20, 1319–21). The matricide itself is vividly represented. Orestes and Pylades are said to enter the palace like Furies (1388), holding "newly-whetted murder in their hands" (1394). Klytaimestra cries out within, asking Orestes to pity his mother (1410–1411), while Elektra urges her brother on with the horrific line, "Strike, if you have strength, a second blow!" (1415). When the act is completed, and Orestes appears on stage, Elektra notes that his "bloody hand drips with sacrifice to Ares" (φοινία δὲ χεὶρ στάζει θυηλῆς Ἄρεος: 1422–23).[21]

Klytaimestra's murder of her husband is mentioned in many of the passages just cited, and in others as well (for example, in 124–26, 558, 779, 1411–12). As a result of the murder, Agamemnon is "the most hostile of mortals" (δυσμενεστάτῳ βροτῶν) to Klytaimestra, who killed him (407–8; cf. 433, 440–41, 444–45, 454–56: ἐχθροὺς . . . ἐχθροῖσιν); she in turn has also become her children's greatest enemy (τὰ μητρός, ἥ μ' ἐγείνετο, ἔχθιστα συμβέβηκεν: 261–62; ἐχθίστοισιν ἀνθρώπων ἐμοί, φονεῦσι πατρός: 815–16; cf. 638, 647, 979), a "mother who is no mother" (μήτηρ ἀμήτωρ: 1154). This state of affairs results in the internal conflict Klytaimestra expresses when she learns of Orestes' supposed death: "It is a painful thing, if I am to save my life by means of my own ills" (767–68). Even though Orestes has become her enemy, she cannot, she says, hate the child she has borne (770–71).

The murder of husband by wife has resulted in other evils as well. Elektra is forced to live with her *authentai*, Aigisthos and her mother, who have killed her father (1190). She laments (262–76) the fact that she is forced to share a house with them, that Aigisthos pours libations at the hearth where he killed Agamemnon, and that she is forced to see the greatest *hybris* of all, the killer of her father[22] sleeping in his bed with his victim's wife. She accuses her mother of sleeping with her husband's killer and of making children with him (ἥτις ξυνεύδεις τῷ παλαμναίῳ . . . καὶ παιδοποιεῖς: 587–89), and of having married her enemy (ἐχθροῖς γαμεῖσθαι: 594). Elektra also accuses her sister Khrysothemis of associating with the murderers of her father (358) while betraying her dead father and her *philoi* (368).

Other acts of harm to *philoi* are alluded to more briefly. Agamemnon was guilty of killing his own daughter, Iphigeneia (530–32). The story of Amphiaraos, who was betrayed by his wife, Eriphyle, and whose death was avenged by their son Alkmeon, is mentioned at 837–48 as a mythological example that parallels the story of Agamemnon, Klytaimestra, and Orestes.[23]

In *Elektra*, as in *Libation Bearers*, xenia plays a role in the matricide. Orestes, Pylades, and the Pedagogue pretend to be *xenoi*, in the sense of strangers (44, 1442, 1450), who also claim a *xenia* relationship with Klytaimestra and Aigisthos as the messengers of Phanoteos, the "greatest spear-friend" (μέγιστος . . . δορυξένων: 46) of the latter. As the supposed envoy of this *xenos* (801) of Aigisthos and Klytaimestra, the Pedagogue is welcomed by Klytaimestra: "*Xenos*, you would come as a *philos* worthy of much good" (797). Finally, as she lures Aigisthos into the palace to his death, Elektra ironically refers to Klytaimestra as the *proxenos* ("protector of a *xenos*") of the disguised Orestes (1451).

Although *Libation Bearers* ends with the pursuit of Orestes by the Furies, they are notably absent from Sophocles' play.

■ Sophokles' *Oedipus the King*.   Oidipous was given an oracle stating that he would kill his father and marry his mother. Fearing this, he fled Polybos and Merope of Korinth, who had brought him up as their own child, and came to Thebes, after killing a man whom he met on the way. In Thebes, he married Queen Iokaste and acquired the throne. When the action begins, a plague is attacking Thebes. An oracle states that the plague can be stopped only by punishing the murderer of the former king. Oidipous searches for this person, and his inquiries lead him to discover that he himself has killed the former king, who was his father, while the woman he has married is his mother. Iokaste commits suicide and Oidipous blinds himself.

In this play, Oidipous harms his parents, without knowledge of the relationship, and then learns that he has done so, in a recognition leading to a state of enmity. Although the central *pathê*, the patricide and incest, occur before the beginning of the stage action, Oidipous himself recounts the patricide (798–813), and the incestuous couple and their children appear on stage. Other *pathê* are Iokaste's suicide and Oidipous's self-blinding, both reported in detail by the Messenger. Oidipous's sufferings after his blinding are represented on stage.

The patricide and incest are repeatedly emphasized. Before the recognition, oracles and prophecies stress these acts. First, Teiresias tells Oidipous, who fails to understand, that he is "living most shamefully with his closest *philoi*" (σὺν τοῖς φιλτάτοις αἴσχισθ' ὁμιλοῦντ': 366–67), that he is an enemy to his own (415–16), and that he will be found to be both brother and father to his own children, son and husband to his mother, wife-sharer and murderer to his father (457–60). We hear next of the two oracles, one to Laios (an oracle Iokaste believes to be worthless: 720–22, 851–58) stating that he will be killed by his own child (713), and one to Oidipous prophesying that he will commit patricide and incest (791–93, 994–96). As a result of this oracle, Oidipous fears to return to those he believes to be his parents (823–27). After learning the details of Laios's death, however, he also fears that in invoking a curse on the murderer of Laios he has cursed himself, and that he is *authentês* to Iokaste, having killed her former husband (813–22). When he learns that Polybos is dead, Oidipous rejoices that part of the oracle has proved false (964–72), but he still fears his mother's bed (976). A slightly different version of the oracle to Laios, according to which the child of Laios will kill its parents (1176), is reported by the Herdsman. This man speaks more truly than he knows, for Iokaste, as well as Laios, is now dead because of Oidipous.

When Oidipous discovers the truth, the oracles are revealed to have been fulfilled. Oidipous says that he was born from, has lived with, and has killed the wrong people (1184–85), and the Chorus lament Oidipous's marriage, in which the son plowed the furrows his father sowed, and begetter and begotten are one (1208–15). In the Messenger's report of the suicide of Iokaste and the blinding of Oidipous, the incest is described in graphic terms. Iokaste calls it a child-making in which she conceived children by her own child (1247–50), and Oidipous speaks of Iokaste as the "maternal field of himself and of his children" (1256–57). No details of Oidipous's bloody self-blinding are spared (1268–79). Oidipous, the Messenger concludes, accuses himself of patricide and incest (1288–89).

When Oidipous reappears on stage, he refers to his self-blinding as an act done αὐτόχειρ ("with one's own hand"), using a word that frequently refers to kin murder (1331). He states that he wishes he had died when his parents exposed him, for then he would not have been a great grief to his *philoi*, the murderer of his father and the bridegroom of his mother (1355–61). He invokes the crossroads where the earth drank his father's blood, which is his own blood shed by his own hand (τοὐμὸν αἷμα τῶν ἐμῶν χειρῶν ἄπο / ἐπίετε πατρὸς: 1400–1401), and the marriage that revealed the most shameful deeds (αἴσχιστ' . . . ἔργα: 1408), calling it an incestuous and murderous kinship (αἷμ' ἐμφύλιον: 1406)[24] in which fathers, brothers, children, wives, and mothers are confused (1405–7). He rightly calls his daughters his closest *philoi* (φίλοιν, τὰ φίλτατ': 1472, 1474), for he is both brother and father to them (1481–85, 1496–99). The patricide is also mentioned in this final section (1441, 1496–97). The play ends before Kreon decides what Oidipous's fate is to be, but we know from Teiresias's prophecy that he will be driven out of the land by the double curse of father and mother (417–18), a curse that has turned out to be identical to the one that Oidipous invoked on himself in ignorance.

■ Euripides' *Elektra*.   See the plot summary at the beginning of section I.B.

This play, like Aiskhylos's *Libation Bearers*, is centered on Orestes' matricide. However, it treats the subject very differently, emphasizing the ambiguous ethical qualities of the deed. The matricide is represented in very negative terms. Apollo's oracle is blamed by Orestes (971–73, 979, 1190–93) and by Kastor (1245–46, 1296–97, 1302). The horror of the act is highlighted in a number of ways. When it takes place, the audience hears Klytaimestra crying out within, "Children, by the gods, do not kill your mother" (1165), and immediately afterwards, Orestes and Elektra appear "stained with the newly shed blood of their mother" (1172–73). Orestes refers to the murder as "polluted" (μυσαρά: 1179), and Elektra also expresses regrets, leading the Chorus to say that she is only now thinking piously (1198–1205). Orestes recounts the deed in vivid terms, dwelling on Klytaimestra's supplication of her son (1206–17) and his own inability to look at her (1221–22). Kastor sums up the ethical qualities of the act by telling Orestes, "She has received justice, but you have not acted justly" (1244).

Particularly shocking to a Greek audience would have been Elektra's eager participation. When the disguised Orestes asks her if she would dare to kill her mother, she answers, "Yes, with the same ax with which she killed my father" (279), and she adds, "May I die, having shed my mother's blood" (281). She undertakes to prepare for the matricide (647), and when Orestes hesitates, Elektra urges him on (967–987). According to the Chorus, it is she who did terrible things when her brother was not willing (δεινὰ δ' εἰργάσω, φίλα, κασίγνητον οὐ θέλοντα: 1204–5). Elektra herself says that she is responsible (αἰτία: 1182), and (1224–25), that she encouraged her brother and held the sword with him (ξίφους τ' ἐφηψάμαν ἅμα).

Other acts of violence against *philoi* figure less prominently in the play.[25] Klytaimestra's murder of her husband is mentioned frequently (86–87, 122–23, 276, 479–81, 599–600, 745–46, 1065–66, 1093–95, 1155–64, 1170–71). Agamemnon's body was outraged by being thrown out of the house instead of receiving burial (288–89). Klytaimestra sleeps with her husband's murderer (211–12), and Aigisthos lives in his house and dishonors his grave (319–31). In the background is Agamemnon's murder of his daughter Iphigeneia, for which Klytaimestra blames her husband (1011–29), and the quarrel of Atreus and Thyestes (699–726). Finally, Kastor alludes to Ares' murder of his cousin Halirrhothios, son of Poseidon, who raped Ares' daughter (1258–62).

Orestes' murder of Aigisthos is represented as an act of just vengeance against an enemy (πολέμιον), for which Elektra crowns her brother as victor (880–85). However, even this act is presented in a somewhat negative light: Orestes kills his enemy during a sacrifice after accepting *xenia* from him. Aigisthos invites Orestes to share his hearth (συνεστίους . . . γενέσθαι), takes him by the hand (χερὸς λαβών), and refers to him and the Messenger as *xenoi* (783–96). Orestes' negative reciprocation of *xenia* contrasts sharply with the hospitality and guest-gifts Orestes himself received from the Farmer and the Old Man (*xénia*: 359, 414; cf. 493–500). Moreover, Elektra's abuse of Aigisthos's corpse (907–56), of which even she is ashamed (900–902), is uncomfortably similar to the outrages committed against Agamemnon's corpse and grave.

■ Euripides' *Orestes*. The action takes place a few days after Orestes, with the help of Elektra and Pylades, has killed his mother. The Argive people are about to vote on their punishment. Brother and sister supplicate Menelaos, asking for help, but he instead sides against them and with his father-in-law, Tyndareos. Pylades speaks in defense of the siblings before the Argives, but they decide that Orestes and Elektra must die. Orestes, Elektra, and Pylades take vengeance on Menelaos by stabbing Helen, who, however, mysteriously vanishes, and by threatening to kill her daughter Hermione. Apollo reconciles the quarreling *philoi*.[26]

The consequences of matricide are the subject of *Orestes*. Orestes is tormented by his mother's Furies; he and Elektra are condemned by the Argives to die for this deed, and many quarrels among kin result from it. Although the matricide is frequently alluded to, the act is not recounted in detail; Tyndareos merely asks Orestes how he felt when Klytaimestra bared her breast in supplication (526–28). Elektra has less direct responsibility for the murder than she does in Euripides' *Elektra*, because it is Pylades who held the sword with Orestes (1235).[27] The ethical quality of the deed is characterized in similar terms in both plays, for in *Orestes* also, Klytaimestra is said to have suffered justly, although it was not right for her to die at Orestes' hands (538–39). The two plays are also similar in their negative representations of Apollo. In *Orestes*, both Elektra (28–31, 191–93) and Orestes (591–95) blame the god, and Apollo himself takes responsibility (1665).

The *Orestes*, however, differs from the other plays about this subject in that many other *pathê* among kin occur or are about to occur in the stage action. Grandfather (Tyndareos) harms grandchildren (Orestes and Elektra) by urging the Argives to punish them. Uncle (Menelaos) harms nephew and niece (Orestes and Elektra) by refusing to protect them (1056–57, 1462–64). Nephew and niece (Orestes and Elektra) attempt to kill aunt (Helen), an act recounted in detail by the Phrygian slave and made to appear more horrible by the fact that when Orestes approaches Helen he pretends to be a suppliant (1414–15). Cousins (Orestes and Elektra) threaten to kill cousin (Hermione).

Enmity among kin also figures in more minor ways. It forms the mythological background of the story of the house of Atreus, which began with the enmity of Atreus and his brother Thyestes (11–18, 811–18, 996–1010). The frequent mention of the Argives as descendants of Danaos (872, 933, 1250, 1279, 1621) may also hint at the Danaïds' murder of their husbands in the remote past.[28] In the more recent past, Agamemnon sacrificed his daughter Iphigeneia (658), and Klytaimestra in turn murdered her husband (25–26, 195, 366–67). Pylades is guilty of killing Klytaimestra, his aunt by marriage,[29] and he was exiled by his father for his part in the murder (765–67). Finally, when both siblings are condemned to kill themselves, Elektra urges her brother to put her to death, a suggestion he rejects, telling her to die instead by her own hand (1035–40).

In this play, as in *Andromakhe*, the same people are both *philoi* and enemies. Orestes and Elektra are enemies of their mother. Although they consistently act as friends of each other, one of the most important aspects of their relationship is their complicity in matricide. Similarly, their friend and cousin Pylades shows his loyalty by his complicity in harming other kin. Moreover, his help in the matricide has caused his father to exile him. Hermione is the friend of her aunt Klytaimestra, by whom she was brought up (63–65), but she is now living with her cousins, who murdered this aunt. Menelaos is the uncle of the matricides and the brother-in-law of the murdered woman, while Tyndareos is the grandfather of Orestes and Elektra and the father of the woman they have killed. Alliances shift and change under these circumstances. When Orestes and Elektra fail to gain the support of Menelaos and Tyndareos, they act as enemies to Menelaos and his wife, Helen, and daughter, Hermione. After Apollo reconciles the enemies (νείκους τε διαλύεσθε: 1679), former enemies become friends as Orestes marries Hermione, becoming the son-in-law of Menelaos. However, Apollo himself is both friend and enemy. He reconciles enemies and brings about a happy ending (1670), yet his oracle is to blame for the matricide that caused the enmities in the first place.

I.C. *Sibling Harms Sibling (3 Plays)*

■ Aiskhylos's *Seven Against Thebes*.　The sons of Oidipous, Eteokles and Polyneikes, are disputing the rule of Thebes; Eteokles defends the city, against which Polyneikes is leading an invading army. Eteokles assigns a defender to fight against an attacker at each of six gates of the city and meets his own brother at the seventh gate. The city is saved, but brother kills brother. [Antigone resolves to bury Polyneikes, in spite of a decree against this.][30]

This is the last play in a trilogy, of which the first two plays, now lost, were *Laios* and *Oidipous*. The primary *pathos* is fratricide: each brother kills the other, with knowledge of the relationship. The horror and pollution of this act are stressed throughout the play: "When two men of the same blood die in mutual slaughter, the pollution does not grow old" (ἀνδροῖν δ' ὁμαίμοιν θάνατος ὧδ' αὐτοκτόνος, οὐκ ἔστι γῆρας τοῦδε τοῦ μιάσματος: 681–82; see also 672–75, 718, 734–40, 805, 811, 850, 888–99, 930–40, 971–72). Even though the deaths take place offstage, they are forcefully presented to the audience when the bodies are brought on at 848.[31]

This central *pathos* is associated with a number of other *pathê* among *philoi*. The Chorus recount the history of three generations of the royal house of Thebes. First, Laios, in disobedience to Apollo's oracle, begot Oidipous, who killed his father and begot on his own mother children whom he cursed. Oidipous's curse, they fear, will be fulfilled in the mutual fratricide of those children (720–91). Thus, the events represented in this play are the result and culmination of a serious of terrible events within the family: Eteokles and Polyneikes are the children of the incestuous marriage of Oidipous (753–57, 926–30), who killed his own father (751–52, 783), and the fratricide is the fulfillment of the curse of Oidipous, the presence of which is felt throughout the play (70, 655, 695–97, 709, 720–26, 766, 785–91, 886–87, 898, 946, 955, 975–76 = 987–88). Moreover, the attack of Polyneikes on Thebes is itself portrayed as patricide and matricide against the land that is both father (πατρῴας χθονός, "fatherland": 668) and mother (τεκούσῃ μητρί, "the mother that bore him": 415; cf. 477, 580–89, 640). Both brothers have destroyed their fathers' house (876, 880–85) and done evil to the citizens of Thebes (923).[32] Eteokles' realization that his father's curse is being fulfilled (πατρὸς δὴ νῦν ἀραὶ τελεσφόροι: 655) is a recognition leading to a state of enmity, in which Eteokles understands that his father has acted as an enemy to him and that he in turn is about to act as an enemy to his brother. This recognition, however, does not change the direction of the action, but confirms its ongoing progression toward bad fortune.

■ Euripides' *Iphigenia in Tauris*.   This play is discussed in chapter 2.

■ Euripides' *Phoenician Women*.   After discovering that he had committed patricide and incest, Oidipous cursed the two sons of his incestuous marriage.[33] Eteokles and Polyneikes have quarreled over the rule of Thebes. As the play begins, Polyneikes is leading a foreign army to attack the city, which is defended by Eteokles. The city is saved, but the two brothers kill each other in single combat. Iokaste kills herself over their bodies.

The play represents the fulfillment of the curse of Oidipous (1425–26, 1556–59), which entails the destruction of his house (379, 624, 1495–97). This curse is inherited from Laios and passed on to Oidipous's children (1611). Laios disobeyed the oracle telling him not to beget children (17–22, 868–69) and then tried to kill his son by exposing him (1600–1601). Oidipous, in turn, killed his father and begot on his own mother children whom he killed with curses (32–68, 1043–54, 1608–11). Even before Laios, however, the history of the Theban royal house was tainted with kin murder. After Kadmos killed the snake of Ares and sowed the earth with its teeth (657–69), the Spartoi (Sown Men) rose from the earth and, in acts that the Chorus describe in terms reminiscent of fratricide and incest, soaked it with blood as they killed one another, after which they returned to the earth:

> ἔνθεν ἐξανῆκε Γᾶ
> πάνοπλον ὄψιν ὑπὲρ ἄκρων
> ὅρων χθονός· σιδαρόφρων
> δέ νιν φόνος πάλιν ξυνῆψε Γᾳ φίλᾳ.
> αἵματος δ᾽ ἔδευσε Γαῖαν, ἅ νιν εὐαλίοισι
> δεῖξεν αἰθέρος πνοαῖς. (670–75)

> Then the Earth sent up a vision of armed men above the uppermost limits of the land. And iron-minded murder joined them again to dear Earth. It soaked with blood the Earth that had shown them to the bright breezes of the air.[34]

In the action represented on stage, Kreon's son Menoikeus dies because, according to Teiresias, one of the race of the Spartoi, from whom Kreon is descended, must pay with his life for the murder of the snake (930–44).

The central *pathos* is the fratricide, on which attention is continually focused by means of allusions to the curse of Oidipous; by Teiresias's prophecy of their fratricide (880); by the brothers' expressions of their desire to kill one another (610, 622, 754–56); by the choral ode at 1284–1307, by the Messenger's report (1356–1424), according to which each of the brothers prays to succeed in killing the other (1365–69, 1373–76); and finally, by the corpses brought on stage at 1480.[35]

Euripides' play, however, has a more episodic structure than does Aiskhylos's *Seven Against Thebes*, allowing many other acts of harm to *philoi* to take place. Oidipous is dishonored by his sons (63–65, 872–77), Eteokles is unjust to his brother in refusing to share the rule (491–93), and Polyneikes attacks Thebes, an act that makes him an enemy of his land (270–71), of the earth that nourished him (626), of his city (432–33, 609), of his own family (617), and of his fellow Thebans (357–58). Eteokles' denial of burial to Polyneikes (775–77) is enforced by his uncle Kreon (1627–34), who also exiles Oidipous, an act the latter says is a death sentence (1621). Menoikeus and Iokaste kill themselves, and Antigone threatens to act like her relatives the Danaïds[36] by killing her cousin Haimon on their wedding night if she is forced to marry him (1675). Finally, it is possible to see a veiled allusion to the sacrifice of the daughters of Erekhtheus in Teiresias's statement that he has just returned from helping Erekhtheus in his war against Eumolpos (852–57).[37] Polyneikes' statement sums up the central idea of the play: "How terrible, mother, is the enmity of kindred *philoi*" (ὡς δεινὸν ἔχθρα, μῆτερ, οἰκείων φίλων: 374).[38]

I.D. Harm to Other Blood Kin (2 plays)

■ Aiskhylos's *Prometheus Bound*.   Prometheus, because he has helped mortals, is bound to a rock by his nephew Zeus.[39] He is visited by Oceanos and the daughters of Oceanos, and by Io, whose future sufferings and deliverance he prophesies. After Prometheus states that he alone knows how Zeus can be saved from being deposed, Hermes threatens him with further tortures if he does not reveal the secret to Zeus. Prometheus refuses and is given further punishments by Zeus.

In this play, harm to divine *philos* by *philos* is central to the plot. Violation of *philia* among the gods is important in many other ways as well.[40] All of the gods are related, and Zeus is called "father" by the other gods (4, 17, 40, 947, 984). In Aiskhylos's version, Zeus's injuries to Prometheus are particularly terrible because he is Prometheus's nephew. In Hesiod, Prometheus is the son of the Titan Iapetos, brother of Oceanos, and, like Zeus, he is the grandson of Ouranos and Gaia (*Theogony* 507–10, 132–34). According to Hesiod, therefore, Prometheus is Zeus's cousin. In the *Prometheus Bound*, however, Prometheus is himself a Titan, as the son of Gaia (209–10), Zeus's grandmother.[41]

Relationships by blood and marriage are also important in the words and actions of those who visit Prometheus. Hephaistos is reluctant to help punish Prometheus because of his kinship (συγγενῆ θεόν: 14; cf. 39) with the Titan. Hermes, as the son of Zeus, whom he calls "father" at 947, is Prometheus's great-nephew. Oceanos is doubly related to Prometheus, as blood kin and as father of his wife, Hesione (558–60).[42] He visits Prometheus as kin (ξυγγενές . . . γένους: 290–91) and states that no one is a more "steadfast friend" (φίλος . . . βεβαιότερος: 297) of Prometheus. Oceanos attempts to act as a friend by interceding with Zeus on Prometheus's behalf, although Prometheus forbids this (325–96). The Oceanids, who come in *philia* (127), mention their relationship by marriage to Prometheus, stating that they are the sisters of his wife (558–60). They immediately sympathize with Prometheus, who is "pitiable to his *philoi*" (246), and they join with him in indignation over his unjust punishment (ξυνασχαλᾷ: 162, 243). At the end of the play, the Oceanids willingly share in his torments (ξυγκάμνουσαι: 1059), refusing to leave when he is threatened with further punishments. Their final words express a hatred for traitors (1069). Io is the niece of the Oceanids, as Prometheus points out (κασιγνήταις πατρός: 636), and therefore related to Prometheus himself. In addition, because she is the bride of Zeus, her mortal descendants will be even more closely related to Prometheus.

Prometheus's relationship with Zeus varies between friendship and enmity. Prometheus has been Zeus's political friend (τὸν Διὸς φίλον: 304): he helped him win the throne, taking Zeus's side in the civil war (στάσις: 200) against the Titans (199–225). Prometheus then became the enemy of Zeus and his allies (37, 120–21, 975, 1041) because of his too-great friendship with mortals (λίαν φιλότητα βρότων: 123; cf. 28). As a result, Zeus now inflicts outrages (αἰκείασιν: 94; λύμαις: 148) on him. Zeus also punished Prometheus's Titan kin (κασιγνήτου: 347, ξυνομαιμόνων: 410) for opposing him in the war. Nevertheless, Prometheus prophesies that one day Zeus will again enter into friendship (φιλότητα: 191) with him.

Zeus is involved in unfortunate relationships with other *philoi* also. He took over the throne of his father Kronos (πατρῷον . . . θρόνον: 228) after a war with him. Zeus then hid Kronos and his allies in Tartaros, following Prometheus's advice (219–21). As a result, Kronos cursed Zeus (910–12). In seeking a marriage with Io, Zeus treats her more like an enemy than a friend, driving her from her father's home against her will and that of her father (ἐξήλασέν με κἀπέκλῃσε δωμάτων, ἄκουσαν ἄκων: 670–71) and arousing Hera's enmity against her (592, 704). The descendants of the troubled marriage of Zeus and Io will be involved in troubled marriages of their own, since the Danaïds will flee from marriages with their cousins (συγγενῆ γάμον ἀνεψιῶν: 855–56) and all but one of them will kill her husband (862–67). Moreover, according to Prometheus's prophecy, Zeus is destined to lose his throne because of a marriage that will give him a child mightier than its father (764–68). Only Prometheus, Zeus's kin and enemy, can save him from this fate.

■ Sophokles' *Antigone*.   After the sons of Oidipous, Eteokles and Polyneikes, kill one another in battle over the rule of Thebes, Kreon, the new ruler, decrees that no one shall bury Polyneikes on pain of death. Antigone buries her brother and is condemned to death by her uncle Kreon. After being immured in a cave, she commits suicide, and Haimon, Kreon's son and her betrothed, kills himself over her body after a failed attempt to stab his father. Kreon's wife, Eurydike, also kills herself, blaming her husband for her son's death.

There are many *pathê* in the stage action of this play, all involving harm to *philoi*.[43] Kreon harms his nephew Polyneikes in refusing him burial, and his niece Antigone in condemning her to death. Kreon's condemnation of Antigone leads to other *pathê*: Antigone's suicide, Haimon's attack on his father, Haimon's suicide, and the suicide of Eurydike. All of these suicides are vengeance suicides directed against Kreon.[44] When Antigone hangs herself, she brings on the pollution that Kreon had tried to avoid by providing her with some food when immuring her (775–76). Haimon kills himself in anger at his father's murder of his fiancée (1177), and Eurydike kills herself at the house-hold altar (1301),[45] charging Kreon with the murder of his son (1312–13), and calling him a "child-killer" (παιδοκτόνῳ: 1305). Kreon fully accepts responsi-bility for the death of Haimon, calling the Chorus to look on the kin killer and the killed (ὦ κτανόντας τε καὶ θανόντας βλέποντες ἐμφυλίους: 1263–64) and repeating that he has killed his son and wife (ὅς, ὦ παῖ, σέ τ᾽ οὐχ ἑκὼν κατ-έκτανον / σέ τ᾽ αὖ τάνδ᾽: 1340–41; cf. 1319). Haimon's aborted attack on his father (1231–34) is condemned by Aristotle (*Po.* 14.1453b37–1454a2) as an act that is *miaron* (polluted) and "without *pathos*," because someone is about to act, with knowledge of the *philia* relationship, but does not. Seen as a prelude to his vengeance suicide, however, Haimon's act makes better dramatic sense than Aristotle indicates.

Kreon errs by acting impiously both in refusing burial to the dead and in burying the living (1068–73), and he later recognizes his mistake ("I know it," ἔγνωκα: 1095). This error is closely bound up with a failure to act as *philos* to his own kin, followed by a recognition of this mistake. Kreon states that he now rules Thebes because he is next of kin to Polyneikes and Eteokles (174), but he also states that he does not count as a *philos* the enemy of his country (187–88), that an enemy is never a *philos*, even in death (522), and that Antigone must die no matter how closely related she is in blood (486–88). When Kreon later realizes that he has erred, he understands that his errors (ἁμαρτήματα: 1261; αὐτὸς ἁμαρτών: 1260) have led to kin murder (1263–64). Thus, Kreon's error in failing to treat his kin as *philoi* is similar to that of Oidipous, who harmed his kin in ignorance. Antigone makes a mistake simi-lar to that of Kreon in failing to acknowledge as *philoi* those who do not act with her in honoring blood kin. For this reason, she rejects her sister Ismene, calling her an enemy (ἐχθίων: 86, ἐχθαρῇ: 93), and she refuses to consider the claims of her uncle Kreon. She dies lamenting that she is bereft of *philoi* (876–82).

In the background of the stage action is the history of Oidipous and his sons. Ismene forcefully reminds her sister of their father's infamy and self-blinding (49–52), of the suicide of Oidipous's mother and wife (53–54), and of their brothers' mutual fratricide:

τρίτον δ᾽ ἀδελφὼ δύο μίαν καθ᾽ ἡμέραν
αὐτοκτονοῦντε τὼ ταλαιπώρω μόρον
κοινὸν κατειργάσαντ᾽ ἐπαλλήλοιν χεροῖν. (55–57)

Third, our two brothers in one day,
two wretched self-killers, with each others' hands
brought about a common doom.

The misfortunes of the house of Oidipous are frequently mentioned elsewhere as well (for instance, at 144–47, 171–72, 594–603, 857–66).

Other instances of kin killing are also alluded to. Kreon is responsible for the death of another son, Megareos.[46] The Chorus also allude to a number of mythological exempla that involve kin murder, in at least some version of the myths (944–87). Danaë and her son Perseus were cast adrift in a chest by Danaë's father, Akrisios, who in turn was later killed by his grandson Perseus. Lykourgos killed his son Dryas, and in one version of the myth, Kleopatra blinded her sons, the Phineidai.[47]

II. Reciprocal Relationships (9 Plays)

In nine plays, *philoi* harm or threaten *philoi* in the reciprocal relationships of marriage, *xenia*, and suppliancy.

II.A. *Marriage (2 Plays)*

■ Aiskhylos's *Agamemnon*.   Agamemnon has sacrificed his daughter Iphigeneia in order to sail to Troy. He returns after a victory and is killed by his wife Klytaimestra and her lover Aigisthos.

In the main *pathos*, wife deliberately kills husband. This act is vividly represented in the play as about to occur, as actually taking place, and as an event in the past. First, Kassandra prophesies (1100–29) Klytaimestra's murder, "unbearable to *philoi*, incurable" (1103), of her "husband of the same bed" (ὁμοδέμνιον πόσιν: 1108). She repeats the prophecy, saying that "the female is murderer of the male" (1231–32), "breathing Ares against her *philoi*" (1235–36). Next, the audience hears Agamemnon cry out within the palace that he has been struck (1343, 1345). Finally, Klytaimestra recounts the deed she has just committed, standing over the body of her husband and boasting that she struck him three times, rejoicing in the bloody drops with which he spattered her as crops rejoice in rain (1379–98). She boldly proclaims, "This is Agamemnon, my husband, a corpse, the work of this right hand, crafter of justice" (1404–6). In another violation of decency, Klytaimestra, in response to the Chorus's questions, says that she, who murdered her husband, will also give him burial (1541–54).

In this play, in contrast to the accounts in Homer, where it is usually Aigisthos who is responsible for the actual killing (see chapter 1, section 2, with note 35), Klytaimestra does the deed and her lover merely helps in the planning (1604, 1609, 1614, 1627, 1634–35, 1643–46). The Chorus complain to Aigisthos that because the wife did the actual deed, there is pollution of the land and of its gods (χώρας μίασμα καὶ θεῶν ἐγχωρίων: 1645). Although Aigisthos is kin to Agamemnon (1583–85), in stressing the pollution that results from husband-murder and asking Aigisthos why he did not do the deed himself (1643–44), the Chorus imply that Aigisthos's murder of Agamemnon would have created less pollution.

Klytaimestra and Aigisthos are also guilty of adultery, of which she openly boasts (1435–37), even stating, in a line that continues to shock modern editors, that the murder of Kassandra gives her a sexual thrill (1447).[48] The Chorus accuse Aigisthos of adultery at 1626, and Kassandra alludes to it at 1258–59.

The central act of husband-killing is closely linked to past acts of kin murder. Klytaimestra says that she killed her husband in vengeance for his sacrifice of their daughter Iphigeneia (1417–18, 1432–33, 1525–29, 1555–59), and the Chorus narrate this act in the Parodos (205–47). For his part, Aigisthos helped plan the murder in revenge for the crimes of Agamemnon's father, Atreus, against Atreus's brother Thyestes, Aigisthos's father. According to Aigisthos (1583–1602), Atreus first exiled Thyestes, and then, when his brother returned to his hearth as suppliant (προστρόπαιος ἑστίας: 1587), gave him as guest-gift (ξένια: 1590) the flesh of his own children to eat (παρέσχε δαῖτα παιδείων κρεῶν: 1593). Thyestes then cursed the house of Atreus (1598–1602). Aigisthos sees himself as fulfilling this curse in avenging his father Thyestes (1577–82, 1603–11). Although Klytaimestra's main concern is for Iphigeneia, she also believes herself to be the ἀλάστωρ ("avenging spirit"), who punishes "Atreus, the cruel giver of the feast" (1497–1504). The feast of Thyestes is also alluded to by Kassandra, who recoils from the "kin murders" (αὐτοφόνα κακά: 1091) in the house and who has a vision of the children eaten by their father (κλαιόμενα τάδε βρέφη σφαγὰς, / ὀπτάς τε σάρκας πρὸς πατρὸς βεβρωμένας: 1096–97). She paints an especially vivid picture at 1219–22:

παῖδες θανόντες ὡσπερεὶ πρὸς τῶν[49] φίλων,
χεῖρας κρεῶν πλήθοντες οἰκείας βορᾶς
ξὺν ἐντέροις τε σπλάγχν', ἐποίκτιστον γέμος,
πρέπουσ' ἔχοντες, ὧν πατὴρ ἐγεύσατο.

Children, it seems, whom their own relatives have killed;
their hands are full of meat—their own flesh served as food,
a pitiable burden! I can see them holding up
the vitals and the entrails, which their father tasted.

                                        (trans. Ewans 1995)

Kassandra also sees Aigisthos's role in Agamemnon's murder as an act of vengeance for Atreus's deed (1223–25), as does the Chorus (1338–40, 1505–12). However, Kassandra alone briefly mentions the adultery of Thyestes with Atreus's wife (1193) that began the bloody cycle in the version of the story this play appears to follow.

Frequent allusions to Orestes' future matricide remind us that Agamemnon's murder is not the end of the chain of kin murders. Kassandra prophesies that an avenger will come, the "mother-killing offspring, avenger of his father" (1281), and the Chorus also speak of vengeance, first in general terms (1429–30, 1533–36, 1562–64), then stating clearly their hope that Orestes will come as murderer (φονεύς) of both Aigisthos and Klytaimestra (1646–48, cf. 1667). Klytaimestra, however, hopes to ward off further kin murders (θανά-τοις αὐθένταισιν; μανίας μελάθρων ἀλληλοφόνους: 1567–76).

Finally, Paris's violation of *xenia* is in the background of the Trojan War. It is Zeus Xenios who sends the sons of Atreus against Paris (60–62, 362–64), who shamed the table of *xenia* by stealing a woman (399–402; cf. 700–704). The marriage of Paris has destroyed his own *philoi* (1156).

■ Sophokles' *Women of Trakhis*.   Herakles has been away from home for a long time, forced to undergo labors. When he is about to return home, his wife Deianeira learns that he has fallen in love with another woman, Iole, whom he is bringing home as a captive. Deianeira gives Herakles a drug she thinks is a love charm but that turns out to be poison. When she learns that her husband is dying, she kills herself. Before he dies, Herakles persuades his son Hyllos to carry him to a funeral pyre and to marry Iole.

The main *pathos* is the killing of husband by wife. Deianeira kills Herakles unintentionally because of *hamartia* (ἥμαρτεν οὐχ ἑκουσία: 1123)[50] and recognizes later what she has done (712–13). This act of husband-killing is the center of a web of other interconnected acts of violence against *philoi*. Deianeira acts because Herakles has treated her badly in bringing another woman, who will be more than a slave (367), to live with her, sharing her bed and marriage (539–46). Moreover, Iole's capture is the last of a series of events connected with violation of *xenia*. According to Likhas, when Herakles was a guest (δόμους ἐφέστιον, ξένον παλαιόν: 262–63) in the home of Eurytos, king of Oikhalia and Iole's father, Eurytos insulted Herakles and threw him out of the house. In revenge, Herakles killed Iphitos, Eurytos's son, by throwing him from the walls of Tiryns, Herakles' home, when the young man was not paying attention. Zeus punished him for killing Iphitos by trickery. Later on, Herakles sacked Oikhalia and killed Eurytos and his sons (262–83). Although Likhas's story leaves out Iole's part in Herakles' attack on Oikhalia, this does not change the fact that Eurytos violated his *xenia* relationship with Herakles and that Herakles, in turn, killed Iphitos while he was visiting Herakles' home.[51]

Deianeira's husband-killing also results in other acts of violence against *philoi*. Herakles, mad with pain because of the poison, murders his faithful friend Likhas (777–84), and Deianeira commits suicide, partly because her son curses her (808–12, 932–33).[52] Without knowing that she is already dead, Herakles also curses his wife, wishing that she might die just as she killed him (1037–40) and that he himself had killed her (1133). In what Jan Coenraad Kamerbeek calls "perhaps the most savage passage in Greek Tragedy," Herakles asks Hyllos to bring Deianeira to him for punishment, so that he can see whether his son is pained more by his father's or his mother's sufferings

(1066–69).[53] Even when he learns that Deianeira did not intend to kill him, Herakles says nothing to show that he, like Hyllos, forgives Deianeira; he does not mention her from 1143 on.

Herakles' sufferings lead, in turn, to the terrible orders he gives Hyllos, telling his son to bring about his father's death. Hyllos is to place Herakles on the pyre with his own hand (αὐτόχειρα: 1194), or his father will be a curse to him even in the underworld (1201–2). After Hyllos expresses horror at the idea of becoming his father's murderer (φονέα γενέσθαι καὶ παλαμναῖον σέθεν: 1207), Herakles allows his son to escape pollution—technically, at least—by avoiding actually touching the pyre (1211–15). But the horror of the deed remains. Herakles also orders his son to marry Iole, the woman who is part cause (μεταίτιος) of the deaths of both his parents (1233–37). Hyllos is also *authentês* to Iole because Herakles killed her father and brothers. When Herakles again threatens his son with a curse (1239–40), Hyllos yields, saying that he must learn to act impiously (ἐκδιδαχθῶ δῆτα δυσσεβεῖν: 1245).[54] He agrees to obey both orders but places the responsibility on his father (1249–50). Herakles not only asks his son for death, he makes the same request of others. He calls the Greeks, whom he saved from many dangers, "most unjust" because they will not give him death (1010–16). He calls on Hades, as the brother of his father, Zeus, to put him to sleep (1040–43), and on his father to kill him with his thunderbolt (1087–88).

Herakles' death is complex and paradoxical, being a release from sufferings and labors (1170–71, cf. 79–81, 166–68, 821–30), which he himself desires. Responsibility for this death is equally problematic. Of the many who share in Herakles' death (Iole, the cause of Deianeira's decision to use the poison; Nessos, who gave Deianeira the poison; Deianeira, who administered the poison; Hyllos, who takes his father to the pyre; and Zeus, who does not help his son), who is ultimately responsible? According to Hyllos, it is Zeus, who looks with indifference on his son's sufferings (1264–74). According to Herakles, however, it is Nessos, his enemy. Herakles has the authority of a prophecy of Zeus, stating that a dead man would kill him (1159–63). Yet, if "none of these things is without Zeus" (1278), it is after all Herakles' father who fulfills the prophecy.

II.B. Xenia *(3 Plays)*

■ Sophokles' *Philoktetes.*   This play is discussed in chapter 4.

■ Euripides' *Hekabe.*   Hekabe has seen Troy sacked by the Greeks, who killed her husband and sons and enslaved her and her daughters. In the stage action, a remaining daughter, Polyxene, is sacrificed by the Greeks at Akhilleus's tomb, and her last living son, Polydoros, is killed by Polymestor, a *xenos* to whom he had been sent for safekeeping. Hekabe takes vengeance on Polymestor by blinding him and killing his sons.

This play is concerned with violation of an established *xenia* relationship.[55] Polymestor kills his *xenos* Polydoros, and Hekabe in turn takes vengeance on Polymestor and his sons. The murder of Polydoros is alluded to throughout the play. The young man's ghost speaks the Prologue, telling how the *xenos* of his father (ξένος πατρῷος) killed him and threw his body into the sea, where he lies unburied (25–30). Hekabe has an evil dream concerning her son (54, 68–82) and realizes that it is fulfilled (703–7) when she recognizes that her Thracian *xenos* has killed her son (710–20). This is a recognition leading to a state of enmity. Vengeance for the murder occupies the rest of the play.

Hekabe interweaves the representation of these central *pathê* with many other allusions to *philia* and its violation.[56] Hekabe suffers as a slave after the Trojan War, a conflict that began when Paris married Helen (629–56, 943–51), thus violating his *xenia* relationship with Menelaos, and ended with Akhilleus's murder of Priam at an altar (23). Hekabe supplicates Odysseus in vain, asking him to spare her daughter's life, claiming that he owes her a debt (ἀντιδοῦναι: 272) since she once saved his life when he was her suppliant in Troy (239–78). She also claims that it is contrary to accepted law to kill a woman he has saved after dragging her from an altar (288–92). Odysseus, however, answers that he owes a greater debt to Akhilleus, his *philos* (311), and says that she, as a barbarian, has no true concept of *philia*: "The barbarians do not believe *philoi* to be *philoi*" (328–29).

After she discovers that Polymestor has killed Polydoros, Hekabe supplicates Agamemnon, asking him to punish Polymestor, "the most impious *xenos*," who did "the most impious deed" after frequently receiving hospitality at the table of *xenia* (790–94).[57] She argues that the law requires those who kill *xenoi* to be punished (799–805). Hekabe also attempts to persuade Agamemnon that because his relationship with Kassandra is a kind of marriage, Polydoros is in fact his brother-in-law (κηδεστήν: 834). The Chorus remark that the laws of necessity make enemies *philoi* and *philoi* enemies (848–49). Agamemnon, however, argues that Polymestor is friendly (*philios*) to the Greeks, while Polydoros is an enemy (858–60). In persuading Agamemnon to let her take vengeance on Polymestor, Hekabe cites women who have overcome men: the Danaïds and the Lemnian women (886–87), who killed their husbands and male kin.

The unsuspecting Polymestor still claims to be a friend of the Trojans. He enters with the words, "O Priam, dearest [φίλτατ'] of men, and you the dearest woman [φιλτάτη], Hekabe" (953–54). He agrees to send his bodyguard away, telling her, "You are dear [φίλη] and this army of the Greeks is friendly [προσφιλές] to me" (982–83). Hekabe pretends to reciprocate, echoing Polymestor's own words in addressing him as "dearest" (φίλτατ': 990) and in saying to him: "O loved (φιληθείς) as you are now loved (φιλῇ) by me (1000)." Her revenge is appropriately reciprocal. After luring Polymestor into her tent on the pretext of treating him as a trusted *philos* (ὡς δὴ παρὰ φίλῳ: 1152), she acts just as he did, killing the children of her *xenos*. In addition, she blinds him.

In the final debate, the blinded Polymestor claims friendship with the Greeks, calling Agamemnon "dearest" (φίλτατ': 1114) and making his defense on the grounds that he was acting out of *philia* to the Greeks: since Priam's son was an enemy to the Greeks, Polymestor was doing Agamemnon a favor in killing him (1175–76). Hekabe's accusation begins with an echo of Odysseus's words to her at 328–29: "The barbarian race could never be *philon* [dear] to the Greeks" (1199–1201), apparently not realizing that the words apply to herself as well as to Polymestor. She goes on to state (1202–3) that Polymestor is neither blood kin (συγγενής) to the Greeks nor a relation by marriage (κηδεύσων). She claims that Polymestor was guilty of murdering a *xenos* at his hearth (1216), that he killed Polydoros only after Troy fell, and that he has kept the Trojan gold given him by Priam along with Polydoros, which shows that he is not a true *philos* to the Greeks (1208–23). She argues, moreover, that Agamemnon will show himself to be evil if he supports an impious *xenos* (1232–35). When Agamemnon agrees with Hekabe, stating that the Greeks consider it shameful to kill a *xenos* (1247–48), Polymestor loses his case. Before he dies, however, he prophesies Agamemnon's own death at the hands of his wife (1277–81).

■ Euripides' *Helen*.   While the Trojan War was being fought over a phantom Helen, the real Helen was taken by Zeus's orders to Egypt to be kept safe for her husband, Menelaos, by King Proteus. The play opens after Proteus's death. His son Theoklymenos is pursuing Helen, whom he wants to marry against her will. She takes refuge at Proteus's tomb. Menelaos arrives, shipwrecked, recognizes his wife, and learns that she has not betrayed him. Husband and wife are protected by Theonoë, the sister of Theoklymenos. With the help of Helen's divine brothers, the Dioskoroi, Helen and Menelaos escape from Egypt by trickery and sail to safety in Sparta.

Euripides' *Helen* is best understood as a play concerning *xenia* and its violation. Zeus gave his daughter Helen to Proteus, the king of Egypt, to keep her safe for her husband while he was away at Troy fighting to regain the phantom Helen (44–48, 909–11, 964). Since this action created a *xenia* relationship between Helen and Proteus, the relationships among Zeus, Proteus, and Helen are much the same as those among Priam, Polymestor and Polydoros in the *Hekabe*. Proteus's *xenia* relationship has been inherited by Proteus's son Theoklymenos, who, however, violates it by attempting to force Helen to marry him.[58] Even though the term *xenia* is never used of these relationships, they are clearly represented as such.

In addition to being essential to the main events of the plot, *xenia* relationships figure in more minor ways in the *Helen*. The play is concerned with the Trojan War, which began with Paris's violation of *xenia* in Menelaos's house, an act alluded to at 229–35 and 691. Not only does Theoklymenos violate his *xenia* relationship with Helen, he kills all Greek *xenoi* he catches (155), according to Helen, and the Old Woman states that he will give Menelaos death for a guest-gift (*xénia*) if he catches him (480). Although Menelaos escapes this fate, he says that he was driven like a beggar from Theoklymenos's door (790).

Theonoë, on the other hand, acts like her just father Proteus (μιμοῦ τρό-πους πατρὸς δικαίου: 940–41; cf. 920) in protecting her *xenoi*, Helen and Menelaos, from her brother Theoklymenos. When Theonoë discovers the couple, Helen appeals to her, arguing that Proteus would want his daughter to give back (ἀποδοῦναι πάλιν) what belongs to another (915–17). Theonoë agrees, telling Menelaos, "I would do wrong if I did not give back [sc. Helen]. For if he [sc. Proteus] were living, he would give her back [ἀπέδωκεν] to you, and you to her" (1010–12). For this reason, she honors Menelaos's request to save a *xenos* (954) by not revealing his presence. In protecting her *xenoi*, Helen and Menelaos, Theonoë also honors suppliants at her father's tomb (961), who threaten to kill themselves there (980–87), just as she honors her own suppliant, Helen (894). The play ends with a reference to theoxeny (the hosting of gods by mortals), as Kastor prophesies that the deified Helen, together with her brothers the Dioskoroi, will have *xénia* from mortals (ξένια τ' ἀνθρώπων πάρα / ἕξεις μεθ' ἡμῶν : 1668–69).[59]

In both major and minor incidents, then, *Helen* is structured around *xenia* and its violation. Theoklymenos's violation of *xenia* in order to gain the real Helen mirrors Paris's violation of *xenia* that gave him the phantom Helen. On the other hand, Theonoë's respect for *xenoi* and suppliants is the counterpart of Proteus's justice and piety in protecting Helen and of his tomb when it serves as a refuge for the suppliants and *xenoi*, Helen and Menelaos. On the divine level, the Dioskoroi help mortals who are threatened *xenoi*, and they receive *xénia* in return.

Another major concern in the play is the harm that has been done to her *philoi* by the false Helen, that is, by her false reputation as an adulteress. Helen has not, of course, really betrayed her husband, and Menelaos's recognition of Helen's identity also involves the recognition that she is a true *philê*, who has remained faithful to him (566–624). Even though Helen did not harm her *philoi*, however, her name did so (42–43, 1653). For one thing, her evil reputation has injured the Greeks at Troy or on their way home (72–74, 383–85, 1122–36). Teukros, as a result of the war, was exiled by his father, who blamed him for the death of his brother, Aias (90–94). Helen's reputation has also harmed her mother, who killed herself for shame; her brothers, who are reported to have committed suicide because of her (133–42, 200–210, 280: φονεὺς αὐτῆς ἐγώ, 284–85, 686–87); and her daughter Hermione, whom no one will marry (282–83, 688–90, 933). Menelaos suffers from his vain labors in Troy and from his wanderings on his return (520–27, 603), and Helen herself suffers from an unjust evil reputation and from living in exile as a slave in a barbarian land (270–76, 694–95, 1147–48).

In minor events, several acts of harm to *philoi* are averted. Theoklymenos threatens to kill his sister Theonoë (1632) but is immediately persuaded by Kastor not to do so (1682). Menelaos and Helen swear that they will kill themselves rather than survive each other (835–40; cf. 1401–2), and Menelaos says that he will kill Helen and then himself (842). The play also contains a few allusions to mythological exempla in which *philoi* harm *philoi*: Kallisto and Merope (375–83), Oinomaos, Pelops, and Atreus (386–92).[60]

II.C. *Suppliancy (4 Plays)*

■ Aiskhylos's *Suppliants*.   This play is discussed in chapter 3.

■ Sophokles' *Oedipus at Kolonos*.   Oidipous, in ignorance, committed patricide and incest. After discovering what he had done, he blinded himself. When the play opens, he is living in exile from Thebes, attended in his wanderings by his daughter Antigone. Oidipous and Antigone come to a sacred grove near Athens, whose king, Theseus, accepts Oidipous as suppliant. Oidipous's daughter Ismene arrives from Thebes to tell Oidipous that his sons, Eteokles and Polyneikes, have quarreled over which of them is to rule in Thebes. Eteokles has exiled Polyneikes, who is preparing to attack his brother with a foreign army. Moreover, Ismene says, Kreon, because of an oracle, wants to gain possession of Oidipous's body after his death. Theseus protects Oidipous and his daughters when Kreon threatens them. Polyneikes then supplicates his father, asking for help in his war against Eteokles, but Oidipous refuses and curses both his sons. He then dies in a mysterious manner after promising benefits to Athens.

It has been argued that *xenia* is the central issue in *Oedipus at Kolonos*, and that Theseus accepts Oidipous as *xenos* when he settles him in Athens.[61] This argument would have more weight if there were some evidence for the renewal of a previously existing *xenia* relationship between the two men or for the initiation of a new one.[62] There is, however, no evidence that Oidipous is given status as a *xenos* in Athens and no indication of *xenia* ritual. The final handclasp between Theseus and Oidipous's daughters (1631–35) hardly constitutes a ratification of a *xenia* compact between Theseus and Oidipous.[63]

On the other hand, there is abundant evidence for the primary importance of supplication in this play. Oidipous supplicates Theseus, asking the king to protect Oidipous and his daughters against Kreon and the Thebans. Theseus agrees and defends Oidipous against his enemies, thereby acknowledging him as *philos*. In return, he and Athens receive great benefits. As Peter Burian has shown, this play follows the pattern of the suppliant plot, in which "[t]he suppliant, in flight from a powerful enemy, seeks refuge in a foreign land. He must win the support of his host, who, when the enemy approaches, undertakes to save him even at the cost of war. The battle ends favorably for the suppliant's cause, and his safety is assured."[64]

The importance of and frequent references to supplication in *Oedipus at Kolonos* support this interpretation. Oidipous is the suppliant of the Eumenides (44, 634), and he and Antigone supplicate the Chorus (142, 241, 275). After the Chorus raise (ὥσπερ με κἀνεστήσαθ': 276) the suppliant

Oidipous by giving him a pledge of safety (ἔλαβες τὸν ἱκέτην ἐχέγγυον: 284), Oidipous remains a suppliant of the Eumenides (487) until Theseus arrives to consider Oidipous's "suppliant petition" (προστροπὴν: 558) to the city and himself and at last agrees to settle Oidipous in his land (637).[65] In defending Oidipous, Theseus condemns Kreon for "plundering what belongs to me and to the gods, by force leading off wretched suppliant people" (συλῶντα τἀμὰ καὶ τὰ τῶν θεῶν, βίᾳ / ἄγοντα φωτῶν ἀθλίων ἱκτήρια: 922–23). Oidipous blames Kreon for attempting to kidnap a suppliant (1008) and at the same time supplicates the Eumenides, asking for help against his aggressor (1010–12). The end of the play concerns Oidipous's reciprocation of the favors given him by Theseus and Athens.

Suppliants and pursuer are kin by blood and marriage, for Kreon is Oidipous's uncle and brother-in-law and the uncle of Antigone and Ismene, who are said to suffer terrible things at the hands of their kin (δεινὰ τλασᾶν . . . πρὸς αὐθαίμων πάθη: 1077–78). Although Oidipous and the Athenians are not kin, Antigone asks the Chorus to treat her as kin (ὥς τις ἀφ' αἵματος ὑμετέρου προφανεῖσα: 245–46), and the sympathy between Oidipous and Theseus is increased by the fact that they have both been *xenoi* in foreign lands (562–68).[66]

In a secondary suppliant action, Polyneikes is first a suppliant at the altar of Poseidon (1156–59, 1171, 1278), asking to speak to his father.[67] When Oidipous refuses, Theseus asks him to "consider whether his suppliant seat does not compel" Oidipous to hear his son (θάκημ' ἐξαναγκάζει: 1179). After being raised from the altar (1286–88), Polyneikes supplicates his father (1309, 1327), but he is rejected. Antigone then supplicates her brother (1414), asking him not to attack Thebes, but she also is rejected.

Harm to *philoi* is important in many other ways in this play.[68] Oidipous's patricide and incest are frequently alluded to (220–23, 266–74, 510–48, 944–46, 960–1002, 1077–78), and the consequences of these acts continue into the present of the stage action: the Chorus, fearing that he will harm the city (226–36), tell Oidipous to leave the sanctuary; the Thebans refuse to receive or bury him in their city (407, 600–601); and Oidipous, knowing he is polluted, refuses to touch Theseus (1130–36). Although Oidipous benefits his unrelated *philoi*, the Athenians, he curses Kreon (864–70, 951–53), states that Polyneikes' treatment of his father is equivalent to murder (1361), and curses his sons (787–90, 1370–96), condemning them to mutual fratricide. This latter curse, however, is not a simple act of harm to kin; because it is conditional on the fratricidal war's taking place (εἴπερ: 1371), it is instead a curse on those who violate *philia*.[69] It is Polyneikes and Eteokles themselves who bring the curse to fulfillment (1424–25).

■ Euripides' *Children of Herakles*. After Herakles' death, his children, together with his mother, Alkmene, and nephew, Iolaos, are pursued by their father's enemy, Eurystheus, Alkmene's cousin, who wants to kill them. They take refuge at an altar in Marathon, where King Demophon protects them.

Eurystheus is defeated in battle, captured, and put to death, while the children are saved.

This play, like others in this category, focuses on a suppliant action, in which suppliants are acknowledged as *philoi* and protected. Unlike Theseus in Euripides' *Suppliants* and Pelasgos in Aiskhylos's *Suppliants*, Demophon is not represented as hesitating and agonizing over the decision to protect the suppliants, although he does refuse to perform human sacrifice in order to obtain victory.[70] He says that he will not "pollute the gods" (μὴ μιαίνοντος θεούς: 264) by failing to protect the suppliants, and that his greatest reason for helping them is the altar of Zeus at which they sit (238–39). In this play, however, the danger of pollution to the person supplicated is overshadowed by the pollution and violence committed and threatened by Eurystheus. Iolaos says at the beginning of the play that Eurystheus wants to kill Herakles' family (13; cf. 466–67, 1002–3), and immediately after his speech, the Herald announces that the suppliants must go to Argos to be stoned to death (59–60). When he does violence to Iolaos (βιαζόμεσθα: 71, 79), knocks him down (75–76), and drags him from the altar (79), the Herald "pollutes the suppliant wreaths" and is guilty of "dishonoring the gods" (71–72, 78). Demophon, in turn, threatens physical violence against the Herald at 270.[71] The Herald refers to the suppliants as "runaway slaves" (δραπέτας: 140), and his desire to remove them from the altar by force is continually stressed (79, 106, 196, 224–25, 955).[72]

The play ends with a reversal of roles. When Alkmene, a former suppliant, wants to kill Eurystheus (959–60), both the Servant and Eurystheus himself argue that it is against Greek law to kill a prisoner of war (961–72, 1009–15), who is a suppliant (προστρόπαιον: 1015).[73] Alkmene, however, is no more willing than was Eurystheus to respect a suppliant, and our text ends with her order to kill Eurystheus and throw him to the dogs.[74]

Blood kinship plays a major role in *Children of Herakles*. Eurystheus, as he himself states, is Alkmene's cousin and therefore kin to Herakles (987–88) and his children. Thus, both Eurystheus's attempt to kill Herakles' family and Alkmene's murder of Eurystheus are acts of harm to kin.[75] On the positive side, Iolaos, Herakles' nephew, has freely chosen to accompany the children in their flight because he respects ties of kinship (6–9). The suppliants come to Marathon because Demophon is their kin (37), and Iolaos makes an appeal for protection on the basis of this kinship, reciting a lengthy genealogy (207–13) to show that Theseus, Demophon's father, and Herakles were the children of cousins (αὐτανεψίων: 211).[76] Iolaos supplicates Demophon, urging him to "become kin and *philos* to these [children]" (γενοῦ δὲ τοῖσδε συγγενής, γενοῦ φίλος: 229), that is, to act as kin, and when he does so, Iolaos states, "We have found these men to be *philoi* and kin" (ηὕρομεν φίλους καὶ ξυγγενεῖς τούσδ᾽: 304–5).

The self-sacrifice of Herakles' daughter Makaria, who gives her life to appease the gods and save her family, is a minor *pathos*. A paradigmatic reversal occurs when the Messenger states that Eurystheus, who was coming to sack Athens, has instead suffered the opposite—defeat and capture (931–35).[77]

■ Euripides' *Suppliants*.   After Polyneikes and his Argive army were defeated in their war against Thebes, Kreon refused burial to the Seven who had attacked Thebes. In the stage action, the mothers of the dead Seven and Adrastos, king of Argos, supplicate Theseus, king of Athens, asking him for help in obtaining burial for their sons. He agrees and defeats Thebes in war. The dead sons are given funeral rites.

This suppliant drama, like Aiskhylos's *Suppliants*, gives a particularly strong emphasis to the relationship between suppliant and supplicated. The Thebans' status as suppliants contains an implicit threat of pollution,[78] while Theseus's initial refusal to help threatens their safety. Acknowledgment of *philia* occurs when Theseus agrees to protect the suppliants (334–65). Blood kinship is an important aspect of the relationship between suppliant and supplicated. Theseus is a blood *philos* of the Argives who supplicate him, a fact that is repeatedly emphasized. The Chorus of Argive women state, "We have the same ancestral blood [πατρῷον αἷμα] as you" (264). Theseus is descended through his mother Aithra from Pelops (4–7, 263), to whom the Argive race is related through their descent from Danaos (130, 1150, 1190, 1220), descendant of Io, daughter of Inakhos (372, 628–30). The women also appeal to Zeus as their ancestor through Io (628–31).[79] Aithra's part in the supplication increases the emphasis on kinship. Aithra's role is complex: she is herself supplicated by the women (42–43, 68–69), and she acts as their representative to Theseus.[80] Although Theseus's mother is not actually a suppliant, her similarity to the suppliants whose part she takes is emphasized by her physical position: seated at the altar (93, 290) and encircled by suppliant branches (32–33, 102–3). In taking the suppliants' part and identifying with them, she makes their supplication resemble the supplication of son by mother. Aithra also makes an appeal of her own on personal grounds when she tells Theseus, "Since you are mine, child, do not do this" (320). When Theseus agrees, at Aithra's request, to help the suppliants, he tells them to take their branches away from her, "so that I may lead her to the house of Aigeus, touching her dear hand" (360–61). In leading his mother from the sanctuary to his house, Theseus performs an action that is equivalent to the raising and leading of a suppliant. Theseus also has a *xenia* relationship with Polyneikes (928–31), although this is not mentioned until the eulogy.

Although Adrastos and the Argive women do not flee harm from their own kin, they are deeply involved in the plight of Polyneikes, whose burial Kreon, who is both the ruler of Thebes (16–19, 358, 400) and Polyneikes' uncle, forbids. Adrastos became involved in the war against Thebes—although it was forbidden by the gods (155–60), after he married his daughters to Tydeus, who had shed kindred blood, and to Polyneikes, who had left Thebes to avoid fratricide in fulfillment of his father's curse (144–50). These marriages turned out to be bitter ones (832). Led by Adrastos and his son-in-law, Polyneikes (14–16), the Argives attacked Thebes, which was ruled by Eteokles, and were defeated, in a war in which the sons of Oedipus, Eteokles and Polyneikes, killed one another (ἀδελφῇ χειρί: 402). Kreon's refusal of burial to his nephew Polyneikes and to Polyneikes' allies leads to the suppliant action of this play. Thus, through their alliance and kinship by marriage with Polyneikes, Adrastos and the other Argives are involved in his fratricidal death and in the harm done to him by his kin, who forbid his burial. All, as the Chorus state, have shared in the fate of Oidipous (1078–79), and "the Erinys who causes many groans, leaving the house of Oidipous, has come to us" (835–36).

The suicide of Evadne, who leaps into her husband's funeral pyre, is a minor *pathos*, similar to that of Herakles' daughter in Euripides' *Children of Herakles*, in which *philê* harms *philê* (herself).

III. Exceptional Plays (6 Plays)

I have classified six plays as exceptional, because their main *pathê* do not at first appear to be primarily concerned with harm to blood kin or to *philoi* in reciprocal relationships. Closer analysis, however, reveals that harm to *philoi* is in fact an important issue in all but one of these tragedies.

■ Aiskhylos's *Persians.*   While Xerxes, king of Persia, is away leading an army against Greece, his mother the Queen, and his countrymen wait for news. A Messenger announces defeat. Xerxes' mother calls on her dead husband, King Dareios, whose ghost reveals that his son's defeat was predicted by oracles. Xerxes returns and all mourn.

On the most obvious level, *Persians* appears to represent enemy (Greeks) harming enemy (Persians). According to this interpretation, it does not have a tragic plot, by Aristotle's criteria (*Po.* 14.1453b17–18), for it does not arouse pity and fear, nor is it a play in which *philos* harms *philos*. However, Xerxes' act of attacking Greece can also be seen as unintentional harm of his own kin and other *philoi*. Intending to gain glory and make conquests, he has instead caused his own ruin and that of his country. It is this aspect of the defeat that Aiskhylos emphasizes, by setting the play in Persia, among those who have stayed at home and taken no part in the war, rather than in Greece, at the scene of the battles. Throughout the play, Xerxes' defeat is represented as an act that has harmed himself; his mother, who is the major dramatic figure; his kindred Persians, who are represented by the Chorus; and even his father Dareios, whose ghost appears. This view of the play best accounts for the emotional impact it would have had on a Greek audience. Instead of being glad that their enemies have been defeated, the Athenians would have felt pity and fear for the innocent victims who suffer from the mistakes of their *philos*.

The play also represents Xerxes as having harmed his *philoi* by stressing the kinship of all the Persians, through their common ancestry. Xerxes belongs to the "golden race" (80), because he is descended from Perses, the son of Danaë and of Zeus, who came to her in a shower of gold.[81] In the corrupt lines 145–46, the Chorus make the same point—that Xerxes and the other Persians are related through their common ancestor.[82] When the Chorus address the

Queen, Xerxes' mother (156, 157), as "mother" (215) and Dareios as "father" (662), they give them titles that not only are respectful but also reflect a genealogical truth, because the Persians are one race (Περσικῷ γένει: 516, Περσῶν γενεᾷ: 911; γέννας: 946; γένος τὸ Περσᾶν: 1013), as are the barbarians as a whole (βαρβάρων γένει: 434). Given these relationships, the many occurrences of *philos* and its cognates (for example, three times in 647–48 in reference to Dareios) have connotations of kinship.

Interpreted as an action in which *philos* harms *philos*, *Persians* has a complex plot, with reversal and recognition.[83] The action of the play is summarized by the Queen: "My son, thinking that he would exact vengeance for them [sc. those killed at Marathon], brought on such a great number of woes" (476–77; cf. 942–43: δαίμων . . . μετάτροπος ἐπ' ἐμοί). According to this view, Xerxes' statement at 931–34, "Here am I, lamentable; I have become a wretched evil to my race [γέννᾳ] and fatherland [γᾷ τε πατρῴᾳ]," is a recognition that he has been an enemy to his *philoi*. Mae Smethurst correctly notes that this play does not evoke pity and fear in the best way because no recognition scene is enacted on stage and because Xerxes is not a figure with whom the audience would identify.[84] Nevertheless, what takes place is a true recognition, however inferior, in that Xerxes' statements indicate that he has undergone "a change from ignorance to knowledge."

Dareios agrees with Xerxes, stating that his son has proved to be "the spring of evils to all his *philoi*" (743), and the Chorus say that he is "the great ruin of the Persians" (μεγάλατε Περσᾶν: 1016).[85] The Persians pity Xerxes for the misfortunes he has suffered, but they also blame him for the destruction of the army. The Queen states that Xerxes emptied the whole plain of Asia (κενώσας: 718), and Dareios says that his son destroyed the youth of the allies (ἀπώλεσεν: 733), unlike Dareios himself, who never cast such a great evil on the city (κακὸν τοσόνδε: 781). The Chorus plainly state that unlike Dareios, who never destroyed men (οὔτε . . . ἀπώλλυ: 652) and who did not cause evil (ἀκάκας: 855, ἄκακε: 663), Xerxes destroyed the army (ἀπώλεσεν: 551), killed the Persian youth, and crammed Hades with Persian dead (ἦβαν Ξέρξᾳ κταμέναν, Ἅιδου σάκτορι Περσᾶν: 923–24). They recite (955–1001) a lengthy catalog of the dead whom Xerxes left behind (ἀπέλειπον: 963; ἔλιπες ἔλιπες: 985). The long final lament (908–1077) and procession escorting Xerxes into the palace (1038, 1068) is a kind of funeral in which the whole family of the Persians, led by Xerxes, join in mourning the dead.

■ Sophokles' *Aias*.   This play is discussed in chapter 6.

■ Euripides' *Alkestis*.   Alkestis, who has agreed to give her life so that her husband Admetos may live, dies on the fated day. Immediately after her death, Herakles arrives and is received as a *xenos* by Admetos, who does not tell his guest what has happened. When he discovers the truth, Herakles rescues

Alkestis from death and brings her back to her husband. Admetos recognizes his wife and receives her back into his house.

That this is an exceptional play, in which the central *pathos* does not represent harm to *philos* by *philos*, may have something to do with the fact that *Alkestis* was performed in fourth place instead of the usual satyr play and has many features associated with satyr plays, such as captivity and liberation, emergence from the underworld, and concern with *xenia*.[86] Although harm to *philoi* is not central to the plot, *philia* is nevertheless an important issue in this play, whose subject is *philia* between husband and wife, parent and child, host and guest, mortal and god.[87]

Xenia is particularly important in *Alkestis*. Apollo rewards Admetos for his piety as a *xenos* (6–12), and Admetos receives Herakles, his "best *xenos*" in Argos (559–60), even though he is in mourning, an act for which he is called *philoxenos*, "*xenos*-loving," by Herakles (830, 858) and the Servant (809; cf. πολύξεινος . . . οἶκος: 568–69). Herakles blames Admetos (μέμφομαι: 1017) for concealing the truth, but he nevertheless rescues Alkestis in gratitude for his act of extraordinary *xenia* (ὑπουργῆσαι χάριν: 842, 854–60). In contrast to Admetos, the model host, stands Diomedes, to whom Herakles is journeying when he first arrives. This *xenos* (484) is the owner of the man-eating horses Herakles must capture, and the clear implication of the Chorus's words is that he feeds his guests to these monsters (484–96).

Alkestis's excellence in *philia* to her husband corresponds to Admetos's excellence in *xenia*. Admetos reveres her *philia* (279), and the Chorus call her "a wife not [merely] dear but most dear" (οὐ φίλαν ἀλλὰ φιλτάταν γυναῖκα: 230–31) She is "best" (ἀρίστη: 83, 151), "fair-famed" (εὐκλεής: 150, 938), and "most noble of all" (993). For her self-sacrifice she should be honored like the gods and will be said to have become a "blessed daimon" (995–1005). Moreover, Alkestis's position as wife is like that of a *xenê*, for she is not kin (συγγενής) but a foreigner (ὀθνεία: 532–33, 646, 810–11), who was received into the house on the occasion of her marriage. When she returns from Hades, she is again received into Admetos's house as an apparent *xenê* (1117), in a scene recalling the marriage ceremony.[88] In contrast to Alkestis's excellent *philia* as wife stand the defective *philia* relationships of Admetos and his blood kin. Admetos quarrels with his father Pheres, who refused earlier to die in his son's place. Admetos says that he is not Pheres' son (641), that he will not care for his parents in old age or bury them (662–65), and that he would disinherit his father if it were possible (737–38). In turn, Pheres accuses his son of murdering his wife (φονεύς: 730; κατακτάς: 696) by allowing Alkestis to die in his stead. A counterpart, on the divine level, of these quarrels among mortal kin is the quarrel, briefly mentioned, between Apollo and his father Zeus. Zeus killed Apollo's son Asklepios, and Apollo in turn killed the Kyklopes, for which act Zeus forced him to serve Admetos (3–7, 121–30).

Alkestis, then, presents positive models of *philia* but also clearly delineates their negative counterparts, in which host kills guest, parents and children attack one another, and husband murders wife. Even though violence against *philoi* is not a serious threat in this play, acts that benefit *philoi* are dramatically effective in large part because they are vividly contrasted with negative possibilities.

■ Euripides' *Andromakhe*.   This play is discussed in chapter 5.

■ "Euripides'" *Rhesos*.   Greeks and Trojans are camped in the field the night after Hektor has driven the Greeks back toward their ships. After Hektor sends Dolon as a spy to learn what the enemy is doing, the Thracian king, Rhesos, arrives with his army to help the Trojans defeat the Greeks. While Rhesos is sleeping, Odysseus and Diomedes kill Dolon and, with Athena's help, Rhesos. Rhesos's mother, the Muse, prophesies her son's deification.

The *Rhesos* is the only extant tragedy in which enemy kills enemy in the main action and in which violation of *philia* is not an important issue in either minor events or mythological allusions. Nevertheless, the idea of *philos* harming *philos* plays an interesting minor role in the form of the mutual recriminations of Trojans and Thracians. Hektor complains that Rhesos has not arrived in Troy to help until very late, although he is a kindred barbarian (ἐγγενής ὤν βάρβαρος: 404; cf. 413) and owes a debt of gratitude to Hektor, who made him king of Thrace (406–12). Rhesos is also a *xenos* of Hektor (336–37). In return, the Thracian Charioteer accuses the Trojans of killing the Thracians, their *philoi* (803, 838) and military allies (συμμάχους: 839–42). Both accusations are without substance. Rhesos has the excuse of another war to explain his late arrival in Troy (422–33), and the Charioteer's accusation is false: Rhesos, as the Muse explains, was killed by enemies (ἐχθρῶν: 893). Two other instances of violation of *philia* are also hinted at in the Muse's speech. She comes close to accusing Hektor of harming a *philos* when she complains that Rhesos went to his death at Troy because the embassies of Hektor persuaded him to help his *philoi* (935–37). Hektor, however, points out that he could hardly have done otherwise than ask for his friends' help (954–57), and the Muse herself appears to think that Athena is more to blame than Hektor when she accuses the goddess of killing Rhesos (945), although Athena owed gratitude to the Muses and to Rhesos's cousin Orpheus (938–49).

Whatever the truth may be about the authenticity and date of the *Rhesos*,[89] these minor allusions to violation of *philia* are of interest. Homer (*Il.* 10.299–563) stresses the exploits of Odysseus and Diomedes in killing Dolon (338–464) and slaughtering Rhesos and the Thracians (469–525). In the *Iliad*, the Thracians never suspect that they have been harmed by Trojans. In fact, however, the Trojan Dolon is responsible for their fate, because in telling Odysseus about the positions of the Trojans and their allies (433–41), Dolon singles the Thracians out as ideal victims.[90] In contrast to the epic, the *Rhesos* stresses the idea of treachery rather than heroic exploits. After he leaves the Trojan camp, Dolon does not return and is not mentioned by the Trojans except in two lines (863–64). The death of Dolon, so vividly recounted in the

Iliad, is compressed into a mere three lines in the play (591–93). The killing of Rhesos by his enemies is colored in the play, as it is not in the epic, by the Charioteer's accusation of treachery. These accusations and the Trojan defenses occupy a significant portion of the text, taking up one-half of the dialogue between Hektor and Rhesos, and one third of the Charioteer episode.[91]

In contrast to the *Iliad*, then, *Rhesos* emphasizes both the possibility of violation of *philia* and the fact that it does not occur. Hektor and the Charioteer make accusations of violation of *philia* that are shown to be false. The Muse also begins to accuse Hektor, then backs away from her accusations to blame Athena instead. The *Rhesos*, like the *Iliad*, avoids violation of *philia*, but unlike the epic, this play appears to call attention to its own avoidance of such events. It is also noteworthy that these false accusations of violation of *philia* occur in a play set in Troy, a city that does not fit the typical tragic pattern of the city that is saved by the destruction of a leader. The *Rhesos* is the exception that proves the rule.

■ Euripides' *Trojan Women.* Hekabe has seen Troy captured by enemies, her husband and sons killed, and her daughters made slaves of the victors. She herself is waiting to be taken into slavery. She suffers further misfortunes: the enslavement of her daughter Kassandra, the sacrifice of her daughter Polyxene, the enslavement of her daughter-in-law Andromakhe, the murder of her grandson Astyanax, and the sight of the escape from punishment of Helen, who caused the war. She prepares Astyanax for burial and is led from her burning city into slavery.

In the main action of *Trojan Women*, enemy (Greek) harms enemy (Trojan). However, Euripides arouses pity and fear in response to these non-tragic events by representing the Greeks as harming their enemies in ways that violate both divine and human laws. The acts of the Greeks are made to appear similar to harm to *philoi* in that they are represented as being impious and as undermining two of the reciprocal relationships that are the very basis of civilization: suppliancy and marriage.

In the Prologue, the gods state that the Greeks have incurred divine wrath in several ways. They killed Priam at the altar of Zeus (16–17); they raped Kassandra, a virgin dedicated to Apollo, thereby "neglecting the will of the gods and piety" (41–44); they committed *hybris* against Athena and her temple when Aias dragged Kassandra away by force (69–70); and they sacked temples and tombs (95–97). The mortal dramatic figures also stress the impiety of the acts of the Greeks. Hekabe says that she saw with her own eyes Priam slaughtered (κατασφαγέντ') at the altar of the household god, Zeus Herkeios (481–83); the Chorus sing of slaughterings around the altars (σφαγαὶ δ' ἀμφι-βώμιοι: 562), and of the "impious slaughter" (ἀνοσίοις σφαγαῖσιν: 1316) of pious Priam; and Andromakhe mentions corpses flung out for the vultures beside the temple of Athena (599–600). These impious acts color our view of the murders of the innocent victims, Polyxene and Astyanax. Moreover, Andromakhe compares the killing of Astyanax to cannibalism when she tells the Greeks to "feast on his flesh" (775), and Hekabe calls the sacrifice of Polyxene "impious slaughter" (ἀνοσίων προσφαγμάτων: 628). The impious violations of the suppliant status of Priam and Kassandra also contrast shockingly with the ultimately successful suppliancy of Menelaos by the guilty Helen (1042–48).

The Greeks have also perverted and destroyed the institutions of marriage and the family. Helen's adulterous relationship with Paris, the "deceiver of his host" (ξεναπάτης: 866), leads to her betrayal of her country and house (947) and to the destruction of the legitimate marriages of the women of both Troy and Greece. Kassandra's speech at 353–405 points out many of these connections. For the sake of Helen, who left her husband of her own free will, Agamemnon killed his daughter Iphigeneia, and he in turn will be killed because of his slave-bride Kassandra, a wife as fatal as Helen. Kassandra's "marriage" will also lead to Klytaimestra's death at the hands of her own son. Other Greek families, Kassandra notes, were destroyed by the war when soldiers died in Troy without seeing their sons, without wives to prepare the corpses for burial, and without children to tend the ancestral tombs of their fathers. In this play, not only do the Greeks destroy Andromakhe's marriage to Hektor, but her very virtues as a wife lead to increased misery. Andromakhe's fame as a good wife has caused her to be chosen as slave-wife by Neoptolemos, who, as the son of her husband's murderer (657–60), is her *authentês*. Similarly, Hektor's nobility is the cause of his son's death (742–43).[92]

The gods are, for the most part, represented as the agents of justice, who punish mortals guilty of impiety, but there is an occasional reference to a darker side of the relations of gods and mortals. Zeus, who is "ancestral father" (γενέτα πάτερ: 1288–89)[93] of the Trojans, as the father of Dardanos, their ancestor, has betrayed (προύδωκας: 1062) his descendants and the kin of his love-object Ganymede (820–47) in failing to protect their city.

Appendix B: Violation of *Philia* in the Fragments of the Major Tragedians

The preceding chapters and appendix A have shown that harm to *philoi* is an important aspect of the plots of nearly all of the extant tragedies. Is this merely an accident of the plays that happen to have survived, or is harm to *philoi* an essential aspect of the genre of Greek tragedy? Any attempt to answer this question must take into consideration the plays known to us only by means of fragments or testimonia. Because this evidence is at best incomplete and at worst confusing and contradictory, any reconstruction is necessarily speculative. H. Friis Johansen and Edward Whittle make an excellent point: "It may be well to affirm here and now that the reconstruction of a play of which only a few brief fragments survive cannot safely be assumed to have any significant resemblance to the lost original, however plausibly it uses all the available evidence. . . . It cannot reasonably be expected to do more than demonstrate a theoretical possibility."[1] In spite of these inherent limitations, there is sufficient evidence, especially in the case of the three major tragedians, to allow for some plausible conclusions about the kinds of subjects treated by this genre. In most of the lost plays by Aiskhylos, Sophokles, and Euripides, as in their extant tragedies, some kind of harm to *philoi* appears to have been a central issue. The chief exceptions to this rule are plays about epic subjects: Akhilleus, Odysseus, and Palamedes. However, even in the case of these and other exceptional plays, the *pathê* are often assimilated in some way to harm to *philoi*. For example, in the *Niobe*, where harm to *philoi* is not a central issue, Aiskhylos mentions the divine ancestry of the children of Niobe, who are killed by their kindred gods, and in his *Myrmidones*, he emphasizes Akhilleus's responsibility for the death of Patroklos, who, unlike the Homeric hero, is Akhilleus's beloved.

A few words about methodology are necessary. I divide the plays into four mutually exclusive categories:

Category I (discussed in section 1 below), consists of a number of groups, each of which consists of plays about the same subject (for example, "House of Atreus Myths," "Medeia Myths"). Violation of *philia* occurred in at least half of the plays in each of these groups. The groups are listed in English alphabetical order according to their subject.

Category II (discussed in section 2) consists of individual plays in which violation of *philia* occurred. These plays are listed, in English alphabetical order, under the types of *philia* relationships that were violated: blood kinship and reciprocal relationships.

Category III (discussed in section 3), like category I, consists of groups of several plays about the same subject (for example, "Akhilleus Myths," "Odysseus Myths"). However, this category differs from category I in that violation of *philia* is either uncertain or unlikely in more than half of the plays in each group. These groups are listed in English alphabetical order according to the subject of each group.

Category IV (discussed in section 4), like Category II, is composed of individual plays, listed in English alphabetical order. In this category, however, as in category III, violation of *philia* is either uncertain or unlikely.

My classifications in this appendix may seem somewhat arbitrary, since many plays represented more than one kind of harm to *philoi*. However, I have classified plays according to the relationship that appears to have been most important, when this can be determined. When it is not possible to decide which of several *philia* relationships was most significant in a play, I choose whichever relationship is closest. For example, if a play contains violation of both the parent-child relationship and of *xenia*, I classify it according to the former. When a group contains a large number of plays, a brief summary is given after each group discussed. Where the evidence suggests that the central *pathos* did not take place among any of the *philia* relationships discussed in this study, I classify the play as "unlikely." If not enough is known about the play to allow for categorization, I classify the play as "uncertain." Before each group of plays or type of relationship discussed, I list the total number of plays in the group, the number of plays in which specific kinds of *philia* relationships were violated, and the number of plays in which violation of *philia* is uncertain or unlikely; for example, in category I, "Aias Myths (4 Plays): Suicide, 1; Parent-Child, 2; Unlikely, 1," and in category II: "Blood Kinship (10 Plays): Parent-Child, 5; Sibling-Sibling, 2; Other Blood Kin, 1; Some Form of Harm to Blood Kin, 2."

In this appendix and in appendix C, I adopt some new categories of *philia* relationships in addition to those used in discussing the extant plays. Under "Blood Kinship" I add the subcategory, "Some Form of Harm to Blood Kin." In addition to "Blood Kinship" and "Reciprocal Relationships," I include a third category, "Other," which comprises the subcategories "Suicide," "Domestic Animals," and "Some Form of Harm to *Philos*." These new categories are intended to take into account the greater variety of *pathê* in the fragments and our greater uncertainty about relationships represented. The subcategories of parent harming child and child harming parent include harm to grandparents and grandchildren. Plays focusing on amphimetric strife, that is, a dispute involving two wives of one man and their respective children, or stepparents and stepchildren, are included in the subcategory of marriage.[2]

I have not attempted an exhaustive study of the literature on each of the plays but have for the most part limited my research to a few major surveys: for Aiskhylos, Radt and Mette;[3] for Sophokles, Radt; Pearson; Lloyd-Jones; and Dios;[4] and for Euripides, Nauck; Webster; Mette; Collard, Cropp, and Lee; and Austin.[5] For Aiskhylos and Sophokles I discuss the plays listed by Radt 1977 and 1985 under "Fragmenta certis fabulis adscripta"; for Euripides, the plays in Mette 1981–82. I omit the plays bracketed by these scholars and those they entitle as satyr plays. Plays about which too little is known to allow for even plausible hypotheses are listed separately (section 5). Although I occasionally cite primary sources for the fragments and testimonia, in most cases, instead of burdening the reader with long lists of citations, I summarize the views of these scholars, referring the interested reader to them for sources, discussion, and the Greek text complete with the papyrological symbols omitted here. I use transliterations of the Greek titles to refer to the plays, giving translations of the titles after they are first mentioned. Surveys of the relevant myths, plot summaries, and translations help to make this chapter and the next accessible to non-specialists. The conclusion (section 6) provides a statistical summary of the evidence.

1. Category I. Subject Groups With Violation of *Philia*

Plays are listed according to groups.[6] Each group consists of plays about the same subject. Violation of *philia* occurred in at least half of the plays in each group.

> *Aias Myths (4 Plays): Suicide, 1; Parent-Child, 2;*
> *Unlikely, 1*

In the mythological tradition, Aias and Odysseus compete for the arms of Akhilleus, and Odysseus wins by a trick. As a result, Aias goes mad and attacks the herds of the Greek army, under the impression that he is killing and injuring his human enemies among the Greeks. After he regains his sanity and realizes what he has done, he commits suicide. When Aias's brother, Teukros, the bastard son of their father Telamon, returns to Salamis without Aias, Telamon exiles him.

In addition to Sophokles' *Aias*, we know something about four other plays that dramatized this story: Aiskhylos's *Aias* trilogy, *Hoplon Krisis*, *Threissai*, and *Salaminiai* (*Judgment of Arms*, *Thracian Women*, and *Salaminian Women*), and Sophokles' *Teukros*. Aiskhylos's *Hoplon Krisis* was about the contest for the arms of Akhilleus in which Odysseus is victorious over Aias, the *Threissai* about Aias's suicide, and the *Salaminiai* about the return of Teukros to Salamis after his brother's death and his exile by their father, Telamon.[7] The subject of Sophokles' *Teukros* was also the return of Teukros without his brother.[8] The *Hoplon Krisis* does not appear to have offered much scope for violation of *philia*, but the other three plays certainly do, since Aiskhylos's *Threissai*, like Sophokles' *Aias*, concerned a suicide, and the two other plays represented the exile of a son by his father.

Amphiaraos, House of, Myths (6 Plays):
Child-Parent, 1; Xenia, 3; Uncertain, 2

A number of plays dramatized the story of Amphiaraos, his wife, Eriphyle, and their son, Alkmeon. That this unhappy family was as good a subject for tragedy as that of Oidipous is shown by Aristotle, *Poetics* 1453a20, who lists among good tragedies those about Alkmeon.

There are two main stories in the tradition.[9] The first resembles the Orestes story: a wife causes the death of her husband, and is in turn killed by her son. Amphiaraos hides and refuses to go to war against Thebes, knowing that if he goes he will die. Amphiaraos's wife, Eriphyle, however, is bribed with a golden necklace to betray her husband so that he is forced to go. Before his departure, Amphiaraos makes his son, Alkmeon, promise to avenge his death, and Alkmeon subsequently kills his mother. The second story concerns events after the matricide. Maddened by his mother's Furies, Alkmeon goes to Psophis, where he is purified by Phegeus, and marries his host's daughter Arsinoë, to whom he gives the necklace with which Eriphyle had been bribed. After this, Alkmeon marries Akheloön's daughter, Kallirrhoë, who wants the necklace and refuses to live with him unless she gets it. Alkmeon tricks his former father-in-law and host Phegeus into returning the necklace, but when he learns the truth, Phegeus orders his sons to kill Alkmeon.

The matricide and events leading up to it were the subject of Sophokles' *Epigonoi (The Afterborn)*.[10] Fragment 187R, in which Alkmeon trades insults with Adrastos, the brother of Eriphyle, concerns the matricide:

ΑΛΚΜΕΩΝ: ἀνδροκτόνου γυναικὸς ὁμογενὴς ἔφυς.
ΑΔΡΑΣΤΟΣ: σὺ δ᾽ αὐτόχειρ γε μητρὸς ἥ σ᾽ ἐγείνατο.

ALKMEON: You are kin to a woman who killed her husband.
ADRASTOS: And you are the murderer of the mother who bore you.

Sophokles may have written two other tragedies about this story: the *Amphiareos*, if there was a tragedy of this title in addition to a satyr play,[11] and the *Eriphyle*, identified by some with his *Epigonoi*.[12]

The events subsequent to the matricide were the subject of Sophokles' *Alkmeon*,[13] and Euripides' *Alkmeon dia Psophidos (Alkmeon in Psophis)*.[14] In these two plays, a son-in-law and *xenos* was killed after betraying his wife and his father-in-law, who was also his host. A fragment referring to the matricide is attributed to by some to *Alkmeon dia Psophidos*, by others to Euripides' *Alkmeon ho dia Korinthou (Alkmeon in Corinth)*: μητέρα κατέκταν τὴν ἐμήν ("I killed my mother": frag. 68N).[15]

Still another story about Alkmeon was the subject of Euripides' *Alkmeon ho dia Korinthou*. Alkmeon, in the time of his madness, has two children by Manto, daughter of Teiresias. He gives them to Kreon, king of Corinth, to bring up. The girl, Teisiphone, being very beautiful, is sold by Kreon's wife, who fears that Kreon will sleep with her. Alkmeon, not recognizing her, buys her to be his servant. He later gets his son back also.[16] This play, then, concerned betrayal by a *xenos*.

Of the six Amphiaraos plays, Sophokles' *Epigonoi* concerned matricide, and three plays—Sophokles' *Alkmeon* and Euripides' two *Alkmeon* plays— were about violation of *xenia*. In two of these plays, the *xenoi* were related by marriage. Uncertainties about genre and separate identity surround Sophokles' *Amphiareos* and *Eriphyle*.

Antenor Myths (2 Plays): Xenia, 2

The subject of Sophokles' *Helenes Apaitesis* (*The Demand for Helen's Return*) was the embassy of Odysseus and Menelaos at Troy to demand Helen's return.[17] In the Homeric version, the Greeks are not only rejected but in danger of their lives (Il. 11.136–42). Only Antenor receives them as guests and saves them from death.[18] The play, like the epic, is likely to have been concerned with threats to ambassadors who are also *xenoi*.

Sophokles' *Antenoridai* (*The Sons of Antenor*) is usually thought to have been concerned with a sequel to this story. At the capture of Troy, a leopard's skin is placed in front of the door of Antenor, as a warning that his house is to be spared, and he escapes to Thrace. Antenor is spared because of his hospitality to the Greek envoys, the subject of the *Helenes Apaitesis*.[19] This also was a play about threats to a *xenos*.

Athamas Myths (7 Plays): Parent-Child, 6;
Uncertain, 1

Athamas and his family were the subject of a number of plays. There are three versions of this story,[20] in all of which some kind of harm to *philoi* is prominent. In the simplest, Athamas and his wife Ino are driven mad by Hera. Athamas kills one son, whom he mistakes for a deer, and Ino kills the other by throwing him into boiling water (Apollodoros, *Library* 3.4.3) This story may have been the basis for Aiskhylos's *Athamas*[21] and for one of Sophokles' *Athamas* plays.[22]

Euripides' *Ino* was based on the more complex story given in Hyginus, *Fabulae* 4. In this version, Athamas's killing of his son is preceded by amphimetric strife:

> Athamas in Thessaly had two sons, Learchos and Melikertes, by Ino. She went as a Bacchant to Parnassos. . . . Athamas, thinking she was dead, married Themisto and had two sons by her. When he found that Ino was alive, he had her brought back. Themisto thought she was a captive . . . and confided to her her scheme for killing Ino's children, telling her to dress them

in black and the other pair in white. Ino switched the clothing so that Themisto killed her own children and then when she discovered her error committed suicide. Athamas went mad and killed his son Learchos; Ino threw herself in the sea with Melikertes and became a goddess.[23]

In the third version, that of Hyginus, *Fabulae* 2–3, Athamas first has two children by Nephele, and then marries Ino. She tricks him into sacrificing his and Nephele's son, Phrixos, but the plot is revealed and Phrixos escapes. Athamas is then about to put Ino and their son to death, but they are saved by Herakles or Dionysos. Further adventures follow. Some version of this story was the subject of Euripides' *Phrixos* 1 and 2[24] and of one of Sophokles' *Athamas* plays.[25]

Although these plays followed somewhat different versions of the Athamas story, in all six of them, parent killed or was about to kill child. About the seventh play, Sophokles' *Phrixos*, there are only conjectures.[26]

Atreus, House of, Myths (12 Plays): Parent-Child, 8; Sibling-Sibling, 2; Uncertain, 2

The many acts of violence against kin in the house of Atreus are well known from the extant plays: Aiskhylos's *Oresteia*, Sophokles' *Elektra*, and Euripides' *Elektra*, *Orestes*, *Iphigenia in Aulis*, and *Iphigenia in Tauris*. These plays focus on Agamemnon's sacrifice of his daughter Iphigeneia, Klytaimestra's murder of her husband, Orestes' matricide, and Iphigeneia's averted fratricide. The Iphigeneia story was also the subject of Aiskhylos's *Iphigeneia*[27] and of Sophokles' play of the same title.[28] The *Klytaimestra* attributed to Sophokles, if there was such a play,[29] may have been about the husband-killing, although this is uncertain.[30]

Other plays represented events in the generation before Agamemnon, that of Atreus and his brother Thyestes. Atreus and Thyestes quarrel, and Thyestes sleeps with his brother's wife. In revenge, Atreus kills Thyestes' children and serves them to him as food. These events are alluded to in the extant plays.[31] Subsequent events are less well known. Thyestes rapes Pelopia, his own daughter, and she bears him Aigisthos. This child is brought up by Atreus, who believes him to be his own son. Atreus orders Aigisthos to kill Thyestes, but recognition of father, mother, and son occurs, and Pelopia kills herself.[32] Some parts of the Atreus-Thyestes story were the subject of Sophokles' *Atreus*, or *Mykenaiai* (*Mycenian Women*), of his three *Thyestes* plays,[33] and of Euripides' *Thyestes*.[34] Euripides' *Kressai* (*Cretan Women*) may also have dramatized this history, although this is uncertain.[35] Euripides' *Pleisthenes* may have been based on another story about kin murder in the house of Atreus. Thyestes, after being exiled by his brother, brings up Atreus's son Pleisthenes as his own. Thyestes sends Pleisthenes to kill Atreus, but Atreus instead kills him, believing him to be Thyestes' son.[36]

The bastard and legitimate children of Agamemnon were the subject of another play. Sophokles' *Khryses* may have dramatized the story of a bastard son of Agamemnon. Khryseis, Agamemnon's captive mentioned in *Iliad* 1, bears him a son, Khryses, but conceals his paternity. When he is grown, Iphigeneia and Orestes arrive at his island after the events recounted in Euripides' *Iphigenia in Tauris*; they are pursued by Thoas, who demands their surrender. Khryses is about to give up his siblings to their enemy when his mother reveals his paternity. Khryses then helps his half brother, Orestes, to kill Thoas.[37]

Sophokles' *Polyxene* was concerned not only with the sacrifice of Polyxene to the dead Akhilleus after the capture of Troy, but also (frag. 522R) with a quarrel in Troy between Agamemnon and his brother, Menelaos, about sailing away from Troy.[38] Menelaos wants to sail away at once, while Agamemnon wants to stay and appease Athena,[39] who is angry over Lokrian Aias's impious violation of the suppliant Kassandra.[40] This quarrel is mentioned in *Odyssey* 3.130–50,[41] where it is a minor incident without violence. In the play it was certainly more important, and may well have been more serious.

Of the twelve Atreus plays, ten were concerned with different kinds of serious harm, actual or imminent, committed by parent against child (Aiskhylos's and Sophokles' *Iphigeneia* plays, Sophokles' *Atreus* and his three *Thyestes* plays, and Euripides' *Pleisthenes* and *Thyestes*) or by sibling against sibling (Sophokles' *Khryses* and *Polyxene*). The subject of Sophokles' *Klytaimestra* may well have been husband-murder, but its existence is uncertain, as is the plot of Euripides' *Kressai*.

Danaos Myths (2 Plays): Marriage, 2

Aiskhylos's *Aigyptioi* and *Danaïdes* were about some aspect of the Danaïds' murder of their husbands. See chapter 3, section 7.

Dionysos Myths (7 Plays): Parent-Child, 3; Marriage, 1; Unlikely, 1; Uncertain, 2

Six plays by Aiskhylos were about Dionysos. The subject of the *Edonoi* (*Edonians*) was the punishment of Lykourgos by Dionysos. In *Iliad* 6 there is no kin killing; Lykourgos attacks the nurses of Dionysos and is punished with blindness (130–40). It is likely, however, that in Aiskhylos, Lykourgos was punished by being driven mad so that he killed his son at an altar.[42]

Kin murder also occurred in other Dionysos plays by Aiskhylos. *Pentheus* had a plot similar to that of Euripides' *Bacchae*, in which son is torn apart by mother.[43] Although the plot of *Xantriai* (*The Wool Carders*) is unknown, it also is likely to have focused on harm to blood kin. Some speculate that it was about the death of Pentheus,[44] although Mette[45] suggests that its subject may have been the *sparagmos* (tearing apart) of the son of Leukippe by his mother and the other daughters of Minyas.

Killing of "wife" by "husband" was the subject of Aiskhylos's play with the two titles *Semele* and *Hydrophoroi* (*The Water Carriers*). Semele, pregnant with Dionysos by Zeus, is tricked into making the god promise to appear to her as he does to Hera. When Zeus does so, she is killed by the divine light-ning.[46] The view that wife-killing was a central issue is supported by fragment 221R: "Zeus, who killed him": Ζεύς, ὅς κατέκτα τοῦτον. Dodds explains τοῦτον as referring to Dionysos, supposed to have been killed with his mother when she was struck by Zeus's lightning. The idea of wife-killing is even clearer in Hartung's reading, ταύτην ("her," sc. Semele).[47]

In the other Dionysos plays by Aiskhylos, violation of *philia* is unlikely or uncertain. In *Bassarai* (*The Bakkhantes*) or *Bassarides*, Orpheus was torn apart by Bakkhai for dishonoring Dionysos,[48] but there is no evidence for kin mur-der. Nothing is known about the *Bakkhai*, and some identify it with another of Aiskhylos's Dionysos plays.[49] The subject of *Trophoi* (*Nurses*) was Medeia's renewal of the youth of the nurses of Dionysos and their husbands.[50] According to Mette,[51] this was a satyr play. If it was a tragedy, there is no indica-tion of what the pathos might have been.

Three of these plays, then (*Edonoi*, *Pentheus*, and *Xantriai*), involved harm to child by parent, and *Semele* was concerned with murder within a kind of marriage relationship. *Bassarai* appears to have been a play about theo-machy (a mortal fighting a god) and punishment. Too little is known about *Bakkhai* and *Trophoi* to allow for classification.

Domestic Animal Myths (2 Plays)

In two plays, a man was killed by his own animals. This event resembles harm to *philos* by *philos* in that domestic animals are like members of the house-hold. The parallel underlies *Iliad* 22.66–71, where Priam expresses horror at the thought of being eaten by the dogs he raised to be at his table, and is explicit in Euripides' *Bacchae* 337–41, where Pentheus's fate is compared to that of Aktaion.[52] In Aiskhylos's *Glaukos Potnieus* (*Glaukos of Potniai*), Glaukos was eaten or torn apart by his own horses, either after he trained them to eat humans or because he offended Aphrodite.[53] The subject of Aiskhylos's *Toxotides* (*The Archer Maidens*), as fragment 244R makes clear, was the pun-ishment of Aktaion, who was turned into a stag and torn apart by his own dogs: "The dogs completely destroyed the man who was their master" (κύνες διη-μάθυνον ἄνδρα δεσπότην).[54]

Erekhtheus, House of, Myths (5 Plays):
Parent-Child, 2; Marriage, 1; Uncertain, 2

Euripides' *Erekhtheus* was about the sacrifice of a child by her parents. Because a large number of fragments survive, we have a clear idea of the plot. When Erekhtheus, king of Athens, is attacked by an enemy, an oracle tells him that he must sacrifice his daughter to gain victory. He and his wife Praxithea agree to do so.[55] Several passages explicitly refer to the sacrifice. In fragment 360 Cropp, Praxithea consents to the sacrifice: ἐγὼ δὲ δώσω παῖδα τὴν ἐμὴν κτανεῖν ("I will give my child to be killed": 4); τὴν . . . ἐμὴν . . . δώσω κόρην θῦσαι πρὸ γαίας ("I . . . will give . . . my girl to be sacrificed for my country": 38–39), and in fragment –/370 K,[56] Athena gives Praxithea instructions about the burial and cult of her daughter: ἥν τῆσδε χώρας σὸς προθύεται [πόσι]s ("whom your husband sacrifices on behalf of this land": 66). Euripides' *Ion* also alludes to this sacrifice (277–78).

Sophokles' *Prokris* probably concerned the story of Prokris, daughter of Erekhtheus, and her husband Kephalos, who kills her by mistake. Pausanius 10.29.6 notes that everyone tells the story of how Prokris died at the hands of her husband,[57] and Euripides' *Hypsipyle* (frag. I iv Bond, 2–3) states that Prokris's husband killed her (Πρόκριν τὰν πόσις ἔκτα).

Euripides' extant *Ion* recounts the story of Ion, son of Kreousa, who is a daughter of Erekhtheus. In this play, mother and son are about to kill one another, in ignorance of their relationship. Some scholars[58] think that this was also the subject of Sophokles' *Kreousa*, although others disagree.[59] Nothing is known about Sophokles' *Ion*, if in fact it is not to be identified with *Kreousa*.[60]

Finally, Aiskhylos's *Oreithyia* concerned a daughter of Erekhtheus, who is taken away by Boreas.[61] There is no indication of harm to *philos*, but so little is known that we can draw no conclusions from this fact.

Euripides' *Erekhtheus* certainly concerned the killing of a child by her parents, and Sophokles' *Kreousa* is also likely to have focused on harm to child by parent. The subject of Sophokles' *Prokris* was the killing of a wife by her husband. About two plays, Sophokles' *Ion* and Aiskhylos's *Oreithyia*, there are too many uncertainties to allow for classification.

Ixion Myths (4 Plays): Marriage, 4

Two plays of Aiskhylos, *Ixion* and *Perrhaibides* (*The Perrhaibians*),were about Ixion's murder of his father-in-law. Ixion marries the daughter of Eioneos, promising a large bride-price, but to avoid paying, he kills his father-in-law. No one wants to give him purification, "for he was the first to kill a relative" (πρῶτος γὰρ ἐμφύλιον ἄνδρα ἀπέκτεινεν). Finally Zeus purifies him, where-upon Ixion tries to sleep with Hera and is punished.[62] This latter crime involves violation of *xenia*. Euripides' *Ixion* ended with Ixion's punishment for his intended rape of Hera.[63] Sophokles also wrote an *Ixion*, which must have dramatized some aspect of this story, but we know nothing of the details of its plot.[64] Since Ixion was well known as the first killer of kin (by marriage), I place all four plays in the category of harm to relatives by marriage.

Laios, House of, Myths (4 Plays): Child-Parent, 3; Other Blood Kin, 1

The third play of Aiskhylos's tetralogy about the house of Laios, *Seven Against Thebes*, survives. The first two plays, *Laios* and *Oidipous*,[65] were concerned in some manner with Oidipous's incest and patricide. In *Seven Against Thebes* 742–57, Apollo is said to have told Laios that Laios would save his city if he died childless. He disobeys and begets Oidipous, who kills his father and begets children with his mother. Many think that this was the subject of *Laios*.[66] The *Oidipous* had the same subject as Sophokles' *Oedipus the King*, according to Mette,[67] but others connect it with the death of Oidipous, as told in Sophokles' *Oedipus at Kolonos*.[68] In any case, it is certain that patricide, incest, and fratricide figured prominently in all three tragedies of the tetralogy.

Euripides also wrote an *Oidipous*, but we know little about how he handled the story.[69] The play began with a reference to Laios's disobedience to Apollo: Laios "once begot a child against Phoibos's will."[70] Oidipous is blinded by the servants of Laios (frag. 541N), perhaps at the command of Kreon.[71] One fragment mentions the patricide: "at the meeting of three roads . . . killing my father" (τριπλαῖς ὁδοῖς / . . . κταν]ὼν φυτοσπόρο(ν)).[72] Violation of a suppliant may also have figured in the play. In fragment 554a Snell, someone says that he or she would not hesitate to remove an unjust man from an altar.[73]

Euripides' *Antigone*, like Sophokles' extant play, focused on the aftermath of the Theban war, when Kreon forbids the burial of Polyneikes, who had attacked the city, and Antigone, daughter of Oidipous, buries her brother in defiance of her uncle's order. Webster sums up the evidence: "What was common to the two plays [sc. Sophokles' and Euripides' *Antigone*] must have been that Antigone was discovered burying Polyneikes, but in Euripides (as our authorities say) she had the assistance of Haimon and was given in marriage to him and bore him the child Maion." He speculates that Haimon and Antigone were caught, Kreon threatened them with death or ordered Haimon to kill Antigone, and Dionysos saved them.[74] In any case, this play concerned the consequences of fratricide, and enmity between niece and uncle.

Three of the Laios plays were about harm to parent by child (Aiskhylos's *Laios* and *Oidipous* and Euripides' *Oidipous*). Euripides' *Antigone* concerned harm to niece by uncle.

Medeia Myths (6 Plays): Child-Parent, 2; Parent-Child, 2; Sibling-Sibling, 2

The Medeia story contains many instances of harm to *philoi*. Medeia kills her brother, tricks the daughters of Pelias into killing their father, kills her own children, and nearly succeeds in tricking Aigeus into killing his son Theseus. The child-murders take place in Euripides' *Medea*, which also mentions the fratricide (166–67) and the daughters of Pelias (486–87). A number of other plays also were about one or more of these incidents of kin killing.

In Sophokles' *Kolkhides* (*The Women of Kolkhis*), Medeia helped Jason to capture the Golden Fleece[75] and escape from Kolkhis: in so doing she killed her own brother.[76] That the fratricide occurred is clear from fragment 343R: Σοφοκλῆς δὲ ἐν Κολχίσι φησὶ κατὰ τὸν οἶκον τοῦ Αἰήτου τὸν παῖδα (sc. Ἄψυρτον) σφαγῆναι ("Sophokles says that she [sc. Medeia] killed the son of Aietes (sc. Apsyrtos) in the house"). Sophokles' *Skythai* (*The Scythians*) was also concerned with the Argonauts, and many believe that it also contained Medeia's murder of her brother Apsyrtos.[77] The killing of Pelias by his daughters was the subject of two plays: Sophokles' *Rhizotomoi* (*The Root Cutters*)[78] and Euripides' *Peliades* (*The Daughters of Pelias*).[79]

The Aigeus story was the subject of Euripides' *Aigeus*. After killing her children, Medeia flees to Athens and marries Aigeus. She persuades Aigeus to poison Theseus, claiming that the young man, whom Theseus does not know is his son, is plotting against the throne. When he is about to drink the poison, Aigeus recognizes Theseus, takes away the poison, and casts Medeia out of Attica.[80] Many believe that the same events were the subject of Sophokles' *Aigeus*.[81]

Of the six Medeia plays, two (Sophokles' *Kolkhides* and *Skythoi*) were concerned with Medeia's fratricide, two (Sophokles' *Rhizotomoi* and Euripides' *Peliades*) with the patricide by the daughters of Pelias, and two (Euripides' and Sophokles' *Aigeus*) with Aigeus's poisoning of his son Theseus. Medeia's child-murders, interestingly, were central to none of these.

Melanippe Myths (2 Plays): Parent-Child, 1;
Marriage, 1

Euripides wrote two plays about Melanippe: *Melanippe he Sophe* (*Wise Melanippe*) and *Melanippe Desmotis* (*Captive Melanippe*). The evidence is summarized by M. J. Cropp. In *Wise Melanippe*,

> the young Melanippe has borne twin sons by Poseidon and tried to hide them from her father Aeolos in a stable; when discovered they are taken for cow-born monsters which must be destroyed, and she tries to protect them without incriminating herself, by arguing that they must be some unknown girl's natural children. The twins . . . survive . . . the outcome for Melanippe is not known.[82]

During the course of the play,

> presumably the truth emerged . . . Aeolus threatened to punish her . . . and Melanippe asserted her innocence. . . . Hygin. *Fab.* 186 . . . starts with Melanippe blinded and incarcerated by her father and the infants exposed and rescued by herdsmen. One cannot tell if this reflects the end of *Wise Mel.*, the background of *Capt. Mel.*, or both . . . . Many scholars (including . . . Webster [1967] 149) conclude that Hippo [Melanippe's mother] averted the threatened punishment of Melanippe in Wise Mel., but it could be that Aeolus acted drastically against his daughter (e.g. by blinding her), and that Hippo appeared only in time to reveal his error. (241).

Harm to blood kin was certainly important in this plot. One fragment of *Wise Melanippe* stresses the grandfather's threat to murder his grandchildren: εἰ δὲ παρθένος φθαρεῖσα ἐξέθηκε τὰ παιδία καὶ φοβουμένη τὸν πατέρα, σὺ φόνον δράσεις ("But if a girl exposed the children because she had been raped and was in fear of her father, will you then commit murder?")[83] Amphimetric strife was prominent in *Captive Melanippe*. According to Cropp,

[K]ey features were the rearing of the twins by a royal couple [King Metapontus and Queen Theano], a foiled plot by their stepmother to have them killed as they approached adulthood, and the liberation of Melanippe by her sons from the bondage which gives the play its subtitle. . . . It remains unclear whether Melanippe was blinded by her father and healed by Poseidon (as Hyginus relates), or blinded by the Queen [Theano] and healed by Poseidon, or not blinded at all.[84]

The murder of the twins when they approached adulthood was attempted in an ambush by Theano's brothers (243). After this plot failed, "the Queen either committed suicide . . . or was killed by the twins . . . and the twins liberated Melanippe" (244). Although the twins were unrelated to Theano and her brothers, there were overtones of threats to kin in this episode because the sons of Melanippe believed that Theano's brothers were in fact their own uncles:[85]

τὼ δ' εἰσιδόντε δίπτυχον θείοιν κάρ[α
. . . εἶπον . . .
. . . "Μητρὸς ὦ κασίγνη[τοι φίλης,
τί δρᾶτ'; ἀποκτείνοντες ο[ὓς ἥκιστα χρῆν
φωρᾶσθε . . ."

But the twins, catching sight of their two uncles
. . . said . . . , "Brothers of <our dear> mother, what are you doing?
You are caught in the act of killing those <you should least kill>."
(frag. 495 Cropp 7–8, 15–17; Cropp's translation)

Although only *Wise Melanippe* certainly was concerned with harm to blood kin, the idea of kin murder was prominent in *Captive Melanippe* also. Moreover, the latter play was certainly about amphimetric strife, a kind of strife within the marriage relationship.

Meleagros Myths (2 Plays): Parent-Child, 1; Uncertain, 1

The Meleagros story is recounted in *Iliad* 9.543–99. Because Meleagros kills the brother of his mother, Althaia, she calls on the gods to give death to her son. Meleagros in turn is angry at his mother's curses and refuses to defend his people in battle. After rejecting the supplications of many, Meleagros at last yields to that of his wife and returns to the fight. Euripides followed a somewhat different version of this myth in his *Meleagros*. Althaia knows that Meleagros is fated to live as long as a brand is kept safe. After Meleagros kills his uncles, Althaia in vengeance burns this brand and thereby kills her son.[86] What in Homer is merely a curse that does not kill becomes, in Euripides, the killing of son by mother. It is not known how Sophokles treated the story in his *Meleagros*, but it probably followed the Homeric story fairly closely.[87] It should be noted that although Sophokles, unlike Homer, may have recounted the death of Meleagros in battle, this version is not necessarily inconsistent with the story of the burning brand.[88]

Niobe Myths (2 Plays): Other Blood Kin, 1;
Unlikely, 1

Niobe is the daughter of Tantalos, son of Zeus, and the wife of Amphion, another son of Zeus. In Homer, she boasts that she is superior to Leto, since she has borne more children than the goddess. Leto's two children, Artemis and Apollo, then kill Niobe's many children, and Niobe herself is turned to stone (Il. 24.602–17). That this story was the subject of Sophokles' *Niobe* is confirmed by the papyrus hypothesis summarizing the plot.[89] This play, then, appears to have represented a straightforward case of theomachy and punishment; at least, we know nothing to suggest otherwise.[90] On the other hand, fragment 162R of Aiskhylos's *Niobe* contains a hint that harm to kin might have been emphasized in this play. Niobe says,

οἱ θεῶν ἀγχίσποροι,
⟨οἱ⟩ Ζηνὸς ἐγγύς, ὧν κατ' Ἰδαῖον πάγον
Διὸς πατρῴου βωμός ἐστ' ἐν αἰθέρι,
κοὔ πώ σφιν ἐξίτηλον αἷμα δαιμόνων

Those who are close kin to the gods,
who are near to Zeus, of whom on the Idaian hill
the altar of father Zeus is high in the aither,
and in whom the blood of divinities has not yet faded away.

These words might have referred to Niobe's children, killed by the gods from whom they were descended. However, Eva Keuls gives good arguments for the view that the fragment alludes to the punishment by Apollo of Amphion and his brother Xethos. After Apollo and Artemis kill his and Niobe's children, Amphion attacks the temple of Apollo and is in turn killed by him. Amphion and his brother are then immortalized as Dioskouroi.[91] In any case, the lines suggest that the play may have stressed the gods' killing of their own blood kin. The fact that Niobe's father Tantalos was one of the dramatic figures in this play[92] may be some evidence in favor of the view that kin killing was emphasized, since he is associated in myth with harm to kin. There are also parallels in the extant plays. Harm to *philoi* among the gods is central to Aiskhylos's *Prometheus Bound*, and in Euripides' *Medea* 1255–57[93] the Chorus mention the divine ancestry of Medeia's children as she is about to kill them.

Paris Myths (2 Plays): Sibling-Sibling, 1;
Parent-Child, 1

The story of Sophokles' *Alexandros* is given in Hyginus, *Fabulae* 91. The infant Paris is exposed after the pregnant Hekabe has a dream of ill omen. Raised by shepherds, he returns to Troy and defeats his brothers in games. When his brother Deiphobos is about to kill him in anger at being defeated, Paris takes refuge at an altar. Kassandra declares that he is Priam's son, and Priam recognizes him.[94]

Euripides' *Alexandros* had a similar plot, but in his version, Paris's mother is about to kill him when recognition prevents the terrible deed. The papyrus hypothesis summarizes the plot. Priam exposes Paris because Hekabe has a dream of ill omen, and the child is brought up by a shepherd. Hekabe, grieving over her lost child, persuades Priam to hold games in his honor. Paris participates in the games and wins. This infuriates Deiphobos's friends, who bid Hekabe consider how she will kill him (κατηξίωσαν τὴν Ἑκάβην ὅ[π]ω[ς ἂ]ν αὐτὸν ἀποκτεί[νη‹ι›]). Kassandra, however, recognizes her brother and prophesies about the future. Hekabe, who wishes to kill him, is prevented from doing so.[95] The truth is at last revealed by the shepherd, and Hekabe regains her son.

Peleus, House of, Myths (3 Plays): Xenia, 2; Uncertain, 1

Peleus is involved in a number of misfortunes involving harm to *philoi*. After killing his brother Phokos (an event alluded to in Euripides' *Andromakhe*, 687), he flees to Phthia, where Eurytion purifies him and gives him his daughter in marriage. However, Peleus accidentally kills Eurytion and flees again, this time to Akastos, who purifies him. Here also Peleus is unfortunate. "Akastos' wife, Astydameia, attempted to seduce him. When he refused her she accused him falsely; Akastos believed her and threw him out into the forest unarmed, but the gods saved him by giving him a sword."[96] The enmity of Peleus with Akastos and his sons continues into Peleus's old age. He is exiled by Akastos or his sons, and subsequently vengeance is taken by Peleus's grandson Neoptolemos. Sophokles' *Peleus* is generally agreed to have been concerned with the events of Peleus's old age.[97] Scholars are divided, however, over whether Euripides' *Peleus* also was about the events of Peleus's old age or about the Akastos story from his youth.[98] In either case, Peleus was involved in enmity with the *xenos* who purified him.

Other adventures of Peleus's grandson, Neoptolemos, were the subject of Sophokles' *Hermione*. The story was similar to that recounted in Euripides' *Andromakhe* (esp. 966–86). Hermione is first betrothed to Orestes, then taken from him and given to Neoptolemos. When Neoptolemos is killed at Delphi, she returns to Orestes.[99] Euripides' play was concerned with many kinds of harm to *philoi*, as chapter 5 showed. Although it is uncertain how Sophokles' version differed from that of Euripides, it is possible that some form of harm to *philos* figured in his play as well.

Pelops, House of, Myths (4 Plays): Some Form of Harm to Philoi, 3; Uncertain, 1

Pelops and his family were the subject of a number of plays. Although we know nothing about the plot of Sophokles' *Tantalos*,[100] Pearson suggests that it was about Tantalos's part in the theft of Zeus's golden dog and his subsequent punishment.[101] In myth, Tantalos is guilty of serving his son Pelops to the gods as food, but there is no evidence for or against this incident being represented in Sophokles' play.

Pelops's marriage to Oinomaos's daughter Hippodameia was the subject of Sophokles' *Oinomaos*, but we do not know how he treated this story.[102] There are a number of variants to the myth. In Apollodoros's account,[103] Oinomaos challenges the suitors of his daughter Hippodameia to a chariot race and kills those he overtakes, either because he himself is in love with her or because of an oracle that his son-in-law will kill him. Pelops succeeds in winning Hippodameia because she, who is in love with him, asks Oinomaos's charioteer, Myrtilos, who is in love with her, to assist Pelops. Myrtilos removes the linchpins from Oinomaos's chariot, causing it to crash, and Oinomaos dies cursing him. Myrtilos in his turn curses Pelops, who throws him into the sea after he tries to rape Hippodameia. Apollodoros also cites a variant according to which Pelops kills Oinomaos (*Epit.* 2.7); this is the version followed by Euripides in *Iphigenia in Tauris* 823–25 (see chapter 2, section 1). Whatever version Sophokles followed, his play certainly dramatized some form of harm to *philos*: incest, murder of father-in-law, or violation of *xenia*. Fragment 473aR suggests that the murder of *xenoi* may have figured in another way in the play, for Sophokles' Oinomaos is said to have covered the temple of Poseidon with the skulls of the *xenoi* who wooed his daughter (τῶν ξένων τῶν ἡττωμένων τοῖς κρανίοις ἐρέφειν τὸν τοῦ Ποσειδῶνος νάον). While these *xenoi* may simply have been strangers, it is possible that Oinomaos was represented as a murderer of those in a formal *xenia* relationship who was himself killed by a *xenos*.

Euripides' *Oinomaos* also was about the story of Oinomaos, Pelops and Hippodameia, although the details of the plot are unknown. According to Webster, "[I]ts relation to Sophocles' play . . . is unclear. . . . If Euripides did treat the same part of the story, it looks as if he completely changed the emphases and made Oinomaos an unhappy father who was outwitted by the unscrupulous Pelops."[104] It is likely that some form of harm to *philos* was an issue.

The subject of Euripides' *Khrysippos* was Laios's rape of Pelops's bastard son. Amphimetric strife is central to Hyginus's version of the myth: "Laius, son of Labdacus, carried off Chrysippus, illegitimate son of Pelops, at the Nemean Games because of his exceeding beauty. Pelops made war and recovered him. At the instigation of their mother Hippodamia, Atreus and Thyestes killed him. When Pelops blamed Hippodamia, she killed herself."[105] Webster, however, holds that Euripides followed a version according to which the boy kills himself from shame.[106] According to Apollodoros,[107] the rape occurred when Laios was a guest of Pelops. Laios "while living in the Peloponnese, was received as *xenos* by Pelops, and having fallen in love with his son, Khrysippos, while teaching him to drive a chariot, he carried him off" (ὁ δὲ ἐν Πελοποννήσῳ διατελῶν ἐπιξενοῦται Πέλοπι, καὶ τούτου παῖδα Χρύσιππον ἁρματοδρομεῖν διδάσκων ἐρασθεὶς ἀναρπάζει). Whatever version Euripides dramatized, it is likely that his play contained one or more instances of harm to *philoi*.

Three of the four Pelops plays are likely to have involved some form of harm to *philoi*, although the great variety of myths does not allow for certainty about the particular kind of relationship that was involved. In the case of Sophokles' *Tantalos*, there is too little evidence to allow for classification.

Perseus Myths (9 Plays): Child-Parent, 1; Parent-Child, 4;
Some Form of Harm to Blood Kin, 1;
Suppliancy, 2; Unlikely, 1

The story of Perseus begins and ends with acts of violence between Perseus and his grandfather. Akrisios, king of Argos and the father of Danaë, receives an oracle saying that he will be killed by his daughter's child. When she has a child by Zeus, he puts her and the child into a chest and casts it into the sea. Danaë and her son, Perseus, however, are rescued in Seriphos by Diktys and taken to his brother, Polydektes, king of the island. Some time later, Polydektes, who wants to rape Danaë, sends Perseus away, telling him to bring the head of the Gorgon Medusa. Danaë takes refuge at an altar from which she is rescued by Perseus, who turns Polydektes to stone with the Gorgon's head. Later on, Perseus accidentally kills his grandfather, Akrisios, in games at Larissa.[108]

Many plays were concerned with one part or another of this history. Three titles—*Akrisios*, *Danaë*, and *Larisaioi* (*The Men of Larissa*)—were attributed to Sophokles. The finale of the Perseus story was the subject of Sophokles' *Larisaioi*. In this play, Akrisios, the father of Danaë, leaves Argos and goes to Larissa because of an oracle that he will be killed by his daughter's son. Perseus finds his grandfather in Larissa and makes himself known to him. Before his departure, Perseus competes in a local contest and accidentally wounds Akrisios with a discus. Akrisios dies as a result.[109] The *Danaë* is likely to have concerned the first part of the story. Pearson suggests that a fragment of this play refers to Akrisios's attempt to kill Perseus, speculating that after the birth of Perseus, Danaë pleads with her father that she was forced, and that he replies,

οὐκ οἶδα τὴν σὴν πεῖραν· ἓν δ' ἐπίσταμαι·
τοῦ παιδὸς ὄντος τοῦδ' ἐγὼ διόλλυμαι. (frag. 165R)

I know nothing of the attempt you tell me of, but only that, if this child
lives, I am undone.[110]

Much disagreement surrounds the *Akrisios*, which is sometimes identified with the *Danaë*, sometimes with the *Larisaioi*.[111] If Radt is right in listing it as a separate play, it probably was concerned with some instance of the kin killing associated with the Perseus myth.

Euripides' *Danaë* was about the birth of Perseus and exile of mother and son.[112] In Euripides' *Diktys*, according to Webster,

> Polydektes, King of Seriphos and brother of Diktys, fell in love with Danaë and was prevented from seducing her by her son Perseus who had grown up. Polydektes sent Perseus to fetch the Gorgon's head as his part in an *eranos* or as a wedding present for Hippodameia. When Perseus returned to Seriphos, "he found that the violence of Polydektes had caused Danaë and Diktys to take refuge on an altar [καταλαβὼν προσπεφευγυῖαν τοῖς βωμοῖς μετὰ τοῦ Δίκτυος τὴν μητέρα διὰ τὴν Πολυδέκτου βίαν]; he entered the palace and when Polydektes had summoned his friends, he showed them the Gorgon's head and they were changed into stone." He then made Diktys king.[113]

This play, if Webster is right, was concerned with threats to a suppliant. In addition, one fragment concerns amphimetric strife:

ὄντων δὲ παίδων καὶ πεφυκότος γένους
καινοὺς φυτεῦσαι παῖδας ἐν δόμοις θέλεις,
ἔχθραν μεγίστην σοῖσι συμβάλλων τέκνοις. (frag. 338N)

When you already have children and a family
you wish to beget new children in your house,
bringing the greatest enmity to your children.

Webster (64) interprets this as an argument to Polydektes against marrying Danaë.

Perseus was also the subject of Aiskhylos's *Phorkides* (*The Daughters of Phorkys*) and *Polydektes*. The *Phorkides*, which featured the story of Perseus's killing of the Gorgon Medusa after having stolen the single eye shared by the Graiai, the guardians of the Gorgons,[114] is unlikely to have been concerned with harm to *philoi*. *Polydektes* is known only from the Catalogue, but most believe that it followed *Phorkides* in the Perseus tetralogy,[115] and Mette thinks it concerned the story of Perseus after his return to Seriphos with the Gorgon's head.[116] If so, it is possible that Aiskhylos's play, like Euripides' *Diktys*, had to do with threats to a suppliant.

The rescue of Andromeda from a sea monster, an episode in which Perseus becomes involved while on his expedition to capture the Gorgon's head, was the subject of Sophokles' and Euripides' *Andromeda* plays. Andromeda is the daughter of Kassiopeia and Kepheus. In Euripides' play "Kassiopeia had boasted that Andromeda was more beautiful than the Nereids, and Poseidon therefore ordered Kepheus to expose her to the monster."[117] She was rescued by Perseus.[118] Several fragments allude to Kepheus's exposure of his daughter:

ἄνοικτος ὃς τεκών σέ τὴν
πολυπονωτάτην βροτῶν
μεθῆκεν Ἅιδα πάτρας ὑπερθανεῖν. (frag. 120N)

Pitiless he who, having begotten you,
who are the most wretched of morals,
gave you up to Hades to die for your country;

γοᾶσθέ μ' . . . ὡς . . . πέπονθα . . . ἀπὸ δὲ συγγόνων . . . ἄνομα πάθεα
(frag. 122N, 1036–39)

Weep for me . . . how I have suffered . . . at the hands of kin . . . lawless sufferings;

. . . τὸν δὲ πατέρα Κηφέα,
ὅς σ' ἐξέθηκεν, ἀπολέσειαν οἱ θεοί. (frag. 167 Mette [1981–82, 50])

May the gods destroy your father Kepheus,
who exposed you.

Sophokles' *Andromeda* was about the same events, although the details of his
treatment are not known.[119] Fragment 126R mentions human sacrifice.

Of the nine Perseus plays, four—Euripides' *Danaë*, and Sophokles'
Akrisios, Danaë, and *Larisaioi*—were concerned with acts of violence among
blood kin. Sophokles' and Euripides' *Danaë* concerned harm to grandchild
by grandparent; Sophokles' *Larisaioi* was about harm to grandparent by grandchild, and Sophokles' *Akrisios* was about some form of harm to blood kin.
Sophokles' and Euripides' *Andromeda* plays were concerned with the violence
done to Andromeda by her father. Euripides' *Diktys* probably represented violence to a suppliant, which may also have been the subject of Aiskhylos's
Polydektes. It seems unlikely that Aiskhylos's *Phorkides* centered on harm to
philoi.

Phaethon Myths (2 Plays): Marriage, 1; Uncertain, 1

Substantial fragments are preserved from Euripides' *Phaethon*, allowing for a
reconstruction of the plot with some probability. Collard reconstructs the
action:

> Merops is married to Clymene, daughter of Oceanus; he believes Phaethon,
> her son from a premarital union with Helios, to be his own, for she has not
> told Merops the truth—nor told the youth himself, perhaps not until the
> mutilated Prologue scene. The time is the day-dawn when Merops will
> marry Phaethon to a goddess. But Phaethon distrusts Clymene's news of his
> true parentage and resists marriage; he cannot however avoid discussing the
> marriage with Merops, but resolves to go immediately afterwards to Helios's
> nearby house, to test his mother's truthfulness by using the single promise
> which Helios gave her at their union.[120]

Phaethon then asks Helios to be allowed to drive the chariot of the sun.
During the drive he is killed by a lightning bolt: "[T]he fatal drive may have
been shown as no more than a straightforward test of Clymene's claim, or both
that and a foolish demand" (199). His smoldering body is brought in; Klymene
conceals it from Merops, but he discovers it. "The Chorus sing their alarm that
Clymene's concealment from Merops of Phaethon's parentage and now of his
death may bring her execution. . . . The missing end of the play . . . was probably a dangerous scene between a vengeful Merops and a defensive
Clymene . . . a god would have interrupted to rescue Clymene" (197).

Fragment 781 Collard clearly indicates that both Klymene and the Chorus fear that her husband will kill her. She hides her son's body in fear of her husband (216–23) and invokes Helios, telling him that he has destroyed her by killing her son:

ὦ καλλιφεγγὲς Ἥλι᾽, ὥς μ᾽ ἀπώλεσας
καὶ τόνδ᾽· Ἀπόλλων δ᾽ ἐν βροτοῖς ὀρθῶς καλῃ,
ὅστις τὰ σιγῶντ᾽ ὀνόματ᾽ οἶδε δαιμόνων. (224–26)

O Helios with your lovely light, how you have destroyed me, and the one here! "Apollo" you are rightly called among men where any knows the silent meaning of gods' names! (Collard's translation)

Shortly after this, the Chorus tell Klymene to supplicate her father Oceanos, asking him to protect her from her husband:

ὦ δυστάλαινα τῶν ἀμετρήτων κακῶν,
Ὠκεανοῦ κόρα,
†πατρὸς ἴθι πρόσπεσε γόνυ λιταῖς σφαγὰς
σφαγὰς οἰκτρὰς ἀρκέσαι σᾶς δειρᾶς.† (280–83)

So cruelly wretched in your measureless tragedy, daughter of Oceanus! †Go and fall at your father's knee in prayer to him to hold back slaughter, piteous slaughter, from your throat!†

The first of these passages (frag. 781.224–26) suggests that the play may have been about Helios's responsibility for the death of his son and for the dangers incurred by his son's mother. This interpretation is supported by Cicero's linking of the fatal promise given by Helios with that of Neptune to Theseus, which leads to the death of Theseus's son Hippolytos.[122] More important, however, is the threat of husband to wife. It is probable that the climax of the play was Merops's attempted retaliation against Klymene.[123]

About Aiskhylos's *Heliades* (*The Daughters of the Sun*) we know little. The plot probably concerned Phaethon's fatal drive and the mourning of his sisters, the Heliades.[124] Diggle speculates: "[I]f the Aeschylean Helios was bound by no promise (the promise is the result of the matrimonial entanglements which are almost certainly the invention of Euripides), then it is as likely that he refused the request as that he acceded to it. If he did refuse, then the Heliades may have lent Phaethon their secret aid."[125] It is possible that this play, like Euripides' *Phaethon*, emphasized some kind of harm to kin. However, we do not have enough information to determine the likelihood of this.

*Phineus Myths (4 Plays): Parent-Child, 2; Some
Form of Harm to Philos, 1; Uncertain, 1*

Three different versions of the early history of Phineus are given in the scholion to Sophokles' *Antigone* 981 (frag. 645R of Sophokles' *Tympanistai* [*The Drummers*]). Phineus marries Kleopatra, the daughter of Boreas, and has two children by her. In one version, after Kleopatra's death, Phineus's second wife blinds the children of Kleopatra and shuts them up in a tomb. In another version, after Kleopatra's death, Phineus's second wife falsely accuses Kleopatra's sons of trying to rape her. Phineus believes her and himself blinds his and Kleopatra's sons. In the third version, Phineus puts Kleopatra aside and marries a second wife. In anger, Kleopatra then blinds her own sons.[126] There are also several different versions of Phineus's later history. According to one account, Phineus's sons are cured of their blindness and take vengeance on their stepmother for blinding them. In other sources, Phineus, after being blinded (either in punishment for his treatment of his sons or for some other reason) and then tormented by the Harpies, is finally rescued by the Argonauts.[127]

Sophokles' two plays *Phineus 1* and *Phineus 2* and, most believe, his *Tympanistai*, about which little is known,[128] were about some aspects of some version of this complicated tradition. The fragments of *Phineus 1* and 2 indicate that these plays concerned the blinding of the sons of Phineus, the blinding of Phineus himself, and the Harpies.[129] According to two fragments, Phineus is blinded for harming his own sons: "Sophokles [says] that he [sc. Phineus] blinded the sons of Kleopatra . . . persuaded by the slanders of Idaia, their stepmother" (Σοφοκλῆς δέ, ὅτι τοὺς ἐκ Κλεοπάτρας υἱοὺς ἐτύφλωσε . . . πεισθεὶς διαβολαῖς Ἰδαίας τῆς αὐτῶν μητρυιᾶς: 704R); "Sophokles in the *Phineus* says that he [sc. Phineus] was blinded because he killed his own children" (Σοφοκλῆς δὲ ἐν Φινεῖ πηρωθῆναι αὐτόν φησιν, ὅτι τὰ ἴδια τέκνα ἀνεῖλεν: 705R).[130]

The details of the plot of Aiskhylos's *Phineus* are not known,[130] although the Harpies are alluded to in fragments 258R and 259aR and mentioned in 260R. It is possible that, like Sophokles' plays, its subject was Phineus and his sons.

Of the four Phineus plays, Sophokles' *Phineus 1* and 2 probably concerned Phineus's harming of his sons, and Sophokles' *Tympanistai* was about either the same subject or amphimetric strife. Too little is known about Aiskhylos's *Phineus* to allow any classification.

Phoinix Myths (2 Plays): Parent-Child, 1; Uncertain, 1

Euripides' *Phoinix* concerned the story of Akhilleus's mentor recounted in *Il.* 9.447–80. In Homer's version, Phoinix lies with the concubine of his father, who, when he discovers what has happened, curses his son with childlessness. Phoinix contemplates patricide but is restrained by fear of blame (458–61),[132] and leaves his native land. In Euripides' version, however, Phoenix, after being falsely accused by the concubine, is not merely cursed but blinded by his father.[133]

The plot of Sophokles' *Phoinix* is unknown.[134] Its subject is generally thought to have been the story of the concubine,[135] but even if this is true, there is no evidence to indicate whether Sophokles' version was closer to that of Homer or that of Euripides.

Prometheus Myths (2 Plays): Other Blood Kin, 2

The subject of Aiskhylos's extant play, *Prometheus Bound*, is Prometheus's punishment by Zeus. The other two tragedies in the tetralogy, *Prometheus Pyrphoros* (*Prometheus the Fire Carrier*) and *Prometheus Lyomenos* (*Prometheus Unbound*), are generally agreed to have concerned Herakles' shooting of the eagle that tortured Prometheus, Prometheus's revelation of the prophecy concerning Zeus, his release, and the reconciliation of Zeus and Prometheus.[136] The extant play and, we may infer, the two other tragedies in the tetralogy were deeply concerned with harm to *philoi*, since they were about the enmity between the kindred gods Prometheus and Zeus (see appendix A). That kinship played a role in the other plays is also suggested by fragment 193R, line 1, of *Lyomenos*, where Prometheus addresses a Titan as "sharer in our blood" (*socia nostri sanguinis*).[137] Prometheus's words about Herakles in fragment 201R of *Lyomenos*, "This is the dearest child of a father who is my enemy" (ἐχθροῦ πατρός μοι τοῦτο φίλτατον τέκνον), also hint at the importance of kinship in this play, for they mark out Herakles as son of Zeus but friend of Prometheus, Zeus's enemy.

Protesilaos Myths (2 Plays): Suicide, 1; Unlikely, 1

Two plays dramatized with the story of Protesilaos, the first Greek to be killed at Troy. In Sophokles' *Poimenes* (*The Shepherds*), Protesilaos is killed by Hektor, and Akhilleus kills the Trojan, Kyknos.[138] There is no evidence that the plot was concerned with harm to *philoi*, although Pearson suggests that it is "barely possible" that it contained the story of Laodamia, the wife of Protesilaos, who killed herself after his death.[139] Euripides' *Protesilaos*, on the other hand, was about harm to *philoi*. Aside from the Aias plays, this is the only play we know of in which suicide seems to have been the central *pathos*. After his death, Protesilaos is allowed to return to the upper world for a short time to see his wife. When he leaves again, she is overcome by grief and embraces a statue of Protesilaos. Her father discovers what she is doing and orders the statue burned. Laodamia kills herself in grief.[140]

Telephos Myths (7 Plays): Parent-Child, 2; Other Blood Kin, 1; Suppliancy, 3; Uncertain, 1

The history of Telephos is particularly rich in events in which *philos* harms *philos*. Kin murder, incest, and threats to suppliants abound.

Euripides' *Auge* concerned the birth of Telephos. Auge, daughter of Aleos, is raped by Herakles. Aleos exposes the resulting child, Telephos, and imprisons his daughter in a chest. Herakles then rescues mother and son.[141]

The rape occurs while Herakles is a *xenos* of Aleos: "After Aleos had feasted him (268N²), love and wine led him to abandon reason and rape Auge. . . it was an injustice but an involuntary injustice (269 [N²] . . . 265N²)."¹⁴² In the fragments cited by Webster, Herakles admits that Aleos was his host ("You thought fit to sacrifice in my honor": καὶ βουθυτεῖν γὰρ ἠξίους ἐμὴν χάριν: 268N), whom he wronged ("I agree that I wronged you, but the wrong was not voluntary": ὁμολογῶ δέ σε ἀδικεῖν, τὸ δ' ἀδίκημ' ἐγένετ' οὐχ ἑκούσιον: 268N). This play, then, concerned violation of *xenia* as well as harm to blood kin.

Sophokles' *Telepheia* trilogy focused on harm to blood kin in Telephos's later history. In this slightly different version of the early history, Aleos receives an oracle stating that if his daughter has a child, the child will kill Aleos's sons. Accordingly, after Auge becomes pregnant by Herakles, Aleos attempts to kill her. She survives, however, and gives birth to Telephos, who kills his maternal uncles in a manner unspecified by our sources. Sophokles' *Aleadai* (*The Sons of Aleos*) was about some aspects of this story.¹⁴³ Sophokles' *Mysoi* (*The Mysians*) concerned Telephos's later adventures, after he arrives in Mysia. As a reward for helping Teuthras against his enemies, Telephos is married to his adoptive daughter, who, unbeknownst to Telephos, is actually his mother Auge. On the wedding night, Auge, who wants to remain faithful to the memory of Herakles, is about to kill Telephos, and he in turn is about to kill her in vengeance for her failed attempt. Recognition prevents kin killing and incest.¹⁴⁴ The third tragedy in Sophokles' *Telepheia* was *Telephos*. It probably dramatized the threatened violation of a suppliant, the events recounted in Euripides' *Telephos*.¹⁴⁵

Cropp gives the story of Euripides' *Telephos*:

> Wounded by Achilles, he [sc. Telephos] was directed by an oracle to Argos to be healed by him and become the Achaeans' destined guide to Troy. . . . Telephus learns from Apollo . . . that he can only be healed "by the same spear that wounded him." . . . He comes to Agamemnon and "on Clytemnestra's advice" seizes Orestes from his cradle threatening to kill him if the Achaeans will not treat his wound. They have received an oracle that they cannot take Troy "without Telephus's leadership" . . . so they ask Achilles to heal him. Achilles replies that he is ignorant of medicine, but Odysseus perceives that the destined healer is the spear itself. Telephus is cured with its filings. . . . He refuses to help them in sacking Troy because he is Priam's son-in-law, but consents to guide them and after doing so returns to his homeland.¹⁴⁶

Telephos's threat to Orestes at the altar, frequently represented in vase paintings, was the climax of the play.¹⁴⁷

There is no consensus about which aspect of the Telephos story was the subject of Aiskhylos's *Mysoi*.¹⁴⁸ Most scholars hold that events subsequent to the wounding were the subject of his *Telephos*, although there is widespread disagreement about how this play differed from Euripides' play of the same name.[149] According to Cropp, Aiskhylos's play differed from that of Euripides in putting less stress on the threats to the hostage Orestes: "the threatening was Euripides' striking innovation."[150] Aiskhylos probably adapted Thucydides 1.136, in which Themistokles in his flight from Greece supplicates King Admetos, on the queen's advice, taking Admetos's son and sitting at his hearth without threatening him.[151] If Cropp is right, Euripides made more explicit the threats that are implied by any suppliancy or hostage taking.

Of the seven Telephos plays, Euripides' *Auge* and Sophokles' *Mysoi* were about harm to child by parent, and Sophokles' *Aleadai* concerned harm to uncle by nephew. The *Telephos* plays of Euripides and Aiskhylos were suppliant plays, and this is also likely to have been the case for Sophokles' *Telephos*. The subject of Aiskhylos's *Mysoi* is uncertain.

Temenos, House of, Myths (3 Plays): Child-Parent, 1; Sibling-Sibling, 1; Xenia, 1

Euripides wrote two plays about Temenos. In myth, this man is murdered by his sons because he shows more favor to Deiphontes, the husband of his daughter, Hyrnetho, than to them. The sons then try to get Hyrnetho away from Deiphontes by accusing him of various crimes. When she refuses, they carry her off, and Deiphontes pursues them. In the ensuing struggle, Hyrnetho is accidentally killed by her brother Phalkes. *Temenos* may have been about the murder of Temenos, and *Temenidai* (*The Sons of Temenos*) was concerned with the story of Hyrnetho.[152] One fragment of the latter contains accusations of maltreatment of *xenoi* and kin; it may be part of the sons' false accusation against Deiphontes:[153]

ὡς σκαιὸς ἀνὴρ καὶ ξένοισιν ἄξενος
καὶ μνημονεύων οὐδὲν ὧν ἐχρῆν φίλου.
σπάνιον ἄρ' ἦν θανοῦσιν ἀσφαλεῖς φίλοι,
κἂν ὁμόθεν ὦσι. (736N.1–4)

What a fool is the man, both a bad friend to *xenoi*,
and remembering nothing that he ought of a friend.
It is a rare thing even for kin
to be true friends to the dead.

Euripides' *Arkhelaos* was about a son of Temenos and concerned both harm to kin and harm to *xenos*. The story is given in Hyginus, *Fabulae* 219.[154] Arkhelaos is exiled by his brothers and goes to Makedonia, where King Kisseus promises him his kingdom and marriage to his daughter if he protects Makedonia from an enemy. Arkhelaos does so, but Kisseus goes back on his promise and tries to kill Arkhelaos. The latter learns of the plot and instead kills Kisseus. This play, if it focused on the Kisseus episode, was concerned with violation of *xenia*.

Theseus, House of, Myths (6 Plays): Parent-Child, 2;
Suppliancy, 2; Unlikely, 1; Uncertain, 1

A number of plays were concerned with this Athenian hero and his family. Sophokles' *Aigeus* and Euripides' *Aigeus* (both discussed above, with the Medeia plays) dramatized the episode in which Aigeus is about to kill his son, Theseus, in ignorance. The subject of Euripides' *Theseus* was the story of Theseus and the Minotaur, but we do not know the details.[155] Webster suggests that the play represented Ariadne's betrayal of her country for love of Theseus.[156] Aiskhylos's *Eleusinioi* (*The Eleusinians*) had a plot similar to that of Euripides' *Suppliants*, in which Adrastos and the mothers of the fallen Seven supplicate Theseus, asking for help in burying their sons. In Aiskhylos's *Eleusinioi*, Adrastos and Theseus bring about the burial of the dead not by resorting to armed combat, as in Euripides, but by means of persuasion.[157] Aiskhylos's *Argeioi* (*Men of Argos*) may have been concerned with the same subject.[158] Later events were the subject of Sophokles' *Phaidra*, which probably resembled the extant *Hippolytos* of Euripides, in which stepmother accuses stepson of rape and father causes death of son.[159] Euripides' *Hippolytos Kalyptomenos* (*Hippolytos Veiled*) also treated this subject, although in a somewhat different manner from his extant play.[160]

On the other hand, there is no evidence of harm to *philoi* in the *Peirithous*. The attribution of this play is disputed: Mette, Nauck, and Page hold it to be Euripidean, while Snell lists it among the plays of Kritias.[161] In this plot, Peirithous goes to Hades with Theseus to woo Persephone and is punished by being bound to a rock. Theseus, not wanting to abandon his friend, voluntarily remains in Hades. Herakles then rescues them both.[162] Fragment 595N (= Kritias frag. 6 Snell) refers to the chains of *aidôs* (αἰδοῦς ἀχαλκεύτοισιν ἔζευκται πέδαις) that bind friend to friend.[163] Here, then, companion suffers along with companion, but there is no evidence of harm to *philoi*.

Two of the Theseus plays (Sophokles' *Phaidra* and Euripides' *Hippolytos Kalyptomenos*) were concerned, like Euripides' extant *Hippolytos*, with harm to child by parent. Aiskhylos's *Eleusinioi* and *Argeioi* were suppliant plays. The *Peirithous* is unlikely to have involved harm to *philoi*. Too little is known about Euripides' *Theseus* to allow for any kind of judgment.

Tyro Myths (2 Plays): Suppliancy, 2

Sophokles' two plays *Tyro 1* and *Tyro 2* were about Tyro, the daughter of Salmoneus. Tyro bears two sons to Poseidon and exposes them. They are rescued, and when they grow up they recognize their mother and kill her stepmother, Sidero, who has been mistreating Tyro. Sidero, who has taken refuge at Hera's sanctuary, is killed at the altar.[164] Radt believes that Apollodoros, *Library* 1.9.8 (ἐπ' αὐτῶν τῶν βωμῶν αὐτὴν κατέσφαξε: "He killed her at the very altars"), contains a quotation of Sophokles' play: ἐπ' αὐτῶν (τῶν) βωμῶν ("at the very altars": frag. 669a).[165] These plays, then, were about amphimetric strife between stepmother and stepdaughter and they focused on the killing of a suppliant at an altar. Another story about the same Tyro may have been the subject of Sophokles' *Sisyphos* (which see).

2. Category II. Individual Plays With Violation of *Philia*

Plays are listed individually, according to types of *philia* relationships violated.[166]

> *Blood Kinship (10 Plays): Parent-Child, 5; Sibling-*
> *Sibling, 2; Other Blood Kin, 1; Some Form of*
> *Harm to Blood Kin, 2*

■ Euripides' *Aiolos* (Sibling-Sibling).   This play concerned the story of the incestuous love affair, followed by suicide, of two children of Aiolos, Kanake and Makareus.[167] Webster summarizes the papyrus hypothesis: "Makareus raped his sister Kanake; she tried to conceal the birth of the child by pretending to be ill. . . . The young man persuaded his father to let his sons marry his daughters. Aiolos drew lots, and the lot gave Kanake to another of the sons."[168] According to Webster, "the other accounts go on immediately after the rape to Aiolos's discovery of it, his sending Kanake a sword with which she commits suicide; Makareus won Aiolos over but only arrived to discover Kanake dying and himself committed suicide" (157–58).

This story is of particular interest because it is also briefly mentioned in the *Odyssey*:

> [T]welve children were born to him [sc. Aiolos] in his palace,
> six of them daughters, and six sons in the pride of their youth, so
> he bestowed his daughters on his sons, to be their consorts.
> And evermore, beside their dear father and gracious mother,
> these feast, and good things beyond number are set before them;
> and all their days the house fragrant with food echoes
> in the courtyard, but their nights they sleep each one by his modest
> wife, under coverlets, and on bedsteads corded for bedding.
> (*Od.* 10.5–12: Lattimore)

Homer's Aiolos presides over a harmonious family who spend their days feasting, like the Olympian gods. The incest is represented in a matter-of-fact way, as an obvious and logical way of disposing of equal numbers of male and female children. Euripides' story, in contrast, stressed the disastrous consequences of incest, compounded by the birth of an illegitimate child and ending in a double suicide.

■ Euripides' *Alope* or *Kerkyon* (Parent-Child).   It is generally agreed that the subject of Euripides' play was some version of the story given in Hyginus,

Fabulae 187. Alope, the daughter of Kerkyon, has a child by Poseidon which is exposed but then rescued by a shepherd. Kerkyon discovers that his daughter has borne a child and orders her to be shut her up in a dungeon and killed (*filiam iussit ad necem includi*), and the child is again exposed. Later, Theseus kills Kerkyon.[169] In this play, then, father killed daughter and was about to kill grandchild.

■ Euripides' *Antiope* (Other Blood Kin).   Euripides' *Antiope* represented the story of a niece tormented by her uncle and his wife. After being raped by Zeus, by whom she has twin sons, Antiope marries Epopeus of Sikyon. Her uncle, Lykos, then kills Epopeus, and he and his wife, Dirke, take Antiope into captivity and maltreat her. When they are grown, Antiope's sons recognize their mother and rescue her. They kill Dirke but are prevented by Hermes from killing Lykos.[170]

■ Sophokles' *Eurypylos* (Parent-Child).   The story on which this play was based is similar to that of Eriphyle and Amphiaraos. (See "Amphiaraos Myths.") Eurypylos is the son of Astyokhe, sister of Priam, and of Telephos, son of Herakles. By means of a golden vine, Priam bribes Astyokhe to send her son to help defend Troy. After Eurypylos goes to Troy, he is killed by Neoptolemos.[171] In Sophokles' play, not only is mother responsible for the death of son (in frag. 210R, 40–46, Astyokhe says that she suffers justly), Priam also holds himself responsible for the death of his nephew and *xenos*, as is clear from fragment 210R, 70–79:

ὁ δ' ἀμφὶ πλευραῖς καὶ σφαγαῖσι [κ]είμενος,
πατ[ὴρ] μὲν οὔ, πατρῷα δ' ἐξαυδ[ῶ]ν ἔπη,
Πρία[μος] ἔκλαιε τὸν τέκνων ὁμ[αί]μονα,
τὸν [π]αῖδα καὶ γέροντα καὶ νεαν[ί]αν,
τὸν οὔτε Μυσὸν οὔτε Τηλέφου [κα]λῶν,
ἀλλ' ὡς φυτεύσας αὐτὸς ἐκκαλούμ[εν]ος·
"οἴμοι, τέκνον, πρ[ο]ύδωκά σ' ἐσχάτη[ν ἔ]χων
Φρυξὶν μεγίστην ‹τ'› ἐλπίδων σωτη[ρία]ν.
χρόνον ξενωθεὶς οὐ μακρὸν π[ολ]λῶν κακῶν
μνήμην παρέξεις . . ."

Embracing his wounded sides,
though not a father, speaking a father's words,
Priam lamented his children's kinsman,
calling him child, old man, and youth,[172]
neither Mysian nor son of Telephos,
but invoking him as though he himself had begotten him:
"Alas, child, I betrayed you by holding you to be the last
and greatest salvation of the hopes of the Phrygians.
Though you were not my *xenos* for long, you will furnish
memory of many evils. . . ."

■ Sophokles' *Hipponous* (Some Form of Harm to Blood Kin).   Although nothing certain is known about the plot of this play,[173] it may have been connected with the story of Hipponous, king of Olenos, and father of Periboia. When he finds his daughter to be pregnant, Hipponous sends her to Oineus with a secret message ordering her be killed. According to one account, Oineus himself is the father of her child.[174] In any case, if the play was about Periboia, it probably concerned some form of harm to kin.

■ Aiskhylos's *Kallisto* (Some Form of Harm to Blood Kin).   It is uncertain which version of the Kallisto myth Aiskhylos followed. Radt cites Hesiod fragment 163MW, which gives two versions of the story, both concerned with harm to *philoi*.[175] In one version, Kallisto, companion of Artemis, is raped by Zeus and turned into a bear by the goddess, in which form she gives birth to a son. Kallisto is later about to be killed by her son, but Zeus rescues her, "because of kinship," and places her among the stars (ὑπὸ δὲ τοῦ ἰδίου υἱοῦ διωκομένην . . . καὶ ἀναιρεῖσθαι μέλλουσαν . . . ὁ Ζεὺς διὰ τὴν συγγένειαν αὐτὴν ἐξείλετο). In the second version also, Zeus rapes Kallisto. Her father, Lykaon, then hosts (ἐξένιζεν) Zeus and serves him the child as food. Zeus punishes Lykaon and puts the child back together again. Later, son marries mother, in ignorance (ἀγνοήσας τὴν μητέρα †γῆμαι†) and they are about to be put to death for this crime. Zeus rescues them "because of kinship" (διὰ τὴν συγγένειαν), just as in the first version.

■ Euripides' *Kresphontes* (Parent-Child).   For harm to kin in this play, we have the authority of Aristotle: "In the *Kresphontes*, Merope is about to kill her son; she does not kill him, but recognized him" (ἐν τῷ Κρεσφόντῃ ἡ Μερόπη μέλλει τὸν υἱὸν ἀποκτείνειν, ἀποκτείνει δὲ οὔ, ἀλλ' ἀνεγνώρισε).[176] According to Hyginus, Merope is about to kill Kresphontes because she believes that he is her son's murderer.[177] Hyginus's account is confirmed by Arist. *NE* 1111a11–12: οἰηθείη δ' ἄν τις καὶ τὸν υἱὸν πολέμιον εἶναι ὥσπερ Μερόπη ("One might also think that one's son is an enemy, as Merope does").

■ Euripides' *Oineus* (Sibling-Sibling).   The subject of this play was the enmity between two brothers, Oineus and Agrios, and their descendants. In the myth, Agrios, or his sons, or both, deprive Oineus of his rule and take over his kingdom. Diomedes, the son of Tydeus and grandson of Oineus, then kills his grandfather's enemies. According to some accounts, he restores his grandfather to power; in another account, two of the sons of Agrios escape him and kill Oineus at the hearth of Telephos: "Lying in wait at the hearth of Telephos in Arkadia, they killed the old man" (ἐνεδρεύσαντες περὶ τὴν Τηλέφου ἑστίαν τῆς Ἀρκαδίας τὸν πρεσβύτην ἀπέκτειναν).[178] A central scene in this play, if Webster is right, represented Agrios threatening Oineus at an altar.[179] Fragment 566N, which mentions the triumph of gain over kinship ("For the sake of gain, even kinship suffers": κέρδους δ' ἕκατι καὶ τὸ συγγενὲς νοσεῖ), may have alluded to an episode in which kin harmed kin. An episode of harm to kin outside the plot is alluded to in fragment 558N, where Diomedes mentions the fratricide committed by his father Tydeus:[180]

> . . . ἔνθεν αἷμα συγγενὲς φυγὼν
> Τυδεύς, τόκος μὲν Οἰνέως, πατὴρ δ᾽ ἐμός,
> ᾤκησεν Ἄργος . . .

> . . . where, fleeing after shedding kindred blood,
> Tydeus, child of Oineus, and my father,
> settled in Argos . . .

■ Euripides' *Tennes* (Parent-Child). Although the attribution of this play is debated, its subject is not in doubt. The stepmother of Tennes accuses him of attempted rape to his father, Kyknos, who tries to kill Tennes by shutting him up in a chest and casting him adrift at sea. Tennes, however, lands on an island and is saved. At the command of Apollo, Kyknos names the island Tenedos and kills his wife, who has slandered Tennes.[181] In this plot, then, amphimetric strife is about to lead to murder of son by father.

■ Sophokles' *Tereus* (Parent-Child). The subject of this play was the story of Prokne and Philomela, daughters of Pandion. Tereus marries Prokne and they have a child, Itys. Tereus then rapes Prokne's sister, Philomela, and cuts out her tongue to prevent her from telling her sister what he has done. Philomela however, reveals what has happened by weaving a picture. Prokne then kills Itys and serves him up as food to Tereus, who, when he finds out, is about to kill the sisters. The gods, however, turn them all into birds.[182] Aristotle refers to this story in *Poetics* 16.1454b36–37: "In Sophokles' *Tereus*, [recognition comes about by means of] the voice of the shuttle" (see frag. 595R). This play was especially rich in harm to *philoi*. Brother-in-law raped sister-in-law; mother killed son; father ate son; husband tried to kill wife and sister-in-law.

Reciprocal Relationships (4 Plays): Marriage, 1;
Suppliancy, 1; Xenia, 1; Some Form of Harm to
Philoi, 1

■ Euripides' *Alkmene* (Marriage). This play dramatized the story of Amphitryon's wife, Alkmene, with whom Zeus also sleeps. Amphitryon becomes suspicious of his wife and is about to burn her on the altar at which she has taken refuge when Zeus sends a storm to put out the fire and save her.[183] In this play, then, a wife, who was also a suppliant at an altar, was about to be killed by her husband.

■ Sophokles' *Aias Lokros* (*Lokrian Aias*) (Suppliancy). This play was concerned with Aias's abduction of Kassandra from Athena's temple after the defeat of the Trojans, and with his subsequent escape from punishment, perhaps by taking refuge at Athena's altar.[184] In fragment 10cR (P. Oxy. 3151),

Athena compares someone, Aias most likely, to Lykourgos, who killed his son at an altar.[185] Thus, violation of an unrelated suppliant would seem to be compared to kin murder in this play.

■ Aiskhylos's *Herakleidai* (*The Sons of Herakles*) (Some Form of Harm to Philos). There are two kinds of conjectures about the subject of this play. Some believe that its subject was the same as that of Euripides' play of the same title, in which the children of Herakles are pursued by their kin Eurystheus and saved after supplication. Others argue that it was about the events covered in Sophokles' *Women of Trakhis*.[186] If the former theory is accepted, the play was about threats to suppliants by a relative; if the latter, it was about husband-killing.

■ Sophokles' *Helenes Harpage* (*The Rape of Helen*) (Xenia). Even though only the title of this play remains, it is sufficient to give the subject of the play: Paris's abduction of Helen from Sparta.[187] The title, then, suggests that the play dealt was about violation of *xenia*.

3. Category III. Subject Groups Without Violation of *Philia*

Plays are listed according to groups.[188] Each group consists of plays about the same subject. Violation of *philia* is uncertain or unlikely in more than half of the plays in each group.

> *Akhilleus Myths (8 Plays)*: Xenia, 1; *Suppliancy*, 1;
> *Uncertain*, 3; *Unlikely*, 3

These eight plays are of particular interest because some of them dramatized episodes also treated in the *Iliad*: the death of Patroklos and the ransom of Hektor. In the epic, Akhilleus is indirectly responsible for the death of Patroklos because he sends his friend to battle in his armor. Akhilleus deeply mourns the death of Patroklos, and he blames himself for not defending his friend: "May I die at once, since I was not going to help my companion when he was killed" (*Il.* 18.98–99). There is, however, no suggestion that Akhilleus is a kind of murderer. Moreover, the fact that Patroklos was brought up in Peleus's house as a suppliant-exile (*Il.* 23.84–90) is not stressed in the epic, and there is no erotic relationship between the two men. In the episode of the ransoming of Hektor, there is much emphasis on the danger to Priam from his enemy Akhilleus, but little stress on the danger to Akhilleus from the wrath of the gods.[189]

Aiskhylos wrote a trilogy[190] about Akhilleus: *Myrmidones* (*The Myrmidons*), *Nereides* (*The Daughters of Nereus*), and a play titled either *Phryges* or *Hektoros Lytra* (*The Phrygians* or *The Ransom of Hektor*). The subject of

Myrmidones was Akhilleus's refusal to fight (frag. 132R) and the death of Patroklos while dressed in Akhilleus's armor (frags. 135–39R). In Aiskhylos, in contrast to the Homeric account, Akhilleus and Patroklos are lovers,[191] and their relationship may have been an important aspect of the play. It is also possible (although the fragments give no evidence for this) that the two men were cousins in this play, as they were in Hesiod.[192] Moreover, one fragment likens Patroklos's death in Akhilleus's armor to the death of an eagle shot by a feathered arrow:

> ὧδ' ἐστὶ μύθων τῶν Λιβυστικῶν κλέος,
> πληγέντ' ἀτράκτῳ τοξικῷ τὸν αἰετὸν
> εἰπεῖν ἰδόντα μηχανὴν πτερώματος·
> "τάδ' οὐχ ὑπ' ἄλλων, ἀλλὰ τοῖς αὐτῶν πτεροῖς ἁλισκόμεσθα." (139R)

> This is the famous story which the Libyans tell;
> an eagle, when a bow-shot arrow pierced it, said
> —seeing this feathered thing which caused his death—
> "so not by any other hands, but by our own
> plumage we die."[193]

Thus, while this play seems to have been concerned with harm to an unrelated companion, the idea expressed in the passage just quoted, like the erotic relationship between the two men, goes a long way toward assimilating to kin murder Akhilleus's act of sending Patroklos to battle: Patroklos and Akhilleus were both responsible for the former's death.[194]

In the *Nereides*, the second play of Aiskhylos's trilogy, the Nereids brought Akhilleus his new arms,[195] and he may then have fought Hektor.[196] The subject matter makes it unlikely that this play was about harm to *philoi*. Aiskhylos's third play, *Phryges*, was concerned with the ransom of Hektor, as its alternative title, *Hektoros Lytra*, indicates.[197] Hermes, in ordering Akhilleus to give Hektor's corpse to Priam, warns him against the wrath of the gods and avenging Justice:[198] ἡμῶν γε μέντοι νέμεσις ἐσθ' ὑπερτέρα, / καὶ τοῦ θανόντος ἡ Δίκη πράσσει κότον ("However, our [sc. the gods'] nemesis is more powerful, and Justice collects payment for the wrath of the dead": frag. 266R, 4–5).[199] This fragment suggests that, unlike the epic treatment (see chapter 1, section 2), this play may have stressed the dangers Akhilleus incurred by maltreating Hektor's corpse and refusing to give it up to the suppliant Priam.

We know little about Sophokles' *Phryges* (*The Phrygians*) and *Syndeipnoi* or *Syndeipnon* (*Those Who Dine Together*, or *The Dinner*). Many think that *Phryges*, like Aiskhylos's play of the same name, concerned the ransom of Hektor. However, this is far from certain.[200] The *Syndeipnoi* dramatized either the quarrel between Akhilleus and Odysseus mentioned in *Odyssey* 8.75–82 or a quarrel between Akhilleus and Agamemnon at Tenedos.[201] There is no evidence that this quarrel between unrelated companions was in some way assimilated to a quarrel among *philoi*. Sophokles' *Troilos* concerned Akhilleus's killing of Troilos at Apollo's temple while Troilos is exercising horses.[202] The setting is suggestive, and it is possible that this act was represented as the killing of a suppliant,[203] but there is no direct evidence for this.

The papyrus hypothesis[204] of Euripides' *Skyrioi* (The Men of Skyros) gives part of its plot. Thetis places the young Akhilleus, disguised as a girl, in the house of Lykomedes of Skyros in hopes that he will avoid death at Troy. Lykomedes, not knowing who he is, brings him up with his daughter Deidameia, whom Akhilleus impregnates in secret: ὁ δ[ὲ λαθρραῖ— / ος [ὑπο]κλέψας τὴν Δηιδά[μειαν ἔγ— / κυ[ον ἐπ]οίησεν ("And he, stealing her away in secret, made Deidameia pregnant"). The hypothesis goes on to state, before breaking off, that as a result of an oracle the Greeks sent Diomedes to do something. Euripides' play, then, was about Akhilleus's violation of *xenia*. The subject of Sophokles' *Skyrioi* is disputed, some arguing that it dramatized the hiding of Akhilleus at Lykomedes' house and his recognition by Odysseus, others holding that it concerned the taking of Neoptolemos, the son of Akhilleus and Deidameia, to Troy.[205]

We can be fairly certain, then, that Euripides' *Skyrioi* was about harm to *xenoi*, and it is likely that Aiskhylos's *Phryges* was a suppliant play. The evidence we have for the other six Akhilleus plays, however, does not indicate that harm to *philoi* was an important element. Playwrights may have tended to create more "epic" plots about Akhilleus, the epic hero. On the other hand, it is possible that complete texts of these apparently exceptional plays would indicate that some of them actually did feature some form of harm to *philoi*. Although harm to *philoi* is uncertain in three plays, Sophokles' *Phryges* may have been a suppliant drama like Aiskhylos's and Euripides' *Suppliants*; Sophokles' *Troilos* may have concerned violation of a suppliant, and Sophokles' *Skyrioi* may have dramatized violation of *xenia*. Harm to *philoi* is unlikely in Aiskhylos's *Nereides* and *Myrmidones* and in Sophokles' *Syndeipnoi*. However, in the *Myrmidones*, Aiskhylos appears to have gone a long way toward assimilating harm to an unrelated companion to harm to a *philos*, and it is possible that Sophokles did the same in the *Syndeipnoi*. Perhaps most significant is the fact that there is no clear evidence that any of these tragedies focused on harm of enemy by enemy. In contrast, harming enemies is central to the epic treatments of these same subjects.

Bellerophon Myths (3 Plays): Xenia, 1;
Uncertain, 1; Unlikely, 1

Euripides' *Stheneboia* concerns violation of *xenia*. The hypothesis gives the plot. Proitos, king of Tiryns and husband of Stheneboia, purifies Bellerophon (αὐτὸς μὲν ἥγνισε τοῦ μύσους), who has fled Korinth because of a murder. Stheneboia is in love with their *xenos* Bellerophon (ἡ γυνὴ δὲ αὐτοῦ τὸν ξένον ἠγάπησε), and when he refuses her, she accuses him falsely to her husband. Proitos tries to have Bellerophon killed, but is unsuccessful; after various episodes, Bellerophon kills Stheneboia.[206] According to Apollodoros 2.3.1, the murder Bellerophon committed in Korinth was that of his brother.[207]

Some of the fragments concern Bellerophon's *xenia* relationship with Proitos and his refusal to injure his host by yielding to Stheneboia's desires. He speaks the Prologue:

ξένον γὰρ ἱκέτην τῆσδ' ἔμ' ἐλθόντα στέγης

. . . .

ἐγὼ δὲ θεσμοὺς Ζῆνά θ' ἱκέσιον σέβων
Προῖτόν τε τιμῶν, ὅς μ' ἐδέξατ' εἰς δόμους
λιπόντα γαῖαν Σισύφου φόνον τ' ἐμῆς
ἔνιψε χειρὸς αἷμ' ἐπισφάξας νέον
οὐπώποτ' ἠθέλησα δέξασθαι λόγους,
οὐδ' εἰς νοσοῦντας ὑβρίσαι δόμους ξένος,
μισῶν ἔρωτα δεινόν, ὃς φθείρει βροτούς.

[F]or when I came under his roof here as guest and suppliant . . . I have reverence however for Zeus the god of suppliants and his laws, and honour for Proetus who received me in his house after I left Sisyphus's land, and who cleansed bloodshed from my hands with a sacrifice of fresh blood over them; I have never yet been willing to entertain that talk of hers, nor to violate a troubled household while I am its guest, from my hatred of the dangerous love which destroys people. (frag. 661, Collard, lines 7, 15–21; Collard's translation)

In fragment 664 Stheneboia speaks of "the Corinthian *xenos*," and in fragment 667 someone asks, "Who honors a man who deceives his *xenos*?" (τίς ἄνδρα τιμᾷ ξεναπάτην;).[208]

Stheneboia is based on an incident in *Iliad* 6.155–95. In the epic version, Proitos conquers Bellerophon in war; he is not Bellerophon's host, nor has Bellerophon committed murder. After Proitos's wife falsely accuses Bellerophon, Proitos drives Bellerophon out of his country and sends him to Lykia to be killed, because *sebas* (reverence) prevents his killing him directly (167). The story has a happy ending, for Bellerophon obtains the king's daughter and half of the Lykian kingdom.

Some have claimed that Sophokles' *Iobates* concerned some aspect of the Stheneboia story; others deny this or are dubious.[209]

Euripides' *Bellerophontes* represented an event subsequent to the Stheneboia story, Bellerophon's flight to heaven. It is uncertain what relationship the latter story had to the former. Collard's analysis is helpful:

> The high-point, perhaps the climax of the action, was Bellerophon's attempt to scale Heaven on Pegasus the winged horse, in order to confront the gods with their apparent injustice. But Pegasus threw him off; he re-appeared crippled by the fall and in rags, and may have died at the play's end. . . . This much of the action can be established. . . . [I]t is not known whether Euripides was "completing" the story of Bellerophon her [sc. Sthenoboea's] killer by showing him here humiliated by the gods for his inhumanity to her. . . . Euripides innovated with Stheneboea's killing and in *Bell.* he may have used the version in which she took her own life from shame . . . before the play began. . . . The central fact of the play for us is the Pegasus-flight, but accounts of the myth vary in giving Bellerophon's motive in seeking to reach the gods and remonstrate.[210]

Although harm to *philoi* may have been a central concern in this play, as it was in *Stheneboia*, this seems unlikely, given the evidence we have.

In the case of the Bellerophon plays, then, there is one instance of violation of *xenia*, one uncertainty, and one play in which there is clear evidence of theomachy but not of harm to *philoi*.

Hypsipyle Myths (6 Plays): Xenia, 1; Uncertain, 5

There are three main myths about Hypsipyle treated in the fragments. First, when the other Lemnian women kill their male relatives, Hypsipyle manages to avoid killing her father, Thoas. Second, when the Argonauts arrive in Lemnos, she sleeps with Jason and bears two sons to him. Third, Hypsipyle, now nurse of the infant son of Lykourgos and Eurydike of Nemea, accidentally causes the death of the child.

The murder of the Lemnian men by their wives may have been the subject of Aiskhylos's *Lemniai* or *Lemnioi* (*Lemnian Women* or *Lemnian Men*),[211] although if the play was entitled *Lemnioi* it is possible that it was about Philoktetes, who was abandoned on Lemnos by his fellow Greeks.[212]

Aiskhylos's *Hypsipyle* concerned the story of the Lemnian women and Jason and his Argonauts. The Argonauts arrive in Lemnos and are forcibly prevented from sailing until they swear to sleep with the women.[213] Even though harm to *philoi* does not appear to have been prominent in this play, the murder of the Lemnian men was in the mythological background. Aiskhylos's *Kabeiroi* was also about the Argonauts, and some speculate that it concerned the Lemnos episode.[214] In Sophokles' *Lemniai*, the Lemnian women actually joined battle with the Argonauts.[215] Pearson conjectures that the climax of the play was the departure of Jason, Hypsipyle's lover, and that it may have ended with Hypsipyle's being sold into slavery by the Lemnian women after they discover that she has not killed her father Thoas when the other women killed their male *philoi*.[216] If this is correct, the subject of the play may have been violation of *philia* in the form of desertion of "wife" by "husband."

The sequel to the Lemnian episodes was the subject of Euripides' *Hypsipyle*, of which many lines survive. Hypsipyle tells of her flight from Lemnos following her refusal to kill her father when the other Lemnian women kill their husbands (frag. 64 Bond, 72–82). She is now nurse of the infant son of Lykourgos and Eurydike of Nemea. Hypsipyle's sons by Jason, from whom she has been separated, arrive, and she receives them as *xenoi* into her master's house. However, mother and children do not recognize one another. When Amphiaraos arrives with others going to Thebes, he asks her to show him where he can obtain water for a sacrifice. She puts down the baby to help him, and it is killed by a snake.[217] Eurydike is about to have Hypsipyle put to death in the belief that she killed the child deliberately (frag. 60 Bond, 35–36) when Amphiaraos arrives and witnesses on her behalf. After a stay of execution followed by imprisonment, Hypsipyle recognizes her sons and is saved.[218]

Although the central *pathos* of this play is not an act of harm to kin, the fragments allow us to see that *philia* nevertheless played an important role.

Hypsipyle claims that she is like a mother to the child of whose murder she is accused:

ὡς τοῦ θανεῖν μὲν οὕνεκ' [οὐ μέγα στέν]ω,
εἰ δὲ κτανεῖν τὸ τέκνον οὐκ ὀρθ[ῶ]ς δοκῶ,
τοὐμὸν τιθήνημ', ὃν ἐπ' ἐμαῖσιν ἀγκάλαις
πλὴν οὐ τεκοῦσα τἄλλα γ' ὡς ἐμὸν τέκνον
στέργουσ' ἔφερβον, ὠφέλημ' ἐμοὶ μέγα. (frag. 60 Bond, 8–12)

I do not greatly lament that I am to die,
but I do care if I am unjustly thought to have killed the child,
my nursling, whom I loved and nourished in my arms,
a great benefit to me, in all respects my own,
save that I did not give birth to it.

Hypsipyle's relationship to Amphiaraos is also portrayed as a kind of *xenia* characterized by mutual favors. When she supplicates him, asking him to rescue her from imminent death, she reminds Amphiaraos that the child was killed because she led him to the water he needed:

[κ]αιρὸν γὰρ ἥκεις τοῖς ἐμοῖσιν ἐν κακοῖς,
[ῥ]ῦσαί με· διὰ γὰρ σὴν ἀπόλλυμαι χάριν.
μέλλω τε θνήσκειν, δεσμίαν τέ μ' εἰσορᾷς
πρὸς σοῖσι γόνασιν, ἣ τόθ' εἱπόμην ξένοις. (frag. 60 Bond, 27–30)

You have arrived in good time, in my present dangers,
to save me, since for your sake I perish.
I am going to die, and you see me bound
at your knees, who at that time attended [you and your men, as my] *xenoi*.

Finally, if Godfrey Bond correctly reconstructs the portions of the play not covered by the papyrus fragments, Hypsipyle's rescue appears to be connected in some way with the sons whom she received as *xenoi* into her master's house without knowing their identity.[219] Although Page speculates that the sons may have been appointed as executioners of Hypsipyle, there is no textual evidence to support this.[220]

Thus, *Hypsipyle* appears to have been in some respects like *Alkestis*. Hypsipyle extended *xenia* to her sons and to Amphiaraos and was saved by those whom she had welcomed. The play was also concerned with violation of *xenia* in that Hypsipyle was falsely accused of violation of a relationship with her nursling that resembled *xenia*. She was, moreover, about to be put to death by Eurydike, who was much like a *xenê* to her.

Aiskhylos's *Nemea* was also concerned with this story of Hypsipyle and the death of the child.[221] We cannot say, however, whether or not his version had overtones of harm to *philoi*, as that of Euripides did.

Of the six *Hypsipyle* plays, only Euripides' *Hypsipyle* was concerned with violation of *xenia*. The other five may well have represented some form of harm to *philoi* also, but we do not have enough information to decide.

Memnon Myths (3 Plays): Unlikely, 3

The story of Memnon was given in the lost epic *Aithiopis*. During the Trojan War, Memnon kills Antilokhos and is in turn killed by Akhilleus. He is then made immortal by his mother Eos.[222] Aiskhylos and Sophokles each wrote a *Memnon* about this story, but we know nothing of the specifics. If Mette's conjecture is correct and Aiskhylos's play featured the combat between Memnon and Antilokhos,[223] this play had an epic plot, in which enemy killed enemy. Aiskhylos's *Psykhostasia* (*The Weighing of Souls*) is generally thought to have focused on an episode prior to the combat of Memnon and Akhilleus. Zeus weighs the souls of Memnon and Akhilleus in a scale while Thetis and Eos stand by, each pleading for her son's life.[224] It seems likely, then, that this play was concerned with enemy killing enemy. It is worth noting, however, that one Memnon myth resembled Sophokles' *Eurypylos*, in which Astyoke is bribed with a golden vine to send her son to Troy. According to Servius, Memnon's father, Tithonos, accepted the same bribe to send his son to Troy.[225]

Minos Myths (6 Plays): Marriage, 1; Xenia, 1;
Uncertain, 4

Minos of Krete figured in a number of plays. Euripides' *Kretes* (*The Men of Krete*) was based on the story of Pasiphaë, the wife of Minos, who falls in love with a bull. Daidalos constructs an artificial cow for her so that she can mate with the bull, and she subsequently gives birth to the Minotaur. Minos's "imprisonment of her [sc. Pasiphaë], and her intended death . . . are Euripides' innovation in the myth."[226] The play perhaps ended with Pasiphaë's miraculous release by a god, the arrest and imprisonment of Daidalos and his son Ikaros by Minos, and their escape.[227] The surviving fragments clearly refer to Pasiphaë's love for the bull and to Minos's intended punishment:

> . . . ἐς τί γὰρ βοὸς
> βλέψασ' ἐδήχθην θυμὸν αἰχίστῃ νόσῳ;
> . . . .
> . . . πρὸς τάδ' εἴτε ποντίαν
> κτείνειν δοκεῖ σοι, κτε[ι]ν'· (frag. /472e K, 11–12, 35–36: Collard)

> What was there I saw in a bull to eat at my heart, in such shameful affliction?
> . . . .
> So then, if you have decided to kill me in the sea, go on, kill me!
> (Collard's translation)

In this play, then, wife deceived husband, who in turn attempted to put her to death.

In Sophokles' *Kamikoi* (*The Men of Kamikos*), Minos pursues Daidalos after his escape from prison, where he was sent after helping Theseus escape from the labyrinth. Daidalos is received by King Kokalos at Kamikos, where Minos discovers him. Kokalos promises to turn Daidalos over to Minos and receives Minos as *xenos* (ἐξένισεν αὐτόν:).[228] The daughters of Kokalos prevent the surrender of Daidalos to his enemy by boiling Minos in his bath.[229] This story, then, was about treachery to a *xenos*, whether Daidalos or Minos or both.

About Sophokles' *Daidalos* we know nothing certain; some believe it to have been a satyr play.[230] Talos, a bronze robot that guarded Krete for Minos and kept strangers from approaching, appeared in it.[231] If Talos was a central figure, it is possible that violation of *xenia* was an important issue in the play.

Finally, three plays were concerned with the story of Glaukos, son of Minos. In Aiskhylos's *Kressai* (*The Cretan Women*), Sophokles' play with the title *Manteis* (*Prophets*) or *Polyidos*, and Euripides' *Polyidos*, the child Glaukos, son of Minos and Pasiphaë, falls into a vessel of honey and dies. Minos requires the seer Polyidos, who found the body, to bring the boy back to life and shuts him up in the tomb with the corpse. Polyidos there discovers a magic herb by means of which he restores the child to life.[232] This is not an obvious case of violation of *philia*. It is possible, however, that if Polyidos was the guest of Minos, the plots of these plays involved harm to a *xenos*.

Of the six Minos plays, one (Euripides' *Kretes*) was about harm between husband and wife, and one (Sophokles' *Kamikoi*) was concerned with harm to a *xenos*. Certainty is not possible in the case of the other four plays (Aiskhylos's *Kressai*, Sophokles' *Daidalos* and *Manteis*, and Euripides' *Polyidos*), although violation of *xenia* may have been an issue in one or more of them.

Odysseus Myths (9 Plays): Parent-Child, 1; Child-Parent, 1; Uncertain, 4; Unlikely, 3

Several plays dramatized the story of Odysseus after his return to Ithaka. Aiskhylos wrote a trilogy that probably included, in some order, *Ostologoi* (*The Bone Gatherers*), *Penelope*, and *Psykhagagoi* (*The Summoners of Dead Souls*).[233] The *Ostologoi* was probably about the burial of the suitors after Odysseus killed them.[234] Harm to *philoi* does not immediately appear to have been prominent in this plot. It is possible, however, that the play was about the maltreatment of the suppliant Odysseus (see *Od.* 19.303–4) by the suitors. Fragment 179R mentions the *hybris* of Eurymakhos to Odysseus:

⟨ΟΔ⟩ Εὐρύμαχος †οὐκ ἄλλος† οὐδὲν ἧσσον ⟨—⟩
ὕβριζ᾽ ὑβρισμοὺς οὐκ ἐναισίμους ἐμοι·

<ODYSSEUS>: Eurymakhos and no other, no less <—>
committed unseemly outrages against me.

Although nothing certain is known about the plot of the *Penelope*,[235] Mette speculates that it concerned the homecoming of Odysseus.[236]

Aiskhylos's *Psykhagagoi* is particularly interesting because it contains an instance of a striking exception to the rule that tragedy tends to focus on those versions of the myths in which harm to *philoi* occurs. This play is probably based on the *Nekyia* of *Odyssey* 11, in which Odysseus speaks with the souls of dead.[237] In fragment 275R, Teiresias prophesies that Odysseus will be killed by a fishbone dropped on his head by a bird. This is clearly a transformation of the story of Odysseus's death in the epic *Telegony*, in which he was killed in ignorance by Telegonos, his son and Kirke's.[238] In this prophecy, at least, Aiskhylos avoided the kin murder of an earlier version. It seems unlikely that this play centered on harm to *philoi*.

Two of Sophokles' plays about Odysseus certainly were about harm to kin. In the *Euryalos*, father kills son. After his return to Ithaka, Odysseus has a son, Euryalos, by Euippe, with whom he slept while being entertained as a guest by her father. When Euryalos grows up, his mother sends him to Odysseus, who happens to be absent. Penelope learns who he is and induces Odysseus to kill him, saying that Euryalos is plotting against him.[239] The subject of Sophokles' *Odysseus Akanthoplex* (*Odysseus Wounded By the Spine*) was the killing of Odysseus by his son. Telegonos, the son of Kirke, kills his father Odysseus in ignorance; recognition follows.[240]

Other Odysseus plays by Sophokles seem less likely to have focused on harm to *philoi*, although so little is known about them that we cannot be certain either way. In *Odysseus Mainomenos* (*The Madness of Odysseus*), Odysseus pretends to be mad in order to avoid going to Troy. However, by threatening the infant Telemakhos, Palamedes reveals that he is really sane.[241] The subject of *Nausikaa* or *Plyntriai* (*The Women Washing Clothes*) was the story, recounted in *Odyssey* 6, of Odysseus's meeting with Nausikaa when he arrives in the land of the Phaiakians and is given hospitality by her.[242] In the Homeric version, there are no serious threats to a *xenos*, but this might have been an issue in Sophokles' play. Pearson identifies the *Niptra* (*The Footwashing*) with *Odysseus Akanthoplex*; Radt lists the two as separate plays. If *Niptra* was a separate play, it concerned the washing of Odysseus's feet by the nurse Eurykleia (*Od.* 19).[243] In the *Odyssey*, the nurse recognizes her master when she sees his scar and is about to reveal his presence to his enemies. Odysseus prevents her, saying, "Why do you wish to destroy me?" (τίη μ' ἐθέλεις ὀλέσαι: 19.482).[244] It is possible that Sophokles' play dramatized this action as a threat to a suppliant.

Finally, Sophokles' *Lakainai* (*The Lakonian Women*) was concerned with an episode at Troy: the stealing of the statue of Athena from Troy by Odysseus and Diomedes.[245] Fragment 799R, if it belongs to this play,[246] appears to be taken from a speech of Odysseus attacking Diomedes on the occasion of a quarrel between the two on their return from the theft. Odysseus tries to murder Diomedes in order to enjoy sole credit for the theft, but Diomedes sees the flash of the sword in time to escape and makes Odysseus walk in front of him.[247] Odysseus's speech in this fragment mentions kin killing and cannibalism committed by Diomedes' father Tydeus:

ἐγὼ δ' ἐρῶ σοι δεινὸν οὐδέν, οὔθ' ὅπως
φυγὰς πατρῴας ἐξελήλασαι χθονός,
οὔθ' ὡς ὁ Τυδεὺς ἀνδρὸς αἷμα συγγενὲς
κτείνας ἐν Ἄργει ξεῖνος ὢν οἰκίζεται,
οὔθ' ὡς πρὸ Θηβῶν ὠμοβρῶς ἐδαίσατο
τὸν Ἀστάκειον παῖδα διὰ κάρα τεμών

I will say nothing terrible to you, neither how
you were driven into exile from your father's land
nor how Tydeus, having shed the blood
of a kindred man, settled in Argos as a *xenos*,
nor how before Thebes he made a savage feast,
cutting open the head of the son of Astakeios.

The speech alludes to two unsavory incidents in the history of Tydeus, son of Aitolian Oineus. After killing a relative, he fled to King Adrastos in Argos. Moreover, Tydeus engaged in an act of cannibalism at Thebes.[248] The mention of these incidents may be some indication that harm to *philoi* figured in the play in other ways also, although the evidence we have points to a plot centered on harm between unrelated companions.

Of nine Odysseus plays, then, only two (Soph. *Euryalos* and *Odysseus Akanthoplex*) certainly were concerned with harm to *philoi* and were completely unlike the Homeric epics in this respect. In the other tragedies, harm to *philoi* is either uncertain (Ais. *Penelope* and Soph. *Odysseus Mainomenos*, *Nausikaa*, and *Niptra*) or unlikely (Ais. *Psykhagogoi* and *Ostologoi* and Soph. *Lakainai*). Although it is possible that these other plays also dramatized harm to *philoi* to a greater extent than our surviving evidence indicates, it is interesting to note that most of these tragedies about an epic hero appear, like the Akhilleus plays, to have followed an "epic" treatment of their subject matter in giving little prominence to harm to *philoi*.

Palamedes Myths (5 Plays): Unlikely, 5

Each of the three tragedians wrote a tragedy entitled *Palamedes*, each of which was about betrayal of companion by unrelated companion. Odysseus is angry with Palamedes because it was he who proved Odysseus to be sane when Odysseus feigned madness to avoid going to Troy (see Soph. *Odysseus Mainomenos*). During the Trojan War, Odysseus falsely accuses Palamedes of treachery and plants barbarian gold in his tent in order to substantiate his charges. As a result, Palamedes is killed by the Greek army.[249] Sophokles' *Nauplios Katapleon* (*Nauplios Sailing In*) and *Nauplios Pyrkaeus* (*Nauplios Lighting Fire*) concerned subsequent events when Palamedes' father Nauplios takes vengeance for the death of his son. In *Pyrkaeus*, Nauplios lures Greek ships to their destruction by lighting a beacon. The *Katapleon* probably concerned another form of vengeance, perhaps Nauplios's debauching of the wives of the Akhaians, by, for example, helping Aigisthos to seduce Klytaimestra.[250] These plays, then, also focused on enmity among unrelated companions, and there is no evidence to show that they might have assimilated the relationship between companions to one of kinship or *xenia*.

Philoktetes Myths (3 Plays): Xenia, 1; Uncertain, 2

Aiskhylos and Euripides wrote tragedies titled *Philoktetes*, both of which had a plot similar to that of Sophokles' extant play: Philoktetes' bow was taken by Odysseus, either by theft or force, and Philoktetes was brought to Troy.[251] The appearance of Neoptolemos in this story was Sophokles' innovation.[252]

In Euripides' *Philoktetes*, Diomedes, not Neoptolemos, accompanied Odysseus.[253] As is the case in Sophokles' extant play, a major issue seems to have been the betrayal of a *xenos*. In fragment 790N, Odysseus "pretends to be a friend of Palamedes, and Philoktetes invites him into his cave,"[254] saying, "The things within are vile to see, *xenos*" (δύσμορφα μέντοι τἄνδον εἰσιδεῖν, ξένε).[255]

In Aiskhylos's *Philoktetes*, Odysseus was "shrewd and crafty,"[256] and he deceived Philoktetes by means of a false story.[257] This play also was concerned with the deception of a companion, although we cannot be certain whether or not a *xenia* relationship was also established, as was the case in Sophokles' extant play and probably in Euripides' tragedy as well.

Finally, Sophokles' *Philoktetes ho en Troiai* (*Philoktetes in Troy*) was concerned with the sequel to his *Philoktetes*. Its subject was probably the cure of Philoktetes and his killing of Paris.[258] Nothing in the fragments indicates that harm to *philoi* was an issue. It is possible, however, that a hint is given in Sophokles' *Philoktetes*, where Herakles prophesies that Philoktetes and Neoptolemos will take Troy together (1434–37) and warns them against committing impious acts during the sack of the city: "Keep this in mind: when you sack the land, be reverent toward the gods" (τοῦτο δ' ἐννοεῖθ', ὅταν πορθῆτε γαῖαν, εὐσεβεῖν τὰ πρὸς θεούς: 1440–41). This is a clear reference to Neoptolemos's killing of Priam at the altar of Zeus.[259] Although Philoktetes himself does not appear to have been guilty of such things in myth, it is possible that the play dramatized the impious deeds of others.

Sisyphos Myths (2 Plays): Unlikely, 1; Uncertain, 1

Aiskhylos wrote two plays about Sisyphos: *Sisyphos Drapetes* and *Sisyphos Petrokylistes* (*Sisyphos the Runaway* and *Sisyphos the Stone Roller*), of which the first probably and the second possibly were satyr plays.[260] I include only *Petrokylistes* as a tragedy. In this play, in which there is no evidence for harm to *philos*, Sisyphos was punished in the underworld by being forced to roll a stone uphill in vain.[261]

We know nothing about the plot of Sophokles' *Sisyphos*.[262] Among the possibilities discussed by Pearson is the story of Tyro: "Sisyphus, in feud with his brother Salmoneus, was told by Apollo that, if his brother's daughter Tyro should bear children to him, they would avenge him on Salmoneus. But Tyro, hearing of their destiny, destroyed the children whom Sisyphos had begotten."[263] Although it is possible, then, that the subject of this play was enmity between brothers and child-killing, I classify the play as "uncertain."

Trojan Horse Myths (2 Plays): Unlikely, 2

The subject of Sophokles' *Sinon* is the story recounted in Virgil, *Aeneid* 2.57–233, which may follow the play fairly closely.[264] According to the *Aeneid*, after the Greeks construct the Trojan Horse and pretend to sail away, the Greek Sinon allows himself to be captured by Trojans, and accuses the Greeks of treachery in order to persuade the Trojans to bring the horse into the city. Laokoön, a priest of Apollo who warns the Trojans not to bring the horse into Troy, is killed by snakes. In Sophokles' *Laokoön*, the Trojans are feasting in the belief that the war is over when Laokoön and his son are attacked by the serpents. Alarmed by the omen, Aeneas and his family leave Troy for Ida.[265] Ancient sources give versions in which Laokoön is punished for offending Apollo in one way or another,[266] none of which appear to be connected with harm to *philoi*.

4. Category IV. Individual Plays Without Violation of *Philia*

In these six plays, listed individually, violation of *philia* is uncertain or unlikely.[267]

Uncertain, 4; Unlikely, 2

■ Aiskhylos's *Aitn(ai)ai* (*The Women of Aitna*) (Uncertain).   This subject of this play was a love affair between Zeus and the nymph Thaleia. After being impregnated by Zeus, she is hidden in the earth through fear of Hera and from there bears two children.[268] This story does not appear to have anything to do with harm to *philoi*, but so little is known about the play that we cannot be certain how it treated this subject.

■ Aiskhylos's *Epigonoi* (*The Afterborn*) (Uncertain).   The subject of this play is usually thought to have been the conquest of Thebes by the sons of the attackers defeated in the extant *Seven Against Thebes*.[269] Nothing is known about how this story was treated.

■ Aiskhylos's *Kares* or *Europe* (Unlikely).   This play concerned the death and burial of Sarpedon, the son of Zeus and Europe, who was killed by Patroklos.[270] The story, drawn from *Iliad* 16 (419–507, 666–83), appears to be concerned with harm to enemy by enemy.

■ Euripides' (?) *Rhadamanthys* (Uncertain).   Snell attributes this play to Kritias; Mette and Austin attribute it to Euripides.[271] The little that is known about the plot is given in the preserved end of the papyrus hypothesis: Kastor is killed with Polydeukes in single combat; Rhadamanthys is pleased with the victory, but mourns his daughters; and Artemis appears ex machina, orders Helen to give divine honors to both dead brothers, and says that the daughters of Rhadamanthys will become goddesses.[272] This does not give us enough information about the story to allow for a reconstruction, and I have found no other trace of the myth.

■ Sophokles' *Thamyras* (Unlikely).   In *Iliad* 2.594–600, Thamyras boasts that he can sing better than the Muses, competes with them and is punished as a result, being blinded and deprived of his musical art.[273] This story would appear to be one of theomachy and punishment,[274] but we do not know how it was handled in Sophokles' play.

■ Sophokles' *Triptolemos* (Uncertain).   It is not known which of the stories about Triptolemos was the subject of this play. One conjecture is that it concerned an incident of violation of *xenia*. When Triptolemos, while traveling to teach people about agriculture, comes to King Kharnabon, he is at first hospitably received but later treated cruelly and nearly killed.[275]

Of these six plays, Aiskhylos' *Kares* and Sophokles' *Thamyras* seem unlikely to have dramatized harm to *philoi*. In the case of the other four, this is uncertain.

5. Plays Not Discussed

I have not discussed some tragedies because too little is known about them or because their existence is too uncertain. The following plays are listed in Radt 1985 (Aiskhylos), Radt 1977 (Sophokles), or Mette 1981–82 (Euripides); I include their notations for dubious plays, "?" and "??," but do not list the plays they exclude from the corpus by bracketing. Nor do I list alternate titles or plays identified in the titles as satyr plays (for example, *Ikhneutai Satyroi*). Plays are listed by author in alphabetical order of the Greek titles.

Aiskhylos

Alkmene
Argo
Atalante
Glaukos Pontios (probably a satyr play: Radt 1985, 142)
Thalamopoioi (perhaps a satyr play: Radt 1985, 193; Mette 1963, 183)

Aiskhylos (cont.)

Hiereiai
Kyknos?
Neaniskoi
Prometheus Pyrkaeus (satyr play: Radt 1985, 321)
Propompoi
Ten(n)es?
Phrygioi?

Sophokles

Admetos?
Aithiopes
Aikhmalotides
Amphitryon
Andromakhe
Auge?
Akhaion Syllogos
Bakkhai?
Dolopes
Helenes Gamos
Eris (satyr play: Radt 1977, 188)
Eumelos
Eurysakes
Erigone
Theseus
Iambe?
Iberes?
Inakhos (most think this is a satyr
    play: see Radt 1977, 247–48)
Ino?
Iokaste?
Iphikles
Kerberos
Kretes?
Minos
Mousai
Nai(a)des?
Neaniskoi?

Sophokles (cont.)

Neoptolemos?
Xoanephoroi?
Oikles
Oileus?
Oineus?
Oinone?
Pandora or *Sphyrokopoi* (satyr play:
    Pearson 1917, 2.135; Dios 1983,
    248; Radt 1977, 388)
Pelias?
Priamos
Ptokheia?
Tyndareos
Hydrophoroi
Phaiakes
Phthiotides
Oreithyia?

Euripides

Andromakhe II??
Glaukos: see *Polyidos*
Epeios
Kadmos?
Likymnios
Pandion??
Pelopides??
Phryges?

6. Conclusion

The preceding analysis has shown that harm to *philoi* was an important aspect of the lost tragedies of Aiskhylos, Sophokles, and Euripides, just as it is of the extant plays. Sections 1–4 above discussed 182 plays. In forty-one of these, the kind of *pathos* involved was uncertain. This leaves 141 plays for which the available evidence indicates that harm to *philos* was certain, likely, or unlikely. The table below summarizes the kinds of *philia* relationships within which harm occurred in these 141 plays:

    I. Blood kinship (69 plays)
        A. Parent harms child (43 plays)
        B. Child harms parent (9 plays)
        C. Sibling harms sibling (8 plays)
        D. Harm to other blood kin (6 plays)
        E. Some form of harm to blood kin (3 plays)

II. Reciprocal relationships (37 plays)
   A. Marriage (12 plays)
   B. *Xenia* (14 plays)
   C. Suppliancy (11 plays)
III. Other (9 plays)
   A. Suicide (2 plays)
   B. Domestic animals (2 plays)
   C. Some form of harm to *philos* (5 plays)
IV. Unlikely (26 plays)
 V. Uncertain (41 plays)

In sum, harm to blood kin (I) occurred in sixty-nine plays, or 49 percent of those in which the kind of *pathos* can be determined with some likelihood. Harm within reciprocal relationships (II) and other kinds of harm to *philoi* (III) occurred in an additional forty-six plays. Harm within all kinds of *philia* relationships occurred, then, in 115 of the plays, or 82 percent of those in which the *pathos* can be determined with some likelihood. In contrast, harm to *philoi* was unlikely in only twenty-six plays, or 18 percent of those in which the *pathos* can be determined. It is possible that if we had the complete text, some of these plays also would be seen to be about some form of harm to *philoi*, for in many cases where substantial fragments remain, harm to *philoi* is stressed in sometimes unexpected ways (for example, Ais. *Niobe*).

Appendix C: Violation of *Philia* in the Fragments of the Minor Tragedians

Much less is known about tragedies by dramatists other than Aiskhlyos, Sophokles, and Euripides. The evidence usually consists only of titles, which are themselves often of doubtful attribution and in fragmentary form, or of brief fragments that give little indication of the contents of the play. Any theories about the nature of most of these plays must necessarily be speculative. Nevertheless, the evidence, such as it is, is consistent with the view that the three major tragedians were not atypical in focusing on harm to *philoi*.

The evidence discussed here falls into three categories: section 1 lists titles, in English alphabetical order, that suggest harm to *philoi*, in the case of plays for which there is no evidence for this but the title; section 2 discusses plays for which evidence other than titles (for example, fragments or testimonia) suggests harm to *philoi*; and section 3 presents evidence against harm to *philoi*. I do not list plays for which the evidence is too slight to allow for even speculative conclusions. Appendix C concludes (section 4) with a comparison of fourth- and fifth-century tragedies of the *minores* (minor playwrights). This section includes tables and statistics. Cross-references to titles and myths (for example, "see Atreus Myths") are to the titles and groups of plays discussed in appendixes A and B. The survey in this chapter is based on Bruno Snell's edition of the minor tragedians through the fourth century, beginning with Thespis and ending with Phanostratus.[1] Doubtful plays and authors (those Snell either lists under *dubia* or marks with "?") are included and indicated with Snell's notation "?" or with my "perhaps"; plays bracketed by Snell are omitted. I follow Snell's designations of some authors by Roman numerals (for example, Astydamas I and Astydamas II). With the single exception of the *Helle*, mentioned by Aristotle, I have not taken the *adespota* (fragments of unknown authorship included in Snell-Kannicht 1981) into account, since the dates are often unknown. In this appendix I follow Snell's Latinate spelling in referring to the tragedians, although I transliterate the Greek titles of the plays.

My classifications in this appendix, as in appendix B, may seem somewhat arbitrary, since the myths on which many of the plays are based involved more than one kind of harm to *philoi*. In these cases, I classify plays according to the relationship that appears to have been most important in the play, when this can be determined. When it is not possible to decide which of several *philia* relationships was most significant in a play, I choose whichever relationship is closest. For example, if a play contains violation of both the parent-child relationship and of *xenia*, I classify it according to the former. Where the evidence suggests that the central *pathos* did not take place among any of the *philia* relationships discussed in this study, I classify the play as "unlikely." Where not enough is known about the play to allow for categorization, I do not include it.

In this appendix, as in appendix B, I adopt some new categories of *philia* relationships in addition to those used in discussing the extant plays. Under "Blood Kinship" I add the subcategory "Some Form of Harm to Blood Kin." In addition to "Blood Kinship" and "Reciprocal Relationships," I include a third category, "Other," which comprises the subcategories, "Suicide" and "Domestic Animals." These new categories are intended to take into account the greater variety of *pathê* in the fragments, and the greater uncertainty about relationships. The subcategories of parent harming child and child harming parent include harm to grandparents and grandchildren. Plays focusing on amphimetric strife, that is, a dispute involving either two wives of one man and their respective children or stepparents and children, are included in the subcategory of marriage.[2]

1. Titles Suggesting Harm to *Philoi* (78 Plays)

In many of the plays by the less well known dramatists, the titles provide our only evidence that harm to *philoi* may have been an issue. Attempting to reconstruct a plot from a title alone is, of course, extremely hazardous. For example, if we had nothing but the title of Aiskhylos's *Libation Bearers*, we would not guess that matricide occurred, while the title of Carcinus's *Medeia* would lead us to believe, probably falsely, that child-murder occurred in this play (see section 4). However, plays about which more is known can be of some limited help in establishing possibilities. Accordingly, I list titles if evidence from the extant and fragmentary plays of Aiskhylos, Sophokles, or Euripides supports the view that the relevant myths may have been about harm to *philoi*. In a few cases—for example, *Teknoktonos* (*The Child-Killer*)—the title itself indicates that harm to *philos* occurred.

In this section, as in appendix A, I list plays under broad categories of *philia* relationships (for example, "Blood Kinship," "Reciprocal Relationships"); the categories are further subdivided to indicate the specific kind of relationship (for example, "Parent Harms Child," "Marriage"). The number of plays within each category and subcategory is given in parentheses after each category and subcategory heading. Within the subcategories, plays are listed by title, followed by the number of plays of that title, the name(s) of the author(s), and brief comments on the myths, for example: "*Alope* (1). Choerilus."

I. *Blood Kinship* (51 *Plays*)

I.A. *Parent Harms Child* (25 *Plays*)

Alope (1). Choerilus. In Euripides' *Alope*, Kerkyon kills his daughter Alope and tries to kill his grandson. It should be noted, however, that Carcinus II follows a different version (see section 4).

Athamas (1). Astydamas II. Athamas kills his son: see "Athamas Myths."

Auge (1). Aphareus. In one version of the myth, Auge, the mother of Telephos, is married to her son in ignorance and is about to murder him. See "Telephos Myths."

Bakkhai (3). Iophon (Snell gives the alternate titles *Bakkhai* and *Pentheus*), Xenocles I, perhaps Cleophon. In Euripides' *Bacchae*, son is killed by mother.

Dymainai or *Karyatides* (1). Pratinas. Since the title means "Bakkhai," this play was probably concerned with Dionysos, in whose myths parent frequently harms child; see "Dionysos Myths."

Kyknos (1). Achaeus I. In Eurpides' *Tennes*, Kyknos tries to kill his son, who has been slandered by his stepmother.

Lykaon (2). Xenocles I, Astydamas II. In one version of the Kallisto myth, Zeus rapes Kallisto, who bears a child. Afterward, her father Lykaon hosts the god and serves him the child as food; see Aiskhylos's *Kallisto*. However, another Lykaon, who may or may not be associated with harm to *philoi*, figures in the *Azanes* of Achaeus I.

Lykourgeia (1). Polyphrasmon. It is possible that Lykourgos killed his son at an altar in Aiskhylos's *Edonoi*. See "Dionysos Myths."

Meleagros (1). Sosiphanes Syracusanus. Meleagros kills his uncles and is in turn killed by his mother. See "Meleagros Myths."

Pentheus (1). Thespis. Pentheus is killed by his mother. See "Dionysos Myths."

Phoinix (3). Ion (*Phoinix* 2, and perhaps *Phoinix*), Astydamas II. In Euripides' version, Phoinix is blinded by his father. See "Phoinix Myths."

Phrixos (2). Achaeus I and perhaps Timocles (Snell lists *Phrixoi* under dubia). In the myth, Phrixos is about to be killed by his father. See "Athamas Myths."

Teknoktonos (1). Apollodorus. The title of this play (*The Child-Killer*) indicates that its subject was child-murder.

Telephos (3). Iophon, Agathon, and perhaps Cleophon. In one version of the myth, Auge, the mother of Telephos, is married to her son in ignorance and is about to murder him. See "Telephos Myths."

Tereus (or *Epops*) (1). Philocles I. Tereus rapes his sister-in-law and is punished by being made to eat his own child. See Sophokles' *Tereus*.

Teukros (2). Ion, Euaretus (*Teukroi*). Teukros is exiled by his father. See "Aias Myths."

I.B. *Child Harms Parent (13 Plays)*

Akanthoplex (1). Apollodorus. Odysseus is killed by his son Telegonos in Sophokles' *Odysseus Akanthoplex*.

Alkmeon (2). Agathon, Timotheus. Alkmeon kills his mother Eriphyle. See "Amphiaraos Myths."

Oidipous (7). Achaeus I, Philocles I, Xenocles I, Nicomachus I, Theodectas, perhaps Timocles (*Snell* lists *Oidipodi* under *dubia*), Meletus II (Snell lists *Oidipodeia*). The patricide and incest figure in Sophokles' *Oedipus the King* and in other plays. See "Laios Myths."

Orestes (2). Euripides II, Aphareus. The matricide figures prominently in the extant plays. See "Atreus Myths."

Peliades (1). Aphareus. The title suggests that this play was about the daughters of Pelias, whom Medeia tricks into boiling their father. See "Medeia Myths."

I.C. *Sibling Harms Sibling (2 Plays)*

Oineus (2). Philocles I, Chaeremon. Prominent in this myth is enmity between two brothers, Oineus and Agrios, and their descendants. See Euripides' *Oineus*.

I.D. *Harm to Other Blood Kin (1 Play)*

Antigone (1). Astydamas II. In Sophokles' and Euripides' plays of this title, Antigone is condemned to death by her uncle for burying her brother. See "House of Laios Myths."

I.E. *Some Form of Harm to Blood Kin (10 Plays)*

Iason (1). Antiphon. This play may have dramatized some aspect of the Medeia story, in which many forms of harm to *philoi* occur. See "Medeia Myths."

Medeia (4). Euripides II, Theodorides (Snell lists *Medeiai*), perhaps Melanthius I and Morsimus. Medeia kills her brother and her own children, and does other evil acts. See "Medeia Myths."

Perseus (1). Pratinas. Perseus's grandfather Akrisios tries to kill him as an infant and is in turn killed by his grandson. See "Perseus Myths."

Thyestes (4). Agathon, Apollodorus, Chaeremon, and perhaps Cleophon. Thyestes seduces his brother's wife, eats his own children, and has a child by his daughter. See "Atreus Myths."

II. *Reciprocal Relationships (23 Plays)*

II.A. *Marriage (16 Plays)*

Aerope (2). Agathon, Carcinus II. Aerope is the wife of Atreus, whom his brother Thyestes seduces, in punishment for which Atreus serves Thyestes' children to their father as food. See "Atreus Myths."

Agamemnon (1). Ion. Klytaimestra kills her husband Agamemnon in Aiskhylos's play.

Alkmene (3). Ion, Astydamas II, Dionysius. In Euripides' play of the same title, husband is about to kill wife, whom he suspects of adultery.

Alphesiboia (3). Achaeus I, Timotheus, Chaeremon. Alphesiboia, the first wife of Alkmeon, punishes him after he deserts her.[3] See "Amphiaraos Myths."

Amphiaraos (2). Carcinus II and Cleophon may have written plays with this title.[4] Amphiaraos is killed as a result of the betrayal of his wife Eriphyle. See "Amphiaraos Myths."

Danaïdes (1). Phrynichus. In Aiskhylos's *Danaïd* trilogy, wives kill husbands.

Ixio[ni] (title restored by Snell) (1). Callistratus. Ixion kills his father-in-law. See "Ixion Myths."

Phaethonti (1). Theodorides. In Euripides' *Phaethon*, husband threatens wife.

Semele (2). Diogenes Atheniensis, Carcinus II. In Aiskhylos's *Semele* (which see), "husband" kills wife.

II.B. Xenia *(3 Plays)*

Helene (2). Theodectas, Diogenes Sinopensis. Helen betrays her husband, and Paris violates *xenia* in carrying her off from Menelaos's house. See Sophokles' *Helenes Harpage*.

Khrysippos (1). Diogenes Sinopensis. The title suggests that violation of *xenia* or fratricide may have occurred in this play, which may have been about Laios's rape of Pelops's son Khrysippos. See Euripides' *Khrysippos*, "Pelops Myths."

II.C. *Suppliancy (4 Plays)*

Hiketides (1). Apollodorus. The title (*The Suppliants*) suggests that this was a suppliant play.

Hektoros Lytra (1). Dionysius. This tragedy, like Aiskhylos's play titled either *Phryges* or *Hektoros Lytra*, may have been about the ransom of Hektor by the suppliant Priam.

Tyro (2). Astydamas II and perhaps Carcinus II. In Sophokles' *Tyro* plays, a suppliant is killed at an altar.

III. *Other (4 Plays)*

III.A. *Suicide (1 Play)*

Aias (1). Astydamas II (Snell lists as *Aias Mainomenos*). In Sophokles' *Aias*, Aias commits suicide. See also the *Aias* plays of Carcinus II and Theodectas (section 2, III.A).

III.B. *Domestic Animals (3 Plays)*

Aktaion (3). Phrynichus, Iophon, perhaps Cleophon. Aktaion is killed by his own dogs in Aiskhylos's *Toxotides*. See "Domestic Animal Myths."

2. Evidence Other than Titles for Harm to *Philoi* (32 Plays)

These plays are grouped by category and subcategory. With the exception of three plays by Diogenes Sinopensis (*Thyestes*, *Atreus*, and *Oidipous* in I.B.), each play is listed by title, if known, and discussed separately.

I. *Blood Kinship (23 Plays)*

I.A. *Parent Harms Child (11 Plays)*

Adonis. Dionysius. Fragment 1, because it mentions the birthing of a wild boar (σύαγρον ἐκβόλειον), allows us to infer something about the plot, including the fact that incest is likely to have been an issue. In the myth, the pregnant Myrrha is changed into a tree. A boar cuts through the tree and releases her son Adonis; when he is changed into a boar, Ares kills him.[5] Moreover, Myrrha (or Smyrna) is pregnant by her father, who, in some versions, tries to kill her.[6]

Alkmeon. Astydamas II. Aristotle is our authority for this play, which he cites as an example of a terrible deed done in ignorance and followed by recognition of *philia*. In contrast to Sophokles' *Oedipus the King*, where the deed is done "outside the drama," in the *Alkmeon*, the deed is done "in the tragedy itself."[7] According to Webster: "Alkmaion was driven mad by his father's command to kill his mother and killed her in his madness."[8]

Dionysos. Chaeremon. One fragment suggests that this play had the same plot as Euripides' *Bacchae*:[9] Πενθεὺς ἐσομένης συμφορᾶς ἐπώνυμος ("Pentheus, having a name suited to his future suffering": frag. 4).

Medeia. Diogenes Sinopensis. The Medeia of Diogenes Sinopensis was said to have known how to restore health by her cleverness and because of this to have gotten the reputation of restoring youth by boiling flesh.[10] This suggests that his *Medeia* may have been about the daughters of Pelias, whom Medeia tricked into boiling their father.

Medeia. Neophron. Fragment 2 clearly shows that this play was concerned with Medeia's murder of her children. Medeia says,

> οἴμοι, δέδοκται· παῖδες, ἐκτὸς ὀμμάτων
> ἀπέλθετ᾽· ἤδη γάρ με φοινία μέγαν
> δέδυκε λύσσα θυμόν. ὦ χέρες χέρες,
> πρὸς οἷον ἔργον ἐξοπλιζόμεσθα· (10–13)

> Alas, it has been determined. Children, go away from my sight. For already murderous madness has entered my great spirit. O hands, hands, for what deed are we armed.

Meleagros. Antiphon. Fragments allude to the boar that is the cause of strife between Meleagros and his *philoi*. The dispute culminates in the murder of son by mother: see "Meleagros Myths."

Pleuroniai. Phrynichus. Fragment 6 concerns Meleagros:

> κρυερὸν γὰρ οὐκ
> ἄλυξεν μόρον, ὠκεῖα δέ νιν φλὸξ κατεδαίσατο
> δαλοῦ περθομένου ματρὸς ὑπ᾽ αἰνᾶς κακομαχάνου

> He did not escape cruel death, but the swift flame devoured him when his terrible, evil-devising mother burned the brand.

We do not know whether or not the story of the death of Meleagros at the hands of his mother was the focus of this play, and the past tenses would seem to indicate that the play was concerned with later events.[11] The fragment shows, however, that kin murder had some role in the play.

Theseus. Achaeus I. Fragment 18a is taken by Snell to allude to a bull: ὀξ-υπρώρῳ (ταύρῳ): "to a sharp-horned (bull)." Snell cites Latte, who suggests that this refers to the bull that killed Theseus's son Hippolytos as a result of Theseus's curse.[12] (See Euripides' *Hippolytos*.) Although this is very slim evidence for the plot, it is the best we have.

[*Unknown title*.] Melanthius I (Snell testimonium 2). Hesione is said to have been bound and set out to be eaten by a sea monster in some play of Melanthius. Since Hesione in myth is sacrificed by her father Laomedon and rescued by Herakles (Apollodoros 2.5.9), this story is much like that of Perseus and Andromeda. See "Perseus Myths."

[*Unknown title*.] Sosiphanes Syracusanus. In fragment 6, Phoenix is said to have been punished undeservedly by his father (cf. Eur. *Phoinix*).

[*Unknown title*.] Theodectas. In a fragment of a play of unknown title, Thyestes is referred to: ἀλλ᾽ ὦ τάλαν Θυέστα, καρτέρει δάκνων / ὀργῆς χαλινόν ("But, O wretched Thyestes, endure, biting the bit of your anger": frag. 9). Georgia Xanthakis-Karamanos comments: "In view of the reference to Thyestes it was suggested that Theodectes wrote a play of that name. If this is correct, it can be plausibly assumed from the content and the advisory tone of the passage that the words were addressed to Thyestes after the recognition of his appalling act."[13] In other words, it is likely that the subject of this play was Thyestes' eating of his children.

I.B. *Child Harms Parent (9 Plays)*

Alkmeon. Theodectas. One fragment shows this play to have been about Alkmeon's matricide: Ἀλκ: τὴν μὲν θανεῖν ἔκριναν, ἐμὲ δὲ μὴ κτανεῖν (Alk: "They judged that she [sc. Alkmeon's mother] should die, but that I should not have killed her": frag. 2.4). According to Xanthakis-Keramanos, the plot was the same as that of Euripides' *Alkmeon dia Psophis* and Sophokles' *Alkmeon*: "having slain his mother Eriphyle, and being driven mad by the Erinyes, Alcmeon flees Argos and comes at last to Psophis in Arcadia where he is purified by King Phegeus . . . and marries the king's daughter Alphesiboea."[14]

Atreus, Oidipous, Thyestes. Diogenes Sinopensis. Diogenes wrote a *Thyestes*, an *Atreus* in which he is said to have defended cannibalism, and an *Oidipous* in which he was said to have approved of patricide and incest.[15]

Helle. Author unknown. According to Aristotle, in this play, son is about to betray mother when he recognizes her.[16]

Oidipous. Carcinus II. Fragment 1f is thought by many to allude to the exposure of Oidipous as an infant. This, as well as the title, suggests that the play was about some of the well-known acts of harm to *philoi* treated in Sophokles' play. See further section 4.

Orestes. Carcinus II. In this play, Orestes was compelled to agree that he killed his mother (frag. 1g).

Orestes. Theodectas. This play contains a clear reference to the matricide:

> δίκαιόν ἐστιν, ἥτις ἂν κτείνῃ πόσιν,
> ‹ταύτην θανεῖν, υἱόν τε τιμωρεῖν πατρί› (frag. 5)
>
> It is just for the woman who kills her husband
> ‹to die, and for a son to avenge his father›.[17]

Tydeus. Theodectas. In discussing the fourth kind of recognition, that from reasoning, Aristotle cites Theodectas's *Tydeus*: ὅτι ἐλθὼν ὡς εὑρήσων τὸν υἱὸν αὐτὸς ἀπόλλυται ("[a man reasons] that coming to find his son, he himself perishes": *Po.* 16.1455a8–10: frag. 5a). Richard Janko explains, "[P]resumably Tydeus came looking for his son and was about to be killed by him, in ignorance of his identity, but was saved when he said he had come to find his son Diomedes."[18]

I.C. *Sibling Harms Sibling (2 Plays)*

Iphigeneia he en Taurois? Polyidus? Polyidus is said by Aristotle to have written (ἐποίησεν) a play based on the same story as that of Euripides'

Iphigenia in Tauris (*Po.* 17.1455b8–12), in which sister is about to kill brother.[19]

Medeia. Dicaeogenes. Fragment 1a states that Medeia's brother, who is named Apsyrtos in other versions of the story, was called Metapontios in Dicaeogenes' play. Since Medeia kills her brother in Kolkhis, this is some slight evidence that the play was about fratricide. See "Medeia Myths."

I.D. Harm to Other Blood Kin (1 Play)

Likymnios. Xenocles I. In this play, certain words appear to have been spoken by Alkmene after she learns that her grandson Tlepolemos has killed her brother Likymnios.[20] The story is recounted in *Iliad* 2.661–62, where Likymnios is Tlepolemos's father's uncle.

II. Reciprocal Relationships (6 Plays)

II.A. Marriage (3 Plays)

Aigyptioi. Phrynichus. Fragment 1, stating that Aigyptos arrived in Argos with his sons, suggests that this play, like Aiskhylos's *Danaïd* trilogy, was about the murder of the sons of Aigyptos by their wives.

Lynkeus. Theodectas. Aristotle is our source for this play: "In the *Lynkeus* the one [sc. Lynkeus] being led away to die, and Danaos following to kill him, it happened in the event that the one [sc. Danaos] died, but that the other [sc. Lynkeus] was saved" (*Po.* 1452a27–29). Whatever else happened in this plot, it is clear that it focused on strife between Danaos and his son-in-law Lynkeus, the only one of the Aigyptiads to be spared by his wife.[21]

[*Unknown title.*] Sosiphanes Syracusanus. Fragment 4 states that Menoikeus was killed by Laios. Menoikeus is the father of Iokaste, the wife of Laios (Apollodoros 3.5.7).

II.B. Xenia (1 Play)

Unknown title. Phrynichus. In fragment 14, a beheading is ironically compared to the giving of *xénia*:

τό γε μὴν ξείνια δούσας, λόγος ὥσπερ λέγεται,
ὀλέσαι κἀποτεμεῖν ὀξέι χαλκῷ κεφαλάν.

Giving guest gifts, so it is said,
he destroyed and cut off his head with sharp bronze.

Snell (1971, 77) cites Crusius, who compares Herodotos 7.35, where Xerxes cuts the heads off those who built the first bridge over the Hellespont after it was smashed in a storm, and Aiskhylos, *Persians* 369 [–71], where he threatens to cut off heads for another reason. It is possible that the act was portrayed in Phrynichos's play as a violation of *xenia*.

II.C. *Suppliancy (2 Plays)*

Akhilleus Thersitoktonos. Chaeremon. Akhilleus kills Thersites because the latter blamed him for his alleged love of the Amazon Penthesileia. This causes *stasis* in the Greek army. Afterwards, Akhilleus sacrifices to Apollo, Artemis, and Leto and is purified of the murder by Odysseus (frag. 1b). According to Snell, the murder happened in a temple in this play, and Louis Séchan argues, on the basis of an Apulian vase in Boston, that Thersites was killed after he interrupted a sacrifice.[22] The sacred location and Akhilleus's subsequent need for sacrifice and purification give some reason to believe that Thersites was killed while supplicating.

Heracleidai. Pamphilus? Suppliancy figured in this play, which, like Euripides' *Children of Herakles*, recounted the story of the Herakleidai, pursued by Eurystheus, supplicating the Athenians.[23]

III. *Other (3 Plays)*

III.A. *Suicide (3 Plays)*

Aias. Carcinus II. In this play, Aias laughed at Odysseus, who said that one should do just things (frag. 1a). This play, then, is likely to have concerned the judgment of arms and Aias's suicide.

Aias. Theodectas. Theodectas also wrote on *Aias*, in which Odysseus spoke to Aias. The subject of this play is likely to have been the same as that of the *Aias* of Carcinus II.

Alope. Carcinus II. Alope's father, Kerkyon, commits suicide after he finds out that his daughter has been seduced by Poseidon (frag. 1b).

3. Evidence Against Harm to *Philoi* (29 Plays)

For a few plays, the title or some other evidence suggests that harm to *philoi* was unlikely to have been a central issue. I group these plays according to subject.

Antaios Plays (3 Plays)

In Phrynichus's *Antaios* or *Libyes* (frag. 3a), Herakles is said to have wrestled with Antaios the Libyan. This would appear to be an act in which enemy fights enemy, although we do not know how it featured in the plot. Since the Antaios of myth kills strangers, it is possible that violation of *xenia* was a central issue.[24]

Aristias also wrote an *Antaios*, and, if Snell correctly restores the title, Archestratus did also.

Bellerophon Plays (1 Play)

The *Bellerophontes* of Astydamas II is unlikely to have concerned harm to *philoi*, judging from the evidence of the other fragmentary plays. See "Bellerophon Myths."

Historical Plays (3 Plays)

In the *Phoinissai* of Phrynichus, the defeat of Xerxes was announced. This suggests that the play may have been about the defeat of enemy by enemy.[25] Phrynichus's *Miletos Halosis* was about a historical event, the capture of Miletus by its enemies.[26] Because Theodectas's *Mausolos* probably dramatized a flattering story about the contemporary ruler of this name, or perhaps about an ancestor of the same name, it is highly unlikely to have focused on harm to *philoi*.[27]

Medeia Plays (1 Play)

In the *Medeia* of Carcinus II, the child-murder was probably avoided (see section 4).

Odysseus Plays (4 Plays)

Since most of the Odysseus plays of Aiskhylos, Sophokles, and Euripides did not focus on harm to *philoi*, it is a plausible guess that this was not the subject of the *Odysseus* plays of Apollodorus and Chaeremon, of Philocles I's *Penelope*, or of Ion's *Laertes*. However, some Odysseus plays were about patricide, and it is possible that Collard is right in taking this to be true of Chaeremon's *Odysseus*.[28]

Palamedes Plays (3 Plays)

Philocles I and Astydamas II both wrote plays titled *Nauplios*. In Astydamas's play, Nauplios appears to have spoken to his dead son Palamedes,[29] who was killed because of the treachery of Odysseus, an unrelated fellow Greek. (See "Palamedes Myths.") Astydamas II also wrote a *Palamedes*.

Philoktetes Plays (3 Plays)

The *Philoktetes* of Achaeus I, of Philocles I, and of Theodectas, in which Neoptolemos figured (frag. 5b), may have concerned harm to an unrelated companion. See "Philoktetes Myths."

Theseus Plays (1 Play)

The *Peirithous* of Achaeus I may have resembled Euripides' play of the same title in having no concern with harm to *philoi*. See "Theseus Myths."

Trojan War Plays (10 Plays)

The title *Priamos* of Philocles I and those of Iophon's *Iliou Persis* and Cleophon's <*Iliou*> *Persis*, if there was such a play,[30] indicate Trojan War plays, in which it is likely that enemy harmed enemy. The *Hektor* of Astydamas II was about the duel, recounted in *Iliad* 22, between Hektor and Akhilleus. In fragment 1i.5–6, Hektor asks for Akhilleus's captured armor, and fragment 2a refers to the duel.[31] Iophon, Astydamas II, Carcinus II, perhaps Cleophon, Diogenes Sinopensis, and Aristarchus Tegeates wrote plays titled *Akhilleus*. These may well have been plays in which enemy harmed enemy. On the other hand, Akhilleus betrayed *xenia* by raping Deidameia, the daughter of his host, in Euripides' *Skyrioi*. See "Akhilleus Myths."

4. Conclusions: Tragedy of the Fourth and Fifth Centuries

The scarcity of the remains makes conclusions about the minor tragedians even more hypothetical than are those about the fragmentary plays of Aiskhylos, Sophokles, and Euripides. Nevertheless, the evidence we have supports the view that these tragedies also focused on terrible events among *philoi*. Sections 1–3 discussed or listed 139 plays. The table below summarizes the kinds of *philia* relationships, if any, within which harm may have occurred.

Minores: All Plays

    I. Blood kinship (74 plays)
        A. Parent harms child (36 plays)
        B. Child harms parent (22 plays)
        C. Sibling harms sibling (4 plays)
        D. Harm to other blood kin (2 plays)
        E. Some form of harm to blood kin (10 plays)

    II. Reciprocal relationships (29 plays)
        A. Marriage (19 plays)
        B. *Xenia* (4 plays)
        C. Suppliancy (6 plays)

    III. Other (7 plays)
        A. Suicide (4 plays)
        B. Domestic animals (3 plays)

    IV. Unlikely (29 plays)

Total: 139 plays

In sum, harm to blood kin (I) occurred in seveny-four plays, or 53 percent of those in which the kind of *pathos* can be determined with some likelihood. Harm within reciprocal relationships (II) and other kinds of harm to *philoi* (III) occurred in an additional thirty-six plays. Harm within all kinds of *philia* relationships occurred, then, within 110 of the plays, or 79 percent of those in which the *pathos* can be determined with some likelihood. In contrast, in only twenty-nine plays, or 21 percent of those discussed or listed, is harm to *philoi* unlikely to have occurred. These statistics are very similar to those for the fragmentary plays of Aiskhylos, Sophokles, and Euripides (see appendix B, section 6).

Some scholars have claimed that fourth-century tragedy was significantly different from that of the fifth century. To see if this is true with respect to plots of the *minores* in which violation of *philia* occurred, it is helpful to separate the statistics for the fourth century (the playwrights listed in Snell 1971, vi–vii, from Empedocles through Phanostratus) from those for the fifth century and earlier (playwrights from Thespis through Demetrius).

Minores: Plays of the Fifth Century and Earlier

    I. Blood kinship (34 plays)
        A. Parent harms child (21 plays)
        B. Child harms parent (6 plays)
        C. Sibling harms sibling (1 play)
        D. Harm to other blood kin (1 play)
        E. Some form of harm to blood kin (5 plays)

    II. Reciprocal relationships (10 plays)
        A. Marriage (8 plays)
        B. *Xenia* (2 plays)
        C. Suppliancy (0 plays)

    III. Other (2 plays)
        A. Suicide (0 plays)
        B. Domestic animals (2 plays)

    IV. Unlikely (13 plays)

Total: 59 plays

In plays of the earlier period, harm to blood kin (I) occurred in thirty-four plays, or 58 percent of those in which the kind of *pathos* can be determined with some likelihood. Harm within reciprocal relationships (II) and other kinds of harm to *philoi* (III) occurred in an additional twelve plays. Harm within all kinds of *philia* relationships occurred, then, in forty-six of the plays, or 78 percent of the plays in which the *pathos* can be determined with some likelihood. In contrast, harm to *philoi* is unlikely to have occurred in only thirteen plays, or 22 percent of the plays discussed or listed.

Minores: Fourth-Century Plays

    I. Blood kinship (40 plays)
        A. Parent harms child (15 plays)

    B. Child harms parent (16 plays)
    C. Sibling harms sibling (3 plays)
    D. Harm to other blood kin (1 play)
    E. Some form of harm to blood kin (5 plays)

II. Reciprocal relationships (19 plays)
    A. Marriage (11 plays)
    B. *Xenia* (2 plays)
    C. Suppliancy (6 plays)

III. Other (5 plays)
    A. Suicide (4 plays)
    B. Domestic animals (1 play)

IV. Unlikely (16 plays)

Total: 80 plays

In fourth-century plays, harm to blood kin (I) occurred in forty plays, or 50 percent of those in which the kind of *pathos* can be determined with some likelihood. Harm within reciprocal relationships (II) and other kinds of harm to *philoi* (III) occurred in an additional twenty-four plays. Harm within all kinds of *philia* relationships occurred, then, in sixty-four of the plays, or 80 percent of those in which the *pathos* can be determined with some likelihood. In contrast, harm to *philoi* is unlikely to have occurred in only sixteen plays, or 20 percent of those discussed or listed.

The evidence, then, goes against the theory of Xanthakis-Karamanos that fourth-century tragedy differed significantly from fifth-century tragedy in its treatment of harm to *philoi*. According to her view, fourth-century tragedy avoided deliberate kin murder to a much greater extent than did fifth-century tragedy: "[A] feeling of humanity and moral sensitivity appears to have induced fourth-century playwrights either to ascribe the deliberate crimes of old tragedy to ignorance ([Astydamas's] *Alcmeon*) or entirely to avoid any murder ([Carcinus II's] *Medea* and *Alope*). . . . The transformation . . . of well-known fifth-century dramatic treatments into milder and more humane versions makes the change of attitude explicit."[32] Neither the evidence she herself cites nor that presented here supports this conclusion.

Xanthakis-Karamanos cites the *Medeia* of Carcinus II, from which the child-killing so prominent in Euripides' play seems to have been absent. Fragment 1e states:

> Another topic is to accuse or defend on the basis of mistakes that have been made. For example, in the *Medea* of Carcinus some accuse her on the ground that she has killed her children. At any rate, they are not to be seen; for Medea made the mistake of sending the children away. But she defends herself on the ground that [it is improbable she has killed them, because] she would have killed Jason [then as well], not [only] the children; for she would have made a mistake in not doing so if she had done the other thing.[33]

According to Xanthakis-Karamanos, Carcinus's account accords with the tradition that Medeia's children were killed by the Korinthians. This playwright "depicted Medea as not only incapable of any deliberate murder of close kin but also as concealing her children, possibly to protect them from murder threatened by other people."[34]

Xanthakis-Karamanos also cites Carcinus's *Alope*. In the Alope story, Kerkyon's daughter Alope was seduced, and her father learned that Poseidon was the aggressor. In Euripides' version, Kerkyon killed Alope and tried to kill her child. In Carcinus's *Alope*, on the other hand, he committed suicide.[35]

Both the *Alope* and the *Medeia* show, in Xanthakis-Karamanos's view, "Carcinus' direct criticism of tragic deeds involving wilful murders of close relatives as these were treated by his great predecessor [sc. Euripides]."[36] The versions are indeed different, but the conclusions are hardly justified. Innovations are frequent in the fifth century also, and in many of Euripides' plays deliberate harm to kin is avoided, even though violation of *philia* is an important issue. In the *Iphigenia in Tauris*, sister avoids killing brother; in the *Hippolytus*, Theseus harms his son in ignorance that the young man is innocent; in the *Helen*, wife remains faithful to husband; and in the *Orestes*, Orestes marries his cousin Hermione instead of killing her. Suicide is itself a form of kin killing.

The Medeia tradition, morever, is much more complex than Xanthakis-Karamanos recognizes. The fourth-century Medeia was often murderous. She certainly killed her children in Neophron's *Medeia* (frag. 2), and in the version of Diogenes Sinopensis, she may have induced the Peliades to kill their father. On the other hand, in portraying a Medeia innocent of deliberate child murder, Carcinus may have been following a common tradition rather than innovating. Indeed, in many versions of the Korinthian story, beginning with that of Eumelus, who may have composed as early as the seventh century, Medeia was innocent.[37] And even if the Korinthians killed her children in Carcinus's version, Medeia was not necessarily blameless. Indeed, in some versions they died because of her neglect.[38]

Xanthakis-Karamanos also cites Fragment 1f of Carcinus's *Oidipous* as evidence for her views: ἡ Ἰοκάστη ἡ Καρκίνου ἐν τῷ Οἰδίποδι ἀεὶ ὑπισχνεῖται πυνθανομένου τοῦ ζητοῦντος τὸν υἱόν. The whole passage reads, "If something [in a narrative] is unbelievable, promise to tell the cause of it immediately and to refer [judgment] to somebody, as Iocasta in the *Oedipus* of Carcinus is always promising when someone is trying to find out about her son."[39] On the basis of this fragment, Xanthakis-Karamanos contrasts Carcinus's plot with that of Sophokles, in which Iokaste gave Oidipous to be exposed. She argues that in Carcinus's play, Iokaste may have tried to save the child. The fragment, according to Xanthakis-Karamanos, "implies that Iocasta, like Andromache and Medea, may have hidden the infant Oedipus from someone (Laius?) who was seeking him out (to kill him?), and had to account (to Laius?) for the child's disappearance."[40] Although Xanthakis-Karamanos concludes that Carcinus's treatment "accords with the milder humanity of the age,"[41] other interpretations are also possible. Webster, for example, draws a different conclusion from the fragment: "This sounds as if Iokaste exposed the infant

Oidipous and had to account for its disappearance to Laios who wanted to kill it."[42]

In the *Alkmeon* of Astydamas II, the matricide was committed in ignorance, with recognition coming later (Arist. *Po.* 1453b29–33). Xanthakis-Karamanos argues plausibly, following Webster, that Alkmeon committed the act in a state of madness, and she believes that this feature of the story was Astydamas's innovation.[43] However, Xanthakis-Karamanos's conclusion that this *Alkmeon* is an instance of a "transformation . . . of well-known fifth-century dramatic treatments into milder and more humane versions" is not justified.[44] Webster notes that Euripides' *Bacchae* has a similar plot,[45] and Herakles kills his family in a state of madness in Euripides' *Herakles*. In both plays, the horrific account of the murders is far from mild and humane.

Thus, the plays Xanthakis-Karamanos cites do not support her conclusions. Instead, the evidence presented in this chapter strongly supports Patricia Easterling's views on the continuity of fourth- with fifth-century tragedy.[46]

This view is also supported by Aristotle's statements in the *Poetics*, in which he clearly indicates that his contemporaries of the fourth century focused on harm to *philoi*:

1. "At first, the poets recounted any chance stories, but now[47] the finest tragedies are composed about few houses, for example, about Alkmeon and Oidipous and Orestes and Meleagros and Thyestes and Telephos, and about others who happened to suffer or do terrible things." (*Po.* 13.1453a17–22)

2. "For this reason, as was said before, tragedies are not about many families. For seeking not by craft but by chance they [sc. tragedians] discovered how to contrive this in their plots. Indeed they are compelled to look to those houses in which these kinds of terrible events occurred." (*Po.* 14.1454a9–13)

In these two passages Aristotle presents his view that tragedians at the time he is writing have learned which families make good subjects for tragedies: those in which *philos* harms or is about to harm *philos* (see *Po.* 14, esp. 1453b19–22). The examples given in the *Poetics* 13 passage are all of figures well known for harm to kin, and many of them are explicitly cited as such in chapter 14: Alkmeon (1453b24; 1453b33), Oidipous (1453b30–31), and Orestes (1453b23–24). Aristotle also frequently cites as examples fourth-century tragedians, giving no indication that their subject matter differed from that of the fifth-century poets.[48]

Notes

Introduction

1. The Greek word *philia* can mean either "kinship" or "friendship." For this and other words often left untranslated, see the glossary.

2. Blundell 1989. *Philia* in the plot: Else 1957, 349–52, 391–98, 414–15; Gudeman 1934, 257–58; Vickers 1973, 63, 230–43. *Philia* in other aspects of tragedy: Goldhill 1986, 79–106; Schmidt-Berger 1973; Scully 1973; Seaford 1990, 1994a; Simon 1988.

3. Seaford 1993, 1994a.

4. E.g., Gudeman 1934, 257–58; Else 1957, 391–98.

Chapter 1

1. On *pathos* and recognition, see further Belfiore 1992a, 134–41, 153–60.

2. Aristotle's examples are given at *Po.* 14.1453b19–22, quoted above. Else discusses *philia* in 1957, 349–52, 391–98, 414–15. See also Belfiore 1992a 72–73.

3. Nothing else is known about the author or plot of this play. Cf. Soph. *Phil.* 1386: "You who want to hand me over to my enemies" (ὅς γε τοῖς ἐχθροῖσί μ' ἐκδοῦναι θέλεις).

4. Lacey 1968, 28; Patterson 1998, 83 (fig. 1), 88–89. Littman 1979, 6 n. 2, argues that the children of children of cousins are included.

5. On the breadth of the concept of *philia* in Aristotle and elsewhere in Greek literature, see Millet 1991, 109–26.

6. Cf. *EE* 1242a1–2. The number of categories and their interrelationships are disputed; I follow Gauthier and Jolif 1970, 2.2, 706–7. On the inclusion of the marriage relationship within the category of kinship *philia*, see Gauthier and Jolif on 1162a16, and note that in *Pol.* 1262a10–11 kinship (συγγένεια) includes both blood kinship and relationship by marriage.

7. Gould 1973, 93. On suppliancy, *xenia*, and kinship, see also Herman 1987.

8. For the central role of reciprocity in *philia* among both kin and non-kin in Greek thought, see Millett 1991, 109–59; Mitchell 1997a, 8–9.

9. The combination of biological and social features in Aristotle's discussions of kinship is analyzed by Price 1989, 164–67; Sherman 1989, 148–51. On the idea that recognition in tragedy involves acknowledgment of a social role, see Simon 1988, 50–51; Belfiore 1992a, 157–60. In Eur. *Heracl.*, Iolaos first demonstrates that the children of Herakles are related to Demophon (207–13) and then urges the king to "become kin and friend" (γενοῦ . . . συγγενής, γενοῦ φίλος, 229). When Demophon shows his willingness to act as kin and friend, Iolaos says, "We have found friends and kin" (ηὕρομεν φίλους καὶ ξυγγενεῖς, 304–5). For a similar view of recognition in Homer, see Goldhill 1991a, 5–6; Murnaghan 1987, esp. 5–6, 22–5. See also Demosthenes 23.56 (*Against Aristokrates*), discussed by Blundell 1989, 38. Konstan (1996 and 1997) provides many useful examples of *philos* in the sense of someone who acts as a friend, although I disagree with him about the meaning of the Greek term: see appendix to chapter 1.

10. On ὀθνεία in Eur. *Alc.* (e.g., 646, 810), see Rehm 1994, 92–93. The bride's continuing ties to her natal family have important legal aspects in the classical period (Hunter 1994, 13–15) and frequently give rise to conflicts in tragedy (Seaford 1990).

11. See Donlan 1982, 145–48; Littman 1979, 15–17.

12. On *amphimêtores* and amphimetric disputes, see Ogden 1996, 19–21, 189–99, who notes, "The structure that above all sowed discord in Greek families was the amphimetric one, i.e. that in which a man kept two women . . . and fathered lines of children from both" (189).

13. Seaford 1990, 168–71.

14. Gould 1973, 93, citing *Od.* 8.546–47 and Hesiod, *Op.* 327–34.

15. See Herman 1987, esp. 41–72.

16. On the distinction between the ritualized friend and the temporary guest, see Donlan 1989, 7.

17. *Il.* 7.287–305. See Herman 1989, 60 n. 56.

18. *Pace* Lateiner 1995, 38–39.

19. Herman 1987, 16–29.

20. Schwartz 1985, 487, 495 (cited by Janko 1992, note on *Il.* 13.624–25), argues that Greek ξεν- words are derived from the Indo-European root meaning "to give in exchange or reciprocity, to requite." See also Smith 1993, 18 n. 5.

21. See Gould 1973, 92–93, citing *Od.* 16.422–23. See also Eur. *Heracl.* 503–6.

22. On the distinction, see Gould 1973, 92–94; Roth 1993, 7 n. 15.

23. See below, chapter 3, section 4.

24. Isokrates, *Panathenaikos* 122, links murder of *xenoi* with murder of parents and brothers, incest and cannibalism. (This passage is quoted by Herman 1987, 124, but incorrectly cited.) For other examples of the association of incest with cannibalism, see Moreau 1979; Seaford 1993, 138 n. 102.

25. In Ais. *Supp.*, Zeus Hikesios is called Zeus Aidoios. On *aidôs* and supplication, see Cairns 1993, 183–85, 189–93, 221–27, 276–87; Glotz 1904, 138–42; Gould 1973, 85–90.

26. Glotz 1904, 138.

27. The evidence is surveyed by Seaford 1994a, 360–62.

28. *Pathê* in epic: *Po.* 1459b7–15; tragedy develops from and is superior to epic: *Po.* 4 and 26; best *pathê*: *Po.* 14. See further Belfiore 1992a, 137–38. Jong 1987, 98, notes that the *Iliad* arouses admiration and sometimes fear, rather than the "pity and fear" aroused by tragedy.

29. Agamemnon is included among Akhilleus's "dear companions" (φίλων ἑταίρων) at *Il.* 19.305.

30. Akhilleus was a cousin of Patroklos, according to Hesiod, *Catalogue of Women*, frag. 212aMW: Eustathius, Hom. 112.44ff. In *Il.* 23.84–90, Patroklos is said to be a suppliant-exile, brought up with Akhilleus in Peleus's house after killing a man in his own country. This relationship, however, is mentioned only in this passage, in which Patroklos's ghost asks for burial. Contrast Ais. *Myrmidones* (see below, appendix B).

31. Lateiner 1993, 182. He also notes, "The suitors . . . usurp social status as *xeinoi*" (181), and "[t]he suitors have purposely neglected the obligation and privilege to reciprocate to men and gods" (182). Cf. Lateiner 1995, 220–21.

32. Thus, Odysseus is not guilty of killing his own guests, *pace* Nagler 1993, esp. 244.

33. This fact is noted by Garvie 1986, x–xi; Griffin 1977, 44; Olson 1995, 161–83; Seaford 1989, 87, with n. 1, 1993, 142–46, 1994, 11–13; Simon 1988, esp. 1–2, 13–26. Seaford 1994a, 11, lists six people in addition to Klytaimestra who kill kin in Homer: Tlepolemos (*Il.* 2.662), Medon (*Il.* 15.336), Epeigeus (*Il.* 16.573), Oidipous (*Od.* 11. 273), Aedon (*Od.* 19.552), and Meleagros (*Il.* 9.567). To these, add two cases in which a woman is bribed to lead a man to his death: Euriphyle, responsible for the death of her husband Amphiaraos (*Od.* 11.326–27, 15. 244–47), and Astyokhe, who betrays her son Eurypylos (*Od.* 11.520–21).

34. Noted by Kirk, 1985, on 101–8.

35. Aigisthos is implicated in the murder of Agamemnon in *Od.* 1.36, 1.298–30, 3.193–98, 3.234–35, 3.248–50, 3.261–75, 3.303–10, 4.91–92, 4.518–37, 11.387–89, 11.409–39, 24.19–22, 24.96–97. Klytaimestra helps in the planning in 3.234–35, 4.91–92, 11.429–30, 11.439. Klytaimestra kills Agamemnon in 11.409–11, 11.453, 24.96–97, 24.199–200.

36. Roussel 1976, 27–34, notes the absence in Homer of large, organized kinship groups.

37. See Saïd 1983 for this idea in Ais. *Eum.*

38. Eur. *Hec.* 1200; cf. *Andr.* 173, 665; Ais. *Pers.* 434. Hall 1989, 161, argues that tragedy presupposes a generic bond between all Greeks and between all non-Greeks. Cf. Plato, *Rep.* 5.470c.

39. On these lines, alleged by Plutarch to have been deleted by Aristarkhos, see Hainsworth 1993, ad loc., and Janko 1992, 25–29.

40. Gould 1973, 79 n. 35, 80–81, followed by Richardson 1993, on 21.74–96, sees the food presented to Lykaon as an act of hospitality and sharing a meal. Akhilleus, however, has not shared food with Lykaon as a host but merely given food as master to slave. Lykaon uses the deliberately ambiguous phrase πὰρ . . . σοὶ . . . πασάμην (76), which, unlike a reference to the "table of *xenia*," does not necessarily imply sharing. On Lykaon's specious arguments, see Parker 1983, 181–82; Yamagata 1994, 42–44.

41. Examples: Ais. *Supp.* 359–60, 385; *Od.* 9.270–71. The view (held by, e.g., Pedrick 1982) that Zeus does not play the same role as protector of suppliants in the *Iliad* that he does in the *Odyssey* ignores both the *Litai* speech in *Il.* 9.502–12, well explained by Thornton 1984, and Priam's request to Akhilleus to have *aidôs* for the gods (*Il.* 24.503).

42. The Kyklops is punished by Odysseus for his abuse of suppliants, but he is not represented as making an agonizing decision, and he says that he has no fear of Zeus (*Od.* 9.273–78).

43. On these issues, see Delcourt 1939; Gould 1973, 100; Parker 1983, 9, 146–47. Parker notes a number of differences between Homeric and classical supplication

(81–88), although he attaches less importance than many to the absence of "pollution" terminology in Homer (130–43).

44. These are "supplications," not "prayers," as Thornton 1984 points out. See also Hainsworth 1993, on 9.501.

45. On the genealogy in Aiskhylos, see below, appendix A.

46. According to the biology of Ais. *Eum.* 658–61, Orestes really is a *xenos* rather than blood kin of his mother.

47. I follow Burian 1971, 1, and Lattimore 1958, 13 n. 2, in categorizing these four as suppliant plays.

48. Mercier's 1990 table of contents lists supplications in all of the plays of Euripides except *Rhes.*, *Alc.*, and *Bacch.*, to which I would add *Bacch.* 1117–21, where Pentheus supplicates Agave. In Ais. *Eum.* (40–45, 91–92, 232, 439–41, 474), Orestes appears as a suppliant, and the Chorus supplicate the gods in the Parodos of *Sept.* (110–11). Supplications also occur in Soph. *Aj.* 1171–84, *OT* (Prologue), and *Phil.* 484–506.

49. For details, see below, chapters 5 and 6, and appendix A.

50. Kopperschmidt 1967, 52, notes a more specific pattern of recognition in suppliant plays, in which an apparent enemy is recognized as savior or vice versa.

51. See also Froidefond 1971, 87: "a real recognition scene." Jones 1999, 24, cites a parallel in Herod. 2.91, where Perseus is said to have "recognized" (ἀναγνῶναι) his kin in Egypt.

52. Avery 1965, 285, notes that Philoktetes uses two words that mean "child," τέ-κνον and παῖς, fifty-two times in this play.

53. I owe this interpretation of the *Helen* to Mikalson 1991, 78, 261 n. 48.

54. Konstan 1996, 1997. I am indebted to Konstan for making a draft of the latter available to me prior to publication and for helpful discussion of this topic, on which we have agreed to disagree.

55. Konstan 1996, 75–78; 1997, 55–56.

56. For example, 1996, 73–74, 76 n.13, 85, and n. 35.

57. Konstan's views have recently been challenged by Mitchell 1997b.

58. Noted by Gauthier and Jolif 1970, ad loc. Konstan's view (1996, 77–78) that Aristotle is distinguishing friends from companions is implausible in view of the fact that most of 8.12 is devoted to kinship *philia*.

59. See also the problematic cases noted by Konstan 1996, 85n. 35.

60. West 1990 attributes these lines to the Chorus, although the MSS give them to Antigone and Ismene.

61. Sommerstein 1989, on 355–56.

62. Konstan 1997, 62–63. His own earlier interpretation—"kin but not kind"—is much preferable: Konstan 1985, 181.

63. The passage is cited by Dirlmeier 1931, 11; Millet 1991, 287 n. 2, citing Cooper 1980, 334n. 2.

Chapter 2

1. Cf. Hartigan 1986, 120.

2. At 390, the generalizing τὸν θεὸν (L) is preferable to τὴν (the emendation attributed in Diggle's apparatus to "the friend of Markland") read by Diggle and G. Murray, which would refer specifically to Artemis.

3. This is also the view of Sansone 1975, 288–89.

4. That τοὺς ἐνθάδ' refers to the Taurians is suggested by "these people" in the translations of Bynner 1959 and Lattimore 1973 and by "les gens du pays" of Grégoire 1964.

5. Although the word *xenos* does not appear in the text, Oinomaos was infamous for his murder of *xenoi* (frag. 473R of Sophokles' *Oinomaos*), and Pelops was a *xenos* of Oinomaos, whether he was merely a stranger or an actual guest of Hippodameia's father. On the similarity of the crimes of stranger-killing and host-killing in this play, see below, section 3.

6. The other versions of the story are surveyed by M. J. O'Brien 1988, 103–5. Apollodoros, *Epit.* 2.7 mentions the variant in which Pelops kills Oinomaos. See below, appendix B, on Sophokles' *Oinomaos*. While some see an allusion to Myrtilos in the reference to horses at 192, I agree with Platnauer 1938, on 192 ff., that the horses are those of the sun.

7. For example, M. J. O'Brien 1988, 105–6.

8. On Agamemnon's murder of Klytaimestra's previous family, see Jouan 1966, 276 n. 2, who notes that Euripides is our most ancient source for this story, although he probably did not invent it. On the *authentês* relationship, see chapter 5 below.

9. The feast of Thyestes is also recounted in detail in Ais. *Ag.* 1219–22, 1583–1602.

10. While 197 is daggered as a corrupt line by Diggle and G. Murray, it is accepted by England 1886 and Grégoire 1964. On the allusion to the feast in this passage, see Sansone 1975, 289 n. 19.

11. Agamemnon's killing is also mentioned at 211–12, 563–65, 853–54, 862, 992, 1083.

12. Reading κτανών with P.

13. Cf. θύω (38), φονέα . . . χεῖρα (586), and 225–26, where the general sense in a corrupt text is that Iphigeneia is concerned with the murder of *xenoi*. These passages show conclusively that Iphigeneia is involved in the murders. Summaries of the evidence and bibliography on the question of whether or not Iphigeneia has actually sacrificed Greeks are given by Sansone 1978, and Strachan 1976.

14. Platnauer 1938 correctly notes that Artemis, not Thoas, is the subject of τίθησι in line 34.

15. For example, Burnett 1971, 58. I agree with Luschnig 1972, 159–60, that Apollo and Artemis share in the guilt of their human protégés.

16. Even though the play does not explicitly state that Gaia is Pytho's mother, this seems to be assumed: see Platnauer 1938 and England 1886, on 1245. Contrast the peaceful succession at Delphi in Ais. *Eum.* 1–8.

17. Cf. Luschnig 1972, 158, Hartigan 1991, 92.

18. The relationship is explained by England 1886, on 918.

19. The friendship between Orestes and Pylades is discussed by Schmidt-Berger 1973, 127–44, who does not, however, adequately appreciate the importance of the kinship and marriage *philia* between the friends.

20. The ambiguity in the same phrase in Soph. *Ant.* 99 is noted by Kamerbeek 1978, ad loc.

21. ἔγκληρος here is equivalent to ἐπίκληρος: see Platnauer 1938, on 682.

22. δόμους οἴκει πατρός (699) means "live as heir in the house of my father"; cf. Ais. *Eum.* 654: δώματ' οἰκήσει πατρός and Sommerstein's (1989) note ad loc., citing Barrett 1964 on Eur. *Hipp.* 1011–11.

23. Harrison 1968; heiress: 9–12, 132–38; posthumous adoption: 90–93. On the heiress in Greek law see also Patterson 1999, 91–103.

24. Harrison 1968, 93; Lacey 1968, 147.

25. Duties to the dead: Lacey 1968, 147–49.

26. Harrison 1968, 137–38; Pomeroy 1997, 123.

27. Pohlenz 1954, 398, and Schmidt-Berger 1973, 139, 141 note that Pylades is Orestes' "other self" but do not discuss his role as husband of Agamemnon's heiress.

28. Schmidt-Berger 1973, 132.

29. Schmidt-Berger 1973, 130.

30. On the idea that good comes from evil in this play, see Burnett 1971, 64; Caldwell 1974–75, 40; Hartigan 1986, 122; Whitman 1974, 28.

31. The brother-sister relationship was an especially close one in Greek society, according to Bremmer 1997, esp. 93–99.

32. On the parallels between the fates of Iphigeneia and Orestes, see M. J. O'Brien 1988, 109, and the works cited in his n. 37.

33. On *kharis* in this scene, see Burnett 1971, 51.

34. On Iphigeneia's pity in this scene, see Vellacott 1984, 167, who notes, "She is the only person in Greek tragedy who has tears for Clytemnestra."

35. See LSJ s.v. προσήκω, II.1.b and III.3.

36. Reading κτανών, with P; cf. 565.

37. τοιοῦτος εἴη τῶν ἐμῶν ὁμοσπόρων ὅσπερ λέλειπται: 611–12. Translation of Lattimore 1973.

38. Discussed by Matthiessen 1964, 131.

39. On redemption of the house through fraternal love, cf. Martinazzoli 1946, 78.

40. There is no good reason to bracket θέλω (993) as Diggle does.

41. Cf. Eur. *Hipp.* 1448–51, where the dying son frees his father from guilt for his death. In Athens, the killer was exempt from legal sanctions if pardoned by the dying victim: Parker 1983, 108 and n. 10.

42. See Platnauer 1938, on 1021.

43. On the divine-human parallel, see Belpassi 1990, 64; Burnett 1971, 48; Whitman 1974, 28.

44. The divine intervention is noted by England 1886 and Platnauer 1938 ad loc.

45. Noted by M. J. O'Brien 1988, 110.

46. See Eur. *Ion* 470, where καθαροῖς is used of the oracle of Apollo in the sense of "clear, free from ambiguity," according to Owen 1939, ad loc.

47. On the differences between the two versions, see Brendel 1950, 33–37; Sansone 1975, 292–93.

48. *Pace* Conacher 1967, 309; Grube 1941, 328–29.

49. On *kharis* here, see Burnett 1971, 66–67.

50. The temple robbing is discussed by Wolff 1992, 314–15.

51. Wolff 1992, 313.

52. My translation, with commas after "festival" and "sacrifice," attempts to preserve the ambiguity of the Greek, in which, *pace* Platnauer 1938, ἄποιν' is in apposition to both the preceding and the following lines.

53. See Wolff 1992, 313–19, on the Halai rites as "compensation by means of substitution" (318).

54. Cf. Caldwell 1974–75, 37: "The rite symbolizes threatened violence . . . and the nullification of this threat" (quoted by Hartigan 1991, 104 n. 49).

55. Myths: Lyons 1997, 143–47, with bibliography; averting of sacrifice: Lyons 1997, 147 (citing Brelich 1969, 257) and Brulé 1987, 182–86, 195–97.

56. Brauronia: Cole 1998, 41.

57. See Burnett 1971, 59–61; Whitman 1974, 28–29.

58. Burnett 1971, 63, is one of the few to mention the fact that the combat is nearly bloodless. To my knowledge, no scholar has noticed that animal sacrifice does not take place.

59. On the similarities, often noted by scholars, and the important but neglected differences, see Belfiore 1992b, esp. 360–61; Hartigan 1991, 105 n. 52.

60. On purification, see Sansone 1975, 286; Whitman 1974, 11, 28; Wolff 1992, 317.

61. Heraklitos frag. 5 DK = Kirk, Raven, and Schofield 1983, frag. 241: their translation. On purification of blood by means of blood, see Parker 1983, 370–74. Other examples from tragedy are Soph. *OT* 100–101, and Eur. *Stheneboia* frag. 661.18 Collard 1995b, on which see his n. 18, p. 93.

62. England 1886, ad loc., compares this cry to the voice of Dionysos in Eur. *Bacch.* 1078 ff.

63. Seaford 1993 and 1994a, appendix C.

Chapter 3

1. Good discussions and summaries of the different views held by scholars are given by Friis Johansen and Whittle 1980, 1:30–40; Garvie 1969, 215–25; MacKinnon 1978.

2. Burian 1971, 71–74; Friis Johansen and Whittle 1980, 1:38–39; Kuntz 1993, 62; R. D. Murray 1958, 66–67.

3. Burian 1974a, 9.

4. Caldwell 1994, 81.

5. Gantz 1978, 287.

6. Lévy 1985, 41; my translation.

7. Moreau 1985, 201; my translation.

8. R. D. Murray 1958, 72. Cf. Garrison 1995, 81–87.

9. Winnington-Ingram 1983, 60.

10. Zeitlin 1988, 253; 1992, 227; cf. Caldwell 1994, 84–86, Lembke 1975, 11.

11. Verdenius's phrase: 1985, 282.

12. τεκμήρια: Friis Johansen and Whittle 1980, on 53–55; 304–5l; 321 n. 1. Distribution of lines at 291–324: Ewans 1996a, 208; Friis Johansen and Whittle 1980, ad loc.

13. See Friis Johansen and Whittle 1980, on 402–3.

14. Diamantopoulos 1957, 225; Friis Johansen and Whittle 1980, on 449.

15. ξενικὸν ἀστικόν θ' ἅμα / λέγων διπλοῦν μίασμα. The pollution is "double" because the women are not only *xenoi* but also *astoi*, that is, Argives, as direct descendants of Io. See Friis Johansen and Whittle 1980, on 618 n. 2 (citing ἀστοξένων: 356), and on 619 n. 1. Cf. Eur. *El.* 795 (ξένους ἀστοῖσι συνθύειν χρεών), *Med.* 222–23; Soph. *El.* 975, OC 13.

16. On the link between suppliancy and kinship in this play, see Zeitlin 1988, 241 n. 15.

17. Cairns 1993, 189–90.

18. On the attribution of this line, see Friis Johansen and Whittle 1980, ad loc.

19. Death at altar: Parker 1983, 183–85; vengeance suicide: Delcourt 1939.

20. Translation of Friis Johansen and Whittle 1980, on 473.

21. "Blackmail": Friis Johansen and Whittle 1980, 1:38; Hester 1987, 10. On the "proclivity to violence" of the Danaïds, see Bakewell 1997, 218.

22. ἱκετῶν ἐγχειριδίοις: 21. Since aggression is implicit in all supplication (Gould 1973, 100), "suppliants' daggers" is appropriate not merely to the particular situation of the Danaïds, who will later kill their husbands (Friis Johansen and Whittle 1980, on 21), but also more generally to all suppliants.

23. On the interpretation of 619, see Friis Johansen and Whittle 1980, ad loc., n. 2.

24. On the attributes of suppliants, see Kopperschmidt 1967, 25–34.

25. Gould's (1973, esp. 77) insistence that physical contact is necessary is challenged by, for example, Goldhill 1991a, 72–75; Pedrick 1982, 135–40.

26. Mercier 1990, 25–26, 306–307.

27. On the gesture of raising with the hand, see Gould 1973, 78–80, 94–95. For the right hand, see section 4. According to Friis Johansen and Whittle 1980, on Ais. *Supp.* 324, the verb *anastêsai* "has the technical sense of inducing suppliants to leave asylum under the promise . . . of protection, immunity or satisfaction."

28. The many Greek constructions with χείρ are easy to confuse with one another: (1) in dative: αἱρεῖν τινὰ χειρί, to take someone with one's hand; (2) in genitive: χειρὸς ἔχειν τινά; to hold someone by their hand; ἀνιστάναι τινὰ χειρός, to raise someone by their hand; τινὰ χερὶ χειρὸς αἱρεῖν, to take someone by the hand with one's hand; (3) in accusative: χεῖρα αἱρεῖν τινός, to take the hand of someone, προσάπτειν χεῖρα, to apply one's hand; (4) with διά: διὰ χερῶν ἔχειν , to hold in one's hands; διὰ δεξιᾶς λαμβάνειν, to take with one's right hand. See LSJ s.v. χείρ II.2–4 and II.6.c; s.v. προσάπτω I.3; Schwyzer 1966, 451.6; Smyth 1920, no. 1346.

29. This distinction, pointed out to me by John Wilkins, is not made in the literature, as far as I know.

30. See Kamerbeek 1984, on 282–86.

31. See also Thucy. 1.126.11. The most detailed version is given in Plut. *Solon* 12.1, where the trial is mentioned, and where the fugitives are said to leave the sanctuary after connecting themselves to the statue of Athena by means of a thread. When the thread breaks, they are killed.

32. On the staging of the play, see Ewans 1996a, 202–22; Friis Johansen and Whittle 1980, ad loc.; Taplin 1977, 192–239.

33. Hands: Friis Johansen and Whittle 1980, on 193 n. 2.

34. Friis Johansen and Whittle 1980, on 208 n. 1.

35. Friis Johansen and Whittle 1980, on 241–42.

36. *Anastasis*: Friis Johansen and Whittle 1980, on 506–23.

37. See Kopperschmidt 1967, 30, citing Soph. *OT* 142 and Eur. *Supp.* 359.

38. Friis Johansen and Whittle 1980, on 506–23, *pace* Gould 1973, 89–90, who cites Schlesinger 1933.

39. The manuscripts read χειρὶ καὶ λόγοις σέθεν, "by [or "for" or "to"] your hand and words," but most editors follow Valckenaer's emendation: καί δή σφε λείπω, χειρία λόγοις σέθεν ("And indeed I leave them [sc. the branches], at hand to [obey] your words"). In the absence of more explicit evidence that Pelasgos takes the women by the hand, it seems best to accept the emendation.

40. As Easterling 1988 argues, tragedy frequently adapts and modifies actual ritual.

41. The importance of *metoikia* in this play is discussed by Bakewell 1997.

42. Zeus Hikesios, Hiktaios, Hikter: 347, 385, 478–79, 616; Zeus Xenios: 627, 671–72; Aidoiou Dios: 192. Mikalson 1991, 74, notes that Zeus Hikesios may be a literary invention of Aiskhylos.

43. On these passages, see Sommerstein 1989, 24–25. On danger to gods by suppliants, see Delcourt 1939, 168; Mikalson 1991, 76 and 260 n. 38; Parker 1983, 146–47. See also Eur. *IT* 972–75.

44. Suppliants frequently appeal to gods on the basis of kinship (Collard 1975, on Eur. *Supp.* 628–30) or some other personal relationship (Kuntz 1993, 59–60). Parker 1996, 156, cites Herod. 7.189, where, during the Persian War, the Athenians are said to have appealed to Boreas as their son-in-law. Many other examples are cited by Jones 1999.

45. See Friis Johansen and Whittle 1980, on 532–33. The language of renewal and kinship also occurs in historical writings: Jones 1999, 7, 42.

46. See Friis Johansen and Whittle 1980, on 403.

47. Voluntary union: Ewans 1996a, 212 n. 25; Zeus's benevolence in *Suppliants*: Boittin 1976, 44; Vürtheim 1928, 51.

48. Bacon 1982, 129–30; Burian 1971, 72–74; Lattimore 1958, 19; R. D. Murray 1958, 35, 56–59. According to Zeitlin 1988, 240, the Zeus-Io union is a "negative paradigm of sexuality" for the Danaïds.

49. On this issue, see Griffith 1983, 189–90, and on 669–82, 703–4.

50. R. D. Murray 1958, vii (cow); 54, 57 n. 3 (gadfly).

51. Zeitlin: "vierge et génisse" (1988, 232, 238). Inconsistently, Zeitlin also refers to the sexual union of Zeus and Io in Argos (1988, 252 n. 34).

52. Froidfond 1971, 107–8; cf. Mazon 1949, 5; correctly, Vürtheim 1928, 37.

53. Ἔπαφος, ἀληθῶς ῥυσίων ἐπώνυμος. Whittle 1964, esp. 2 and n. 5, derives ῥυσίων from ἐρύω "draw," *contra* LSJ s.v. ἐρύω (B) 5: "rescue, save." Cf. Friis Johansen and Whittle 1980, on 412 n. 2.

54. They are so used in the following passages: *Od.* 14.279, 22.372; Ais. *Eum.* 232, *Sept.* (of gods who rescue the Chorus who supplicate [see ἱκέσιον λόχον: 110] them) 92, 130, 165, 303, 318, 824; Soph. *OC* 285; Eur. *Andr.* 575, *IA* 1155–56, *Hel.* 801, 925, 1086, *Med.* 387–88.

55. Friis Johansen and Whittle 1980, on 1067.

56. See Friis Johansen and Whittle 1980, on 630–790, for the antithesis between Zeus and Ares in this ode, and on 98–99 for the translation "armed violence." Contrast *PV* 649–50: Ζεὺς γὰρ ἱμέρου βέλει πρὸς σοῦ τέθαλπται.

57. On the formal parallels between the epiphany of a god and the arrival of a savior of suppliants, see Kopperschmidt 1967, 68 n. 2.

58. The parallel is noted by Bacon 1982, 130. Zeus's touch may also be connected with a tradition of healing and purification by touch, although more evidence would be needed to prove this. See Vürtheim 1928, 35–36; Ais. *Cho.* 1059–60 and Garvie 1986 ad loc., citing *Cho.* 948–51 (with his notes) and *PV* 849 (Zeus touching Io); G. Thompson 1928 on *Cho.* 1057 (= 1059 in other editions).

59. See Gould 1973, 85–90, who connects Io's *aidôs* with supplication (87).

60. See Cairns 1993, 187; Friis Johansen and Whittle 1980, on 578–79. Cairns also argues convincingly (187–88) that the phrase δακρύων δ' ἀποστάζει πένθιμον αἰδῶ (578–79) refers to "the expression of *aidôs* in tears," opposing the view of Friis Johansen and Whittle (1980, on 578–79 n. 3, and on 579 n. 2) that ἀποστάζει means "causes to trickle away," that is, "sheds, i.e. loses, not 'exudes'." On *aidôs* in *Suppliants*, see also Erffa 1937, 86–91.

61. Friis Johansen and Whittle 1980, on 579 n. 2, connect Io's *aidôs* with her role as sexual partner of Zeus. On *aidôs*, women, and sex, see Cairns 1993, 120–26, 185–88, 305–40. On the association of marriage and mourning, see Rehm 1994; Seaford 1987, esp. 112–14.

62. Katz 1991, 134–54, 174–77, argues for an equivalency in the *Od.* between *xenia* and marriage, citing (p. 135) *Life of Pythagoras* 18.84. In her examples, however (Odysseus and Nausikaä, Odysseus and Penelope), the *xenos* is male.

63. Noted by Zeitlin 1992, 207–13, and 1990a, 109–10. On the bride as suppliant, see also Carson 1990, 164.

64. First and third passage cited by Gould 1973, 98. While Gould translates διώκειν as "persecute," there are more parallels for the sense "drive away" (LSJ s.v. διώκω II) and this interpretation better fits the context of supplication. Although this testimony is late, Gould, following Burkert 1962, 150–75, 451–53, holds that the idea goes back at least to the archaic period.

65. Recent studies of the Greek wedding ceremony include those of Oakley and Sinos 1993; Rehm 1994; R. F. Sutton 1989, and 1981, 145–275. Of these, only Oakley and Sinos (34) mention the idea that the bride is a suppliant.

66. On this rite, see R. F. Sutton 1989, 351–59, who argues that a red-figure loutrophoros (plate 34: Boston Museum of Fine Arts 10.223, ARV² 1017.44) illustrates the rite. The chief literary evidence is a scholion to Aristophanes' *Ploutos* 768, quoted by Sutton, 353.

67. A possible connection between the *katakhysmata* and the bride as suppliant is suggested by Gould 1973, 97–98; Oakley and Sinos 1993, 34; Vernant 1965, 130 n. 23.

68. Vogel 1966, 112 n. 1, mistranslates "and we have to touch them by the right hand," which suggests that the reference in διὰ δεξιᾶς is to the bride's right hand. On this construction, see above, note 28. The evidence of the vase paintings, discussed below, confirms my interpretation.

69. Illustrations and discussions: Haspels 1930, 436–44; Jenkins 1983; Mylonas 1945; Neumann 1965, 59–66; Oakley and Sinos 1993, 32 and numerous plates; Rehm 1994, 14–16, 35–40; R. F. Sutton 1981, 181–85, and 1989, 344–45.

70. Mylonas 1945, 563–64.

71. Noted by Flory 1978, 70–71.

72. R. F. Sutton 1981, 182, who, however, gives less emphasis to the legal aspects of the gesture in 1989, 345.

73. R. F. Sutton 1981, 181, notes that most scenes representing the procession on foot show this gesture. The scene in the marriage chamber is depicted on an Attic red-figure loutrophoros (reproduced by Oakley and Sinos 1993, fig. 122: Buffalo Museum of Science, C 23262).

74. For example, Jenkins 1983; Neumann 1965; Oakley and Sinos 1993, 32; R. F. Sutton 1981, 181–84, and 1989, 344–45. On marriage as abduction, see also Sourvinou-Inwood 1973, 1987.

75. On the wedding song see below, section 7, note 129.

76. Examples from Oakley and Sinos 1993, 137 n. 71.

77. Female dancers: Attic black-figure lekythos (Oakley and Sinos 1993, fig. 59: Metropolitan Museum of Art 56.11.1); woman between two satyrs dancing: pithos from Crete ca. 600–550 (British Museum GR 1980.12–28.1). Aithra: Apollodoros *Epitome* 5.22; vase: red-figure KCA with named figures (British Museum, LONBE 458; ARV², 239.16, 237, 238). Jenkins 1983, 138, claims that Athena is shown leading Herakles "hand on wrist," citing a black-figure kylix (British Museum, *BMC Vases* B424, ABV 169, 3, *JHS* 52 [1932], pl. 5). This vase, however, actually portrays Athena grasping Herakles just below the elbow, not "hand on wrist" (personal observation).

78. Tearing clothes and dragging by hair: Ais. *Supp.* 903–9. Jenkins 1983, 141, argues unconvincingly that the representation of a man grasping the edge of a woman's

cloak is "equivalent" to the "hand on wrist" motif, citing a white-ground lekythos (fig. 2: Palermo, ARV², 446, 266).

79. Attic red-figure loutrophoros (Berlin Staatliche Museen F 2372) and red-figure skyphos (ARV² 647, 21). Both are reproduced in Jenkins 1983, 137, fig. 1 (= Oakley and Sinos 1993, figs. 72, 73) and plate 18b.

80. As argued by Sourvinou-Inwood 1987, 143, 147.

81. Rehm 1994, 36–39.

82. R. F. Sutton 1992; 1989; 1981, 169–96, 212–13; quotation: 1989, 346.

83. R. F. Sutton 1981, 184.

84. Frontisi-Ducroux 1996, 83. I am indebted to Marilyn Skinner for this reference.

85. Peitho: Oakley and Sinos 1993, 32–33, and Attic red-figure skyphos (fig. 86: Boston Museum of Fine Arts 13.186); Eros: R. F. Sutton 1981, 186–89.

86. Either hand or wrist: Oakley and Sinos 1993, 45; leading by hand: figs. 79, 90, 91, 94, 106, 110; holding hands: fig. 122. The statement of Oakley and Sinos that the term "is never used in the context of a wedding" (137 n. 71) needs qualifying in view of Eur. *Ion*, 891–95, where Kreusa says that Apollo led her "hand on wrist" to bed (λευκοῖς δ' ἐμφὺς καρποῖσιν χειρῶν εἰς ἄντρου κοίτας . . . ἆγες).

87. Although Βαστάζω can mean "touch" (e.g., Soph. *OC* 1105, with Kamerbeek 1984 ad loc.) the sense of "raise" or "lift" is more common (see LSJ s.v. I.1) and more appropriate here (cf. Eur. *Alc.* 19; Dale 1961, ad loc.). On wedding ritual in this play, see Buxton 1987, 18–22; Foley 1985, 87–88; Halleran 1988, 126–27; Schein 1988, 201–2; Rehm 1994, 84–96.

88. This is especially clear in Oakley and Sinos 1993, figs. 85, 94, 97, 106. In many scenes, the bride "seems to hold out her wrist to him [sc. her husband]": R. F. Sutton 1981, 184.

89. Oakley and Sinos 1993, figs. 72, 73 = Jenkins 1983, fig. 1 (note 79 above).

90. R. F. Sutton 1989, 339, notes that in the classical wedding procession the groom "strides right," leading the bride while "grasping her left hand in his right." Of the fourteen illustrations of groom leading bride in Oakley and Sinos 1993, only two (figs. 86 and 91) represent the man using his left hand to lead the woman. It may be significant that on a red-figure skyphos (fig. 86: Boston Museum of Fine Arts 13.186), the adulterer Paris leads Helen, striding to the left. That Admetos grasps Alkestis with his right hand when he "remarries" her is indicated by Eur. *Alc.* 1115, on which see the works cited in note 87 above.

91. Mercier 1990, 54, 78–80, notes that the raising of a suppliant in literature is seldom marked in words.

92. Right hand: Eur. *IT* 1068; *Hipp.* 333, 605; *Hec.* 342–44, 753; *IA* 909. Examples given by Kaimio 1988, 50–61; Sittl 1890, 165 n. 7, 166 n. 1.

93. It is Priam's right wrist that Akhilleus grasps when they come to an agreement in *Il.* 24.671–72. I am not convinced by Flory's argument that in the *Il.* 24 example Priam is in a position of inferiority (1978, 71 n. 5). On the handclasp, see Herman 1987, 50–54, and for the gesture in tragedy, Kaimio 1988, 26–34.

94. Graces: Eur. *Hipp.* 1148, Barrett 1964 on 1147–50; Herakles: Eur. *HF* 1403; cf. 1375, and see further below in section 4.

95. Suppliant: Soph. *OC* 284, Herod. 5.71; bride: Harrison 1968, 3–12; Ogden 1996, 38.

96. Collard 1975, on 359–61, somewhat misleadingly translates "taking her dear hand in mine." On the construction, see above, note 28.

97. *Med.* 496–98, discussed by Mercier 1990, 278–83.

98. Reading ἐς οἴκους.

99. Mercier 1990, 126–27.

100. Kaimio 1988, 52.

101. ἕδρα is used esp. of the sitting of suppliants: LSJ s.v. II.1. Compare the supplication of Adrastos in Eur. *Supp.*, who also lies on the ground (κεῖται: 22), weeps (21), and covers his head (110–11).

102. See Mercier 1990, 123–24.

103. The parallel is noted, for example, by G. W. Bond 1981, on 1424.

104. Cf. Zeitlin 1992, 213, 215.

105. On Zeus, fertility, and the breath of life, see Zeitlin 1992, 223–25.

106. See Peck 1979, 170 note e, on *aither* and *pneuma*, and 580–89 (appendix B, nos. 10–25) on the role of the *pneuma* in generation.

107. Plato, *Laws* 6.775d7–8. Friis Johansen and Whittle 1980 bracket *Supp.* 282–83, but the lines are accepted by Mazon 1949, Page 1972, Tucker 1889, and West 1990.

108. Among the many scholars who have argued that the play is concerned with changes in the institution of marriage are Detienne 1988, 160; Robertson 1924, 53; Thomson 1946, 305–8; Winnington-Ingram 1983, 71; and Zeitlin 1988, 234, 241–42. Detienne 1988, 163, connects the Pythagorean idea that the wife is a suppliant with the new institution of marriage. Zeitlin 1992, 207–13, and 1990, 109–10, notes parallels between virgin wife and suppliant in the *Suppliants* and in Greek society generally, and cites the Pythagorean comparison of wife to suppliant. However, no one, to my knowledge, has interpreted the relationship between Zeus Hikesios and Io as a prototype of the relationship between husband and suppliant bride.

109. Saïd 1978, 327–33, discusses the *hybris* of suitors and Herald. Ewans 1996a, 216, and Taplin 1977, 216–17, give good arguments for assigning some of the lyrics at 825–71 to the Herald, *pace* West 1990 and Friis Johansen and Whittle 1980, who assign them to a chorus of Egyptians.

110. Goldhill 1991b, 24. Friis Johansen and Whittle 1980, on 908 n. 1, argue convincingly that the Herald touches the women, *pace* Taplin 1977, 216–17.

111. Bacon 1982, 130. On the erotic connotations of *oistros* (gadfly) and *kentron* (goad), see Padel 1992, 120–22.

112. Line 1034, reading θεσμός with the manuscripts and West 1990, who notes a similar use of θεσμίος at 707–8 (where it refers to respect for parents). In *Od.* 23. 296, θεσμός, used of the renewed marriage of Odysseus and Penelope, may refer to wedding ritual: Seaford 1994a, 37 and nn. 33–34 , citing Plut. *Mor.* 138b and Soph. *Ant.* 798. θέμις is used of heterosexual relations in *Il.* 9.134, 276 (= 19.177).

113. I am indebted to Peter Burian for calling this point to my attention.

114. For evidence concerning and possible reconstructions of the rest of the trilogy, see Friis Johansen and Whittle 1980, 1.40–55; Fritz 1962; Garvie 1969, 163–233; Keuls 1974, 43–81; Winnington-Ingram 1983, 55–72.

115. Winnington-Ingram 1983, 63.

116. Among those who have argued for a reconciliation of Zeus with Hera are Zeitlin 1992, 223; 1988, 250. Positing a reconciliation of Aphrodite with Danaïd(s) are Friis Johansen and Whittle 1980, 1:42, 51–55; Fritz 1962, 189–92; Garvie 1969, 226–27; Seaford 1987, 116–17; Winnington-Ingram 1983, 59. My reconstruction differs from previous ones in connecting both reconciliations with Zeus Hikesios.

117. I follow West 1990 and Friis Johansen and Whittle 1980 in distributing 1034 ff. between the Danaïds and a chorus of Argive men.

118. See MacKinnon 1978, 81, on the irresolvable ambiguity of this line, which can also be translated as "desire will enchant one of the children [of Danaos]." MacKinnon argues that *eros* and fertility are inseparable, in Aiskhylos's view.

119. On the reading θεσμός, see above, note 112. Zeus, Hera Teleia, and Kypris are also linked in *Eum.* 213–15, where Apollo affirms the sanctity of marriage.

120. Burkert 1983, 164; J. V. O'Brien 1993, 147.

121. A second marriage is part of the account given by Pindar, *Pyth.* 9.111–16. On the issue of a second marriage, see Friis Johansen and Whittle 1980, 1:45, 51–52; Garvie 1969, 226–27, 230; Keuls 1974, 47–48, 69–74; Seaford 1987, 116–17; Sissa 1990, 153–54.

122. Hera cult: Burkert 1985, 134–35; Heraia: Burkert 1983, 166, 162–63, citing Herod. 1.31 (Kleobis and Biton).

123. The evidence is inconclusive. See Calame 1977, 1: 218 (1997, 119); Zeitlin 1970, 662, with bibliography.

124. Burkert 1985, 133–35; J. V. O'Brien 1993, 54–62.

125. Herod. 2.171. Among those who believe that the trilogy ended with the foundation of the Thesmophoria are Detienne 1988, 173; Robertson 1924; Thomson 1946, 308; Zeitlin 1990, 111–12, 1992, 234–38.

126. On the Thesmophoria, see Burkert 1985, 242–46.

127. The main source is Bakkhylides 11. On this and other premarital myths, see Burkert 1983, 168–79; Calame 1977, 1:209–24, 411–20 (1997, 116–20, 238–44); Seaford 1988.

128. Marriage as yoking: Calame 1977, 1:411–20 (1997, 238–44); J. V. O'Brien 1993, 184–88; Seaford 1988. On Hera βοῶπις, see Burkert 1985, 64, 131; J. V. O'Brien 1993, 134–37.

129. The trilogy may have ended with the institution of the wedding song, in which the reluctance of the bride is dramatized. The wedding song is anticipated in the antiphonal singing of choruses of males and females at the end of the *Suppliants*: Seaford, 1984–85; 1987, 114–17.

130. On text and interpretation of frag. 44R (125M), see Friis Johansen and Whittle 1980, 1.41–42; Garvie 1969, 204–11; Radt 1985.

131. On the *hieros gamos* in this fragment and in Ais. Ag., see Herington 1986.

Chapter 4

1. Scholars have long debated the question of whether Philoktetes, his bow, or both are needed. On the controversy, see Easterling 1978; Gill 1980; Hinds 1967; Hoppin 1981; Machin 1981, 61–103. Pucci 1994, 39, writes insightfully of the "labyrinthine oracles" that have "no authoritative evidence of the truth." Cf. M. Davies 1991, 268–69; Seale 1972, 97.

2. Among those who discuss *philia* in the *Philoktetes* are Blundell 1989, 184–225; Easterling 1978; Gill 1980; Newman 1991; P. W. Rose 1976; Segal 1981a, 292–361; White 1985.

3. Segal 1981b, 133, mentions "the quasi-ritual of the transmission of the bow" (cf. 1981a, 295: "renewal of ritual action;" 321: "quasi-ritual"), but he does not elaborate. Belfiore 1994 and Smith 1993 independently analyzed the play in terms of *xenia* relationships, arriving at different conclusions.

4. These preliminaries are discussed by Herman 1987, 41–58.

5. Herman 1987, 57.

6. Herman 1987, 50.

7. Herman 1987, 59. Konstan 1997, 36–37, challenges Herman's view that *xenia* is initiated by formal rituals, yet he also notes that it is "an institution marked by self-conscious formality" (86). The truth is that *xenia*, like other ancient institutions — marriage, for example — allows for a certain variety and flexibility in ritual.

8. The accent on the first syllable distinguishes this word from the term for the *xenia* relationship: see Herman 1987, 60.

9. Herman 1987, 60 n. 56. On the *Iliad* passage, see also Benveniste 1969, 343.

10. On these characteristics of *xénia* gifts, see Herman 1987, 60–63.

11. Herman 1987, 58–61.

12. Herman 1987, 50.

13. "Stranger-shy" is Webster's rendition of ὑπόπτης, 1970, ad loc.

14. I quote the translation of Lattimore 1965. Some parallels between Philoktetes and the Kyklops, in the *Odyssey* and in Euripides' *Kyklops*, are noted by Greengard 1987, 56, 81–83; Segal 1981a, 297–98, 300–301. On the importance of *xenia* in both of these works, see Konstan 1981, D. F. Sutton 1974. For a good discussion of the relationships among epic, satyr play, and tragedy, see also Seaford 1984, introduction.

15. Kamerbeek 1980, ad loc., calls attention to the emotional effect of the short line and notes the parallel interruptions of the meter made by Philoktetes' cries of pain at 730 ff.

16. This aspect of the relationship between the two men is discussed by Avery 1965, who notes (285) that Philoktetes uses the words τέκνον and παῖς fifty-two times in this play.

17. Kamerbeek 1980, on 248, notes the cruelty of Neoptolemos's pretense of ignorance.

18. ὁ ἀφικούμενος can mean "the stranger, newcomer": LSJ s.v. ἀφικνέομαι. On the irony of the Chorus's words, see Blundell 1989, 194–95.

19. On this beginning of friendship based on common hate, see Blundell 1989, 196; Segal 1981a, 332.

20. Steidle 1968a, 176–81, argues that Neoptolemos feels pity from the very beginning of his encounter with Philoktetes and that his first clear expression of it occurs at 339: ὦ τάλας ("O wretch"). Although these words and the other passages Steidle cites could be taken as evidence for Neoptolemos's pity, I agree with Winnington-Ingram 1980, 283–86, that Sophokles leaves this ambiguous until 759. On the ambiguity, see also Seale 1972: 97–100.

21. *Pace* Taplin (1971, 33, followed by Smith 1993, 35 n. 22), who believes that Neoptolemos touches Philoktetes for the first time at 813.

22. *Teknon*: 236, 249, 260, 276, 284, 300, 307, 327, 337, 466, 468, 484.

23. I assume the attribution of 671–73 to Neoptolemos, following Lloyd-Jones and Wilson 1990a and most other editors.

24. On this passage, and the pun on Philoktetes' name, see Daly 1982, 440–43; Greengard 1987, 60.

25. Harsh 1960, 411, notes that the bow is the "objective symbol of Heracles." On the significance of the bow as a symbol of friendship and *euergesia*, see also Gill 1980; J. A. Johnson 1988; Segal 1977 and 1981a, 318–22; Taplin 1978, 89–93.

26. Seale 1982, 36.

27. J. A. Johnson 1988, 117, notes this.

28. This proverb is quoted by Aristotle, *EE* 1245a30: ἄλλος Ἡρακλῆς, ἄλλος αὐτός. On the bond the bow creates among Philoktetes, Neoptolemos, and Herakles, see Avery 1965, 294–95.

29. Among those who write that Neoptolemos handles the bow during the conversation at 654–73 are Kitto 1956, 118; Knox 1964, 129; Winnington-Ingram 1980, 286. For the correct view, see Seale 1982, 36–37.

30. On tragedy's use and adaptation of ritual patterns, see Easterling 1988.

31. On this interpretation of 772–73, see Kamerbeek 1980, ad loc.

32. The parallel is noted by Jebb 1932, on 774.

33. This gesture is referred to at 942 and repeated at 1291–92: see further section 2.

34. For examples in the visual arts, see Herman 1987, 51–52.

35. See further note 44.

36. Linforth 1956, 132.

37. I follow Webster 1970 in taking Ἡρακλέους as possessive genitive dependent on τόξα, and μου as ablative genitive, with λαβών. Cf. Kamerbeek 1980, ad loc.

38. Jebb 1932, followed by Kamerbeek 1980, ad loc.

39. LSJ lists "apply," "put to" as sense (1) of προστίθημι, citing Euripides *Bacchae* 1110: χέρα προσέθεσαν ἐλάτῃ. I translate it as "giving" to preserve the ambiguity of the word.

40. On Neoptolemos's silences, see Taplin 1978, 113–14.

41. Jebb 1932; Kamerbeek 1980, and Webster 1970, ad loc., note that this refers to Zeus who punishes those who harm suppliants, but they do not see that Zeus Xenios is also in question. The appeal to *xenoi* at 1184 supports my interpretation.

42. For this reading of πέλασσον, see Jebb 1932, ad loc., followed by Lloyd-Jones and Wilson 1990b, 208.

43. Jebb 1932, ad loc., quotes Arndt's translation of *xenos* as "guest-friend." Webster 1970, ad loc., writes that if ξένον is construed with σέβῃ, the words mean: "'if you have any reverence for a stranger,' i.e. you have been my host since my arrival and that should constitute a bond."

44. Philoktetes also mentions an oath to take him home at 941, although all that Neoptolemos gave at 813 was a promise to stay with Philoktetes. As Taplin notes (1971, 38), Neoptolemos is morally committed to take Philoktetes home, even though no oath was given.

45. Steidle 1968a, 178–79, calls attention to the parallel between 526 and 645.

46. See Harsh 1960, 412; Knox 1964, 139–40; Segal 1981a, 320–21.

47. On Philoktetes' act as an expression of *philia*, see R. Newman 1991, 307; P. W. Rose 1976, 79.

48. Kirkwood 1994, 435–36, argues persuasively that the plural φίλων ("friends") includes Neoptolemos, whose actions in forgoing glory to honor his promise help to persuade Philoktetes.

49. The negative aspects of Sophokles' Neoptolemos are stressed by Calder 1971; Kott 1970, 177–85; Machin 1981, 410–19. On Neoptolemos's impiety at Troy, see Blundell 1988, 146; Easterling 1978, 39; Kirkwood 1994, 428; Stinton 1986, 90–91; P. W. Rose 1976, 102 and n. 109.

50. The hypothesis of Eur. *Skyrioi* states that Akhilleus slept with Deidamia in secret. On these plays, see below, appendix B, and Jouan 1966, 204–18. The dates of both are unknown. Fuqua (1976, 44–45, citing Jouan 216–17) argues that the plot of Sophokles' *Skyrioi* is sketched at *Phil.* 343–47.

51. On the Athenian preoccupation with questions of legitimacy, see Ogden 1996, Patterson 1990.

52. On the myth, see Jouan 1966, 204–18, who argues (211) that in Euripides' lost *Skyrioi* a reconciliation between Lykomedes and Akhilleus took place. Webster 1967, 96, also believes that a marriage took place in Euripides' play.

53. According to one myth, Laertes paid the bride price for Odysseus's mother when she was already pregnant by Sisyphos. See Kamerbeek 1980, ad loc., and Webster 1970.

54. Schein 1997, 135 comments on the "impossibility of knowing the truth" in this play. On the veracity of Neoptolemos's story, see also Hamilton 1975; Knox 1964, 191 n. 30; Machin 1981, 77–81; Roberts 1989, 170–71; Taplin 1987, 69–70.

55. See Machin 1981, 76.

56. Ogden 1996, 201–8; 1997, esp. 9–46; Patterson 1990, 68; Teichman 1982.

57. Winnington-Ingram 1980, 308. Cf. Alt 1961; Diller 1939, 245–46; Fuqua 1976, 36; Hajistephanou 1975, 33–38; Kirkwood 1958, 242–43; Lesky 1939, 372; Nussbaum 1976, 43–49; and Ryzman 1991. More nuanced versions of this view are held by Blundell 1988; Erbse 1966; and P. W. Rose 1976, 87–89.

58. Calder 1971.

59. For a survey of the treatment of Neoptolemos in the mythical tradition, much of which is negative, see Fuqua 1976, 35–43.

60. For this view, see Blundell 1988; Fuqua 1976, 54–55; Knox 1964, 122–23. Philoktetes himself is portrayed as holding this view when he states that Neoptolemos has received an education in deceit from Odysseus (971–72, 1013–15).

61. On the similarities and differences between Neoptolemos and Akhilleus, see Blundell 1988, 143–44; Hamilton 1975, 131–32, with bibliography.

62. Cf. Roberts 1989, 174. Davidson 1995 notes many other parallels between *Philoktetes* and the *Odyssey*.

63. Cf. Hamilton 1975, 132; P. W. Rose 1976, 88.

64. Noted by P. W. Rose 1976, 88.

65. See Easterling 1978, 28–29; Greengard 1987, 22–27; Seale 1972, 97–100.

66. Cf. Blundell 1988, 146.

67. Noted by Machin 1981, 417–18. The MSS reading, ὠφελούμενος, is often amended by those who are uncomfortable with the parallel to Odysseus's statement in the prologue (111).

68. Neoptolemos's readiness to use force in this way is sometimes explained away: see Blundell 1989, 189; Knox 1964, 122–23.

69. On the staging, see Seale 1982, 44.

70. See Nagy 1979, 45–49. The verb cognate with *mêtis* is applied to Odysseus at *Phil.* 1114 and 1139.

71. The phrase Ὀδυσσέως βία(ς) ("the force of Odysseus") occurs at 314, 321, and 592. Although Kamerbeek 1980, on 314–16, writes that some explain it as an "epicism," it does not occur in Homer. On this phrase, see Blundell 1989, 208 n. 88, who cites Long 1968, n. 138, and Schein 1984, 135–36, who discusses the association of Herakles with *bia* in the *Iliad*.

72. On Herakles as bastard and patron of bastards, see Ogden 1996, 199–203; Patterson 1990, 63. Herakles' bastardy is closely linked to his mixed divine-mortal status. On this idea in Sophokles' *Women of Trakhis*, see Friis Johansen 1986, esp. 57; on Herakles' ethical ambiguity in that play, see Easterling 1981, esp. 60.

73. On the negative aspects of the bow, see Kamerbeek 1980, ad loc.; Blundell 1989, 204–5, who cites Kott 1970, 176.

74. On Neoptolemos's unfinished story, see Roberts 1989, 173–75; 1988, 190–91.

Chapter 5

1. Vernant 1981, 107.

2. Reading αὐθέντου. The singular of the MSS should not be questioned, since the *authentês* relationship is hereditary.

3. On this passage, see Hall 1989, 188–90.

4. See Aristotle *Top.* 2.7.112b27–113a19.

5. On these two senses of the word, see Gernet 1955, 31–33, and cf. below, chapter 6, note 37. Gernet cites, for the sense "killer of one's own kin," Ais. Ag. 1573, *Eum.* 212; Eur. *HF* 839, *IA* 1190; cf. *HF* 1359.

6. On the *authentês* relationship, see Gernet 1955, 29–38 and Parker 1983, 122–23, both of whom cite Antiphon 5.11. See also Demosthenes 21 (*Against Meidias*) 116–20, with MacDowell 1990, ad loc.

7. This is why, for example, Homer's Danaans express the desire to avenge Helen's rape by sleeping with the wives of the conquered Trojans (*Il.* 2.354–56).

8. The MSS have αὐτοέντην or αὐτοφόντην, synonyms of αὐθέντης.

9. These two examples are quoted by Gernet 1955, 34; cf. Soph. *El.* 585–90.

10. On Neoptolemos in other versions of the myth, see Fuqua 1976, 34–49; Amoroso 1994, 139–40 and n. 2; M. Lloyd 1994, 1. For an excellent discussion of the questions of allusions to events not related in the text and of the prior knowledge of the audience, see Roberts 1997.

11. For the sense "murderer" of αυτο- compounds, see Soph. *OT* 107, cited by Parker 1983, 351. In that passage also, the word has an ironic ambiguity.

12. On extensions of responsibility in Euripides, see M. Lloyd 1994, on 248. Saïd 1978, 412, notes that Neoptolemos treats Apollo as a mortal. No details about Apollo's role in the death of Akhilleus and Neoptolemos's demand for satisfaction are given in this play. For the mythological tradition, see Gantz 1993, 625–28, 690–94.

13. Among those who hold that Neoptolemos's relationship with Hermione creates the central tensions are Aldrich 1961, 68; Craik 1984, 26; Hartung 1852, 5–6; Heath 1987, 102–3; Kovacs 1980, 79–80; Steidle 1968b.

14. Aigisthos was the child of the incestuous union of Thyestes and his daughter: see below, appendix B, "Atreus Myths."

15. Andokides 4, *Against Alkibiades* 22–23. This passage was called to my attention by P. J. Wilson 1996, 319–20, who does not, however, notice the parallel with *Andromakhe.* Furley 1989, 152, speculates that the passage might have been inspired by "a particular play, perhaps that of Sophocles" (that is, the *Atreus* or *Thyestes*).

16. On the centrality of tensions within kinship relationships in this play, see also Phillipo 1995, who, however, errs in holding that the relationship between Andromakhe and Neoptolemos "does not in itself involve a conflict that affects the course of events" (367).

17. On Neoptolemos's absence and importance in the play, see Friedländer 1926, 101; Jong 1990, 10–14; M. Lloyd 1994, 3.

18. Cf. Ferrari 1971, 222.

19. On these distinctions between wife and concubine, see Ogden 1996, 100–106; Patterson 1990, 55 and n. 61; M. Lloyd 1994, 6–9. Lloyd wrongly holds that Hermione has no cause for complaint since Neoptolemos has ceased to sleep with Andromakhe (9).

20. Cf. 170–80, quoted above, section 1. On amphimetric strife, see chapter 1, section 1, and note 12 of that chapter. On conflict over offspring in *Andr.*, see Ogden 1996, 196–97; Seaford 1990, 168–70. Diggle daggers the MSS reading ἔριδας, which does not

correspond metrically with 475. It makes excellent sense here, however, and is printed without daggers by Murray, who instead questions 475.

21. On the importance of motherhood in this play and on Andromakhe's ambiguous relationship to Molossos, see Fantham 1986, 268–70.

22. Cf. Amoroso 1994, 140 n. 3; Storey 1989, 18.

23. Burnett 1971, 136–37, and Michelini 1987, 92–93, note the negative aspects of Andromakhe's complaisance.

24. Burnett 1971, 135.

25. Ogden 1996, 196 n. 49, notes that he is called *nothos* (bastard) at 636, 912, 927–28, and 941–42.

26. On these words and Molossos's ambiguous status, see Pòrtulas 1988, 293.

27. On Hippolytos and other literary bastards, see Ogden 1996, 194–99; Patterson 1990, 65–69.

28. See Barrett 1964, ad loc.; Ogden 1996, 198.

29. Pòrtulas 1988, 287–88, 292–96, citing Vernant 1974; Seaford 1990, 169–70.

30. Ogden 1996, 24, referring to *Il.* 11.101–4. See also Patterson 1990, 49–50.

31. This is the formulation of J. K. Davies 1977–78, 105. On marriage and legitimacy, see also Harrison 1968, 24–29, 61–70; Lacey 1968, 100–118; MacDowell 1978, 86–92; Manville 1990; Ogden 1996; Patterson 1990, 1998.

32. J. K. Davies 1977–78. A good example of a challenge is the case of Phrastor, who tried to legitimize a bastard. See Lacey 1968, 145, 298 n. 80, citing Isaeus 4.18; Ogden 1996, 115, citing Demosthenes 59.59 (*Against Neaira*).

33. See Ogden 1996, 59–62, quoting Plut. *Per.* 37.2–5.

34. Ogden 1996, 72–75, 104, 189–91.

35. Metroxeny: Ogden 1996, 18–19, 62–64, 194–95 (on Eur. *Med.*), 209.

36. Free children: Ogden 1996, 23; Patterson 1990, 54. On Megapenthes, the son of a slave woman, who is Menelaos's apparent heir in *Od.* 4. 3–14, see Patterson 1990, 50 n. 40; Seaford 1994a, 206–7; Vernant 1974, 66–67.

37. Ogden 1996, 37–44, 58, 62 and n. 129, 209.

38. Harrison 1968, 164; MacDowell 1978, 89.

39. Ogden 1996, 125 and n. 246, 177.

40. See K. H. Lee 1975, 10–11; Sorum 1995, 377.

41. ξυντράπεζος is a rare word, but when it or its synonym ὁμοτράπεζος occurs, it refers to someone in a relationship of equality: Plato *Euthyphro* 4c1: ὁμοτράπεζος (of Euthyphro's father); Herod. 9.16.2: ὁμοτράπεζος . . . καὶ ὁμόσπονδος (of a military ally); Xen. *Anab.* 1.9.31.1: φίλοι καὶ συντράπεζοι (of Kyros's friends). Contrast the beggars Odysseus and Iros who are offered food but sit on the ground at the threshold instead of at tables with their hosts (*Od.* 17.339–40, 356–57; 18.17, 32–33).

42. Menelaos's words at 658–59 recall those of the law prohibiting citizens from living with foreigners as wives: οὐκ ἐᾷ . . . συνοικεῖν . . . οὐδὲ παιδοποιεῖσθαι: Demos. 59.16–17, quoted by Lacey 1968, 112 and n. 92, 288.

43. Compare the imprecision of δάμαρ at *Andr.* 4. The same word is used of the concubine Iole in Soph. *Trach.* 428–29: see Easterling 1982, ad loc., and Stevens 1971, ad loc.

44. Cf. Albini 1974, 94.

45. See Burnett 1971, 134.

46. Diggle, following Cobet, brackets 810, where the Nurse reports Hermione's fears that her husband will kill her. Stevens 1971, on 810, writes that "she is surely exaggerating her danger."

47. Cf. Ferrari 1971, 213–14, who notes that Hermione's attack on a suppliant at Thetis's altar is an offense to the family.

48. See Kamerbeek 1943, 57–58.

49. Burnett 1971, 142, notes that Menelaos cannot distinguish friend from enemy and deserts both Hermione and Andromakhe.

50. Cf. 663–66, where, as Sorum notes (1995, 383–84), Menelaos also forgets that Molossos's father is Greek.

51. Orestes tells Hermione of the plot at 993–1008. I agree with Aldrich 1961, 53–54, and M. Lloyd 1994, on 1008, that Orestes himself does the killing: see 997, 1063–65, 1074–75, 1115–16, 1242. In any case, in plotting the murder (993–97) Orestes is *authentês* whether or not he actually holds the sword. Cf. Fontenrose 1960, 220, and compare Eur. *IT* 870–72, where Iphigeneia, who does not do the actual killing in the rites (40), states that her brother was almost killed by her hand.

52. The word *deinon* can mean "terrible" or "wonderful." Cf. Soph. *El.* 770, where Klytaimestra, after learning of the supposed death of Orestes, says δεινὸν τὸ τίκ-τειν ἐστίν ("it is a wonderful thing to give birth"). I am indebted to Richard Seaford for this reference.

53. This refers to a place, not the shrine of Thetis: see M. Lloyd 1994, 9–10; Stevens 1971, on 16–21.

54. Cf. Stevens 1971, on 46: "the shrine expresses in stone . . . pride in the . . . marriage." Ferrari 1971, 213, notes that the shrine represents the sanctity of the race, and the religious center of the house of Neoptolemos.

55. On Thetis's "failed marriage" and its relationship to the play, see Storey 1989, 20–21. Sourvinou-Inwood 1987, 138, goes too far in claiming that "the union of Peleus and Thetis is a paradigm for marriage" in general.

56. Homer's Akhilleus seems to regret his mixed parentage when he expresses the wish that Thetis had remained with the immortals and that Peleus had married a mortal woman (*Il.* 18.86–87). Cf. Eur. *Ion* 506–9, where the children of the unions of gods with mortals are said to be unhappy. Patterson 1990 argues that *nothoi* are the children of mixed or unequal unions (41, 62) and points out (63 n. 88) that the children of a god and a mortal are called *nothoi*, citing Plato, *Apol.* 27d8. The most famous of these children is Herakles, the patron hero of bastards (Ogden 1996, 199–203; Patterson 1990, 63–65). Ogden 1996, 15–17, disputes Patterson's technical definition of the term *nothos* but agrees that it is frequently used of the children of mixed marriages.

57. Ormand 1996, 82.

58. On these sources and their interrelationships, see Lesky 1937, 1956; Reitzenstein 1900; Roscher 1884–1937, 5.783–99; Scodel 1982; Slatkin 1991, 70–77, 118–21. Jouan 1966, 55–92, discusses the influence of these sources on Euripides.

59. *Il.* 18.432–34: Lattimore. On Thetis in the *Iliad*, see Slatkin 1991.

60. On the two versions, see Lesky 1937, 1956; Reitzenstein 1900; Apollodoros, *Library* 3.13.5; Apollonius, *Argon.* 4.790–809.

61. Allen 1946, *Kypria* frag. 2 = Hes. frag. 210 MW = frag. 4 Evelyn-White, all of whom adopt the text of Reitzenstein 1900, 73. M. Davies 1988, frag. 2 follows Luppe. On the passage, see also Lesky 1937, 291.

62. Apollodoros, *Library* 3.13.5, quoted in Reitzenstein 1900, 73. The struggle of Peleus with Thetis is mentioned in many other sources, for example, Pindar, *Nem.* 3.35–36, 4.62–65; Herod. 7.191.2. See Lesky 1937, 289–90. The struggle and metamorphoses are represented in Oakley and Sinos 1993, fig. 130 (Attic red-figure *epinetron*,

Athens National Museum 1629). Other visual representations are listed in Jouan 1966, 75 n. 4.

63. Heyne's correction of Θέτιδος of the MSS.

64. Proklos's summary of the *Kypria* in *Khrestomathia*, M. Davies 1988, 31.5–11 = Allen 1946, 102.13–19 = frag. 1 Evelyn-White.

65. *Kypria*, frag. 1 (Schol. A to *Il.* 1.5): M. Davies 1988, 34–35. Allen 1946, 117–18, has a slightly different text. The scholion goes on to quote seven verses of the poem, translated Evelyn-White, frag. 3.

66. Hes. frag. 204 MW, 98–103, with omission of subscript dots. Evelyn-White, *Catalogues of Women and Eoiae* 2:200.5–10, has a slightly different text. On the meaning of πρόφασιν here, see Scodel 1982, 38 n. 11.

67. The separation of gods and humans may also include a sexual separation, which would prevent the birth of more demigods: see Scodel 1982, 37–38, citing frag. 1.1–14 MW. In frag. 204.101 MW, Rzach's μ[γέη]ι, read by Evelyn-White, makes this explicit. Evelyn-White translates: "that the children of the gods should not mate with wretched mortals."

68. Hes. *Op.* 156–171 West. Lines quoted: 159–60, 167–68. West 1978, on 160, notes that ἡμίθεοι means "children of the gods," not "semi-divine." Line 166, stating that some of the heroes died at Troy, is bracketed by Solmson 1990, defended by West, ad loc.

69. Jouan 1966, 99–100; 1988, 23. On *eris* and Thetis's marriage, see Slatkin 1991, 70–77; on *eris* in *Andr.*, see Albini 1974, 94–95; Ferrari 1971, 229; Storey 1989, 21; John R. Wilson 1979, 7–10. Euripides' use of the Judgment of Paris is discussed by Stinton 1965.

70. Frag. 1093 Nauck. That the mention of Sepias in *Andr.* alludes to the wrestling match is argued by Jouan 1966, 68–71; Lesky 1937, 289–90; Stevens 1971, on 1265, 1278.

71. Cf. Jouan 1966, 70: "le héros s'unit à Thétis malgré sa résistance" (the hero is united with Thetis in spite of her resistance).

72. *Pace* Dunn 1996, 17–18, 135–36. This tailpiece, which also appears in a number of other plays, has often been suspected: see Stevens 1971 ad loc., citing Barrett 1964, on Eur. *Hipp.* 1462–66, who argues that it is a later addition in *Andr.* Even if this is so, the coda may have been added because Peleus's last speech reminded an actor or a scribe of the metamorphosis. Dunn 1996, 24–25, and Roberts 1987 argue that this coda has a legitimate dramatic function as a closural device, although it is not directly relevant to the action.

73. See Jouan 1966, 41–43, citing *El.* 1282–83, *Hel.* 36–41 and 1639–42, *Or.* 1639–42.

74. See passages no. 6 and no. 7 and note 68 above; cf. Eur. *IA* 172, where the heroes about to sail for Troy are called "demigods" (ἡμιθέων).

75. Cf. Sorum 1995, 386.

76. See Storey 1989, esp. 23–24, on the chain of *eris* and murder.

77. If we may trust a hopelessly corrupt text, Hermione is mentioned explicitly at 1192.

78. On this idea, see Schein 1984; Slatkin 1991, 99–103, 42: "preserving a hero from death means denying him a heroic life."

79. Cf. Eur. *Hipp.* 1396, where Artemis says that it is not *themis* for a god to shed tears. Peleus will indeed bury Neoptolemos at Delphi (1240, 1277), but his abrupt ces-

sation of mourning complicates the emotional impact of the end of the play. On exclusion from mourning and funeral rites in other plays, see Roberts 1993.

80. On this cult, see Fontenrose 1960; M. Lloyd 1994, 2–3; Méridier 1927, 91–92.

81. Cf. Boulter 1966, 52.

82. Eur. *Hipp.* 1028. Hippolytos is given this *kleos* in cult, "not falling without name" (οὐκ ἀνώνυμος πεσών: 1429).

83. The Molossians are listed among barbarian tribes in Thucydides 2.80 (see Hall 1989, 180–81). Robertson 1923 argues that the *Andromakhe* was a gift to Tharyps, the boy-king of Molossia.

84. For these duties of a legitimate heir, see Harrison 1968, 124–32 (inheritance), 77, 123, 130; Lacey 1968, 147–49 (care, burial, cults); MacDowell 1978, 109–13; Parker 1983, 110 (vengeance).

85. According to LSJ ἀνάστατος means both "driven from one's house and home" and "ruined."

86. On these two passages, see John R. Wilson 1979, 9.

87. Seaford 1993; 1994a, esp. chapter 9.

88. On the parallels between events in Troy and those in Phthia, see Sorum 1995; M. Lloyd 1994, 6.

89. As Scodel notes (1982, 35–36), Greek myth is generally silent about the period after that of the sons of the Trojan heroes, who represent the end of the heroic age.

90. Unfortunately both of these passages are corrupt. Some support for 1222 ("I no longer have a city": οὐκέτ᾽ ἐστί μοι πόλις) may be found in Eur. *Hipp.* 1184, where Hippolytos uses nearly the same words as he departs for exile ("This city is no longer mine": πόλις γὰρ οὐκέτ᾽ ἔστιν ἥδε μοι).

91. He perhaps underscores this point by throwing away his scepter at 1223, as suggested by K. H. Lee 1975, 7–8, citing Steidle 1968b, 124.

92. Saïd 1984, esp. 51.

Chapter 6

1. Linforth 1954, 24, 25.

2. Heath 1987, 181, is one of the few to state this assumption explicitly: "Extending life that is ruined beyond hope is shameful, cowardly; it follows that it will be *kalon* ["noble"] to curtail life."

3. *Phaedo* 62b, taking φρουρᾷ at b4 to mean "garrison." Questions of interpretation are discussed by Gallop 1975, 83–85.

4. Loraux 1987a, 8, 7. While these conclusions are correct, Loraux should be read with caution. See the reviews of Knox 1988 and Skinner 1988. Others who note the unheroic nature of male suicide include Golder 1990, 14; Kott 1970, 57; Sorum 1986, 373; Zeitlin 1990, 73, 82.

5. Garrison 1991, 1995, to which I am indebted for many of the examples discussed below. In addition to Garrison, I have found most valuable the studies of Daube 1972; Delcourt 1939; Garland 1985; Gernet 1955; Hirzel 1908; Katsouris 1976; Loraux 1987a; Walcot 1986. Hooff 1990 is rightly criticized by Garrison 1991, 1 n. 3.

6. Garrison 1995, 3 (= 1991, 4).

7. Durkheim 1951, 44, 227, followed by Garrison 1991, 2–4, 1995, 34–44. McClure 1995 contains good criticisms of Garrison's use of Durkheim.

8. Durkheim 1951 argues that woman's "sensibility is rudimentary," while man "is a more complex social being" (215–16), and he believes that all suicides of "lower

societies" (217) or "primitive peoples," including "the Gallic and German barbarians," the Polynesians, the Hindus, and the Japanese (222–24), share common characteristics (217–25).

9. Daube 1972, 401–5.

10. Aiskhines, *Against Ktesiphon* 244, cited by Garrison 1991, 9 (= 1995, 18–19), who cautions that this passage is our only evidence for such treatment of a suicide.

11. Plato, *Laws* 9.873c2–5 (ἑαυτὸν κτείνῃ); *Phaedo* 62c6–7 (αὐτὸν ἀποκτεινύναι); Lysias, *Against Eratosthenes* 96 (φονέας αὐτῶν). See Daube 1972, 403–4; Garrison 1991, 8–9 (= 1995, 17–18); Hirzel 1908, 244–45.

12. Hirzel 1908, 95–98; Valgiglio 1966, 60–61.

13. ὑπεραποθνῄσκειν: Plato, *Symp.* 179b4, Arist. *NE* 1169a20, 25; ὑπερθνῄσκειν: Eur. *Alc.* 155, 682; προθνῄσκειν: Eur. *Alc.* 383, 472, 620, 684, 698, 710.

14. Durkheim 1951, 227, quoted by Garrison 1991, 4 n. 10, who follows him in arguing that self-sacrifice is suicide (1991, 4, 13, 33 n. 123; 1995, 129–31). A better account of Menoikeus's case is given by Loraux 1987a, 41: "in this death there is no clear distinction between sacrifice and suicide."

15. She is "most excellent" (ἀρίστη: Eur. *Alc.* 83, 151, 235, 241, 324, 441) and "noble" (εὐκλεής: 150, 938); cf. Plato, *Symp.* 179b–d.

16. Delcourt 1939.

17. For example, Eur. *Hec.* 1107–8 (συγγνώσθ'), noted by Bowra 1944, 46.

18. *Pace* Garrison 1991, 17 (= 1995, 28): "honorable suicide;" Katsouris 1976, 6 n. 5.

19. Garrison 1991, 14, on the examples discussed by her, 13–14 (= 1995, 23–25).

20. *Od.* 10.49 ff. and *Il.* 18.34 are cited by Garland 1985, 164.

21. Stevens 1986, 335 and n. 42, citing Dover 1974, 168. Walcot 1986, 232, gives a more cautious assessment.

22. See note 4.

23. I count Menoikeus's death as a suicide, because he kills himself with his own hand, but do not include other acts of self-sacrifice (Iphigeneia, Polyxene, Makaria). The cases listed by Garland 1985, 164; Garrison 1991, 20–33; Hooff 1990, 144, with nn. 20, 21, and appendix A; and Katsouris 1976 differ from one another to some extent since each scholar uses different criteria.

24. Delcourt 1939, 161–63, argues that both Haimon and Eurydike commit vengeance suicide and notes the parallel between the suicide of Haimon and that of Aias. See also Griffith 1999, on *Ant.* 1304–5.

25. Lefèvre 1991, 91–95 gives a good account of the long history of the view that Aias's suicide is atonement to Athena, beginning with A. W. von Schlegel at the beginning of the nineteenth century. Among more recent advocates of the atonement view are O'Higgins 1989: 48; Sicherl 1977: 96. See further section 3 and n. 53.

26. On "purifying fire," see Parker 1983, 227 (who does not mention *Her.* 1151–52.) On the funeral pyre as purification, see Eur. *Supp.* 1211 and Collard 1975, ad loc., who cites other passages.

27. See especially Furley 1986, Romilly 1980. This view is well criticized by Yoshitake 1994.

28. Adkins 1966, 218, notes that there is no way of knowing this.

29. These and other parallel passages are cited by Kells 1973, on *El.* 1319 ff.; Seaford 1984, on *Cyc.* 201; Willink 1986, on *Or.* 1152.

30. Humiliation: Errandonea 1958, 30–34; Sorum 1986, 373. Avoidance of further dishonor: Furley 1986, 105; Knox 1979, 151; Poe 1987, 72–73; Seidensticker 1983, 139.

31. See the good discussion of Zanker 1992, 22.

32. On this scene, see Taplin 1978, 108.

33. πρόκειμαι (427) is used of laying out a corpse: see Burton 1980, 22; Kamerbeek 1963, on 427.

34. On this point, see Blundell 1989, 72–88.

35. See Taplin 1979, 125, citing the Attic law on *prodosia* (treason).

36. πένθος is most appropriate to the reactions of his dependents, and it looks ahead to the mourning of Aias's mother in the next strophe.

37. Cf. 840–42, where αὐτοσφαγής is used of both Aias's suicide and the kin murder he invokes on his enemies, and *Ant.* 1175–76, where the Messenger says that Haimon died αὐτόχειρ and the Chorus ask whether the hand was his own or that of his father. αὐτο- compounds are frequently used in tragedy of kin murder: e.g., Eur. *HF* 839, *Med.* 1254, 1269, 1281. On these words, see Daube 1972; Gernet 1955; Loraux 1986; Parker 1983, 122, 350–51; Zeitlin 1982, 20.

38. I follow the interpretation of Kamerbeek 1963 and Stanford 1963, *pace* Jebb 1907, who takes it to mean "with the cattle."

39. Wigodsky 1962, 154, notes the ambiguity: "saved" can mean either "safely alive" or "safely dead." According to Taplin 1979: 126 *sôtêria* refers to Aias's rehabilitation after his death. As Seaford notes (1994b), "salvation" also has mystic connotations. On Aias's rehabilitation after death, see also Burian 1972, March 1991–93, Henrichs 1993.

40. ἄτας and μόρον (848) do not have connotations of defeat and humiliation, *pace* Errandonea 1958, 30. Kamerbeek 1963, on 848, rightly stresses the idea of injustice, contrasting this passage with 643. Easterling 1984, 6, notes that "when he kills himself . . . he seems to have found a way of overcoming his shame."

41. Kott 1970, 69, speculates that he dies at high noon, when the shadow of the sword is shortest. Stanford 1978, 196, states that Aias's prayer (*Il.* 17.645 ff.) to die in the light is answered, and that he goes "proudly and luminously into the darkness of Hades."

42. Stanford 1963, on 865, notes this contrast.

43. Noted by Cohen 1978, 32; Kitto 1956, 193–94; Loraux 1987a, 12; Stanford 1963, on 817–20.

44. Vengeance suicide: Delcourt 1939, followed by Blundell 1989, 71 n. 55; Seidensticker 1983, 139–40; Stanford 1963, 289.

45. Loraux 1987a, 22.

46. On these two aspects of the heroic code, see Blundell 1989.

47. Blundell 1989, 86–88; Eucken 1991, 130; Poe 1987, 82–83; Sorum 1986, 369–70.

48. Cf. 403–4: ποῖ τις οὖν φύγῃ, ποῖ μολὼν μενῶ; ("Where might one flee? Where might I remain?")

49. My views are closest to those of Taplin 1979, who argues that Aias believes his suicide will benefit his friends.

50. Winnington-Ingram 1980, 50–51 notes that "the basic theme is not hierarchy but alternation." Cf. Stevens 1986, 333.

51. DK 12 a 9. Translation of Kirk, Raven, and Schofield, 118. Segal 1981a, 120, also sees connections between Aias's speech and Anaximander, although his conclusions differ from mine. Aias's speech is connected with the philosophy of Herakleitos by Kamerbeek 1963, on 669–77, and 1948, 84–98, 89, 95. A further step is taken by Seaford 1994a, 396, 401, who argues that Aias rejects the Anaximandrian view of "hostile reciprocity," accepting instead a Herakleitean cosmology in which "reciprocal relations"

are replaced by "communality." Against this view of Herakleitos, see Vlastos 1947, 165 ("reciprocity between verbs of change"), and G. E. R. Lloyd 1966, 98 ("reciprocal processes").

52. Vlastos 1947, 172 and 173.

53. The term λουτρά alludes not to the suicide itself, but to a funeral bath: Knox 1979, 134–35, followed by Seaford 1994a, 396, who also notes mystic connotations. The phrasing at 654–58, εἶμι πρός τε λουτρά . . . μολών τε χῶρον, indicates that the λουτρά is a separate act preceding the suicide.

54. There is no difficulty in the application of this term to humans; cf. Soph. *El.* 981. Other examples are given by Taplin 1979, 128; Cairns 1993, 206–14.

55. On vengeance as a kind of negative gift exchange, see Saïd 1984, 48–51, and on the function of time in reciprocal exchanges, see Mauss 1923–24, 92.

56. Cf. March 1991–93, 20.

57. Easterling 1984, 7.

58. Cf. Smith 1993, 116: "Aias's provisions in effect legitimate his Trojan household and unite it with the household of his father."

59. Aias's words suggest that he realizes this in some sense, whether he has prophetic powers as he approaches death (Scodel 1984, 23) or merely an understanding in principle of the general consequences (Taplin 1979, 126).

60. Taplin 1979, 125, gives a good summary of the benefits. See also Easterling 1984, 7, and Seale 1982, 172.

61. Jebb's translation (1967). On the iron-tempering metaphor in *Aias*, see Jebb 1907 on 650 ff., appendix, 229–30, and Kamerbeek 1963, 136. For the thought, cf. Soph. *Ant.* 473–76. The technology is discussed by Forbes 1972, 196–210; H. D. P. Lee 1952, 324–29.

62. See Burkert 1955, 69, who cites *Il.* 5.561, 610; 17.346, 352.

63. Cf. Smith 1993, 119.

64. Stanford 1963, on 863, notes the parallel between the two passages.

65. The whetstone is associated with justice, *moira* ("fate"), and the Erinyes in Aiskhylos (*Ag.* 1535, with commentary of Fraenkel 1962). See also Stanford 1963, who refers to the Aiskhylos passage in connection with *Aias* 1034–5, and compare Soph. *El.* 1394, where νεακόνητον αἷμα is used of Orestes' matricide.

66. Lines 841–42 are convincingly defended by Delcourt 1939, 159–60; Stanford 1963, on 841–2. "Lawlessly" translates ἐκνόμως, Jackson's (1955, 166) emendation of the MSS ἐκγόνων.

67. On suicide as kin killing, in connection with the *Aias*, see Seaford 1996a, 291.

68. On the understanding attained by Aias and Odysseus, see Easterling 1984, 7; Seale 1982, 159. Seale 1982, 173–4, and Taplin 1978, 108–9, note the symbolism of the lifting of the corpse.

69. On the expression of community through cult at the end of the *Aias*, see Seaford 1994a, esp. 398–401, and Easterling 1988, 13–17: I follow her account of the role of Odysseus and the Greek army in Aias's funeral. On allusions to a hero cult in the play, see also Burian 1972, 151–56; Henrichs 1993; March 1991–93; Scodel 1984, 21–22; Seale 1982, 174–76; Segal 1981a, 142–51.

70. ἄριστον: 1340; cf. 1380 and 435, where ἀριστεύσας is used of Telamon.

71. Noted by March 1991–93, 27.

72. I am indebted to Sumio Yoshitake for good discussions on Odysseus's role.

73. Jebb's translation (1907 = 1967).

Conclusion

1. Seaford 1994a, 360–62.
2. Silk 1996a.
3. Silk 1996b, 8–9, quoting Nietzsche in *Ecce Homo* ("The Birth of Tragedy," no. 3), in Silk and Stern 1983, 125.
4. Friedrich 1996, 260.
5. Friedrich 1996, 262, quoting Vernant 1988, 187.
6. Friedrich 1996, 263, quoting Goldhill 1990, 114.
7. Friedrich 1996, 264.
8. Friedrich 1996, 275.
9. Seaford 1996a, 293.
10. Hall 1996b, 296.
11. Mogyoródi 1996, 358.
12. Seidensticker 1996, 377, quoting Szondi 1978, 209.
13. Ewans 1996b, 440.
14. Steiner 1996, 536–37.

Appendix A

1. Kopperschmidt 1967; Taplin 1977, 192.
2. For the suppliant pattern, see Burian 1971 and below on Soph. *OC*.
3. Sommerstein 1989, on 237, notes some inconsistencies concerning the purification.
4. Aktaion is also mentioned at 230, in a line incorrectly bracketed by many editors, and at 1227 and 1291. On the parallel, see Seaford 1996b, on *Bacch.* 337–41, and appendix B below, "Domestic Animal Myths."
5. This plot outline is based on that of the *Odyssey* in *Po.* 17.1455b17–23.
6. On Ixion plays, see G. W. Bond 1981, ad loc., and appendix B.
7. The end of the play is discussed in chapter 3, section 4.
8. 1355–57, trans. Hadas and McLean 1960; cf. 1166, 1240–41. For other stories about people destroyed by their own animals, see appendix B, "Domestic Animal Myths."
9. See Barrett 1964, on 34–37.
10. On the Nurse's abuse of supplication in this passage, see Cairns 1993, 330–31.
11. For Pasiphaë, see appendix B, on Eur. *Kretes*. In the version of the Ariadne story alluded to in *Hipp.*, Ariadne deserts Dionysos for Theseus, and is then killed by the god: Barrett 1964, on 339. On text and sense of 552, see Barrett 1964, ad loc.; on Semele, see appendix B, on Ais. *Semele*.
12. Incorrectly bracketed by Diggle.
13. Incorrectly bracketed by Diggle.
14. See Jouan 1966, 276 n. 2.
15. Else 1957, 350. The *Medea* nevertheless has a simple plot because this minor recognition, unlike one that follows an act done in ignorance, does not change the direction of the action: see Belfiore 1992a, 170–75.
16. On supplication in *Medea*, see Mercier 1990, 275–90; on *philia*, Schein, 1990.
17. Ogden 1996, 194–96, discusses amphimetric strife in this play.
18. On 287 (ἐκ προστροπαίων ἐν γένει πεπτωκότων), see Garvie 1986, ad loc.

19. *Xenia* in this scene and in the *Oresteia* as a whole: Garvie 1986, 224, and Roth 1993.

20. Reading ἐνδίκους σφαγάς at 37, with the MSS.

21. Kamerbeek 1974, ad loc., ably defends the MSS attribution of these lines to Elektra.

22. At 272 the MSS are divided between αὐτοφόντην and αὐτοέντην.

23. Kamerbeek 1974, ad loc.

24. On this phrase, see Dawe 1982, ad loc.

25. Konstan 1985 studies the meanings of *philos* and its cognates in this play.

26. On *philia* in this play, see Burnett 1971, 213–22; Schein 1975; Schmidt-Berger 1973, 145–77.

27. I follow the MSS (other than M²) in attributing the second half of 1235, ἠψάμην δ’ ἐγὼ ξίφους, to Pylades. It is he who is said elsewhere to have acted with Orestes (συνκατέκτανον: 1089; συνδρῶν: 406), while Elektra is said only to have approved (ἐπένευσας) of the deed that was done (εἴργασται) by Orestes (284). She participated (μετέσχον: 32) only in this way. Most modern editors, however, attribute the half-line to Elektra. For discussion see West 1987; Willink 1986, ad loc.

28. Most editors bracket 933.

29. Their kinship is alluded to in general terms at 1233 (συγγένεια). According to one account, Pylades' mother is Anaxibia, the sister of Agamemnon. For this and other versions, see West 1987, ad loc.; Willink 1986.

30. Lines 861–73 and the end of the play (1005–77, bracketed here) are generally thought to be spurious. See Hutchinson 1985, ad loc.

31. On the timing of the bringing on of the corpses and the question of the authenticity of the end of the play, see Taplin 1977, 169–76. Hutchinson 1985, 209, notes the parallel scene in Euripides' *Phoenician Women*.

32. On the equation of the fratricide with Oidipous's crimes of incest and patricide, see the introduction to Bacon and Hecht, 1973, 6–9; Zeitlin, 1982, 20, 29–37.

33. I follow Mastronarde's text (1994) of this play.

34. Cf. 818–21. At 1570–75 similar imagery is used of the fratricidal blood of the brothers. Mastronarde 1994 on ξυνῆψε (673) writes, "Here I would detect a sexual, almost incestuous undertone in the use of the verb: the Spartoi die in their mother's embrace . . .wetting her with blood."

35. Cf. *Sept.* 848, on which see Hutchinson 1985, 209.

36. At 676–89 and 828–29 Epaphos and Io are mentioned as the ancestors of the Thebans.

37. See Mastronarde 1994, 28–29.

38. The importance of kinship in the play is noted by Mastronarde 1994, 7–8, 231 (on 291–92), 505, 545–46 (on 1427–79).

39. The question of authenticity is not relevant to this study.

40. On *philia* in this play, see Griffith 1983, 14–15, and on 39, 162, 225, 611, 1063–70.

41. Griffith 1983, 5, discusses the two genealogies.

42. The exact nature of the relationship is not made clear in the play. According to Hesiod, Oceanos is the son of Ouranos and Gaia. Griffith 1983, on 289, states that in *PV* he is Prometheus's half-brother, as the son of Gaia.

43. On *philia* in *Antigone* see Goldhill 1986, 79–106.

44. Haimon and Eurydike: Delcourt 1939: 161–63; all three: Griffith 1999, on 1304–5.

45. The text is corrupt but the sense is clear.

46. This event is alluded to at 1303 and 1312, although the details are not given. While Megareos should not be identified with Menoikeus, who died to save Thebes, his story is similar: see Griffith 1999, on 1302–3; Kamerbeek 1978, on 995; Roberts 1989, 165.

47. On these myths, see Griffith 1999, on 944–87, Winnington-Ingram 1980, 98–109, and below, appendix B, on the myths about Perseus, Dionysos, and Phineus. The version of the Phineus myth in which Kleopatra blinds her own sons is given in frag. 645R (Soph. *Tympanistai*). Griffith 1999, on 971–73, cites the suggestion by Sourvinou-Inwood 1998, 156–57, that *Ant.* may contain a reference to this version.

48. The MSS reading, εὐνῆς, has been questioned by Fraenkel 1962, Mazon 1925, and West 1990, but is well defended by Denniston-Page 1957, ad loc.

49. τῶν is the reading of τ, followed by Fraenkel 1962, Mazon, 1925, Page 1972. West 1990 reads οὐ.

50. This kind of case is discussed by Aristotle in *EE* 1225b1–6 and *NE* 1111a2–21.

51. In *Od.* 21. 22–30, Herakles is clearly said to kill his guest. Although Sophokles is less explicit, he allows us to infer that Herakles treated Iphitos as a guest, taking him to the walls of Tiryns. M. Davies 1991, xxix, notes that Herakles commits "underhand treachery against a guest."

52. In 933, κατ᾽ ὀργήν refers to Hyllos's anger: Kamerbeek 1959, ad loc.

53. Kamerbeek 1959, on 1066–69.

54. Easterling 1982, ad loc., notes that Hyllos's "deepest sense of what is right and holy must be overridden by his filial duty."

55. On *xenia* in this play, see Nussbaum 1986, 397–421.

56. On *philia* in this play, see Adkins 1966; Collard 1991, 25–27; Mikalson 1991, 79–80; Nussbaum 1986, 406–17.

57. Lines 793–98 are bracketed by Diggle, and Collard 1991, ad loc., gives some good arguments against the authenticity of 793–97. However, the lines are accepted by Murray, and mention of the table of *xenia* makes excellent dramatic sense.

58. These points are made by Mikalson 1991, 78, 261 n. 48.

59. On Helen and theoxeny, see Kannicht 1969, ad loc.

60. On the corrupt text at 388–89 and the possible references to Tantalos's serving of Pelops as food to the gods, see Kannicht 1969, ad loc. For the myths, see appendix B, on Aiskhylos's *Kallisto*, Euripides' *Kresphontes* (Merope), "Pelops Myths," and "Atreus Myths."

61. *Xenia* as central issue: Smith 1993, 134–98; Joseph P. Wilson 1997.

62. Joseph P. Wilson's (1997, 85–86) argument (anticipated by Jebb 1928, ad loc.) that evidence for a previously existing relationship is provided by the word *doryxenos* (632) is unconvincing. The word is used because Oidipous has just offered Theseus a military alliance against Thebes (616–23).

63. As Smith claims, 1993, 197–98. Joseph P. Wilson (1997, 85) admits that *xenia* ritual is absent.

64. Burian 1974b: 409; see also Burian 1971, 1–33, 207–62.

65. On this sequence, see chapter 3, section 1.

66. Noted by Burian 1974b, 415.

67. On this scene, see Easterling 1967.

68. On *philia* in this play, see Blundell 1989, 226–59.

69. See Kirkwood 1986: 114; Winnington-Ingram 1980, 207.

70. Burian 1971, 79–136, discusses the suppliant pattern in this play, which he compares and contrasts with Eur. *Supp.*

71. See Wilkins 1993 on 271, a line Diggle mistakenly attributes to the Herald instead of to the Chorus.

72. See also 97–98, 101–3, 112–13, 243–46, 254, 285–87, cited by Burian 1971, 97–98.

73. Wilkins 1993, on 1014–15, defends Paley's translation of προστρόπαιον as "the murdered man who calls for vengeance" but acknowledges that "[t]here is some hint of the basic sense [of suppliant] here as well," even though "Eurystheus is not literally a suppliant." In this context, however, it makes good sense to take the word to refer to a prisoner of war, who cannot be killed because he has been accepted as a suppliant.

74. On the ending of the play and the lacuna in the text, see Seaford 1994a, 126–29; Wilkins 1993, 192–93.

75. Eurystheus and Alkmene are both descendants of Perseus and Pelops: Wilkins 1993, on 987–88. Wilkins notes (177) that kin killing is "a Perseid specialty," shown in both Alkmene (882, 931, 955, 965, 969, 971) and Eurystheus (13, 60, 466, 1000–1008).

76. The genealogy is given by Wilkins 1993, on 207 ff., who also explains (ad loc.) the sense of αὐτανεψίων at 211. Children of cousins, and perhaps their children as well, were included within the Greek concept of close kinship (*ankhisteia*): see above, chapter 1, note 4.

77. ἔστειχε . . . πέρσων Ἀθάνας. ἀλλὰ τὴν ἐναντίαν δαίμων ἔθηκε καὶ μετέστησεν τύχην. Cf. the example of *peripeteia* in Arist. *Po.* 1452a25–26: "coming to cheer up Oidipous . . . he accomplished the opposite" (ἐλθὼν ὡς εὐφρανῶν τὸν Οἰδίπουν . . . τοὐαντίον ἐποίησεν.)

78. Burian 1971, 146, notes that the threat of pollution is increased by the presence of the suppliants at Demeter's temple during the sacred rites.

79. See Collard 1975, ad loc.

80. See also Burian 1971, 158n. 30.

81. Broadhead 1960, ad loc., refers to Herod. 7.150, where Xerxes derives the name "Persian" from Perses, the common ancestor.

82. This general idea is clear in spite of the problematic MSS reading: Δαρειογενὴς τὸ πατρωνύμιον γένος ἡμέτερον. The scholion M (quoted by Broadhead 1960, ad loc.) explains the last four words as κατὰ πατέρα συγγενὴς ἡμῖν, "kin to us on his father's side."

83. *Persians* is sometimes cited as a clear example of a simple plot, without recognition or reversal: see, e.g., Garvie 1978, 67–71. Saïd 1988 argues convincingly that it contains many reversals. See also Broadhead 1960, xxxv; Hall 1996a, 16 and note on 158.

84. Smethurst 1989, 84.

85. Broadhead 1960, H. J. Rose 1958, and LSJ, "Supplement" take μεγάλατε (the reading of M) to mean "involved in great ruin." However, ἄτη can be used of persons in the sense of "bane" or "pest"—e.g., in Soph. *Ant.* 533 (LSJ II.3.a)—and this reading is supported by the parallel sentiments elsewhere in *Persians*.

86. Captivity and underworld: Seaford 1984, 33–38.; *xenia*: Burnett 1971, 30–46, who interprets the Herakles action, with its emphasis on hospitality, as a little satyr play; Konstan 1990, citing (215n. 17) D. F. Sutton 1974, 162–63.

87. See esp. Goldfarb 1992; Schein 1988; Stanton 1990.

88. On wedding ritual here, see chapter 3, note 87.

89. On these questions, see Fraenkel 1965; Lattimore 1960, introduction; Lesky 1983, 397 and 485n. 4; Ritchie 1964.

90. The view of Fenik (1964, summarized 37–38, 61–63) that the *Rhesos* may be based more on non-Homeric than on Homeric versions of the story has recently been challenged by R. S. Bond 1996. Whatever the play's source is, comparison with *Iliad*

10 is instructive, for it is the only model extant, and it is one with which both the author of *Rhesos* and the original audience were familiar.

91. Hektor-Rhesos dialogue: 388–453, 467–526 (= 126 lines), of which the accusation and defense occupy 393–453 (= 61 lines). Charioteer episode: 728–889 (= 162 lines), of which the accusation and defense occupy 802–7, 833–76 (= 50 lines). The entire play is only 996 lines long.

92. These lines, bracketed by Diggle, are consistent with 657–60.

93. The text is corrupt but the sense clear.

Appendix B

1. Friis Johansen and Whittle 1980, 1.40.

2. See above, chapter 1, section 1, and note 12 in that chapter.

3. Mette 1963; Radt 1985.

4. Dios 1983; Lloyd-Jones 1996; Pearson 1917; Radt 1977. Dios provides an excellent survey, in many ways superior to that of Lloyd-Jones. Thanks are due to André Lardinois for calling this work to my attention.

5. Austin 1968; Collard, Cropp, and Lee 1995; Mette 1981–82; Nauck 1964; Webster 1967.

6. See the introductory section of this appendix for an explanation of this and other categories.

7. Mette 1963, 122; Radt 1985, 205–6, 288–89, 333; see also March 1991–93, 4–7, 8.

8. Lloyd-Jones 1996; Pearson 1917, 2.214, 286–87; Radt 1977, 431.

9. See Nauck 1964, 379–80.

10. Kiso 1984, 27; Mette, 1963, 43; Pearson 1917, 1.130.

11. Pearson 1917, 1.72, lists only a satyr play. Radt 1977, 151, speculates that Sophokles may have written both a tragedy and a satyr play with this title and explains that the spelling is an old form of Amphiaros.

12. Discussion: Dios 1983, 92–93; Lloyd-Jones 1996, 72; Pearson 1917, 1.132; Radt 1977, 183, 189.

13. Dios 1983, 60; Lloyd-Jones 1996, 42–43; Pearson 1917, 1.68–69.

14. Mette 1981–82, 32; Webster 1967, 41.

15. Attribution: Webster 1967, 40; Collard 1995c, 112–13, who follows Kannicht's forthcoming edition in listing this fragment (312aK) with those of Euripides' *Bellerophon*, and in reading κατέκτα, "he killed" (Megapenthes speaks of Bellerophon's killing of Stheneboia).

16. Mette 1981–82, 37; Nauck 1964, 380; Webster 1967, 265.

17. Pearson 1917, 1.87, 121; Radt 1977, 177–78, also citing other conjectures.

18. ἐξείνισσα (*Il.* 3.207) and Σ bT on 205 ff. (1, 396, 69 Erbse): δολοφονεῖσθαι μέλλοντας ἔσωσεν, quoted by Radt 1977, 178. Pearson 1917, 1.121, quotes *Il.* 11.139 ff.

19. Lloyd-Jones 1996, 54–55; Pearson 1917, 1.86–87; Radt 1977, 160–61.

20. See Mette 1963, 162–64. On Ino stories, see also Lyons 1997, 122–24.

21. Mette 1963, 162–63; Radt 1985, 123.

22. Lloyd-Jones 1996, 11; Mette 1963, 164; Pearson 1917, 1.2–4.

23. Webster 1967, 98; cf. Mette 1963, 163, and 1981–82, 140; Nauck 1964, 482.

24. Austin 1968, 101–2; Mette, 1963, 163–64, and 1981–82, 299–301; Nauck 1964, 626–27; Webster 1967, 131–36.

25. Lloyd-Jones 1996, 10–11; Pearson 1917, 1.1–2; Radt 1977, 99–100.

26. Lloyd-Jones 1996, 338–39; Mette 1963, 164; Pearson 1917, 2.322–24; Radt 1977, 491.

27. Smyth 1926, 411; Mette 1963, 95–96.

28. Lloyd-Jones 1996, 138–39; Pearson 1917, 1.218; Radt 1977, 270–71.

29. Dios 1983, 183; Lloyd-Jones 1996, 184; Pearson 1917, 1.219; and Radt 1977, 315, all list this play without bracketing but express doubts about its existence.

30. D. F. Sutton 1984, 31–32.

31. See Ais. *Ag.* 1219–22, 1583–1602; Eur. *El.* 719–36, *Or.* 812–15.

32. Pearson 1917, 1.185–86.

33. Lloyd-Jones 1996, 106–7; Pearson 1917, 1.91–93, 185–87; and Radt 1977, 162, 239–40, who discusses the evidence for three Thyestes plays.

34. Webster 1967, 113–15.

35. Webster 1967, 37–39; Mette 1981–82, 166, is more skeptical.

36. Nauck 1964, 556; Webster 1967, 236–37.

37. Dios 1983, 363–64; Lloyd-Jones 1996, 340–41; Pearson 1917, 2.327–28; and Radt 1977, 494, all express uncertainty about the plot.

38. Lloyd-Jones 1996, 262–63; Pearson 1917, 2.161–63; Radt 1977, 403–4.

39. Pearson 1917, 2.162; Radt 1977, 404.

40. See Dios 1983, 266n. 1002.

41. Pearson 1917, 2.164n. on frag. 522; Radt 1977, 404.

42. See Haslam 1976, 34 and Trendall-Webster 1971, 49 (III.1.13), on Aiskhylos's *Edonoi* (both cited with approval by Radt 1977, 105, on Sophokles' *Aias Lokros* 10c); Smyth 1926, 398; Mette 1963, 138; D. F. Sutton 1975, 360.

43. Smyth 1926, 443; Mette 1963, 145; Radt 1985, 299.

44. Radt 1985, 280–81 cites this and other conjectures.

45. Mette 1963, 147.

46. Mette 1963, 145.

47. Dodds 1960, xxix, and Hartung 1855, 73 ff., cited by Radt 1985, 336, on 221. On Semele as "wife of Zeus," see Lyons 1997, 97.

48. Smyth 1926, 386–87; Mette 1963, 138–40; Radt 1985, 138–39.

49. Radt 1985, 137.

50. Radt 1985, 350, and frag. 246a.

51. Mette 1963, 147.

52. See Seaford 1996b, on 337–41.

53. Smyth 1926, 391; Radt 1985, 148–49, with frag. 39.

54. Smyth 1926, 463; Mette 1963, 134; Radt 1985, 346.

55. Cropp 1995c, 148–49.

56. See Collard, Cropp, and Lee 1995, 11: the form (e.g.) -/370 K indicates a fragment not present in Nauck or Snell that will appear in Richard Kannicht's new *Tragicorum Graecorum Fragmenta*.

57. Dios 1983, 267–68; Pearson 1917, 2.170–71.

58. For example, Pearson 1917, 2.23–24.

59. For surveys of opinions, see Dios 1983, 187–89; Radt 1977, 321.

60. Dios 1983, 178–79; Pearson 1917, 2.23; Radt 1977, 308.

61. Smyth 1926, 474; Mette 1963, 185.

62. Radt 1985, 211 (frag. 89R of *Ixion*), and 300 (on *Perrhaibides*). Cf. Pindar, *Pyth.* 2.32: ἐμφύλιον αἷμα πρώτιστος οὐκ ἄτερ τέχνας ἐπέμειξε θνατοῖς (cited by Smyth 1926, 409), and Ais. *Eum.* 441, 717–18, with Sommerstein's notes (1989).

63. Nauck 1964, 490; Webster 1967, 160.

64. Dios 1983, 145–46; Lloyd-Jones 1996, 134–35; Radt 1977, 267; Snell 1971, 16 (Didascaliae Atheniensis 254).

65. Mette 1963, 34–35; Radt 1985, 231, 287.

66. See Radt 1985, 231.

67. Mette 1963, 35.

68. Radt 1985, 288.

69. Nauck 1964, 532; Webster 1967, 241–46, attempts reconstruction.

70. Φοίβου ποτε οὐκ ἐῶντος ἔσπειρεν τέκνον (539a Snell = adespota 378N); cf. Austin 1968, 59; Webster 1967, 241.

71. Webster 1967, 242.

72. Mette 1981–82, 194: no. 719, frag. 6, 2–3.

73. Also Austin 1968, 64, no. 98. Webster 1967, 243, attributes the words to Kreon.

74. Webster 1967, 182, summarizing the evidence given in Nauck 1964, 404–10.

75. Radt 1977, 316.

76. Pearson 1917, 2.16–17.

77. See Dios 1983, 277–78; Lloyd-Jones 1996, 274–75; Pearson 1917, 2.185–87; Radt 1977, 415–16.

78. Pearson 1917, 2.172, and Radt 1977, 410. Lloyd-Jones 1996, 268–69, is more cautious.

79. Nauck 1964, 550–51; Pearson 1917, 2.172; Webster 1967, 33.

80. Mette 1981–82, 15; Nauck 1964, 363; Webster 1967, 77–79.

81. Dios 1983, 40; Pearson 1917, 1.16; Radt 1977, 123, cites various conjectures.

82. Cropp 1995d, 240.

83. Frag. 485N; translation Cropp 1995d, 252.

84. Cropp 1995d, 242, 243.

85. Cf. Hyginus, *Fab.* 186 (cited by Cropp 1995d, 242), where Theano tells her husband that the children of Melanippe are his.

86. Nauck 1964, 525, and Webster 1967, 234–36, both citing Hyginus, *Fab.* 174, and Apollodoros, *Library* 1.8.2–3.

87. Radt 1977, 345; Webster 1967, 233.

88. Pearson 1917, 2.64–66.

89. Pap. Oxy. 3653: Lloyd-Jones 1996, 228–29, frag. 441aa.

90. Theomachy: Kiso, 1984, 6–10; evidence: Dios 1983, 219–23; Lloyd-Jones 1996, 226–29; Pearson 1917, 2.94–98; Radt 1977, 363–73.

91. Keuls 1978, 51–56. The Amphion story is also mentioned in the papyrus hypothesis to Sophokles' *Niobe* (Lloyd-Jones 1996, 228–30, frag. 441aa, fr. 2).

92. Radt 1985, 266; Taplin 1977, 424.

93. The text is corrupt but the sense clear.

94. Dios 1983, 54–55; Lloyd-Jones 1996, 40–41; Pearson 1917, 1.57–58; Radt 1977, 147.

95. Ἡκάβ[η δὲ ἀποκτ]εῖναι θέλουσα διεκωλύθη: Mette 1981–82, 23–24, no. 54.

96. Webster 1967, 85–86; stories: Dios 1983, 249–50; Jouan 1966, 64–65.

97. Dios 1983, 250–51; Lloyd-Jones 1996, 252–53; Pearson 1917, 2.140–43; Radt 1977, 390–92 and frag. 487; D. F. Sutton 1984, 100–102.

98. Jouan 1966, 64–65; Nauck 1964, 554; Webster 1967, 85–86.

99. Dios 1983, 98–99; Lloyd-Jones 1996, 80–81; Pearson 1917, 1.141–43; Radt 1977, 192.

100. Lloyd-Jones 1996, 286–87; Radt 1977, 430.

101. Pearson 1917, 2.209–10.

102. Lloyd-Jones 1996, 242–43; Radt 1977, 381.

103. *Epit.* 2.3–9, cited by Pearson 1917, 2.121–22.

104. Webster 1967, 115.

105. Hyginus, *Fab.* 85, cited by Mette 1981–82, 308; translation of Grant 1960, 78.

106. Webster 1967, 111.

107. *Library* 3.5.5, cited by Mette 1981–82, 308.

108. Story: Dios 1983, 48, 83–84; Lloyd-Jones 1996, 28.

109. Pearson 1917, 2.47–48; cf. Lloyd-Jones 1996, 29, 200–201; Radt 1977, 334.

110. Pearson 1917, 1.115; his translation, cf. Lloyd-Jones 1996, 29, citing frag. 165. Another theory is cited by Dios 1983, 83–84 and n. 216.

111. Dios 1983, 48, 83–84; Lloyd-Jones 1996, 29, 64; Radt 1977, 136, 173; Pearson 1917, 1.38.

112. Mette 1981–82, 107; Nauck 1964, 453; Webster 1967, 94–95.

113. Webster 1967, 61–62, quoting Apollodoros, *Library* 2.4.3; cf. Nauck 1964, 459–60.

114. Mette 1963, 156; Radt 1985, 362–64, frags. 261, 262.

115. Radt 1985, 118.

116. Mette 1963, 157.

117. Webster 1967, 193; cf. Mette 1981–82, 60; Nauck 1964, 392–93.

118. Reconstruction: Webster 196, 192–99.

119. Dios 1983, 69–70; Lloyd-Jones 1996, 50–51; Radt 1977, 156; Pearson 1917, 1.78–80.

120. Collard 1995d, 196, with omission of references.

121. Translation of Collard 1995d, who notes (238, on line 280): "282–83 are obelized [marked as questionable] because metrically questionable; sense and style are sound."

122. Diggle 1970, 7 and n. 6, citing Cicero, *De Off.* 3.25.94 and *De Nat. Deor.* 3.31.76.

123. Collard 1995d, 202, citing Kannicht 1972, 9. Cf. Diggle 1970, 44, and Webster 1967, 231.

124. Radt 1985, 185.

125. Diggle 1970, 30.

126. Radt 1977, 461.

127. Dios 1983, 352–55; Lloyd-Jones 1996, 334–35; Pearson 1917, 2.311–13.

128. On the *Tympanistai*, see Dios 1983, 321–22; Lloyd-Jones 1996, 308–9; Pearson 1917, 2.262–63; Radt 1977, 458–61.

129. Radt 1977, 484.

130. Phineus's killing of his sons is not consistent with the account given in the previous paragraph, according to which the sons regained their sight. See Pearson 1917, 2.315, on frag. 705.

131. Radt 1985, 359.

132. These lines were excised in antiquity: see, chapter 1, section 2, and note 39.

133. Jouan 1966, 60; Mette 1981–82, 297, no. 1147; Nauck 1964, 621, and frag. 815; Webster 1967, 84–85.

134. Radt 1977, 490.

135. Dios 1983, 358–59; Pearson 1917, 2.320–21.

136. Radt 1985, 306, 329; Griffith, 1983, 282–83, who argues that the subject of *Prometheus Pyrphoros* was Prometheus's theft of fire.

137. See Griffith's note on this passage (1983, 293), and (288) on Kratinus frag. 73 Austin.

138. Dios 1983, 254–56; Lloyd-Jones 1996, 256–57; Pearson 1917, 2.147–48; Radt 1977, 395.

139. Pearson 1917, 2.148.

140. Mette 1981–82, 228; Nauck 1964, 563; Webster 1967, 97–98. Jouan's reconstruction (1966, 317–36) emphasizes the conflict between father and daughter.

141. Koenen 1969; Mette 1981–82, 90; Nauck 1964, 436–37; Webster 1967, 238–41.

142. Webster 1967, 240.

143. Lloyd-Jones 1996, 32–33; Pearson 1917, 1.46–48; Radt 1977, 140–41.

144. Dios 1983, 209–10; Pearson 1917, 2, 70–72; Radt 1977, 349.

145. Dios 1983, 299–303; Radt 1977, 434. Pearson's account is out of date.

146. Cropp 1995a, 17–18.

147. Cropp 1995a, 20, 22; Webster 1967, 46–47.

148. Smyth 1926, 427; Mette 1963, 77–78; Radt 1985, 257–58; Taplin 1977, 423–24.

149. Smyth 1926, 461–62; Mette 1963, 80–82; Radt 1985, 343–44.

150. Cropp 1995a, 22.

151. Cropp 1995a, 19–20, 22.

152. Webster 1967, 254.

153. Webster 1967, 255.

154. Austin 1968, 11; Mette 1981–82, 81; Nauck 1964, 427; Webster 1967, 253, 255–57.

155. Mette 1981–82, 130–34; Webster 1967, 105–9.

156. Webster 1967, 108.

157. Smyth 1926, 396; Mette 1963, 40; Radt 1985, 175.

158. Smyth 1926, 383–84; Mette 1963, 38–40.

159. Dios 1983, 341–46; Lloyd-Jones 1996, 322–23; Pearson 1917, 2.294–96.

160. Barrett 1964, 11–12; Nauck 1964, 491–92; Webster 1967, 64–70.

161. Mette 1981–82, 215–19; Nauck 1964, 546–55; Page 1941, 120–25; Snell 1971, 171. Webster 1967 presumably agrees with Snell, since it is not listed in his index.

162. Nauck 1964, 546–47; Mette 1981–82, 215; Page 1941, 120.

163. Nauck 1964, 549; Snell 1971, 175.

164. Dios 1983, 325–31; Lloyd-Jones 1996, 312–13; Pearson, 1917, 2. 270–74; Radt 1977, 463.

165. Radt 1977, 472, on frag. 669a.

166. For an explanation of this and other categories, see the introductory section of this appendix.

167. Nauck 1963, 365–66; Mette 1981–82, 16; Webster 1967, 157–60.

168. Webster 1967, 157; papyrus hypothesis (Oxy. 2457) now in Austin 1968, 88–89.

169. Nauck 1964, 389–90; Mette 1981–82, 44; Webster 1967, 94.

170. Jouan 1966, 375–77; Mette 1981–82, 67; Page 1941, 61–63; Webster 1967, 205–11.

171. Dios 1983, 100–102; Lloyd-Jones 1996, 84–85; Page 1941, 17; Pearson 1917, 1.146–48; Radt 1977, 195, quotes a version of the story in which Eurypylos's wife, not mother, is bribed.

172. Pearson 1917, 1.158, on 73, explains: "one who, while a boy in years, was both counsellor and warrior."

173. Lloyd-Jones 1996, 137; Radt 1977, 269.

174. See Pearson 1917, 1.216; cf. Lloyd-Jones 1996, 136–37.

175. Radt 1985, 216.

176. *Po.* 1454a5–6, cited by Cropp 1995b, 125; by Mette 1981–82, 157; and by Webster 1967, 137, who also cites *NE* 1111a11.

177. Hyginus, *Fab.* 137, cited by Austin 1968, 41; Cropp 1995b, 121; Mette 1981–82, 157; Nauck, 1964, 497; Webster 1967, 137.

178. Apollodoros, *Library* 1.8.6; Mette 1981–82, 199; Nauck 1964, 536.

179. Webster 1967, 113, 299–300.

180. Mette 1981–82, 200: Tydeus killed his brother Melannipos.

181. The play is attributed to Euripides by Austin 1968, 97; Mette 1981–82, 249; Nauck 1964, 578. Snell 1971, 182–83, attributes it to Kritias; Webster 1967 does not list it in his index; Jouan 1966, 303–8, is uncertain. A new papyrus in Mette 1985, 25–26, provides additional evidence in favor of Euripidean authorship.

182. Lloyd-Jones 1996, 290–91; Radt 1985, 435–37.

183. Nauck 1964, 386; Webster 1967, 92–94.

184. Dios 1983, 35–36; Lloyd-Jones 1996, 12–15; Pearson 1917, 1.8–10.

185. Radt 1977, 105, citing Haslam 1976 and Trendall and Webster 1971, 49 (III 1, 13), on Aiskhylos's *Edonoi.*

186. See Smyth 1926, 404; Lloyd-Jones 1957, 586–90; Mette 1963, 149–51; Radt 1985, 190; Wilkins 1993, xviii–xix.

187. Radt 1977, 181, citing Pearson 1917, 1.123.

188. For an explanation of this and other categories, see the introductory section of this appendix.

189. See chapter 1, section 2.

190. Mette 1963, 112; Radt 1985, 113.

191. Frags. 134a–137R, with Radt's (1985) note on 134a, citing Dover 1978, 197.

192. Frag. 212aMW: see chapter 1, section 2 and note 30.

193. Trans. Ewans 1996a, 109. Cf. Eur. *HF* 1380–81, and G. W. Bond, 1981, on 1381.

194. See the excellent remarks of Croiset 1894, 162–63.

195. Radt 1985, 262.

196. Smyth 1926, 429; Mette 1963, 118.

197. Smyth 1926, 470–71; Radt 1985, 364–66.

198. According to Croiset 1894, 171–72, cited by Radt 1985, 367, on frag. 266. Cf. Smyth 1926, 472; Mette 1963, 119.

199. Croiset's translation (1894, 171), "Mais en nous, dieux, est une Némésis plus puissante," is preferable to that of Mette (1963, 119): "Doch Nemesis ist stärker noch als wir." Radt 1985, 368, on frag. 267, 3–4, also supports the view that ἡμῶν refers to the gods.

200. Dios 1983, 361–62; Lloyd-Jones 1996, 338–39; Pearson 1917, 2.325; Radt 1977, 493.

201. Dios 1983, 286–88; Pearson 1917, 2.198–99; Radt 1977, 425–26.

202. Dios 1983, 317–19; Lloyd-Jones 1996, 306–7; Pearson 1917, 2.253–55; Radt 1977, 453, comments: "Argumentum fuisse videtur Troilus ab Achille ad templum Apollinis Thymbraei interfectus."

203. See Pearson 1917, 2.254, citing Welcker 1939–41, without giving references.

204. Austin 1968, 95–96; see also Jouan 1966, 204–18; Webster 1967, 95–97.

205. See Dios 1983, 279–83; Lloyd-Jones 1996, 276–77; Pearson 1917, 2.191–93; Radt 1977, 418; D. F. Sutton 1984, 118–20.

206. Collard 1995b, 84.

207. Collard 1995b, 90, on line 4 of hypothesis.

208. See Collard 1995b, 96, for discussion of frag. 667.

209. Stheneboia: Lloyd-Jones 1996, 134–35; D. F. Sutton 1984, 63; denial: Collard 1995b, 83; doubts: Pearson 1917, 1.214–15.

210. Collard 1995c, 98–99.

211. Mette 1963, 130–31.

212. Radt 1985, 233.

213. Mette 1963, 131; Radt, 1985, 352.

214. Smyth 1926, 412; Radt 1985, 214. Mette 1963, 131, places it in Samothrace.

215. Lloyd-Jones 1996, 204–5; Radt 1977, 336–37.

216. Pearson 1917, 2.53.

217. G. W. Bond 1963, 11–12 (*xenia*); Page 1941, 79–80; Webster 1967, 211–15.

218. G. W. Bond 1963, 15–19.

219. G. W. Bond 1963, 18–19 and 11, on frag. 2.4 ff.; cf. Webster 1967, 214.

220. Page 1941, 81.

221. Radt 1985, 261–62 and frag. 149a; Mette 1963, 38–39, believes that Hipsipyle's part in the Nemean story is Euripides' invention.

222. Mette 1963, 110.

223. Mette 1963, 111.

224. Mette 1963, 112; Radt 1985, 374–76. Taplin 1977, 431–33, is more skeptical about the evidence.

225. Servius on Verg. *Aen.* 1.489, cited by Gruppe 1906, 681, and Pley 1932, 639.

226. Collard 1995a, 54.

227. Collard 1995a, 55.

228. Apollod. *Epit.* 1.14, cited by Radt 1977, 310, and 311 on frag. 324. Labyrinth: *Epit.* 1.8–9.

229. Lloyd-Jones 1996, 178–79; Pearson 1917, 2.3–4.

230. References: Radt 1977, 171, who lists it as a tragedy.

231. Frags. 160, 161R; Dios 1983, 80–83; Lloyd-Jones 1996, 64–65; Pearson 1917, 1.110.

232. *Kressai*: Mette 1963, 183–85; Radt 1985, 228–29. *Manteis*: Dios 1983, 202–3; Lloyd-Jones 1996, 206–7; Pearson 1917, 2.56–57; Radt 1977, 338–40. Eur. *Polyidos*: Nauck 1964, 558–59; Webster 1967, 161–62. A play titled *Glaukos* by Stobaeus is identified with Eur. *Polyidos* by Nauck 1964, 559, and apparently by Webster 1967, who does not list the *Glaukos* in his index. The fact that Mette 1981–82 cross-references *Glaukos* and *Polyidos* fragments suggests that he also identifies the two plays with one another. I follow Nauck in listing only *Polyidos*.

233. Radt 1985, 113–14.

234. Mette 1963, 127–28; Radt 1985, 291.

235. Radt 1985, 301.

236. Mette 1963, 127.

237. Radt 1985, 371.

238. Mette 1963, 127–28; cf. the ancient sources quoted by Radt 1985, 373, on frag. 275, and M. Davies 1988, 72–73.

239. Lloyd-Jones 1996, 82–83; Pearson 1917, 1.145–46; Radt 1977, 194.

240. Radt 1977, 374–75, citing Arist. *Po.* 14.1453b29–34, which alludes to this play.

241. Lloyd-Jones 1996, 240–41; Pearson 1917, 2.115–16; Radt 1977, 378.

242. Dios 1983, 216–17; Lloyd-Jones 1996, 224–25; Pearson 1917, 2.92; Radt 1977, 361.

243. Pearson 1917, 2.105–10; Radt 1977, 373; survey of opinions: Dios 1983, 229–31.

244. See Belfiore 1988, 191–92, on this passage and Arist. *Po.* 16.1454b29–30.

245. Pearson 1917, 2.34; Radt 1977, 328.

246. Lloyd-Jones 1996, 361, agrees with Welcker 1839–41, 112 ff., 149 ff., in assigning this fragment to the *Lakainai*. Pearson 1917, 2.35–36, 3.38, and Radt 1977, 329, 542 list it among the fragments of uncertain plays. See also discussion of Dios 1983, 389n. 106.

247. Pearson 1917, 2.35–36.

248. See Pearson 1917, 3.38–39, and above on Eur. *Oineus*, esp. frag. 558N.

249. Ais.: Smyth 1926, 441–42; Mette 1963, 106–8; Radt 1985, 295. Soph.: Pearson 1917, 2.131–33; Radt 1977, 386. Eur.: Nauck 1964, 541–42; Webster 1967, 174–76.

250. Lloyd-Jones 1996, 218–19; Pearson 1917, 2.80–83; Radt 1977, 353–54.

251. Radt 1985, 352–53, quoting Dio Chrys. 52, 1.

252. Radt 1985, 354, quoting Dio Chrys. 52, 15; Webster 1970, 6.

253. Dio Chrys. 52, 14, quoted by Radt 1985, 354; Webster 1967, 58.

254. Webster 1967, 59.

255. Cf. frag. 790a Snell, where Philoktetes again addresses his interlocutor as "*xenos*." Mette 1981–92, 288, comments on 790N: "Odysseus gibt sich Philoktet gegenüber als Feind des Odysseus und Freund des von diesem verratenen Palamedes aus." Nauck 1964, 615 quotes Dio Chrys. 59. 8–10: Odysseus pretends to be a friend of Palamedes, who fled to avoid being killed by Odysseus. On Euripides and his sources, see also Jouan 1966, 308–17.

256. δριμὺν καὶ δόλιον: Dio Chrys. 52, 5, quoted by Radt 1985, 353.

257. Dio Chrys. 52, 9, quoted by Radt, 1985, 354; cf. Smyth 1926, 465–66; Mette, 1963, 104.

258. Lloyd-Jones 1996, 332–33; Pearson 1917, 2.307–8; Radt 1977, 482.

259. See above, chapter 4, note 49.

260. See Smyth 1926, 457–58; Mette 1963, 170; Radt 1985, 337, and 1977, 415.

261. Radt 1985, 337.

262. Radt 1977, 415.

263. Dios 1983, 276 and n. 1045; Pearson 1917, 2.184.

264. Pearson, 1917, 2.182; Radt 1977, 414.

265. Lloyd-Jones 1996, 198–99; Pearson 1917, 2.38; Radt 1977, 330. Who exactly was attacked by the snakes is a matter of debate.

266. Pearson 1917, 2.40.

267. For an explanation of this and other categories, see the introductory section of this appendix.

268. Smyth 1926, 381; Mette 1963, 15; Radt 1985, 127–28, on frag. 6.

269. Smyth 1926, 396–97; Mette 1963, 43; Radt 1985, 177.

270. Smyth 1926, 414–15; Mette 1963, 108–10; Radt 1985, 217.

271. Austin 1968, 92; Mette 1981–82, 231; Snell 1971, 178.

272. Austin 1968, 92; Snell 1971, frag. 15, col. 2. Summary: Mette 1981–82, 231.

273. Dios 1983, 111–13; Lloyd-Jones 1996, 102–3; Pearson 1917, 1.176–79; Radt 1977, 234.

274. Kiso 1984, 10–11.

275. Radt 1977, 449–50, note on frag. 604. Other conjectures: Dios 1983, 311–12; Pearson 1917, 2.239–43.

Appendix C

1. Snell 1971. For dates, see his table of contents, vi–viii. I include *Peirithous*, *Rhadamanthys*, and *Tennes* with the plays of Euripides (above, appendix B), although Snell attributes these plays to Critias.

2. On amphimetric strife, see chapter 1, section 1 and note 12. The last two paragraphs are repeated, with slight modifications, from the introductory section of appendix B.

3. See Collard 1970, 26, 31, and Xanthakis-Karamanos 1980, 81, who note that she is named Arsinoë in Eurpides and Apollodoros. Snell 1971, 196, on no. 56, frag. 1, apparently confuses Alphesiboia with Kallirrhoe, Alkmeon's second wife: see Apollodoros 3.7.5–6.

4. Snell 1971, 211, questions Carcinus's play and notes (132 with 246) that all but one (*Mandroboulos*) of the titles he lists under Cleophon should perhaps be attributed to Iophon.

5. Snell 1971, 242.

6. Hyginus *Fab.* 58, Apollodoros 3.14.4.7.

7. *Po.* 14.1453b29–34. Snell 1971, 200, apparently interprets Aristotle to mean that the recognition takes place on the stage: "apparet Alcmeonem matrem mortifero vulnere ictam in scaena agnovisse." However, "in the tragedy" might also include messenger speeches: see Roberts 1992, esp. 146.

8. Webster 1954, 305.

9. Nauck 1964, 783, followed by Snell 1971, 218, on frags. 4–7; cf. Xanthakis-Karamanos 1980, 91.

10. Snell 1971, 255.

11. Snell 1971, 75.

12. Snell 1971, 120, on 18a: "sc. tauro Hippolytum necanti, nam taurus Marathonius abest a sinu Saroni (Latte)." The argument is based in part on the reference to Saronian Artemis in frag. 18.

13. Xanthakis-Karamanos 1980, 136.

14. Xanthakis-Keramanos 1980, 65.

15. Snell 1971, 254–55, who notes (on frag. 1) that the *Thyestes* and the *Atreus* may be the same play.

16. *Po.* 1454a8; Kannicht-Snell 1981, *Helle*, frag. Fii.

17. Snell 1971, 232, restores the second line from the passage in Aristotle's *Rhetoric* (2.24.1401a38–b1) immediately following the quotation of line one: ἀποθνῄσκειν ταύτην, καὶ τῷ πατρί γε τιμωρεῖν τὸν υἱόν ("for her to die, and for a son to avenge his father").

18. Janko 1987, 115; cf. Xanthakis-Karamanos 1980, 58.

19. Aristotle refers to Polyidus as a sophist in *Po.* 16.1455a6, and some question whether the *Po.* 17 passage refers to a playwright (e.g., Snell 1971, 248). However, as Else notes (1957, 509–10), ἐποίησεν clearly indicates that Polyidus was a dramatist.

20. Snell 1971, 153.

21. See chapter 3, section 7, on Ais. *Danaïd* trilogy. Text and interpretation of Aristotle's other citation of this play, *Po.* 18.1455b29–32, are much debated. See Janko 1987, xxv, 119; Webster 1954, 304; Xanthakis-Karamanos 1980, 53–54.

22. Snell 1971, 217, on frag. 1c: "Achilles Thersitem in templo necavit"; Séchan 1926, 531. See also Collard 1970, 26.

23. Snell 1971, 190.

24. Myth: Apollodoros, *Library* 2.5.11, and references in Frazer 1921, 1.222–23n. 2.

25. Roisman 1988, 22, writes that the play "most probably dealt with . . . Xerxes' defeat at Salamis."

26. On the many questions raised by this play, about which nothing is known except the title, see Roisman 1988, Rosenbloom 1993.

27. See Snell 1971, 228, testimonium 6; Webster 1956, 65.

28. Collard 1970, 27, who gives no argument for this view.

29. Snell 1971, 206.

30. See above, note 4. Snell supplies the first word of Cleophon's title.

31. Snell marks both fragments with a double asterisk and a question mark. On the question of attribution of the fragments, see Page 1941, 160–61; Snell 1971, 201–4; Xanthakis-Karamanos 1980, 164–66.

32. Xanthakis-Karamanos 1980, 40.

33. Arist. *Rhet.* 2.23.1400b8–14, trans. Kennedy 1991.

34. Xanthakis-Karamanos 1980, 36. Cf. Grimaldi 1988, 332, on b13–15: "Medea's mistake was in sending the children away, for their absence was the reason for the charge of murder against her."

35. Xanthakis-Karamanos 1980, 37–38.

36. Xanthakis-Karamanos 1980, 38.

37. Graf 1997, 34–35.

38. Johnston 1997, 61n. 54.

39. Arist. *Rhet.* 3.16.1417b16–19, trans. Kennedy 1991.

40. Xanthakis-Karamanos 1980, 45–46.

41. Xanthakis-Karamanos 1980, 46.

42. Webster 1954, 301, followed by Snell 1971, 212: "ὁ ζητῶν Laius post Oedipoda ab Iocasta expositum?" Snell also cites Robert 1915, 492[–93], who sees a reference to Polybos instead of to Laios in the fragment.

43. Xanthakis-Karamanos 1980, 39–40, citing Webster 1954, 305, and 1956, 64n. 1.

44. Xanthakis-Karamanos 1980, 40.

45. Webster 1954, 305.

46. Easterling 1993.

47. "Now" includes but is not restricted to fourth-century tragedy: Else 1957, 389–90. See also Gudeman 1934, 244–45, who notes that later tragedians dramatized the same myths as did those of the fifth century.

48. Chaeremon: 1447b21, 1460a2; Cleophon: 1448a12, 1458a20; Theodectas: 1452a27–29, with 1455b29–32, 1455a8–10; Astydamas II: 1453b32–33; Carcinos II: 1454b22–23, 1455a26–29; Dicaeogenes: 1455a1–2.

Glossary

aidôs   shame, respect, reverent fear

amphimetric strife   conflict involving children of the same father and different mothers, or stepchildren and stepparents

anastasis   raising of a suppliant

aretê   excellence

authentês (pl. *authentai*)   killer of kin

bia   force

eris   strife

euergesia   good service

hetairos   companion

hiketês (pl. *hiketai*)   suppliant

hybris   insolence, outrage, violence, rape

hypothesis   plot summary prefixed to a play in antiquity

kharis   gratitude, favor, positive reciprocity

kleos   glory

metoikos (pl. *metoikoi*)   resident alien

nothos (pl. *nothoi*)   bastard

pathos (pl. *pathê*)   terrible event

philia   kinship, friendship

philos (pl. *philoi*; fem. *philê*, pl. *philai*)   kin, friend

physis   nature

polis   city-state

sôphrosynê   sound-mindedness

sôtêria   salvation

themis   established custom, right

theomachy   the fighting of a mortal against a god

timê   honor

xénia   guest-gifts

xenia   guest-friendship

xenos (pl. *xenoi*; fem. *xenê*, pl. *xenai*; in Homer, *xeinos*, *xeinoi*)   stranger, host, guest

Zeus Hikesios   Zeus of Suppliants

Zeus Xenios   Zeus of Strangers

Works Cited

Adkins, A. W. H. 1966. "Basic Greek Values in Euripides' *Hecuba* and *Hercules Furens*," *CQ* 16: 193–219.

Albini, U. 1974. "Un dramma d'avanguardia: L'Andromaca di Euripide." *Maia* 26: 83–95.

Aldrich, K. M. 1961. *The Andromache of Euripides*. University of Nebraska Studies, n.s. 25. Lincoln.

Allen, T. W. 1946. *Homeri opera*. Vol. 5. Oxford.

Amoroso, F. 1994. "Una lettura progressista dell'*Andromaca* di Euripide." In *Orchestra: Drama, Mythos, Bühne*, ed. A. Bierl and P. von Möllendorff, 139–50. Stuttgart.

Alt, K. 1961. "Schicksal und *Phusis* im Philoktet des Sophokles." *Hermes* 89: 141–74.

Austin, C., ed. 1968. *Nova fragmenta Euripidea in papyris reperta*. Berlin.

Avery, H. C. 1965. "Heracles, Philoctetes, Neoptolemus." *Hermes* 93: 279–97.

Bacon, H. 1982. "Aeschylus." In *Ancient Writers Greece and Rome*, ed. T. J. Luce, 99–155. New York.

Bacon, H., and A. Hecht, trans. 1973. *Aeschylus: Seven Against Thebes*. Oxford.

Bakewell, G. W. 1997. "*Metoikia* in the *Supplices* of Aeschylus." *CA* 16: 209–28.

Barrett, W. S., ed. 1964. *Euripides: Hippolytos*. Oxford.

Belfiore, E. 1988. "*Peripeteia* as Discontinuous Action: Aristotle, *Poetics* 11.1452a22–29." *CP* 83: 183–94.

———. 1992a. *Tragic Pleasures: Aristotle on Plot and Emotion*. Princeton.

———. 1992b. "Aristotle and Iphigenia." In Rorty, 359–77. Princeton.

———. 1994. "*Xenia* in Sophocles' *Philoctetes*." *CJ* 89: 113–29.

Belpassi, L. 1990. "La 'follia' del *genos*: Un' analisi del 'discorso mitico' nella *Ifigenia Taurica* di Euripide." *Quaderni urbinati di cultura classica* 63: 53–67.

Benveniste, E. 1969. *Le vocabulaire des institutions indo-européens*. Vol. 1. Paris.

Bergson, L. 1986. "Der 'Aias' des Sophokles als 'Trilogie'." *Hermes* 114: 36–50.

Betts, J. H., J. T. Hooker, and J. R. Green, eds. 1986. *Studies in Honour of T. B. L. Webster*. Vol. 1. Bristol.

Blundell, M. W. 1988. "The Phusis of Neoptolemus in Sophocles' Philoctetes." *G & R* 35: 137–48.

———. 1989. *Helping Friends and Harming Enemies: A Study in Sophocles and Greek Ethics*. Cambridge.

Boittin, J.-F. 1976. "Figures du mythe et de la tragédie: Io dans le Prométhée Enchaîné." In *Écriture et théorie poétiques*. Paris, 40–56.

Bond, G. W., ed. 1963. *Euripides: Hypsipyle*. Oxford.

———, ed. 1981. *Euripides: Heracles*. Oxford.

Bond, R. S. 1996. "Homeric Echoes in *Rhesus*." *AJP* 117: 255–73.

Boulter, P. N. 1966. "*Sophia* and *Sophrosyne* in Euripides' *Andromache*." *Phoenix* 20: 51–58.

Bowra, C. M. 1944. *Sophoclean Tragedy*. Oxford.

Brelich, A. 1969. *Paides e parthenoi*. Vol. 1. Rome.

Bremmer, J. N. 1997. "Why Did Medea Kill Her Brother Apsyrtus?" In Clauss and Johnston, 83–100.

Brendel, O. J. 1950. "*Iphigenie auf Tauris*." In *Goethe Bicentennial Studies*, ed. H. J. Meesen, 1–47. Bloomington, Ind.

Broadhead, H. D., ed. 1960. *The Persae of Aeschylus*. Cambridge.

Brulé, P. 1987. *La fille d'Athènes: La religion des filles à Athènes à l'epoque classique. Mythes, cultes, et société*. Paris.

Burian, P. 1971. "Suppliant Drama: Studies in the Form and Interpretation of Five Greek Tragedies." Ph.D. diss., Princeton University.

———. 1972. "Supplication and Hero Cult in Sophocles' *Ajax*." *GRBS* 13: 151–56.

———. 1974a. "Pelasgus and Politics in Aeschylus' Danaid Trilogy." *WS* 8: 5–14.

———. 1974b. "Suppliant and Saviour: Oedipus at Colonus." *Phoenix* 28: 408–29.

Burkert, W. 1955. *Zum altgriechischen Mitleidsbegriff*. Ph.D. diss., Friedrich–Alexander–Universität, Erlangen.

———. 1962. *Weisheit und Wissenschaft: Studien zu Pythagoras, Philolaos, und Platon*. Nurenberg.

———. 1983. *Homo Necans: The Anthropology of Ancient Greek Sacrificial Ritual and Myth*. Trans. P. Bing. Berkeley.

———. 1985. *Greek Religion*. Trans. J. Raffan. Cambridge, Mass.

Burnett, A. P. 1971. *Catastrophe Survived: Euripides' Plays of Mixed Reversal*. Oxford.

Burton, R. W. B. 1980. *The Chorus in Sophocles' Tragedies*. Oxford.

Buxton, R. 1987. "Euripides' *Alkestis*: Five Aspects of an Interpretation." In *Papers Given at a Colloquium on Greek Drama in Honour of R. P. Winnington-Ingram*, ed. L. Rodley, 17–30. London.

Bynner, W., trans. 1959. *Iphgenia in Tauris*. In Grene and Lattimore.

Cairns, D. L. 1993. *Aidôs. The Psychology and Ethics of Honour and Shame in Ancient Greek Literature*. Oxford.

Calame, C. 1977. *Les choeurs de jeunes filles en Grèce archaïque*. Rome.

———. 1997. *Choruses of Young Women in Ancient Greece: Their Morphology, Religious Role, and Social Functions*. Trans. of Calame 1977 by D. Collins and J. Orien. Lanham, Md.

Calder, W. 1971. "Sophoclean Apologia: *Philoctetes*." *GRBS* 12: 153–74.

Caldwell, R. 1974–5. "Tragedy Romanticized: The *Iphigenia Taurica*." *CJ* 70: 23–40.

———. 1994. "Aeschylus' *Suppliants*: A Psychoanalytic Study." In *Modern Critical Theory and Classical Literature*, ed. I. J. F. de Jong and J. P. Sullivan, 75–101. Leiden.

Carson, A. 1990. "Putting Her in Her Place: Woman, Dirt, and Desire." In *Before Sexuality*, ed. D. M. Halperin, J. J. Winkler, and F. I. Zeitlin, 135–69. Princeton.

Clauss, J. J., and S. I. Johnston, eds. 1997. *Medea: Essays on Medea in Myth, Literature, Philosophy, and Art*. Princeton.

Cohen, D. 1978. "The Imagery of Sophocles: A Study of Ajax's Suicide." *G & R* 25: 24–36.

Cole, S. G. 1998. "Domesticating Artemis." In *The Sacred and the Feminine in Ancient Greece*, ed. S. Blundell and M. Williamson, 27–43. London and New York.

Collard, C., 1970. "On the Tragedian Chaeremon," *JHS* 90: 22–34.

——, ed. 1975. *Euripides: Supplices*. 2 vols. Groningen.

——. 1991. *Euripides: Hecuba*. Warminster, England.

——. 1995a. "*Cretans*." In Collard, Cropp, and Lee: 53–78.

——. 1995b. "*Stheneboea*." In Collard, Cropp, and Lee: 79–97.

——. 1995c. "*Bellerophon*." In Collard, Cropp, and Lee: 98–120.

——. 1995d. "*Phaethon*."In Collard, Cropp, and Lee: 195–239.

Collard, C., M. J. Cropp, and K. H. Lee, eds. 1995. *Euripides: Selected Fragmentary Plays*. Vol. 1. Warminster, England.

Conacher, D. J. 1967. *Euripidean Drama: Myth, Theme, and Structure*. Toronto.

Cooper, J. M. 1980. "Aristotle on Friendship." In *Essays on Aristotle's Ethics*, ed. A. O. Rorty, 301–40. Berkeley.

Craik, E. M. 1984. "Marriage in Ancient Greece." In *Marriage and Property*, ed. E. M. Craik, 6–29. Aberdeen.

Croiset, M. 1894. "Eschyle imitateur d' Homère dans les *Myrmidons*, les *Néréides*, les *Phrygiens*." *REG* 7: 151–80.

Cropp, M. J. 1995a. "*Telephus*. In Collard, Cropp, and Lee: 17–52.

——. 1995b. "*Cresphontes*." In Collard, Cropp, and Lee: 121–47.

——. 1995c. "*Erectheus*." In Collard, Cropp, and Lee: 148–94.

——. 1995d. "*Melanippe Sophe* and *Melanippe Desmotis*." In Collard, Cropp, and Lee: 240–80.

Cropp, M. J., E. Fantham, and S. E. Scully, eds. 1986. *Greek Tragedy and Its Legacy: Essays Presented to D. J. Conacher*. Calgary.

Dale, A. M., ed. 1961. *Euripides: Alcestis*. Oxford.

Daly, J. 1982. "The Name of Philoctetes: *Philoctetes* 670–73." *AJP* 103: 440–43.

Daube, D. 1972. "The Linguistics of Suicide." *Philosophy and Public Affairs* 1: 387–437.

Davidson, J. F. 1995. "Homer and Sophocles' *Philoctetes*." In *Stage Directions: Essays in Ancient Drama in Honour of E. W. Handley*, ed. A. Griffiths, 25–35. London.

Davies, J. K. 1977–78. "Athenian Citizenship: The Descent Group and the Alternatives." *CJ* 73: 105–21.

Davies, M., ed. 1988. *Epicorum Graecorum Fragmenta*. Göttingen.

——. 1991. *Sophocles: Trachiniae*. Oxford.

Dawe, R. D., ed. 1982. *Sophocles: Oedipus Rex*. Cambridge.

Delcourt, M. 1939. "Le suicide par vengeance dans la Grèce ancienne." *Revue de l'histoire des religions* 119: 154–71.

Denniston, J. D, and D. Page, eds. 1957. *Aeschylus: Agamemnon*. Oxford.

Detienne, M. 1988. "Les Danaïdes entre elles ou la violence fondatrice du mariage." *Arethusa* 21: 159–75.

Diamantopoulos, A. 1957. "The Danaid Tetralogy of Aeschylus." *JHS* 77: 220–29.

Diehls, H., and W. Kranz, eds. 1935–37. *Die Fragmente der Vorsokratiker*. 3 vols. 5th ed. Berlin.

Diggle, J., ed. 1970. *Euripides: Phaethon*. Cambridge.

——, ed. 1981–94. *Euripides: Fabulae*. 3 vols. Oxford.

Diller, H. 1939. "Der griechische Naturbegriff." *Neue Jahrbücher für antike und deutsche Bildung* 2: 241–57.

Dios, J. M. L. de. 1983. *Sófocles: Fragmentos*. Madrid.

Dirlmeier, F. 1931. *Philos und Philia im vorhellenistischen Griechentum*. Ph.D. diss., Ludwig-Maximilians-Universität.

Dodds, E. R., ed. 1960. *Euripides: Bacchae*. 2d ed. Oxford.

Donlan, W. 1982. "Reciprocities in Homer." *CW* 75: 137–75.

——. 1989. "The Unequal Exchange Between Glaucus and Diomedes in Light of the Homeric Gift-Economy." *Phoenix* 43: 1–15.

Dover, K. J. 1974. *Greek Popular Morality*. Oxford.

——. 1978. *Greek Homosexuality*. New York.

Durkheim, E. 1951. *Suicide: A Study in Sociology*. Trans. J. A. Spaulding and G. Simpson. New York. Originally published as *Le suicide* (Paris, 1897).

Dunn, F. M. 1996. *Tragedy's End: Closure and Innovation in Euripidean Drama*. Oxford.

Easterling, P. E. 1967. "Oedipus and Polynices." *PCPS* 13: 1–13.

——. 1978. "*Philoctetes* and Modern Criticism." *ICS* 3: 27–39.

——. 1981. "The End of the *Trachiniae*." *ICS* 6: 56–74.

——, ed. 1982. *Sophocles: Trachiniae*. Cambridge.

——. 1984. "The Tragic Homer." *BICS* 31: 1–8.

——. 1988. "Tragedy and Ritual." *Métis* 3: 87–109. Revised in *Theater and Society in the Classical World*, ed. R. Scodel, 7–24. Ann Arbor, 1993.

——. 1993. "The End of an Era? Tragedy in the Early Fourth Century." In *Tragedy, Comedy, and the Polis*, ed. A. H. Sommerstein et al., 559–69. Bari.

Else, G. F. 1957. *Aristotle's Poetics: The Argument*. Cambridge, Mass..

England, E. B., ed. 1886. *The Iphigeneia among the Tauri of Euripides*. London.

Erbse, H. 1966. "Neoptolemus und Philoktet bei Sophokles." *Hermes* 94: 177–201.

Erffa, C. E. F. von. 1937. *Aidôs und verwandte Begriffe in ihrer Entwicklung von Homer bis Demokrit*. Philologus, suppl. vol. 30, no. 2. Leipzig.

Errandonea, I. 1958. "Les quatre monologues d'Ajax et leur signification dramatique." *Les études classiques* 26: 21–40.

Eucken, C. 1991. "Die thematische Einheit des Sophokleischen 'Aias'." *Würzburger Jahrbücher für die Altertumswissenschaft* 17: 119–33.

Evelyn-White, H. G., trans. 1977. *Hesiod: The Homeric Hymns and Homerica*. Cambridge, Mass.

Ewans, M., ed. and trans. 1996a. *Aischylos: Suppliants and Other Dramas*. London.

——. 1996b. "Patterns of Tragedy in Sophokles and Shakespeare." In Silk 1996a: 438–57.

Fantham, E. 1986. "Andromache's Child in Euripides and Seneca." In Cropp, Fantham, and Scully: 267–80.

Fenik, B. 1964. "*Iliad X*" and the "*Rhesus*": The Myth. Latomus 73. Brussels.

Ferrari, F. 1971. "Struttura e personaggi nella *Andromaca* di Euripide." *Maia*, n.s. 23: 209–29.

Flory, S. 1978. "Medea's Right Hand: Promises and Revenge." *TAPA* 108: 69–74.

Foley, H. P. 1985. *Ritual Irony: Poetry and Sacrifice in Euripides*. Ithaca, N.Y.

Fontenrose, J. 1960. *The Cult and Myth of Pyrros at Delphi*. Berkeley.

Forbes, R. J. 1972. *Studies in Ancient Technology*. 2d ed. Vol. 9. Leiden

Fraenkel, E. 1962. *Aeschylus: Agamemnon.* 3 vols. Oxford.

——. 1965. Review of Ritchie 1964. *Gnomon* 37: 228–41.

Frazer, J. G., ed. and trans. 1921. *Apollodoros: The Library.* Cambridge, Mass.

Friedländer, P. 1926. "Die griechische Tragödie und das Tragische." *Antike* 2: 79–112.

Friedrich, R. 1996. "Everything to Do with Dionysos? Ritualism, the Dionysiac, and the Tragic." In Silk 1996a: 257–83.

Friis Johansen, H. 1986. "Heracles in Sophocles' *Trachiniae.*" *C&M* 37: 47–61.

Friis Johansen, H., and E. W. Whittle, eds. 1980. *Aeschylus: The Suppliants.* 3 vols. Copenhagen.

Fritz, K. von. 1962. "Die Danaidentrilogie des Aeschylus." In *Antike und moderne Tragödie,* 160–92. Berlin.

Froidefond, C. 1971. *Le mirage égyptien dans la littérature grecque d'Homère à Aristote.* Aix-en-Provence.

Frontisi-Ducroux, F. 1996. "Eros, Desire, and the Gaze." In *Sexuality in Ancient Art,* ed. N. B. Kampen, 81–100. Cambridge.

Fuqua, C. 1976. "Studies in the Use of Myth in Sophocles' 'Philoctetes' and the 'Orestes' of Euripides." *Traditio* 32: 29–95.

Furley, D. 1986. "Euripides on the Sanity of Herakles." In Betts, Hooker, and Green, 102–13.

——. 1989. "Andokides 4 ('Against Alkibiades'): Fact or Fiction?" *Hermes* 117: 138–56.

Gallop, D. 1975. *Plato: Phaedo.* Oxford.

Gantz, T. 1978. "Love and Death in the *Suppliants* of Aischylos." *Phoenix* 32: 279–87.

——. 1993. *Early Greek Myth: A Guide to Literary and Artistic Sources.* 2 vols. Baltimore.

Garland, R. 1985. *The Greek Way of Death.* Ithaca, N.Y.

Garrison, E. P. 1991. "Attitudes Toward Suicide in Ancient Greece." *TAPA* 121: 1–34.

——. 1995. *Groaning Tears: Ethical and Dramatic Aspects of Suicide in Greek Tragedy.* Leiden.

Garvie, A. F. 1969. *Aeschylus' Supplices: Play and Trilogy.* Cambridge.

——. 1978. "Aeschylus' Simple Plots." In *Dionysiaca: Nine Studies in Greek Poetry by Former Pupils Presented to Sir Denys Page on His Seventieth Birthday,* ed. R. D. Dawe, J. Diggle, and P. E. Easterling, 63–86. Cambridge.

——, ed. 1986. *Aeschylus: Choephori.* Oxford.

Gauthier, R. A., and J. I. Jolif. 1970. *Aristote: L'éthique à Nicomaque.* Louvain.

Gernet, L. 1955. "Authentes." In *Droit et société dans la Grèce ancienne,* 29–38. Paris. Reprinted from *REG* 22 (1909).

Gill, C. 1980. "Bow, Oracle, and Epiphany in Sophocles' *Philoctetes.*" *G & R* 27: 137–46.

Glotz, G. 1904. *La solidarité de la famille dans le droit criminel en Grèce.* Paris.

Golder, H. 1990. "Sophocles' *Ajax:* Beyond the Shadow of Time." *Arion* 1, 3d ser.: 9–34.

Goldfarb, B. E. 1992. "The Conflict of Obligations in Euripides' *Alcestis.*" *GRBS* 33: 109–26.

Goldhill, S. 1986. *Reading Greek Tragedy.* Cambridge.

——. 1990. "The Great Dionysia and Civic Ideology." In Winkler and Zeitlin, 97–129.

——. 1991a. *The Poet's Voice: Essays on Poetics and Greek Literature.* Cambridge.

——. 1991b. "Violence in Greek Tragedy." In *Violence in Drama,* 15–33. Themes in Drama 13. Cambridge.

Gould, J. 1973. "*Hiketeia.*" *JHS* 93: 74–103.

Graf, F. 1997. "Medea, the Enchantress from Afar: Remarks on a Well-Known Myth." In Clauss and Johnston, 21–43.

Grant, M., trans. and ed. 1960. *The Myths of Hyginus*. University of Kansas Publications, Humanistic Studies no. 34. Lawrence, Kans.

Greengard, C. 1987. *Theatre in Crisis*. Amsterdam.

Grégoire, H., ed. 1964. *Iphigénie en Tauride*. In *Euripide*. Vol. 4. Paris.

Grene, D., and R. Lattimore, eds.1959. *The Complete Greek Tragedies*. Chicago.

Griffin, J. 1977. "The Epic Cycle and the Uniqueness of Homer." *JHS* 97: 39–53.

Griffith, M., ed. 1983. *Aeschylus: Prometheus Bound*. Cambridge.

———, ed. 1999. *Sophocles: Antigone*. Cambridge.

Griffith, M., and D. J. Mastronarde, eds. 1990. *Cabinet of the Muses*. Atlanta, Ga.

Grimaldi, W. M. A. 1988. *Aristotle, Rhetoric II: A Commentary*. New York.

Grube, G. M. A. 1941. *The Drama of Euripides*. London.

Gruppe, O. 1906. *Griechische Mythologie und Religionsgeschichte*. 2 vols. Munich.

Gudeman, A. 1934. *Aristoteles: Peri Poiêtikês*. Berlin.

Hadas, M., and J. McLean, trans. 1960. *Ten Plays by Euripides*. New York.

Hainsworth, B. 1993. *The Iliad: A Commentary*. Vol. 3, *Books 9–12*. Cambridge.

Hajistephanou, C. E. 1975. *The Use of Phusis and Its Cognates in Greek Tragedy with Special Reference to Character Drawing*. Nicosia, Cyprus.

Hall, E. 1989. *Inventing the Barbarian: Greek Self-Definition Through Tragedy*. Oxford.

———, ed. 1996a. *Aeschylus: Persians*. Warminster, England.

———. 1996b. "Is There a *Polis* in Aristotle's *Poetics*?" In Silk 1996a: 295–309.

Halleran, M. R. 1988. "Text and Ceremony at the Close of Euripides' *Alkestis*." *Eranos* 86: 123–29.

Hamilton, R. 1975. "Neoptolemos' Story in the *Philoctetes*." *AJP* 96: 131–37.

Harrison, A. R. W. 1968. *The Law of Athens*. Vol. 1, *The Family and Property*. Oxford.

Harsh, P. W. 1960. "The Role of the Bow in the *Philoctetes* of Sophocles." *AJP* 81: 408–14.

Hartigan, K. V. 1986. "Salvation via Deceit: A New Look at the *Iphigeneia at* [sic] *Tauris*." *Eranos* 84: 119–25.

———. 1991. *Ambiguity and Self-Deception: The Apollo and Artemis Plays of Euripides*. Frankfurt.

Hartung, J. A. 1852. *Euripides' Werke*. Vol. 16, *Andromakhe*, introduction, 5–12. Leipzig.

———. 1855. *Aeschylos' Fragmente*. Leipzig.

Haslam, M. W. 1976. "Sophocles, *Aias Lokros*: P. Oxy. XLIV 3151." *ZPE* 22: 34.

Haspels, C. H. E. 1930. "Deux fragments d'une coupe d'Euphronios." *Bulletin de correspondence hellénique* 54: 422–51.

Heath, M. 1987. *The Poetics of Greek Tragedy*. Stanford.

Henrichs, A. 1993. "The Tomb of Aias and The Prospect of Hero Cult in Sophokles." *CA* 12: 165–80.

Herington, J. 1986. "The Marriage of Earth and Sky in Aeschylus, *Agamemnon* 1388–1392." In Cropp, Fantham, and Scully, 27–33.

Herman, G. 1987. *Ritualised Friendship and the Greek City*. Cambridge.

Hester, D. A. 1987. "A Chorus of One Danaid." *Antichthon* 21: 9–18.

Hinds, A. E. 1967. "The Prophecy of Helenus in Sophocles' *Philoctetes*." *CQ* 17: 169–80.

Hirzel, R. 1908. "Der Selbstmord." *Archiv für Religionswissenschaft* 11: 75–104, 243–84, 417–76.

Hooff, A. J. L. van. 1990. *From Autothanasia to Suicide: Self-Killing in Classical Antiquity*. London and New York.

Hoppin, M. C. 1981. "What Happens in Sophocles' 'Philoctetes'?" *Traditio* 37: 1–30.

Hunter, V. J., 1994. *Policing Athens: Social Control in the Attic Lawsuits, 420–320 B.C.* Princeton.

Hutchinson, G. O., ed. 1985. *Aeschylus: Seven Against Thebes.* Oxford.

Jackson, J. 1955. *Marginalia Scaenica.* Oxford.

Janko, R. 1992. *The Iliad: A Commentary.* Vol. 4, Books 13–16. Cambridge.

Jebb, R. C. 1907. *Sophocles: The Plays and Fragments.* Part 7, *The Ajax.* Cambridge.

———. 1928. *Sophocles: The Plays and Fragments.* Part 2, *The Oedipus Coloneus.* Cambridge.

———. 1932. *Sophocles: The Plays and Fragments.* Part 4, *The Philoctetes.* Cambridge.

———, trans. 1967. *The Complete Plays of Sophocles.* Ed. M. Hadas. New York.

Jenkins, I. 1983. "Is There Life After Marriage? A Study of the Abduction Motif in Vase Paintings of the Athenian Wedding Ceremony." *BICS* 30: 137–45.

Johnson, J. A. 1988. "Sophocles' *Philoctetes*: Deictic Language and the Claims of Odysseus." *Eranos* 86: 117–21.

Johnston, S. I. 1997. "Corinthian Medea and the Cult of Hera Akraia." In Clauss and Johnston, 44–70.

Jones, C. P. 1999. *Kinship Diplomacy in the Ancient World.* Cambridge, Mass.

Jong, I. J. F. de. 1987. *Narrators and Focalizers: The Presentation of the Story in the Iliad.* Amsterdam.

———. 1990. "Three Off-Stage Characters in Euripides." *Mnemosyne* 43: 1–21.

Jouan, F. 1966. *Euripide et les légendes des chants cypriens.* Paris.

Kaimio, M. 1988. *Physical Contact in Greek Tragedy: A Study of Stage Conventions.* Annales Academiae Scientiarum Fennicae, ser. B, vol. 244. Helsinki.

Kamerbeek, J. C. 1943. "L'Andromaque d'Euripide." *Mnemosyne* 11: 47–67.

———. 1948. "Sophocle et Héraclite." In *Studia varia Carolo Guilielmo Vollgraff a discipulis oblata*, 84–98. Amsterdam.

———. 1959. *The Plays of Sophocles. Commentaries.* Part 2, *The Trachiniae.* Leiden.

———. 1963. *The Plays of Sophocles. Commentaries.* Part 1, *The Ajax.* 2d ed. Leiden.

———. 1974. *The Plays of Sophocles. Commentaries.* Part 5, *The Electra.* Leiden.

———. 1978. *The Plays of Sophocles. Commentaries.* Part 3, *The Antigone.* Leiden.

———. 1980. *The Plays of Sophocles. Commentaries.* Part 6, *The Philoctetes.* Leiden.

———. 1984. *The Plays of Sophocles. Commentaries.* Part 7, *The Oedipus Coloneus.* Leiden.

Kannicht, R., ed. 1969. *Euripides: Helena.* 2 vols. Heidelberg.

———. 1972. Review of Diggle 1970. *Gnomon* 44: 1–12.

Kannicht, R., and B. Snell, eds. 1981. *Tragicorum Graecorum Fragmenta.* Vol. 2, *Fragmenta Adespota.* Göttingen.

Katsouris, A. G. 1976. "The Suicide Motif in Ancient Drama." *Dioniso* 47: 5–36. Translation from Greek. Originally published, *Dodone* 4 (1975): 203–34.

Katz, M. A. 1991. *Penelope's Renown: Meaning and Indeterminacy in the Odyssey.* Princeton.

Kells, J. H., ed. 1973. *Sophocles: Electra.* Cambridge.

Kennedy, G. A., trans. 1991. *Aristotle, On Rhetoric: A Theory of Civic Discourse.* Oxford.

Keuls, E. 1974. *The Water Carriers in Hades: A Study of Catharsis Through Toil in Classical Antiquity.* Amsterdam.

———. 1978. "Aeschylus' *Niobe* and Apulian Funerary Symbolism." *ZPE* 30: 41–68.

Kirk, G. S. 1985. *The Iliad: A Commentary.* Vol. 1, Books 1–4. Cambridge.

Kirk, G. S., J. E. Raven, and M. Schofield. 1983. *The Presocratic Philosophers*: A *Critical History with a Selection of Texts*. 2d. ed. Cambridge.

Kirkwood, G. M. 1958. A *Study of Sophoclean Drama*. Ithaca, NY.

——. 1986. "From Melos to Colonus: ΤΙΝΑΣ ΧΩΡΟΥΣ ΑΦΙΓΜΕΘ' . . ." *TAPA* 116: 99–117.

——. 1994. "Persuasion and Allusion in Sophocles' 'Philoctetes'." *Hermes* 122: 425–36.

Kiso, A. 1984. *The Lost Sophocles*. New York.

Kitto, H. D. F. 1956. *Form and Meaning in Drama*. London.

Knox, B. M. W. 1964. *The Heroic Temper: Studies in Sophoclean Tragedy*. Berkeley.

——. 1979. "The Ajax of Sophocles." In *Word and Action: Essays on the Ancient Theater*, 125–60. Baltimore. Reprinted from *HSCP* 65 (1961).

——. 1988. "Attic Exits." Review of Loraux 1987. *New York Times Book Review*, Apr. 28: 13–14.

Konstan, D. 1981. "An Anthropology of Euripides' *Kyklôps*." *Ramus* 10: 87–103. Reprinted in Winkler and Zeitlin 1990, 207–27.

——. 1985. "*Philia* in Euripides' *Electra*." *Philologus* 129: 176–85.

——. 1996. "Greek Friendship." *AJP* 117: 71–94.

——. 1997. *Friendship in the Classical World*. Cambridge.

Koenen, L. 1969. "Eine Hypothese zur Auge des Euripides und tegeatische Plynterien." *ZPE* 4: 7–18.

Kopperschmidt, J. 1967. *Die Hikesie als dramatische Form: zur motivischen Interpretation des griechischen Drama*. Ph.D. diss., Eberhard-Karls-Universität.

Kott, J. 1970. *The Eating of the Gods: An Interpretation of Greek Tragedy*. New York.

Kovacs, P. D. 1980. *The Andromache of Euripides: An Interpretation*. Atlanta, Ga.

Kuntz, M. 1993. *Narrative Setting and Dramatic Poetry*. Leiden.

Lacey, W. K. 1968. *The Family in Classical Greece*. Ithaca, N.Y.

Lateiner, D. 1993. "The Suitors' Take: Manners and Power in Ithaka." *Colby Quarterly* 24: 173–96.

——. 1995. *Sardonic Smile: Nonverbal Behavior in Homeric Epic*. Ann Arbor.

Lattimore, R., trans. 1951. *The Iliad of Homer*. Chicago.

——. 1958. *The Poetry of Greek Tragedy*. Baltimore.

——, trans. 1960. *Rhesus*. Chicago.

——, trans. 1965. *The Odyssey of Homer*. New York.

——, trans. and ed. 1973. *Euripides: Iphigenia in Tauris*. Oxford.

Lee, H. D. P., trans. 1952. *Aristotle: Meteorologica*. Cambridge, Mass.

Lee, K. H. 1975. "Euripides' *Andromache*: Observations on Form and Meaning." *Antichthon* 9: 4–16.

Lefèvre, E. 1991. "Die Unfähigkeit, sich zu Erkennen: Sophokles' *Aias*." *Würzburger Jahrbücher für die Altertumswissenschaft* 17: 91–117.

Lembke, J., trans. 1975. *Aeschylus: Suppliants*. Oxford.

Lesky, A. 1937. "Peleus." *RE* 19.1: 271–308.

——. 1939. "Erbe und Erziehung im griechischen Denkens des fünften Jahrhunderts." *Neue Jahrbücher für antike und deutsche Bildung* 2: 361–81.

——. 1956. "Peleus und Thetis im frühen Epos." *Studi italiani di filologia classica* 27–28: 216–26.

——. 1983. *Greek Tragic Poetry*. Trans. M. Dillon. New Haven.

Lévy, E. 1985. "Inceste, mariage et sexualité dans les *Suppliantes* d'Eschyle." In *La femmé dans le monde méditerranéen*. 1: 29–45. Lyon.

Liddell, H. G., and R. Scott, 1996. *A Greek-English Lexicon*. Rev. H. Jones and R. McKenzie. 9th ed. with rev. suppl. Oxford.

Linforth, I. M. 1954. "Three Scenes in Sophocles' *Ajax*." *University of California Publications in Classical Philology* 15: 1–28

———. 1956. "Philoctetes: The Play and the Man." *University of California Publications in Classical Philology* 15: 95–156.

Littman, R. J. 1979. "Kinship in Athens." *Ancient Society* 10: 5–31.

Lloyd, G. E. R. 1966. *Polarity and Analogy*. Cambridge.

Lloyd, M., trans. 1994. *Euripides: Andromache*. Warminster, England.

Lloyd-Jones, H., ed. 1957. Appendix, and Addendum. In Smyth 1926, 523–603.

———, ed. and trans. 1996. *Sophocles: Fragments*. Cambridge, Mass.

Lloyd-Jones, H., and N. G. Wilson, eds. 1990a. *Sophoclis Fabulae*. Oxford.

———. 1990b. *Sophoclea: Studies on the Text of Sophocles*. Oxford.

Long, A. A. 1968. *Language and Thought in Sophocles*. London.

Loraux, N. 1986. "La main d'Antigone." *Métis* 1: 165–96.

———. 1987a. *Tragic Ways of Killing a Woman*. Trans. A. Forster. Cambridge, Mass.

———. 1987b. "*Oikeios polemos*: La guerra nella famiglia." *Studi storici* 28: 5–35.

Luschnig, C. A. E. 1972. "Euripides' *Iphigenia among the Taurians* and *Helen*: Così è, se vi pare!" *CW* 66: 158–63.

Lyons, D. 1997. *Gender and Immortality: Heroines in Ancient Greek Myth and Cult*. Princeton.

MacDowell, D. M. 1978. *The Law in Classical Athens*. Ithaca, N.Y.

———, ed. 1990. *Demosthenes: Against Meidias*. Oxford.

Machin, A. 1981. *Cohérence et continuité dans le théâtre de Sophocle*. Québec.

MacKinnon, J. K. 1978. "The Reason for the Danaids' Flight." *CQ* 28: 74–82.

Manville, P. B. 1990. *The Origins of Citizenship in Ancient Athens*. Princeton.

March, J. R. 1991–93. "Sophocles' *Ajax*: The Death and Burial of a Hero." *BICS* 38: 1–36.

Martinazzoli, F. 1946. "L'Ifigenia Taurica di Euripide." *La parola del passato* 1: 69–83.

Matthiessen, K. 1964. *Elektra, Taurische Iphigenie und Helena*. Hypomnemata 4. Göttingen.

Mastronarde, D. J., ed. 1994. *Euripides: Phoenissae*. Cambridge.

Mauss, M. 1923–24. "Essai sur le don." *Année sociologique*, n.s. 1: 30–186.

Mazon, P., ed. 1949. *Eschyle*. vol. 1, 5th ed. Paris. (Vol. 2: Paris 1925.)

McClure, L. 1995. Review of Garrison 1995. *BMCR* 95.10.13.

Mercier, C. E. 1990. "Suppliant Ritual in Euripidean Tragedy." Ph.D. diss., Columbia University.

Méridier, L. 1927. *Euripide*. Vol. 2, introduction to *Andromaque*, 90–109. Paris.

Merkelbach, R., and M. L. West, eds. 1967. *Fragmenta Hesiodea*. Oxford.

Mette, H. J. 1963. *Der verlorene Aischylos*. Berlin.

———. 1981–82. "Euripides (insbesondere für die Jahre 1968–1981), Erster Hauptteil: Die Bruchstücke." *Lustrum* 23–24.

———. 1985. "Euripides, Erster Teil: Bruchstücke 1983." *Lustrum* 27: 23–26.

Michelini, A. N. 1987. *Euripides and the Tragic Tradition*. Madison, Wis.

Mikalson, J. D. 1991. *Honor Thy Gods: Popular Religion in Greek Tragedy*. Chapel Hill.

Millet, P. 1991. *Lending and Borrowing in Ancient Athens*. Cambridge.

Mitchell, L. G. 1997a. *Greeks Bearing Gifts: The Public Use of Private Relationships in the Greek World, 435–323 B.C.* Cambridge.

——. 1997b. "*Philia, Eunoia* and Greek Interstate Relations." *Anthichthon* 31: 28–44.

Mogyoródi, E. 1996. "Tragic Freedom and Fate in Sophocles' *Antigone*: Notes on the Role of the 'Ancient Evils' in 'The Tragic'." In Silk 1996a, 358–76.

Moore, J. 1977. "The Dissembling-Speech of Ajax." *YCS* 25: 47–66.

Moreau, A. 1985. *Eschyle: La violence et le chaos*. Paris.

——. 1979. "À propos d'Oedipe: la liason entre trois crimes—parricide, inceste et cannibalisme." In *Études de littérature ancienne*, ed. S. Saïd, F. Desbordes, J. Bouffartique, and A. Moreau, 97–127. Paris.

Murnaghan, S. 1987. *Disguise and Recognition in the Odyssey*. Princeton.

Murray, G., ed. 1902–13. *Euripides: Fabulae*. 3 vols. Oxford.

Murray, R. D. 1958. *The Motif of Io in Aeschylus' Suppliants*. Princeton.

Mylonas, G. E. 1945. "A Signet-Ring in the City Art Museum of St. Louis." *AJA* 49: 557–69.

Nagler, M. N. 1993. "Penelope's Male Hand: Gender and Violence in the *Odyssey*." *Colby Quarterly* 24: 241–57.

Nagy, G. 1979. *The Best of the Achaeans: Concepts of the Hero in Archaic Greek Poetry*. Baltimore.

Nauck, A., ed. 1964. *Tragicorum Graecorum Fragmenta*. Reprint of 2d ed. (1889), with supplement by B. Snell. Hildesheim.

Neumann, G. 1965. *Gesten und Gebärden in der griechischen Kunst*. Berlin.

Newman, R. 1991. "Heroic Resolution: A Note on Sophocles, *Philoctetes* 1405–1406." *CJ* 86: 305–10.

Nussbaum, M. C. 1976. "Consequences and Character in Sophocles' *Philoctetes*." *Philosophy and Literature* 1: 25–53.

——. 1986. *The Fragility of Goodness: Luck and Ethics in Greek Tragedy and Philosophy*. Cambridge.

Oakley, J. H., and R. H. Sinos. 1993. *The Wedding in Ancient Athens*. Madison, Wis.

O'Brien, J. V. 1993. *The Transformation of Hera: A Study of Ritual, Hero, and the Goddess in the Iliad*. Lanham, Md.

O'Brien, M. J. 1988. "Pelopid History and the Plot of *Iphigenia in Tauris*." *CQ* 38: 98–115.

Ogden, D. 1996. *Greek Bastardy in the Classical and Hellenistic Periods*. Oxford.

——. 1997. *The Crooked Kings of Ancient Greece*. London.

O'Higgins, D. 1989. "The Second Best of the Achaeans." *Hermathena* 147: 43–56.

Olson, S. D.. 1995. *Blood and Iron: Stories and Storytelling in Homer's Odyssey*. Leiden.

Ormand, K. 1996. Review of Oakley and Sinos 1993. *CP* 91: 80–84.

Owen, A. S., ed. 1939. *Euripides: Ion*. Oxford.

Padel, R. 1992. *In and Out of the Mind: Greek Images of the Tragic Self*. Princeton.

Page, D. L. 1941. *Select Papyri*. Vol. 3: *Literary Papyri: Poetry*. Cambridge, Mass.

——, ed. 1972. *Aeschyli septem quae supersunt tragoedias*. Oxford.

Parker, R. 1983. *Miasma: Pollution and Purification in Early Greek Religion*. Oxford.

——. 1996. *Athenian Religion: A History*. Oxford.

Patterson, C. B. 1990. "Those Athenian Bastards." *CA* 9: 40–73.

——. 1998. *The Family in Greek History*. Cambridge, Mass.

Pauly, A. F. von, and G. Wissowa. 1894–. *Paulys Realencyclopädie der classischen Altertumswissenschaft*. Stuttgart.

Pearson, A. C. ed. 1917. *The Fragments of Sophocles*. 3 vols. Cambridge.

Peck, A. L., trans. 1979. *Aristotle: Generation of Animals*. Cambridge, Mass.

Pedrick, V. 1982. "Supplication in the *Iliad* and the *Odyssey*." *TAPA* 112: 125–40.

Phillipo, S. 1995. "Family Ties: Significant Patronymics in Euripides' *Andromache*." *CQ* 45: 355–71.

Platnauer, M., ed. 1938. *Euripides. Iphigenia in Tauris*. Oxford.

Pley, J. 1932. "Memnon 1." In *RE* 15: 638–49.

Poe, J. P. 1987. *Genre and Meaning in Sophocles' Ajax*. Beiträge zur klassischen Philologie 172. Frankfurt.

Pohlenz, M. 1954. *Die griechische Tragödie*. 2d. ed. Göttingen.

Pomeroy, S. 1997. *Families in Classical and Hellenistic Greece*. Oxford.

Pòrtulas, J. 1988. "L'*Andromaque* d'Euripide: Entre le mythe et la vie quotidienne." *Métis* 3: 283–304.

Price, A. W. 1989. *Love and Friendship in Plato and Aristotle*. Oxford.

Pucci, P. 1994. "Gods' Intervention and Epiphany in Sophocles." *AJP* 115: 15–46.

Radt, S., ed. 1977. *Tragicorum Graecorum Fragmenta*. Vol. 4, *Sophocles*. Göttingen.

——, ed. 1985. *Tragicorum Graecorum Fragmenta*. Vol. 3, *Aeschylus*. Göttingen.

Rehm, R. 1994. *Marriage to Death: The Conflation of Wedding and Funeral Rituals in Greek Tragedy*. Princeton.

Reitzenstein, R. 1900. "Die Hochzeit des Peleus und der Thetis." *Hermes* 35: 73–105.

Richardson, N. 1993. *The Iliad: A Commentary*. Vol. 6, *Books 21–24*. Cambridge.

Ritchie, W. 1964. *The Authenticity of the Rhesos of Euripides*. Cambridge.

Robert, C. 1915. *Oidipus. Geschichte eines poetischen Stoffs im griechischen Altertum*. 2 vols. Berlin.

Roberts, D. H. 1987. "Parting Words: Final Lines in Sophocles and Euripides." *CQ* 37: 51–64.

——. 1988. "Sophoclean Endings: Another Story." *Arethusa* 21: 177–96.

——. 1989. "Different Stories: Sophoclean Narrative(s) in the *Philoctetes*." *TAPA* 119: 161–76.

——. 1992. "Outside the Drama: The Limits of Tragedy in Aristotle's *Poetics*." In Rorty, 133–54.

——. 1993. "The Frustrated Mourner: Strategies of Closure in Greek Tragedy." In *Nomodeiktes: Greek Studies in Honor of Martin Ostwald*, ed. R. Rosen and J. Farrell, 573–90. Ann Arbor.

——. 1997. "Ending and Aftermath in Ancient and Modern Narrative." In *Classical Closure: Reading the Ending in Greek and Latin Literature*, ed. D. H. Roberts, F. Dunn, and D. Fowler, 251–73. Princeton.

Robertson, D. S. 1923. "Euripides and Tharyps." *CR* 37: 58–60.

——. 1924. "The End of the *Supplices* Trilogy of Aeschylus." *CR* 38: 51–53.

Roisman, J., 1988. "On Phrynichos' Sack of Miletos and Phoinissai." *Eranos* 86: 15–23.

Romilly, J. de. 1980. "Le refus du suicide dans l'Héraclès d'Euripide." *Archaiognosia* 1: 1–10

Rorty, A. O., ed. 1992. *Essays on Aristotle's Poetics*. Princeton.

Roscher, W. H. 1884–1937. *Ausführliches Lexicon der griechischen und römischen Mythologie*. Leipzig.

Rose, H. J. 1957. *A Commentary on the Surviving Plays of Aeschylus*. Vol. 1. Amsterdam. (Vol. 2: 1958.)

Rose, P. W. 1976. "Sophocles' *Philoctetes* and the Teachings of the Sophists." *HSCP* 80: 49–105.

Rosenbloom, D. 1993. "Shouting 'Fire' in a Crowded Theater: Phrynichos's *Capture of Miletos* and the Politics of Fear in Early Attic Tragedy." *Philologus* 137: 159–96.

Roth, P. 1993. "The Theme of Corrupted *Xenia* in Aeschylus' *Oresteia.*" *Mnemosyne* 46: 1–17.

Roussel, D. 1976. *Tribu et cité.* Paris.

Ryzman, M. 1991. "Neoptolemus' Psychological Crisis and the Development of Physis in Sophocles' *Philoctetes.*" *Eranos* 89: 35–41.

Saïd, S. 1978. *La faute tragique.* Paris.

——. 1983. "Concorde et civilisation dans les *Euménides.*" In *Théâtre et spectacles dans l'antiquité: Actes du colloque de Strasbourg, 5–7 novembre 1981,* 97–121. Leiden.

——. 1984. "La tragédie de la vengeance." In *La vengeance: Études d'ethnologie, d'histoire et de philosophie,* ed. G. Courtois. Vol. 4, *La vengeance dans la pensée occidentale,* 47–90.

——. 1988. "Tragédie et renversement: l'example des *Perses.*" *Métis* 3: 321–41.

Sansone, D. 1975. "The Sacrifice-Motif in Euripides' *IT.*" *TAPA* 105: 283–95.

——. 1978. "A Problem in Euripides' *Iphigenia in Tauris.*" *RhM* 121: 35–47.

Schadewaldt, W. 1929. "Sophokles: *Aias* und *Antigone.*" *Neue Wege zur Antike* 8: 61–117. Leipzig.

Schein, S. L. 1975. "Mythical Illusion and Historical Reality in Euripides' *Orestes.*" *WS* 9: 49–66.

——. 1984. *The Mortal Hero: An Introduction to Homer's Iliad.* Berkeley.

——. 1988. "*Philia* in Euripides' *Alcestis.*" *Métis* 3: 179–206.

——. 1990. "*Philia* in Euripides' *Medea.*" In Griffith and Mastronarde: 57–73.

——. 1997. "Divinity and Moral Agency in Sophoclean Tragedy." In *What Is a God? Studies in the Nature of Greek Divinity,* ed. A. B. Lloyd, 123–38. London.

Schlesinger, E. 1933. *Die griechische Asylie.* Ph.D. diss., Giessen.

Schmidt-Berger, U. 1973. *Philia: Typologie der Freundschaft und Verwandtschaft bei Euripides.* Ph.D. diss., Eberhardt-Karls-Universität.

Schwartz, M. 1985. "Scatology and Eschatology in Zoroaster." In *Papers in Honour of Professor Mary Boyce,* 2: 473–96. Leiden.

Schwyzer, E. 1966. *Griechische Grammatik.* 2d ed. Vol. 2. Munich.

Scodel, R. 1982. "The Achaean Wall and the Myth of Destruction." *HSCP* 86: 33–50.

——. 1984. *Sophocles.* Boston.

Scully, S. E. 1973. "*Philia* and *Charis* in Euripidean Tragedy." Ph.D. diss., University of Toronto.

Seaford, R., ed. 1984. *Euripides: Cyclops.* Oxford.

——. 1984–85. "L'ultima canzone corale delle *Supplici* di Eschilo." *Dioniso* 55: 221–29.

——. 1987. "The Tragic Wedding." *JHS* 107: 106–30.

——. 1988. "The Eleventh Ode of Bacchylides: Hera, Artemis, and the Absence of Dionysos." *JHS* 108: 118–36.

——. 1989. "Homeric and Tragic Sacrifice." *TAPA* 119: 87–95.

——. 1990. "The Structural Problems of Marriage in Euripides." In *Euripides, Women, and Sexuality,* ed. A. Powell, 151–76. London.

——. 1993. "Dionysus as Destroyer of the Household: Homer, Tragedy, and the Polis." In *Masks of Dionysus,* ed. T. H. Carpenter and C. A. Faraone, 115–46. Ithaca, N.Y.

——. 1994a. *Reciprocity and Ritual: Homer and Tragedy in the Developing City-State.* Oxford.

——. 1994b. "Sophokles and the Mysteries." *Hermes* 122: 275–88.

——. 1996a. "Something to Do With Dionysos." In Silk 1996a, 284–94.

———. 1996b. *Euripides: Bacchae*. Warminster, England.

Seale, D. 1972. "The Element of Surprise in Sophocles' *Philoctetes*." *BICS* 19: 94–102.

———. 1982. *Vision and Stagecraft in Sophocles*. London.

Séchan, L. 1926. *Études sur la tragédie grecque*. Paris.

Segal, C. 1977. "Philoctetes and the Imperishable Piety." *Hermes* 105: 133–58.

———. 1981a. *Tragedy and Civilization: An Interpretation of Sophocles*. Cambridge, Mass.

———. 1981b. "Visual Symbolism and Visual Effects in Sophocles." *CW* 74: 125–42.

Seidensticker, B. 1983. "Die Wahl des Todes bei Sophokles." In *Sophocle: Sept exposés suivis de discussions*, ed. J. de Romilly, 105–53. Entretiens sur l'antiquité classique 29. Geneva.

———. 1996. "*Peripeteia* and Tragic Dialectic in Euripidean Tragedy." In Silk 1996a, 377–96.

Sherman, N. 1989. *The Fabric of Character: Aristotle's Theory of Virtue*. Oxford.

Sicherl, M. 1977. "The Tragic Issue in Sophocles' *Ajax*." *YCS* 25: 67–98.

Silk, M. S., ed. 1996a. *Tragedy and the Tragic: Greek Theatre and Beyond*. Oxford.

———. 1996b. "General Introduction." In Silk 1996a, 1–11.

Silk, M. S., and J. P. Stern. 1983. *Nietzsche on Tragedy*. Cambridge.

Simon, B. 1988. *Tragic Drama and the Family: Psychoanalytic Studies from Aeschylus to Beckett*. New Haven.

Sissa, G. 1990. *Greek Virginity*. Cambridge, Mass.

Sittl, C. 1890. *Die Gebärden der Griechen und Römer*. Leipzig.

Skinner, M. B. 1988. Review of Loraux 1987. *Style* 22: 677–81.

Slatkin, L. M. 1991. *The Power of Thetis: Allusion and Interpretation in the Iliad*. Berkeley.

Smethurst, M. J. 1989. *The Artistry of Aeschylus and Zeami: A Comparative Study of Greek Tragedy and Nô*. Princeton.

Smith, D. R. 1993. "Tragic Sharers: *Xenia* in Sophokles' *Philoctetes*, *Ajax*, and *Oedipus at Colonus*." Ph.D. diss., Berkeley.

Smyth, H. W. 1920. *Greek Grammar*. Cambridge, Mass.

———. 1926, trans. *Aeschylus*. Vol. 2: *Agamemnon, Libation Bearers, Eumenides, Fragments*. Cambridge, Mass.

Snell, B. 1964. Supplement to Nauck 1964.

———, ed. 1971. *Tragicorum Graecorum Fragmenta*. Vol. 1, *Testimonia et fragmenta tragicorum minorum*. Göttingen.

Solmsen, F., ed. 1990. *Hesiodi Theogonia, Opera et Dies, Scutum*. 3d ed. Oxford.

Sommerstein, A. H., ed. 1989. *Aeschylus: Eumenides*. Cambridge.

Sorum, C. E. 1986. "Sophocles' *Ajax* in Context." *CW* 79: 361–77.

———. 1995. "Euripides' Judgment: Literary Creation in *Andromache*." *AJP* 116: 371–88.

Sourvinou-Inwood, C. 1973. "The Young Abductor of the Locrian Pinakes." *BICS* 20: 12–21.

———. 1987. "A Series of Erotic Pursuits: Images and Meanings." *JHS* 107: 131–53.

———. 1989. "The Fourth Stasimon of Sophocles' *Antigone*." *BICS* 36: 141–65.

Stanford, W. B., ed. 1963. *Sophocles: Ajax*. London.

———. 1978. "Light and Darkness in Sophocles' *Ajax*." *GRBS* 19: 189–97.

Stanton, G. R. 1990. "*Philia* and *Xenia* in Euripides' 'Alkestis'." *Hermes* 118: 42–54.

Steidle, W. 1968a. *Studien zum antiken Drama*. Studia et testimonia antiqua 4. Munich.

———. 1968b. "Euripides' Andromache: Einheit und tragischer Gehalt." In Steidle 1968a, 118–31.

Steiner, G. 1996. "Tragedy Pure and Simple." In Silk 1996a, 534–46.

Stevens, P. T., ed. 1971. *Euripides: Andromache*. Oxford.

——. 1986. "Ajax in the *Trugrede*." *CQ* 36: 327–36.

Stinton, T. C. W. 1965. *Euripides and the Judgement of Paris*. London

——. 1986. "The Scope and Limits of Allusion in Greek Tragedy." In Cropp, Fantham, and Scully, 67–102.

Storey, I. C. 1989. "Domestic Disharmony in Euripides' *Andromache*." *G & R* 36: 16–27.

Strachan, J. C. G. 1976. "Iphigenia and Human Sacrifice in Euripides' *Iphigenia Taurica*." *CP* 71: 131–40.

Sutton, D. F. 1974. "Satyr Plays and the *Odyssey*." *Arethusa* 7: 161–85.

——. 1975. "A Series of Vases Illustrating the Madness of Lycurgus." *Rivista di studi classici* 23: 56–60.

——. 1984. *The Lost Sophocles*. Lanham, Md.

Sutton, R. F., Jr. 1981. "The Interaction Between Men and Women Portrayed on Attic Red-Figure Pottery." Ph.D. diss., University of North Carolina, Chapel Hill.

——. 1989. "On the Classical Athenian Wedding: Two Red-Figure Loutrophoroi in Boston." In *Daidalikon: Studies in Memory of Raymond V. Schoder, S.J.*, 331–59. Wauconda, Ill.

——. 1992. "Pornography and Persuasion on Attic Pottery." In *Pornography and Representation in Greece and Rome*, ed. A. Richlin, 3–35. Oxford.

Szondi, P. 1978. *Versuch über das Tragische*. In *Schriften*, vol. I. Frankfurt.

Taplin, O. 1971. "Significant Actions in Sophocles' *Philoctetes*." *GRBS* 12: 25–44.

——. 1977. *The Stagecraft of Aeschylus: The Dramatic Use of Exits and Entrances in Greek Tragedy*. Oxford.

——. 1978. *Greek Tragedy in Action*. Berkeley.

——. 1979. "Yielding to Forethought: Sophocles' *Ajax*." In *Arktouros: Hellenic Studies Presented to Bernard M. W. Knox*, ed. G. Bowerstock, W. Burkert, and M. C. Putnam, 122–29. Berlin.

——. 1987. "The Mapping of Sophocles' *Philoctetes*." *BICS* 34: 69–77.

Teichman, J. 1982. *Illegitimacy: A Philosophical Examination*. Oxford.

Thomson, G. 1928. *The Oresteia of Aeschylus*. Cambridge.

——. 1946. *Aeschylus and Athens: A Study in the Social Origins of Drama*. 2d. ed. London.

Thornton, A. 1984. *Homer's Iliad: Its Composition and the Motif of Supplication*. Hypomnemata 81. Göttingen.

Trendall, A. D., and T. B. L. Webster. 1971. *Illustrations of Greek Drama*. London.

Tucker, T. G., ed. 1889. *The "Supplices" of Aeschylus*. London.

Valgiglio, E. 1966. *Il tema della morte in Euripide*. Turin.

Vellacott, P. 1984. *The Logic of Tragedy: Morals and Integrity in Aeschylus' Oresteia*. Durham, N.C.

Verdenius, W. J. 1985. "Notes on the Parodos of Aeschylus' *Suppliants*." *Mnemosyne* 38: 281–306.

Vernant, J.-P. 1965. *Mythe et pensée chez les Grecs*. Paris.

——. 1974. "Le mariage." In *Mythe et société en grèce ancienne*, 57–81. Paris.

——. 1981. "Ambiguity and Reversal. On the Enigmatic Structure of *Oedipus Rex*." In J.-P. Vernant and P. Vidal-Naquet, *Tragedy and Myth in Ancient Greece*, trans. J. Lloyd, 87–119. Sussex.

——. 1988. "The God of Tragic Fiction." In J.-P. Vernant and P. Vidal-Naquet, *Myth and Tragedy in Ancient Greece*, trans. J. Lloyd, 181–88. Cambridge, Mass.

Vickers, B. 1973. *Towards Greek Tragedy*. London.

Vlastos, G. 1947. "Equality and Justice in Early Greek Cosmologies." *CP* 42: 156–78.

Vogel, C. J. de. 1966. *Pythagoras and Early Pythagoreanism*. Assen.

Vürtheim, J. 1928. *Aischylos' Schutzflehende*. Amsterdam.

Walcot, P. 1986. "Suicide, a Question of Motivation." In Betts, Hooker, and Green: 231–37.

Webster, T. B. L. 1954. "Fourth Century Tragedy and the Poetics." *Hermes* 82: 294–308.

———. 1956. *Art and Literature in Fourth-Century Athens*. London.

———.1967. *The Tragedies of Euripides*. London.

———, ed. 1970. *Sophocles: Philoktetes*. Cambridge.

Welcker, F. G. 1939–41. *Die griechischen Tragödien mit Rücksicht auf den epischen Cyclus geordnet*. Bonn.

West, M. L., ed. 1978. *Hesiod: Works and Days*. Oxford.

———, ed. 1987. *Euripides: Orestes*. Warminster, England.

———. 1990. *Aeschyli tragoediae*. Stuttgart.

White, J. B. 1985. "Persuasion and Community in Sophocles' *Philoctetes*." In *Heracles' Bow*, 3–27. Madison, Wis.

Whitman, C. H. 1974. *Euripides and the Full Circle of Myth*. Cambridge, Mass.

Whittle, E. W. 1964. "An Ambiguity in Aeschylus: *Supplices* 315." *C & M* 25: 1–7.

Wigodsky, M. W. 1962. "The 'Salvation' of Ajax." *Hermes* 90: 149–58.

Wilkins, J., ed. 1993. *Euripides: Heraclidae*. Oxford.

Willink, C. W. 1986. *Euripides: Orestes*. Oxford.

Wilson, John R. 1979. "*Eris* in Euripides." *G & R* 27: 7–20.

Wilson, Joseph P. 1997. *The Hero and the City: An Interpretation of Sophocles' Oedipus at Colonus*. Ann Arbor.

Wilson, P. J. 1996. "Tragic Rhetoric: The Use of Tragedy and the Tragic in the Fourth Century." In Silk 1996a, 310–31

Winkler, J. J., and F. I. Zeitlin, eds. 1990. *Nothing to Do with Dionysos? Athenian Drama in its Social Context*. Princeton.

Winnington-Ingram, R. P. 1980. *Sophocles: An Interpretation*. Cambridge.

———. 1983. *Studies in Aeschylus*. Cambridge.

Wolff, C. 1992. "Euripides' *Iphigenia among the Taurians*: Aetiology, Ritual, and Myth." *CA* 11: 308–34.

Xanthakis-Karamanos, G.1980. *Studies in Fourth-Century Tragedy*. Athens.

Yamagata, N. 1994. *Homeric Morality*. Leiden.

Yoshitake, S. 1994. "Disgrace, Grief and Other Ills: Herakles' Rejection of Suicide." *JHS* 94: 135–53.

Zanker, G. 1992. "Sophokles' *Ajax* and the Heroic Values of the *Iliad*." *CQ* 42: 20–25.

Zeitlin, F. I. 1970. "The Argive Festival of Hera and Euripides' *Electra*." *TAPA* 101: 645–69.

———. 1982. *Under the Sign of the Shield: Semiotics and Aeschylus' Seven Against Thebes*. Rome.

———. 1988. "La politique d' Éros: Féminin et masculin dans les *Suppliantes* d'Eschyle." *Métis* 3: 231–59.

———. 1990. "Patterns of Gender in Aeschylean Drama: *Seven Against Thebes* and the Danaid Trilogy." In Griffith and Mastronarde: 103–15.

———. 1992. "The Politics of Eros in the Danaid Trilogy of Aeschylus." In *Innovations of Antiquity*, ed. R. Hexter and D. Selden, 203–52. New York.

Index

This index includes the plays of the major tragedians (Aiskhylos, Sophokles, Euripides) discussed in the text and in appendixes A and B, and the most important of the mythological figures discussed in these sections. Plays, playwrights, and figures discussed in appendix C, and modern scholars cited in appendix B, are usually not included. Modern scholars cited elsewhere are included only if they are mentioned in the text or their ideas are particularly relevant. References to, e.g., "Aias myths," are to groups of plays discussed in appendix B.

Index

This index includes the plays of the major tragedians (Aiskhylos, Sophokles, Euripides) discussed in the text and in appendixes A and B, and the most important of the mythological figures discussed in these sections. Plays, playwrights, and figures discussed in appendix C, and modern scholars cited in appendix B, are usually not included. Modern scholars cited elsewhere are included only if they are mentioned in the text or their ideas are particularly relevant. References to, e.g., "Aias myths," are to groups of plays discussed in appendix B.